MODERN
LOVE

MARCUS COLLINS was educated at the universities of Cambridge, Harvard and Columbia before he arrived at Emory University in Atlanta, where he now teaches modern British history.

MODERN LOVE

An Intimate History of Men and Women in
Twentieth-Century Britain

Marcus Collins

Atlantic Books
London

First published in Great Britain in 2003 by Atlantic Books,
an imprint of Grove Atlantic Ltd

This paperback edition published by Atlantic Books in 2004.

1 2 3 4 5 6 7 8 9

A CIP catalogue record for this book is available from the British Library.

ISBN 1 903809 64 9

Printed in Great Britain by
Mackays of Chatham plc, Chatham, Kent

Atlantic Books
An imprint of Grove Atlantic Ltd
Ormond House
26-27 Boswell Street
London WC1N 3JZ

Contents

Acknowledgements

Edward Gibbon decided upon the theme of his peerless history as he sat amid the ruins of Rome's Capitol and listened to the chanting of friars. I found mine in the suitably more prosaic setting of the British Library after coming across a 1920s religious treatise on sexual politics. Perspiration rather than inspiration had seen me through the preceding two years of the project, as I unearthed material on such diverse subjects as mixed clubs, marital problems and pornography. The problem was that it didn't seem like a single project at all. I simply couldn't figure out how each topic related to the others. But this unassuming Christian text gave me my first clue. It argued that the enfranchisement of women had to be accompanied by a corresponding transformation of their personal relationships with men. Harmony between the sexes could be achieved, it believed, through mixing in adolescence, companionate marriage and shared sexual pleasure.

These three elements immediately struck me as much the same matters that I had been exploring in a radically different context in youth clubs, problem marriages and porn. What I had previously regarded as disparate issues now appeared to be part of a common movement to refashion private life in the wake of women's emancipation. My curiosity pricked, I ordered more interwar books and found that the more I read, the more my suspicions were confirmed. I proceeded to search for the origins of these ideas and alighted on certain strands of late-Victorian feminism. Then I sought to find out what had replaced them, and duly discovered alternatives emerging from the postwar women's movement. I also revisited my old material to examine the relationship between the ideal and the real, between hope and experience. Before I knew it, I had a book on my hands.

Now the book is completed, I would like to thank all those people bothered, neglected or otherwise ill-used during its writing. My first thank you, together with the dedication, must go to my mum and dad, who supported me in the way only parents can. My sister and brother-in-law were unfailingly kind hosts during research trips to Cambridge and brainstorming sessions in Rutland, while my brother gave freely of his unrivalled knowledge of sex literature. I owe them all.

David Cannadine was the very model of a thesis sponsor during this work's embryonic stages. My dissertation committee of David Armitage, Victoria de Grazia, Lisa Tiersten, Deborah Valenze and Chris Waters went beyond the call of duty in reading rough drafts and jollying me along my path to completion, as did Atlantic Books' editorial team of Toby Mundy, Bonnie Chiang, Alice Hunt and Penny Gardiner. The entire manuscript was read by the ever-generous Lesley Hall and by my graduate class of 2003 in a less voluntarily but no less valuable manner. Sound advice was provided by my colleagues at Newcastle and Emory during many snatched conversations in the corridors of the Armstrong building and Bowden hall. Academic input also came from Mark Bevir, Joanna Bourke, Kelly Boyd, Stephen Brooke, Deborah Cohen, Anna Davin, Tanya Evans, Paula Fass, Kate Fisher, Martin Francis, Catherine Hakim, Karen Harvey, Julian Jackson, Ayesha Jalal, Winston James, Harriet Jones, Lynn Lees, Chad Ludington, David Lowenthal, Steven Marcus, Chad Martin, Patrick McDevitt, Rohan McWilliam, Tony Morris, Frank Mort, James Obelkevich, Michael Parsons, Bernard Porter, Bill Schwarz, Eve Setch, Simon Szreter and Michelle Tusan. Needless to say, none is responsible for the errors and eccentricities contained in this work.

All my friends had to put up with years of monomania, but special mention is due to Brenda Assael, Art Chapman, Lewis Evans, Nick Harding, Andrea Linell, Joe Meisel and Pat Myers for reading portions of the work; and Nuha Ansari, David Ball, Katja Bromen, James Dellgado, Annette France, Louise Gellman, Ian Grundy, Heather Fishlock, Angelique Habis, Emma Hughes, Jodi Keyserling, Stephen and Nora Lee, Tom Miles, Isabelle Onians, François Quiviger, Felice Ramella, Alex and Debs Reed, Philippe Rosenberg, Ghodsieh Shahin, Michael Slater, Salena Stokes, Jennifer Terni and Kate Wolf for chatting with me about it. Love and thanks also go to Leonie Welberg, in whom I hope.

Institutional support came from Columbia University, the Whiting Foundation, the University of Newcastle and Emory University. The Family Welfare Association, Relate, One Plus One, the Newcastle Centre for Family Studies, the Tavistock Institute of Marital Studies and the Marriage Bureau provided advice and, in certain cases, archival sources on marriage and chapter three could not have been written without the goodwill and hospitality of UK Youth Clubs and the National Association of Clubs for Young People. Research was also conducted at the Public Record Office, the Liverpool Record Office, the Mass-Observation Archive, the London Metropolitan Archives, the Hall-Carpenter Archives, the Imperial War Museum, the Women's Library, the Feminist Library and too many university libraries to bear thinking about.

In this book, I've tried to bridge the gap between academic and general readers. Where this has proved unfeasible – as in the case of some historiographical discussions – scholars are encouraged to consult the extensive endnotes and, if still curious, the dissertation upon which this book is based.[1] Comments, criticisms, suggestions and queries are most welcome from all quarters and can be sent to modernlove@fsmail.net.

Table of Illustrations

Prologue
A Vision of Harmony

A little over a century ago, 'one of the quietest revolutionists ever known' set out his vision of love. As the utopian socialist Edward Carpenter saw it, the Victorian system of separate spheres had introduced 'maximum divergence and absolute misunderstanding' between men and women, the patriarchal structure of society having 'strangely accentuated' their naturally complementary characteristics into an 'absurd caricature of strength on the one hand and dependence on the other.'[1] This immense gulf blighted all relations between the two sexes. In childhood, 'ignorance and darkness and seclusion from each other' allowed them neither to develop rational opinions of the other sex nor to cultivate wholesome sexual desires. 'Feverish' obsessions formed where 'reasonable familiarity' was denied.[2] Each subsequently approached romance with false expectations. Man's work-fetish meant that he never learnt to love and so fell headlong into it, like a 'fly in treacle', while woman harboured an 'unhealthy dream' of being 'folded in the arms of a strong man, and surrendering herself, her life, her mind, her all, to his service.'[3]

Once wed, the asymmetrical lives of husband and wife allowed them little chance to establish that 'intelligent and mutual understanding' which Carpenter deemed essential for any marriage to be worthy of the name. The husband seeking a true 'companion' could not content himself with the 'exasperating trivialities' issuing from his wife's stunted mind.[4] The woman for her part was sacrificed to the 'egoism, lordship and physical satisfaction of the man' and consigned to the soul-destroying drudgery of housework or the pretty redundancy of a ladylike existence.[5] Their hopes thwarted, most couples settled down into a 'dull neutrality' towards each other, serving out their 'life sentence' of wedlock with no hope of reprieve.[6]

'Doubt and conflict and division' also invaded sex, he claimed. In intercourse men and women met as strangers, the painful distance between them yet another product of their divergent upbringings. Well brought-up women to whom 'the subject of sex is probably a sealed book' brought a 'nervous and hysterical' disposition to sexual encounters, calculated to prevent them from obtaining satisfaction.[7] Men were consumed by a contrasting brutishness derived from squalid liaisons with prostitutes. They stripped from sex those elements of affection without which it degenerated into an empty and selfish act. So scarred, each 'approach[ed] the great passion from totally different sides'.[8]

Carpenter believed that things could not continue as they were. The existing division was as artificial as it was acrimonious. Nature decreed that men and women were meant for each other, their 'naturally complementary relation' making them but 'two halves' of a perfect whole. The instinct to marry was a 'natural *fact*' and intercourse demonstrative of an 'unconscious harmony'.[9] Even the function of 'intermediate' homosexuals like himself was to act as the 'interpreters of men and women to each other'. Sometime, somehow, the chasm would be bridged and the 'deep and permanent relation between the sexes' would 'inevitably assert itself again'.[10]

Change in his view waited upon the emancipation of women. A free woman would no longer stand for a lopsided arrangement that kept her economically dependent, sexually ignorant and pitifully subservient to her undeserving man. Equality would not overturn all sex differences, but would do away with unnecessary distinctions and entail some modest revision of masculine and feminine roles. Removing the 'superficial contrast' presently pertaining between the sexes would reveal the 'more vital and deep-rooted differentiations' that lay underneath.[11] Nor would it mean complete autonomy for women, restoring instead that identity of interests hitherto obscured by inequality. Under patriarchy, the two sexes dragged each other down. After emancipation, they would appreciate that 'it is useless for one [sex] to attempt to glorify itself at the expense of the other'. Freedom brought men and women together, it did not push them apart.[12]

Carpenter foresaw a threefold reformation of personal relationships arising from women's emancipation involving heterosocial mixing, companionate marriage and sexual union. Mixing would follow inevitably from the coincidence of the once separate male and female spheres. While work was to remain largely segregated, in coeducational schools and shared leisure activities the sexes would learn to appreciate the peculiar charms of mixed company and to regard each other as equals and comrades. A prime virtue of mixing was to dispel sexual illusions. Unchaperoned working-class girls and boys were less prone to 'ignorance on the one side and licentiousness on the other', while the coeducated saw through the 'glamour' of sex and discerned instead its healthier aspects. As such, both were better equipped for married life.[13]

Companionate marriage formed another element of his recipe for harmony. Companionship as such was no new idea, yet Carpenter charged that the circumscription of courtship, the iniquities of marital law, the dependence of wives and disengagement of husbands made its Victorian version a travesty of the term. Nor was he satisfied to leave the sexual division of labour wholly unchanged. Men would remain the primary wage-earners and women the primary home-makers but, since an 'over-differentiation of the labours of the sexes' perpetuated inequality and mutual misunderstanding, it was desirable for a wife to escape her 'narrow sphere' through performing paid work and for a husband to do his bit around the home, shared parenting included. Any arrangement was permissible provided that it respected the innate differences between the sexes and served to 'enhance and adorn, instead of destroy, their sense of mutual sympathy.'[14] Its inequalities remedied, marriage reverted to its true function as 'that most intimate personal relation of two souls to each other'. 'Real marriage' was a partnership of equals, an exquisite communion in which nothing was withheld, everything shared: a pure, voluntary, joyful 'indwelling-place of Love'.[15]

Carpenter envisaged the new alliance between man and woman to be sealed in sex. The sex instinct in its natural state represented a desire for unity that far surpassed the lesser aims of self-gratification or 'race-propagation'. Oneness was obtained only through respecting the 'laws of equality': that is, by spurning prostitution and the double standard and by recognizing that 'the object of sex is a person' to be treated with a reverence surpassing base lust.[16] Through a sex act devoid of selfishness, elevated above mere procreative purposes and married to a 'tender emotional yearning towards the object of affection', man and woman would come together in the 'deepest soul-union' possible between two human beings. So were mixing, marriage and sex to form three interwoven elements of a 'more healthy relation between the sexes': mixing making for better matches and married love providing the gateway to sexual intimacy. In this manner, and this alone, might love at last truly come of age.[17]

Edward Carpenter was a communist, a mystic, a vegetarian and a self-proclaimed member of the intermediate sex – the archetypal sandal-wearing utopian eccentric – yet his was no voice in the wilderness.

Aspects of his outlook had been prefigured in the key texts of British feminism of the previous hundred years. Mary Wollstonecraft's *A Vindication of the Rights of Woman* (1792) contained the same denunciation of segregation in childhood and adulthood, the same solutions of coeducation and companionate marriage and the same conviction that 'man and woman were made for each other'. Socialist feminist William Thompson's *Appeal of Half the Human Race* (1825) called for 'mutual enjoyment' in sex to replace man's 'mere individual selfish gratification'.[18] Mid-Victorian liberal feminists, though mute on sexual pleasure, anticipated Carpenter's model of marriage almost in its entirety, John Stuart Mill enthusing in 1867 about a 'silent domestic revolution' that allowed the sexes to become 'for the first time in history, really each other's companions'.[19] Carpenter's ideas were echoed by such Continental feminists as the Swede Ellen Key, while many of his proposals were well on the way to enactment in the United States. There coeducation was prevalent, companionship a staple theme of public and private discourse and sex more a matter of pleasure than duty for one 1880s sample of middle-class wives.[20]

The late nineteenth-century milieu in which Carpenter wrote gave him further support. The 1890s were described by one contemporary as a veritable 'epoch of experiment', a decade of 'possibility', the 'central characteristic' of which was a search for 'the most effective, the most powerful, the most righteous way of living'.[21] *Fin de siècle* prognostication fused with feminist reform in the Fellowship of the New Life, the 'little society' of utopian socialists to which Carpenter belonged. The Fellowship backed coeducation, debated free love and provided a tight circle of self-styled 'Forerunners' – Carpenter, novelist Olive Schreiner, sexologist Havelock Ellis and his wife, writer Edith Ellis – with the perfect environment in which to hammer out the proposals encapsulated in Carpenter's *Love's Coming of Age* (1894–6).[22] Their indignation over man's subjection of woman had drawn them together. Their belief that women's emancipation involved 'something deeper' than the elimination of discrimination fuelled their determination to reform private as well as public life. Their ability, moreover, to fashion a 'new politics' out of scattered feminist aspirations gave their theories coherence and influence.[23]

It was as the basis of what I term *mutuality* – the notion that an intimate equality should be established between men and women through mixing, companionate marriage and shared sexual pleasure – that Carpenter's ideas transcended their proud pedigree and contemporary context to set the agenda for the remaking of personal relationships in the twentieth century. At the turn of the century, mutuality provided free-thinking intellectuals with a 'claim to a new sort of moral leadership' and moderate suffragists with intellectual ammunition against their anti-suffragist and militant suffragette adversaries.[24] In the twenties, its sexual maxims inspired the creation of the first birth control clinics by Marie Stopes and Norman Haire. From the forties onwards, mixing began to replace segregation as the norm in youth clubs and state secondary schools. And in the sixties, even the pornography industry became enraptured by a vision of reciprocal sexual desire: testament to the full compass of mutuality's influence.

Love is notoriously tricky to define, one committee of American sociologists describing it as a 'cognitive-affective state characterized by intrusive and obsessive fantasizing concerning reciprocity of amorant feelings by the object of the amorance.' But if we simply define love as an intense sense of attachment, it becomes apparent that mutuality redefined the term. Whereas separate spheres extolled devotion between unequals, mutuality proposed intimacy to be impossible without equality. It was an idea that appeared capable of revolutionizing the three principal forms of personal relationship between men and women: friendship, partnership and intercourse.[25]

Mutuality also helped to define what was 'modern' about twentieth-century Britain. 'Victorian' emerged in the early twentieth century largely as a portmanteau term for all that it rejected: the Victorian husband as 'lord and master' and the Victorian wife as his 'submissive' prop. The Victorian age was tarred with enforcing a 'separation between the sexes' and Victorianism became a byword for 'Prudery'.[26] Counterpoised to this Victorian stereotype was that of a modernity embracing mutuality. Sundry twentieth-century thinkers proclaimed mixing to be a 'commonplace of the modern outlook', the 'modern marriage' to be an 'equal relationship' governed by 'mutual decisions' and the 'modern man' to be seeking 'active companionship... rather than passive submission' in his mate.[27] An 'equality in passion' came to be the *sine qua non* of 'Modern Love'.[28]

This study addresses three fundamental questions. First, how did these changes occur? How did mutuality come to exert in mid twentieth-century Britain an influence comparable to that of separate spheres the century before? Second, what impact did they have? What were the practical effects of mutualists' grand plans for mixing, marriage and sex? And third, what succeeded them? Why does

Carpenter's vision of harmonious cooperation now seem antiquated, even chauvinist and, this being so, what alternatives have emerged?

The answers structure the book. The opening two chapters trace the evolution of the mutual ideal in the fifty years following Carpenter's prophesies, from the 'New Woman' controversy of the 1890s and the turn-of-the-century suffrage campaign to the debates surrounding women's role between the wars. These chapters argue that, although mutuality was a prominent model of personal relationships throughout this period and perhaps the dominant one after the First World War, it never became a consensual creed. Opposition to its proposals for interdependence between the sexes came from anti-feminists favouring the dependence of women, and from radical feminists bent on independence from men.

The social ramifications of mutuality are examined in three case studies concerning mixing, marriage and sex in the mid twentieth century (i.e. the fifty years or so after World War One). The effect of mixing is measured in chapter three, which charts the comparative fortunes of the two major youth club organizations, one of which became mixed while the other did not. Chapter four uses the case-notes and counselling literature of marriage guidance organizations to evaluate companionate marriage through two sets of comparisons: first, between those marital problems encountered by lower working-class patriarchal couples and their mostly middle-class companionate counterparts; and, second, between the expectations created by companionate ideals and their actual impact on mid-century marriages. Mutuality's sexual aspects are touched upon in this chapter and explored further in the next, which explains how sixties soft-core pornography briefly portrayed women and men as being engaged in a joint quest for sexual emancipation.

But the development of mutuality was no straightforward success story, as these and later chapters make plain. Theoretical equality in mixed youth clubs belied their actual domination by boys. The intimacy, equality and sexual satisfaction promised by companionship ran up against the sexual division of labour and the different desires of husbands and wives. And pornographers, when confronted by second-wave feminists who insisted that female sexuality existed independently of male desire, turned against mutuality and women as well. The resulting discrepancy between the ambitions encouraged by mutuality and the problems it engendered provided much of the initial impetus for the women's liberation movement. Chapter six accordingly analyzes how second-wave feminists exposed the flaws of mutuality and sought to replace it with their own autonomous ideal during the 1970s and 1980s. The epilogue suggests, however, that it was not so much feminism as individualism that supplanted mutuality in the 1990s. The same factors that made men and women more similar than ever lessened their perceived need for what the other sex had to offer. A century that had begun with attempts to reform relations between the sexes ended up questioning their very purpose.

'History is hopeless on love,' claims historian John Vincent, and not without reason. Most surviving historical documents are political, not personal, and concern institutions rather than couples, so that we know frustratingly little about, say, what well-to-do Victorians got up to in bed.[29] Yet to acknowledge difficulty is not the same as admitting defeat and researchers have devised a medley of approaches to analyze this intimate yet elusive aspect of the past. Oral historians have circumvented the paucity of sources on everyday family life by generating their own.[30] Demographers have looked for clues about sexual activity in birth rate statistics and the uptake of birth control.[31] Students of social policy have examined how the government has regulated its citizens' private lives.[32] Literary critics have analyzed the fiction of love within its historical context.[33] Social historians have used memoirs, diaries and letters to explore marriages from the inside, and court cases to see what happened when things went wrong.[34] And such theorists as Anthony Giddens and Michel Foucault have provided overarching models of the 'transformation of intimacy', while leaving the empirical spadework to others.[35] The quality, range and volume of research synthesized in recent textbooks reveal the history of love to be far less hopeless a discipline than Vincent allows.[36]

While informed by all these approaches, this work employs another. That is to study the borderline where the public and private intersect: to use the political and institutional sources privileged by Vincent to radically different effect. After all, relationships between men and women produced their own politics, a sexual politics that furnishes the source material for chapters one, two and six.[37] They attracted institutional intervention from organizations such as the youth clubs and marriage counselling agencies studied in chapters three and four.[38] Moreover, they generated more cultural artefacts than practically any other subject, from the girlie mags examined in chapter five to the millennial angst described in the epilogue.[39]

But is mutuality too schematic a concept around which to structure a history of love? The cultural historian Peter Burke has drawn attention to three perils of *Zeitgeist* history: of overestimating the degree of intellectual consensus; of thereby being unable to account for change; and of neglecting the relationship between behaviour and belief.[40] The first danger, that of 'homogenization', has been countered in this book by following Burke's advice to study both 'victors and vanquished, men and women, insiders and outsiders, contemporaries and historians'. Evidence drawn from feminists and anti-feminists, suffragists and suffragettes, Christians and atheists, politicians and pornographers, social workers and social scientists, youth club leaders and youth club members and marriage counsellors and those they counselled, produces exactly the sort of 'polyphonic' history that he favours. Mutuality is accordingly studied not in isolation, but in relation to what preceded, succeeded and competed with it.[41]

The inherent instability of romantic ideals affords one means of accounting for change over time: the second of Burke's concerns. Mutuality supplanted separate spheres by exposing the contrast between noble rhetoric and shameful reality. Yet its own philosophy of love was no less idealistic than that it replaced and, as such, no more capable of realization. The consequent disparity between expectations and outcomes led to mutuality being eclipsed by autonomy and a new set of vainglorious ambitions. And so the process continues. Love, being the most enduring of utopian projects, promises to render perpetual hope and disappointment.

This brings us to the third issue raised by Burke, the relationship between culture and society. While primarily concerned with cultural discourses – that is, with how love was represented – this work also examines how such ideas affected specific social groups. These case studies are by definition suggestive rather than conclusive, but each indicates a disjuncture between theory and practice that provides a further catalyst for change. Chapter four demonstrates how marriage reformers first championed companionship and then questioned it upon encountering its casualties in marital therapy. Chapter six likewise describes how some women's liberationists reassessed their quest for autonomy when faced with its practical consequences. In both cases, ideals at once changed and were changed by related social practices.

One last way of avoiding the pitfalls of *Zeitgeist* history is by recognizing that no single work can hope to capture the spirit of an age. *Modern Love* duly makes no claims to comprehensiveness. Of the two and a half thousand primary sources consulted for this study, only a handful were novels, plays or films in spite (in fact, because) of their having been ably analyzed elsewhere.[42] Regional variations in the dissemination of mutualist ideas and practices are difficult to assess using the sources to hand.[43] The two world wars receive some attention, but merit more than can be allocated to them in a work covering a century.[44] The same can be said for the 1990s, the epilogue simply aiming to show that contemporary history need be no oxymoron. Mutuality's concern with relations between the sexes excludes homosexuals from consideration except where, as in the case of the lesbian separatists appearing in chapter six, they directly challenged heterosexual norms. And, insofar as mutuality constituted a middle-class revolt against middle-class mores, the book focuses principally, but not exclusively, on the bourgeoisie and its bohemian fringe.

Interdisciplinary in its approach, *Modern Love* incorporates elements of social and political history into its cultural history core. Eclectic in its sourcing, it pairs printed texts with archival material drawn from charitable and governmental bodies. Historiographically, it casts new light upon established subjects like suffragism and sexology and exposes such hitherto understudied topics as mixing and the women's liberation movement to sustained scholarly examination. Chrono-logically, it ranges across the entire twentieth century in order to trace the continuities between first-wave feminism and its second-wave successor. And conceptually, it proposes that mutuality represents the missing link between Victorian models of love and our own.

The nature of introductions is to put the cart before the horse by making claims in the absence of supporting evidence. For this, we must return to the world of Edward Carpenter at the twilight of the nineteenth century and the start of the twentieth, when the 'Woman Question' became the subject of urgent public debate. In contention were rival groupings of mutualists, radical feminists and anti-feminists. At stake was the fate of separate spheres. It's here that I'll begin.

I

MUTUALITY
CONCEIVED

The Common Cause

Women's Suffrage

1

Common Cause

The Solution to Sex Antagonism, c. 1890–1918

Edward Carpenter's rhapsodic prophecy of love and harmony failed to materialize over the following two decades. The campaign for women's emancipation engendered unprecedented acrimony once humble petitioning gave way to brazen assertions of equal rights. Cultural strife erupted in 1894 over the 'New Woman', that half-fictional, half-factual nemesis of dainty Victorian femininity. Political conflict intensified three years later with the founding of a nationwide women's suffrage organization. And, as the twentieth century dawned, speculation grew within educated circles that sex war would be 'the biggest thing that civilisation has seen'.[1] 'Men and women appear to have become antagonistic to each other', reported the feminist and novelist Maud Braby in her meditation on *Modern Marriage and How to Bear It* (1908). 'However much they love the individual of their fancy,' the sexes betrayed a 'kind of veiled distrust' towards each other that clouded their every encounter. In his companion volume *Modern Woman and How to Manage Her* (1909), sex writer Walter Gallichan described a generalized 'sex antagonism' infecting not only civic affairs but 'love and ... family life'.[2]

The adversaries in the sex war came from the extremities of the debate over women's emancipation: what I call the radical feminists and the anti-suffragists or antis. One nursery of radical feminism was the social purity movement which, having originated in the 1860s as a crusade against the state regulation of prostitution, expanded via campaigns against paedophilia, white slavery and public vice into an assault by some of its members on 'selfish, lustful, diseased manhood.'[3] Such purity campaigners were matched in their sex antagonism by the Women's Social and Political Union, founded in 1903 by Emmeline Pankhurst and her daughter Christabel. The WSPU's confrontational tactics originated in 1905 as little more than publicity stunts, but soon developed into a commitment to 'Deeds Not Words' that increasingly divided these law-breaking 'suffragettes' from the law-abiding

13

'suffragists' and sanctioned actions verging on terrorism.[4] Their fury at male foot-dragging over granting women the vote led militants to smash windows, trash shopping arcades and slash Old Masters. They defoliated golf courses, pulped mail, snipped telegraph wires, slapped Winston Churchill, stoned Herbert Asquith and bombed the house of David Lloyd George. Imprisoned hunger strikers courted martyrdom and Emily Wilding Davison achieved it under the hooves of the King's Derby steed in 1913. Many suffragettes were not purity campaigners or vice versa.[5] Nor was either grouping uniformly hostile to men. Yet the WSPU's martial rhetoric of a just war waged by virtuous women against vicious men was borrowed from the purity movement and, with Christabel Pankhurst's 1913 call for 'Votes for Women . . . and Chastity for Men', the two looked set to merge into a single cause.[6]

Ranged against radical feminists were the anti-suffragists, who likewise included moderate and extreme factions. Such prominent antis as the statesman Lord Curzon and the novelist Mrs Humphry Ward were neither temperamentally inclined nor so politically maladroit as to pit one sex against another. Moreover, many within the anti-suffragist camp supported such emancipatory causes as divorce reform and women's higher education out of a desire to see men and women 'working hand in hand'.[7] But it was not hard to find anti-suffragists eager to send '*kicks, not kisses*' in women's direction. In sermons and marriage manuals, pamphlets and cartoons, a host of chauvinist and sometimes misogynist diatribes railed against the alleged excesses of female emancipation. And just as radical feminists related the personal to the political, antis advocated a complete programme of women's subordination extending across private and public life.[8]

Both sets of sex antagonists, radical feminists and antis alike, saw themselves as engaged in a titanic struggle between New Women and Old Men. For radical feminists, the New Woman possessed a proud autonomy unknown to her 'home-loving' and 'self-sacrificing' foremothers. Standing in her way was unreconstructed man, a tin-pot despot 'whose favour can only be won by abasement, whose touch is pollution, and whose love is a degradation.'[9] Christabel Pankhurst considered the eventual victor of this 'war of old men against young women' to be beyond doubt. Whereas men presumed superiority, they were in fact moral 'inferiors' to the 'spiritually developed women of this new day' whose triumph was ultimately assured.[10] What would follow was a matter of speculation. The Theosophist Frances Swiney conceded the possibility of some future 'New Adam' sufficiently 'assimilated to the female' for amicable coexistence.[11] But she viewed sexual politics as a zero-sum game whereby women's emancipation entailed men's subordination. Though the sexes would run Swiney's utopia in 'perfect concord', the 'pervading influence' would nonetheless be 'chiefly feminine.'[12] Fellow purity writer Margaret Dalham saw no need of men as lovers, husbands or fathers. She looked forward to a society in which 'women have control of the marriage relation' on the grounds that 'by nature the child is hers, the home should be hers, and the husband accepted, or dispensed with, at her pleasure.' The 'true solution' to the Woman Question was the restitution of matriarchal rule.[13]

Antis simply reversed the charges by identifying New Women as the villains and Old Men as the victims in the ongoing battle over women's emancipation. Whereas radical feminists inveighed against 'aristocratic masculine cruelty', the bitterest anti-suffragists held all women to be 'tyrants' out to institute petticoat government.[14] And while purity campaigners blamed the 'Race Suicide' of a falling birth rate on men's syphilitic loins, antis used the same eugenic rationale to indict emancipated womanhood for forsaking its breeding function. They perceived 'the mannish swagger, the vulgarity of tone, the "slangy" talk, the loud self-assertiveness, the *outré* dress, and the general coarsening' of the New Woman to be signs of a degeneracy spawned by pretensions to equality.[15] Would-be humorist T.W.H. Crosland wanted woman 'relegated to her natural sphere', a sentiment endorsed by a measured tract entitled *Is the British Empire Ripe for Government by Disorderly Women who Smash Windows and Assault the Police?* Only by becoming reconciled to her 'utter dependence on man', it claimed, would a woman find 'joy and happiness and contentment'.[16]

A curious symmetry obtained between these two battalions of sex warriors, at odds on so much else. Both periodically dissociated themselves from a full-blown sex war, the WSPU stating that its was 'not fighting against men, but *for* women' and the Marxist anti-suffragist E. Belfort Bax professing an 'entire absence of any consciousness of sex antagonism in the attitude of men towards women'.[17] But each returned the other's abuse with interest. Crosland suggested that contemporary woman be punished for feminist 'impertinence' by having her every privilege withdrawn:

Less freedom, less pin money, less incense, less deference, less power in the household, a less frequent appearance in public places, fewer dresses and fewer jewels, fewer compliments, might bring the enemy to whatever small senses she possesses.[18]

15

Suffragettes in turn blamed 'unregenerate' men for having 'driven women to be militant'. It was the 'sex filth' elderly men heaped on Mary Richardson as she sold suffragette papers that impelled her to 'hit back, to hit out at anything' and take an axe to the National Gallery's Velásquez 'Venus'. Radical feminists and anti-suffragists were the joint authors of a sex war both ostensibly disowned.[19]

Between these two warring parties stood a body of opinion utterly opposed to sex antagonism. Its political expression was the National Union of Women's Suffrage Societies, the constitutionalist suffrage body that distinguished itself from the militant WSPU in emphasizing the 'shared humanity of both sexes', according to historian Brian Harrison. NUWSS leader Millicent Garrett Fawcett dismissed the very 'possibility of a sex war.' Its propaganda spoke of striving to create 'mutual understanding and respect' between the sexes.[20] Its paper *The Common Cause* categorically rejected the 'setting of women against men', with the editor Helena Swanwick taking pains to deny the inevitability of conflict:

> Certainly there are some blackguards and some lunatics of both sexes. Certainly there is, and perhaps always has been, some antagonism between the sexes. It is the most constant endeavour and the most firm faith of progressive men and women that this antagonism should cease. We do not believe it to be necessary and we do believe it to be altogether bad.[21]

Constitutionalist opposition to sex antagonism stopped short of entering into the wide-ranging debate on personal relationships engaging the radical feminists and antis. With the notable exceptions of Swanwick and Maude Royden, her successor at *The Common Cause*, suffragist leaders were both too 'incurably respectable' and too single-mindedly dedicated to achieving the vote to address such contentious topics as sex and marriage: hence their general acceptance until the 1890s that wives be excluded from the franchise lest strife invade family life.[22]

The broader challenge to the ideas of the sex antagonists came instead from those I term mutualists, a loose collection of intellectuals including in their number the ubiquitous Edward Carpenter, his intimates Olive Schreiner and Edith and Havelock Ellis, the husband-and-wife team of controversialists, Walter Gallichan and C. Gasquoine Hartley, sex reformers Marie Stopes and Stella Browne, doctor Elizabeth Sloan Chesser, philosopher Bertrand Russell, future publisher

Victor Gollancz, theologian W.F. Lofthouse, novelist Sarah Grand, coeducationalist J.H. Badley, anthropologist Jane E. Harrison, Swedish feminist Ellen Key, Helena Swanwick, Maude Royden, George Bernard Shaw (on occasion) and a host of lesser figures concerned with the Woman Question.

Mutualists made poor joiners. Their one stab at organization during this period, the Fellowship of the New Life, attracted only a fraction of them and lasted fifteen years before folding in 1898. Moreover, intellectual affinities did not ensure agreement on every matter.[23] Five general principles nonetheless united them. First was the conviction that men and women were each other's natural equals and intimates. Second came their corresponding abhorrence of sex antagonism in all its forms. That female enfranchisement represented 'merely a reasonable condition for attaining far wider and more fundamental ends' was their third axiom; their disavowal of what came to be called 'Victorian' models of personal relationships, a fourth. All fed into their most audacious proposition: the collapsing of separate spheres.[24]

Separate Spheres

So what were separate spheres and how did they shape the lives of Victorian and Edwardian men and women?[25] On one level, the term recapitulated the hoary notion that 'God and nature' endowed each sex with its own immutable function.[26] Critic and seer John Ruskin famously portrayed man as 'the doer, the creator, the discoverer, the defender' who sallied forth to perform his 'rough work in the open world' under conditions of 'peril and trial'. With woman conversely possessed of a 'modesty of service' best expressed in household management, Ruskin discerned a sacred complementarity: 'Each has what the other has not: each completes the other, and is completed by the other: they are in nothing alike, and the happiness and perfection of both depends upon each asking and receiving from the other what the other only can give.'[27] Symmetry did not mean equality to most of Ruskin's contemporaries, to whom woman was self-evidently the 'weaker sex'. Her physical deficiencies were readily apparent, a naturally delicate frame further enfeebled by the trials of childbirth visited upon the average wife no fewer than six times.[28] Suspect too were her mental faculties. Receptivity made her suggestible, her intuition, irrational, her brain all too subject to the pleadings of heart and womb. Even her much-vaunted moral superiority seemed vulnerable since modesty once lost could never be restored. It and the woman who possessed it had, in Ruskin's words, to be 'protected from all danger and temptation'.[29]

The status accorded to women by respectable Victorians, however demeaning by our lights, appeared progressive by their own when compared to that of any other people, period or place. They looked eastwards to Asian women whose feet were bound or faces swathed in veils, backwards to the sorry plight of the 'savage' woman subjected to hard toil and unbridled lust and downwards to the unrespectable urban poor among whom 'nobody knows ... [or] cares' who was married and 'no form of vice and sensuality causes surprise'.[30] All contrasted sharply with the positive spin supplied by late eighteenth- and nineteenth-century authorities to scientific, religious and moral justifications for male supremacy. Anatomical models depicting females as undeveloped males were replaced by those stressing the sexes' physiological incommensurability.[31] Christians traditionally held woman accursed for Eve's treachery, but Evangelicals spoke of a female spirituality unsullied by the soulless public world. And whereas early modern moralists castigated female lasciviousness, their late eighteenth- and nineteenth-century successors praised woman's capacity to 'purify and refine [man's] sensual nature'. So it was that Victorian moralists conceived of women's subordination in terms not of oppression but protection.[32]

By the turn of the century, however, thinkers of all stripes felt at liberty to appropriate and repudiate aspects of the separate spheres ideal as they pleased. Radical feminists purged Victorian woman-worship of its condescension. Christabel Pankhurst argued that, as the custodian of morality, woman deserved the 'independence which would enable her to play her part of law-giver', while the preservation of her modesty required more restrictions on male behaviour than her own.[33] Anti-suffragists pursued the opposite course of stripping patriarchy of its gallantry by celebrating inequality and jeering at men willing to parley with women in a spirit of 'knowledge and love'. Mutualists sorrowfully observed that the 'sentimental', Ruskinian tone of mid-Victorian chauvinism had given way to a social Darwinian emphasis on 'brute force as the guiding principle of life'.[34]

Mutualist thinking on sex roles bore a certain resemblance to that enshrined in separate spheres. Echoes of Ruskin could be heard in Havelock Ellis' identification of 'fundamentally and eternally distinct' male and female natures and Marie Stopes' assertion that men and women were 'made to love and help each other'. Considering the sexes to be neither interchangeable nor incompatible, they subscribed to what historian Karen Offen terms a 'relational' feminist creed.[35] Yet, for all their belief in innate differences, mutualists found little biological justification for separate spheres. The distinctness of the spheres was in their view 'alleged', segregation 'unnatural' and the interests of the sexes far closer than was ordinarily allowed.[36] Nor could they perceive any complementarity between 'overfed' gentlemen and 'hysterical' ladies, the one being as artificial as the other. The 'coercive differentiations' imposed on women warped 'natural distinctions' to a degree injurious to their relations with men.[37]

Evolutionary theory convinced mutualists that what was natural need not be bestial. What elevated humankind above the proverbial 'beast of the field' was the common ground between males and females extending beyond mere 'sex-duties'.[38] Anti-suffragists and radical feminists were accordingly mistaken to think that women's emancipation would draw them apart from men. As women became a 'little more masculine' in temperament, so men grew to be a 'little more sensitive' if emphatically not effeminate.[39] Partnering the New Woman was the New Man, who had no more use for the 'always fainting, weeping and terrified Emilia or Sophia of a bygone epoch' than had emancipated womanhood for the rakish 'Tom Jones' type populating Georgian novels. With the one jettisoning her timidity and the other his sense of superiority, each sex would ascend 'the same mountain from opposite sides' to meet upon a summit of shared humanity.[40]

Mixing

The mutualist challenge did not stop there, for separate spheres connoted much more than a theory of sex difference. It stood for a whole way of life, a model – part real, part ideal – regulating the whole gamut of relations between men and women as acquaintances, spouses and sexual partners. At its most literal level, separate spheres assigned different social orbits to each sex. The male sphere was that of business and the social affairs conducted in the great institutions of the age. Public schools produced gentlemen, universities refined them, the army hardened them, the professions employed them, parliament represented them and gentleman's clubs afforded them manly pleasures. A culture of fraternity bound men together, finding expression in forms as varied as the Pre-Raphaelite Brotherhood and the 'muscular Christianity' of young Tom Brown.[41] Women's alleged mental and physical limitations excused them from such civic activities as voting, fighting and (wherever possible) paid work and made their sphere primarily domestic. Excursions beyond its confines were especially regulated for unmarried young women out of concern for their moral standing, by which was meant their virginity, their marriageability and their family's good name. On the streets, the rules of etiquette required that a spinster under thirty submit herself to the 'good-natured surveillance' of a chaperon. At home, the intricate rituals of cards and calls shielded her from the advances of unsanctioned male suitors. In balls, the decorousness of the dances and the marking of dance cards prevented improper inferences being drawn from an enthusiastically performed two-step. Self-restraint took care of the rest, a gentleman's 'chivalry' and a lady's self-effacing 'modesty' lending interactions between them their celebratedly stilted air.[42]

Victorian ladies and gentlemen were known to observe such customs in the breach: hence their reputation for humbug. The advice books that codified separate spheres were in any case as much prescriptive as descriptive in character and, for all their strictures, the spheres were fuzzy, overlapping and amenable to change. Men's public role sat oddly with their manifest devotion to the home. The typical middle-class husband defined happiness as 'having his tea beside his own hearth, with his slippers on', according to the visiting French writer Hippolyte Taine.[43] Women were meanwhile undergoing a 'widening' of their own sphere far beyond what could plausibly be considered private. The ancient universities of Oxford and Cambridge began to admit female students in the late 1860s and 1870s. The 1880s saw some relaxation of chaperonage and the emergence of new 'heterosocial spaces' in London's teeming streets, paving the way for a New Woman in the next decade who was unbeholden to wearisome convention. The result was that higher-class women at the end of the nineteenth century probably had greater freedom of movement and involvement in public affairs than ever before.[44]

Even so, incremental change of this kind failed to satisfy mutualists appalled at how residual forms of segregation left women cramped and men coarse. Worst off in their view were ladies confined to a largely feminine family realm. 'Men have drawn ring-fences around women,' complained Helena Swanwick, 'and then twitted them with their narrowness.'[45] Myopia was also thought to mar exclusively male circles. Public schools denied boys the opportunity to form realistic impressions of the other sex. The 'abnormal...male atmosphere' of parliament made MPs legislate on behalf of women known to them only by their 'most superficial characteristics'. The quintessentially masculine arenas of 'the brothel, the race-course, the gaming-table' cultivated in men a 'crudely animal, hard-drinking, hard-swearing, licentious' temperament estranging them still further from housebound women.[46] The obvious antidote to segregation was its opposite. Men's table manners improved in mixed company, and they dispensed with the 'lust of competition and conquest' acquired apart from women in favour of a 'new ethic' of cooperation.[47] And whereas segregated women regarded men either with 'blind reverence' or 'blind hostility', prolonged contact afforded them fewer illusions. Courting evidently had its place in mixed gatherings, but their foremost purpose was to demonstrate that the sexes had more in common than attraction alone.[48]

Mutualists wishing to put their principles to the test established their own miniature mixed communities. Traces of mid nineteenth-century utopian socialism reappeared in the Fellowship of the New Life's plans for communes in a London townhouse and a farm. As before, the aim was to foster an 'honest, natural fellowship of men and women [working] for the same object and on an equal footing'. Yet, again true to precedent, disillusionment followed. The Bloomsbury commune taught its members that 'Fellowship is hell' and survived for only seven years, while the agrarian scheme never got off the ground, largely due to a dearth of female volunteers.[49]

More successful were mutualist ventures in coeducation, a pet idea of such Enlightenment thinkers as Catharine Macaulay and Mary Wollstonecraft and one essayed in the mid nineteenth century by socialist feminist Robert Owen and liberal feminist Barbara Leigh Smith Bodichon.[50] The founding of Bedales (established in 1893, turning coeducational in 1898), King Alfred's, Hampstead (1898) and Keswick (1899) gave coeducation a sounder institutional footing.[51] These independent progressive schools aimed to eradicate 'artificial differences' between the sexes and with them 'man's main excuse for keeping woman in subjection.'[52] Girls and boys were held to have 'nine-tenths of their needs in common', prompting some schools to introduce mixed cricket teams and somewhat androgynous uniforms. Boys at Bedales sewed in the hope of removing 'barriers of contempt', while the libertarian Little Commonwealth of American expatriate Homer Lane witnessed the boys 'willingly, even enthusiastically' cook and clean as the girls performed outdoor chores.[53]

Coeducated pupils were expected to civilize each other, the boys imparting the qualities of 'unselfishness, hardihood, honour' to girls and acquiring 'consideration, gentleness, chivalry' in return. Yet coeducationalists distanced themselves from those feminists who went 'too far in ignoring sex differences' – a besetting sin of hoydenish girls' schools – and accordingly provided some separate vocational and sporting activities.[54] They parried charges of wanton immorality by emphasizing how the 'wholesomeness' of everyday contact checked the 'premature development of the amative emotion'. Havelock Ellis conversely accused girls' schools of fostering lesbian 'pashes' and the fledgling Association for the Promotion of Coeducation of Boys and Girls charged boys' schools with diverting their pupils' instincts into the 'surreptitious, unlicensed and vicious' channels of homosexuality and self-abuse.[55]

The consensus among mutualists over the benefits of mixing in schools and leisure activities did not extend to the workplace. On one side were Walter Gallichan and Olive Schreiner, who argued that the 'sharing by men and women of the same labours' contributed to that 'common habit of thought and interests' intrinsic to the mutual ideal.[56] But Havelock and Edith Ellis and physician Elizabeth Chesser feared that competition over jobs would produce 'sex rivalry and sex war'. Besides being divisive, they considered female incursions into men's work to be unfair on male breadwinners unable to match their low wages and detrimental to women's 'sanity', 'health' and 'charm'. Not wishing to overturn the sexual division of labour entirely, they therefore concentrated their efforts on the reform of private life.[57]

Anti-suffragists and radical feminists raised contrasting objections to mutualist plans for mixing. Antis defended segregation in the name of decency and common-sense. The prominent female signatories to an 1889 'Appeal Against Female Suffrage' advocated restricting women's entry into public life on the grounds that the 'emancipating process' had already reached the 'limits fixed by the physical constitution of women'.[58] Other antis dwelt on the communication barrier between sexes possessing such divergent 'inclinations, feelings and intuitions'. Ernest Crawley maintained in his celebrated anthropological study *The Mystic Rose* (1902) that 'men as a rule prefer to associate with men and women with women' except for such 'functional' purposes as procreation. This accounted for the universal appeal of the man's club for so-called primitives as much as for the denizens of Pall Mall.[59] Mixing also upset antis' devotion to order. Coeducation mocked 'Nature's dictates' by inducing 'masculinity' in girls and 'effeminacy' in boys. Any 'unregulated relations between the sexes' invited the very 'extinction of morality'. Segregation established boundaries; mixing muddled things up.[60]

Radical feminists had their own reasons for cherishing certain aspects of separate spheres. Mid-Victorian feminism had been built largely upon single-sex networks of family and friends and achieved most success through extending women's nominally private sphere into broad expanses of public life. Women's exclusion from male institutions had forced them to create parallel bodies under their own control and spinsters in particular benefited from a range of occupations, from nursing to philanthropy, that permitted them a degree of professional autonomy.[61] Mixing threatened these achievements. Some radical feminists were nonetheless prepared to accept mixed schooling, its long association with feminism convincing even sex warrior Frances Swiney that it taught boys self-control. The opposite case was made by an anonymous contributor to the feminist journal *Shafts*, who predicted that mixed schools would deprive girls of female teachers, male respect and – if coeducational America was any guide – safeguards against illegitimacy and domestic violence.[62] Less dissent arose over other forms of segregation. In employment, playwright Cicely Hamilton considered a woman working alongside men to be more liable to believe in her own 'inherent and essential inferiority'. In leisure, feminists were urged to lend their 'hearty, unflinching support' to clubs 'founded by women for women'.[63] And in politics, radical feminists portrayed the women's movement as an exercise in self-reliance. Here they experienced 'full unfetter[e]d companionship' and a 'sense of unity and mutual confidence' with their own sex rather than in mixed company. 'Sisters of a common sisterhood' learnt to live happily without men.[64]

Mutualists looked sourly on the defence of segregation advanced by sex antagonists. The 'one-sexed world' of the radical feminists held little appeal. Against militant suffragettes' sorority, moderate suffragists welcomed 'comradeship...with men too' in the franchise campaign.[65] For her part, feminist anthropologist Jane Harrison took issue with Ernest Crawley's celebration of male bonding. While accepting that all primitive societies possessed some sort of 'Man's House', she believed its function to be one of crudely regulating male sexual instincts by keeping women out of bounds. She urged men in modern society to surmount their fears in recognition that 'one half of humanity cannot be fully humanised without the other'. The Man's House had had its day.[66]

Companionate Marriage

Separate spheres provided Victorian marriage with a new name for the venerable practice of assigning breadwinning to husbands and housekeeping to wives. Equality within the family was no more contemplated for women than for children. The Anglican marriage service stipulated that a wife 'obey' her husband and most marriage manuals endorsed feminine submission. The law further cemented female subordination through the precept of coverture that, as eighteenth-century jurist William Blackstone explained, withdrew a woman's 'very being or legal existence' upon marriage.[67] Research by Leonore Davidoff, Catherine Hall, John Tosh and, in a Canadian context, Peter Ward indicates that couples took patriarchal authority seriously. 'He always knows my mind, so in future I shall let him make up my mind for me,' wrote the lovestruck Anna Dawson in 1875, while another of Ward's subjects, William Hall, pledged himself willing to 'take charge' of his fiancée for life.[68]

Dependency had its advantages. The law absolved wives of responsibility for debts and of crimes committed in their husbands' presence as well as sparing them the trial of divorce, of which there were only a couple a year before the 1857 reforms and a couple of hundred annually thereafter. Patriarchal rule was often tempered by husbandly magnanimity or wifely guile and, unlike her unmarried sister, a wife enjoyed the right to have sex, rear children, manage a household and come and go much as she pleased.[69] The Victorian middle classes also made a religion of domesticity. Wives were praised to the heavens in panegyrics such as Coventry Patmore's 'The Angel in the House' (1854–6), while many husbands were uncommonly proud to be considered family men. The contribution of one 'Successfully Married Man' to an 1888 newspaper debate on marriage spoke for them all. He considered wedlock to be a 'divine institution' that had made him 'in every way a better man'. The 'salutary and elevating' effect of tending to his wife far outshone the privileges of bachelordom, while marital friction had been overcome by 'self-denial'. 'We seek our pleasures together, and we bear our cares together,' he wrote: 'The centre of my interest in this world is my home, and the centre of my home (which is home indeed) is my wife.'[70]

Such touching sentiments belied the sad truth that matrimony was based not on love but on a legal contract that enshrined inequality. The standing of wives under law had certainly improved since the 1850s in allowing them rights over their property, earnings and children, not to mention their bodies, which could no longer be chastised and imprisoned by husbandly edict. Now legally no 'chattel', a wife nonetheless remained somewhat less than equal so that, for example, the 1857 Matrimonial Causes Act made adultery sufficient grounds for divorce solely for husbands.[71] To mutualists, the subordination of wives by law and custom was not merely unjust but inimical to marital contentment. No woman relished humiliation nor could any self-respecting husband find a wife's 'self-surrender' to be anything but repellent.[72] Moreover, they blamed inequality for the falling marriage rates so troubling to their contemporaries. An aversion to shouldering the wifely yoke inclined emancipated woman to 'misonamic repulsion'. The unenlightened bachelor in turn shied away from committing himself to a woman sufficiently self-possessed to have 'strayed very far from man's ideal'.[73]

No less detrimental to mutualists' idea of true romance was a strictly observed spousal division of labour. 'Man and wife do not, as a rule, live together,' quipped Bernard Shaw: 'they only breakfast together, dine together and sleep in the same room.' He claimed that the average husband knew practically 'nothing' about his wife's life while she, having been rendered 'unfit for human society' by the vacuousness of her domestic routine, was equally ignorant of his working day.[74] For want of mutual sympathy, both partners subjected each other to their own selfish ends: the husband treating the woman with 'self-indulgence', the parasitic wife extracting 'luxury' as her price for belittlement.[75]

The feminist tradition from which mutuality emerged offered two alternatives to patriarchal marriage. Socialist feminists had long championed 'free love', which for all its infamy involved not unbridled promiscuity but monogamous and preferably lifelong cohabitation. They believed that successful partnerships needed no legal interference while unsuccessful ones required recourse to a divorce then prohibited to all but the rich. In this spirit Robert Owen proposed in the 1830s and 1840s that partnerships be 'solely formed to promote the happiness of the sexes' and dissolved in the event of failure.[76] Mid-Victorian liberal feminists dissented, perceiving the greatest threat to their respectability to stem from the 'secret dread' that feminism jeopardized marriage. Besides, the experience of such exemplary feminist couples as the Fawcetts and the Butlers demonstrated that marriage was capable of reform that stopped short of abolition. The 'true domestic ideal' espoused by Josephine Butler retained marriage's permanence but removed its authoritarianism, basing it instead upon 'real affection, equal marriage and virtuous life'.[77]

Of these two options, only a minority of turn-of-the-century mutualists preferred free love. Libertarians insisted that 'no ceremony, religious or civil, can render the bond of mutual affection any more moral than it is by its own natural right', while New Woman Mona Caird advocated that marriage become a private contract.[78] Still more brazen were the anarchist Legitimation League's disavowal of matrimony and maverick W.L. George's promise of 'room for the nymphomaniac' in the forthcoming Feminist State.[79] But most mutualist thinkers, including such socialists as Edward Carpenter and Havelock Ellis, ultimately rejected free love for reasons of pragmatism and propriety. Carpenter accepted that the institution of marriage protected women and children and prevented a 'cheap and continual transfer of affections from one object to another', while Ellis supported free love as an 'abstract social creed' but not as a 'practical possibility' in light of past failures. He had in mind the suicide of his acquaintance Eleanor Marx following her doomed romance with Edward Aveling, but the earlier farrago of the Owenite communes set no more encouraging a precedent.[80]

The best solution therefore appeared that of elevating the 'deplorably low' state of marriage into the 'true union of souls' envisaged by liberal feminists. Justice demanded equality for women so that they no longer had to choose between a free but loveless spinsterhood and a fettered if loving matrimony. Husbands who had 'evolved to the present stage of comradeship and mutual respect' had no use for patriarchal authority, while those 'more domineering' men who craved power proved themselves unworthy of exercising it.[81] Emancipation also required a separate income for wives, whether through a personal allowance, part-time work or state support, thereby abolishing wifely dependency and allowing free rein to the 'untrammelled action of attraction and affection'.[82] Within an ideal mutualist marriage, partners entered into a 'perfect communion' hitherto prevented by the 'patriarchal view of matrimony'. And, as the years passed, 'intertwined memory and affection' fused them into an 'amalgamated personality'.[83] 'Although essential differences must always exist,' explained one contributor to *Shafts*, 'the sexes will become far more closely united in relations of friendship and sympathy within the safeguarded freedom of a wide home-life full of mutual interests and reciprocal duties.'[84]

Radical feminists did not reject the institution of marriage outright.

Ellice Hopkins saw merit in lifelong monogamy, Christabel Pankurst spoke of 'ennobling' matrimony through cooperative housekeeping and separate spousal incomes, and Cicely Hamilton conceded that the 'companionship in marriage of self-respecting man and self-respecting woman' was a 'very perfect thing'.[85] At the same time, they expressed little of the mutualists' confidence that men shared these ambitions. Hopkins thought Mona Caird naive to believe that marriage could be based on emotion rather than duty so long as infidelity flowed from the 'unruly wills and affections of sinful men'. Pankhurst doubted that husbands 'readily surrendered' their economic – and therefore sexual – control, while Hamilton considered men's high-flown talk of loving devotion to be so much 'sentimental balderdash'. 'All men' in her book sought a wife who 'cooks and cooks' but 'never thinks'.[86] The purity campaigners Frances Swiney and Margaret Dalham chose a different tack when contrasting woman's maternal nature with man's 'infinitely' smaller concern for parental responsibilities. He was no 'domestic creature', they argued, but a 'hunter...warrior...breadwinner' and as such merely an 'incident in the home'.[87]

Querying the possibility of companionship caused radical feminists to reevaluate spinsterhood. Single women had formed the backbone of the middle-class women's movement since its inception in the 1850s and were at the forefront of its concerns. While mid-Victorian pleas to alleviate the spinster's plight had not questioned the preferability of marriage, turn-of-the-century radical feminists saw no reason to associate the single state with 'failure'. Cicely Hamilton led the charge with *Marriage as a Trade* (1909) in which, having weighed the 'right to wear on the third finger of the left hand a gold ring' against the manifold drawbacks of wifehood, she expressed herself 'exceedingly glad' that so many women chose, like her, to remain unwed.[88] Christabel Pankhurst credited unmarried women with an 'economic... spiritual and social freedom' denied to wives and endorsed Lucy Re-Bartlett's call for woman to become a *Lysistrata*-like 'celibate striker' unless and until man learnt to behave himself.[89] Christabel's deputy Annie Kenney attributed the WSPU's militancy to the fact that its Young Hot Bloods were 'free and alone...independent of everything and everybody'. Nearly two-thirds of its supporters were unmarried prior to the First World War.[90]

Parallels to radical feminists' aversion to matrimony could be found in such anonymous anti-feminist screeds as *The Celibate's Apology; by A Misogynist* (1914) and the scheme of one 'Grimaud' to impregnate spinsters with men put out to stud. Yet contrary to John Tosh's suggestion of a male 'flight from domesticity' consequent on women's emancipation, most antis strove to uphold family life against feminist assault.[91] They reiterated the separate spheres' nostrum that the institution of matrimony required rules to be followed and roles observed. Spouses were to respect the 'Divine Law, written in the history of the household, written in the Word of God, written in the very nature of man and woman' according to which husbands ordered and wives obeyed. Accord was desirable, but one voice had to prevail and woman's 'handicapped' physique, intellect and will-power made it the man's.[92] The more gallant of anti-suffragists noted that a husband's rights carried responsibilities including the support of his dependants, the curbing of his promiscuous instincts and the upholding of the 'dignity... of true wifehood and motherhood'. Their conclusion was nonetheless the same: 'the wife's state in marriage is certainly more or less one of subjection, perhaps almost of humiliation'.[93]

However much one willed what the other opposed, their shared belief in the incompatibility of marriage and women's emancipation betrayed the similarities between anti-suffragists and radical feminists. The antis' charge that feminists 'only pretend to desire equality [when] what they really aim at is the wife's supremacy' received corroboration from radical feminists' declared intention to replace 'patriarchy' with 'matriarchy' in domestic life.[94] Antis accused The New Woman of 'neglect[ing] her duties at home' in favour of 'demanding rights which woman never thought of before'; unattached suffragettes credited an absence of 'home-life' for their total dedication to the cause.[95] And, as we shall see below, physician William Acton's claim in 1871 that emancipated women considered themselves 'martyrs when called upon to fulfil the [sexual] duties of wives' was echoed a generation later by Frances Swiney's characterization of woman as the 'martyr of organised and systematic sexual wrong-doing.'[96]

Whereas radical feminists happily confirmed anti-suffragists' fears over the future of marriage, mutualists did their best to dispel them. It was not women's emancipation but its denial that accounted for 'marriage troubles and unsatisfactory alliances'. Clip her wings and any woman of 'dignity and worth' was bound to rebel. Allow her 'freedom and scope and happiness', however, and she would gladly embrace her family responsibilities.[97] Shaw identified the true enemies of the 'closeness and sacredness of the marriage tie' to be the anti-suffragists themselves, thanks to their insistence that 'the man's sphere and the woman's sphere are so entirely separate'. Their purblind resistance to reform threatened to destroy the very institution they claimed to defend.[98]

Despite agreeing with radical feminists over the failings of patriarchal marriage, mutualists refused to venerate the 'appallingly barren existence' of spinsterhood. If Christabel Pankhurst chose to be single, so be it, but champion of 'Sane Feminism' Wilma Meikle advised her not to assume that most women would find contentment in a life of 'public activities without domestic happiness'.[99] Most spinsters remained unmarried through misfortune rather than choice at a time when male emigration left a million women 'surplus' to requirements, while those who consciously spurned marriage and motherhood elected a lifestyle that 'nature *abhors*'. Meikle labelled radical feminists 'cowardly' for hiding their fear of sex behind clouds of virtue and shirking their duty to reform marriage from within.[100]

Sexual Harmony

Protecting female chastity was the principal sexual imperative underlying separate spheres. The diaries of Jeanette Marshall document how, as the unmarried daughter of a noted London surgeon, she was forbidden to read of adultery in *The Scarlet Letter* and how her sister's art classes were cancelled soon after she glimpsed a near-naked Indian male model. Interdictions of this kind testify to the Victorians' unease over sexual display. It was not that they were silent on the subject. On the contrary, theorist Michel Foucault has written of a 'veritable discursive explosion', ranging from scientific treatises on sexual dysfunction to sadomasochistic pornography and *exposés* of prostitution.[101] What was absent from these discourses was any reputable association of sex with fun. A new emphasis on the anatomical differences between male and female genitalia resulted in the widespread 'erasure of female pleasure from medical accounts of conception'. The thriving backstreet trade in dirty books illustrated how sexuality had become 'the antonym of respectability'.[102] The great debate over prostitution, meanwhile, confirmed that respectable Victorians were most comfortable talking about sex in relation to immorality and representing women as deviant 'in terms of their visible engagement with pleasure.'[103]

The public suppression of indecency was designed to aid private acts of repression. Men were warned against masturbation and expected, if not actually required, to refrain from pre- or extra-marital sex. Women's supposed innocence made their policing a matter of still greater concern, accounting for the curbs placed on the Marshall sisters mentioned above. A fit between thought and deed cannot be presumed in a society suspected of hypocrisy and quite how higher-class Victorians behaved behind closed doors remains unclear, their notorious reticence on the subject variously interpreted as evidence of prudery or the safeguarding of privacy.[104] What we do know is that public commentary presented sexuality primarily as a problem; that doctors seldom made available information on its pleasurable aspects; that prescriptive literature lauded women for their 'passionlessness'; that religious authorities proscribed intercourse except for the purposes of conception; that the lack of reliable birth control made anything else risky; and that foreign visitors marvelled at how 'deep and sheer' was the divide that separated 'virtue from debauchery' within respectable society. The Victorians' reputation for puritanism was well earned.[105]

Mutualists had no truck with this 'anti-sensual mentality', as the historian Michael Mason has labelled it. They viewed the principal function of sex to be neither procreation nor self-gratification but the creation of an exquisite concord between woman and man. The 'primitive animal instinct' for the propagation of offspring represented the sole end of intercourse only among what Havelock Ellis termed the 'lower races of mankind'.[106] Equally ignoble was the quest for individual pleasure insofar as it conflicted with the 'fusion' of two souls. Spurning the 'repression' of the 'puritan' and the 'excess' of the 'prodigal', his wife Edith called for a reformed sexuality 'wider and deeper and more joyous' than either could possibly imagine. Intercourse in its ideal state constituted an exchange of intimacies, the pooling of identities, the very embodiment of the mutual ideal.[107]

Sexual bonding required men and women to come to terms with their own and each other's natures. Men had to learn how to blend their raw passion with 'consideration for the object of desire'. Women's consent was simply essential, coercion being contrary to 'universal natural law'.[108] Men also had to renounce their privileges under a double standard that, besides being immoral and unfair, encouraged them to expect cheap thrills from prostitutes and 'coldness' in wives. And, once men neither denied female desire nor took it for granted, they had to master the 'art of understanding and pleasing women' by ministering to their singular sexual needs.[109]

The trade-off for men's surrendering their 'unreasonable licence' was that women overcame their 'unreasonable abstinence'. A woman believing herself to be 'ideally pure' was often simply 'sexually cold', claimed Maude Royden, thereby elevating 'a defect into a quality'.[110] She did not know, or was unwilling to admit, that sex was something to be enjoyed rather than endured. She had not, in Helena Swanwick's opinion, accepted that her sex drive was the match of man's:

> the supposed absence of personal feelings on the part of the woman ... is altogether out of accord with the facts of life as one knows it. Women fall in love quite as wholeheartedly as men, and when a woman falls in love with a man, the sentiments that fill her being are not in the first instance consciously racial; they are personal. She desires union with her lover, just as he desires union with her...[111]

It was vital that a woman should recognize that sex was much more than 'mere patient giving': for herself, since ecstasy was hers for the taking; for her husband, who deserved better than a wife who regarded sex with 'horror'; and for a marital bond cemented by sexual union.[112]

Mutuality in intercourse, as in mixing and marriage, promised to create equality and intimacy between the sexes. A 'union of two equals' was possible once the woman claimed her rightful share of pleasure. Intimacy came from that 'self-revelation to, and knowledge of, [one] another' obtained in conjugal union. And, as usual, mutualists made due allowance for the complementarity of man's and woman's natures. His instinct was urgent and aggressive, hers was diffuse, delicate and receptive. It was his role to initiate, hers to invite.[113] Historians such as Margaret Jackson and Sheila Jeffreys perceive this model of heterosexuality to have eroticized women's subordination and sanctioned male aggression. They charge its most famous exponent, Havelock Ellis, with having devised a 'pseudo-scientific' ideology whereby 'women could be controlled and male power maintained' and their views receive some credence from Ellis' conviction that man possessed an instinctual 'delight in domination' and woman a 'delight in submission'.[114]

Closer examination of Havelock Ellis' writings does not, however, support the view that he provided 'a justification of ... a sexuality based on "uncontrollable urges", power and violence.' Rather than arguing that 'men's sexual urges were ordained biologically and could not be controlled', he was adamant that men's wish to exert power in intercourse had to be 'held in check' by a 'consideration of what is pleasing' to women, something upon which women alone were qualified to pronounce.[115] He counselled men not to use women's apparent masochism as an excuse for brutality. 'Violence is bad in every art,' he warned, and a man who did anything contrary to his partner's wishes was guilty of the 'fatal error of yielding to his own impulse of domination.' Equally, Ellis maintained that the sexes' respective courtship roles of hunter and hunted did not make man the predator and woman the prey. Each wooed and was wooed, the woman's powers of attraction possessing all the 'intense energy' of a magnet.[116]

It is also simplistic to represent Ellis as 'prescribing women's passivity' in sex. He considered whatever passivity they exhibited to be 'only... apparent' and 'not... real' and could not abide the idea of a wife 'regard[ing] herself as the passive partner and her pleasure as negligible'.[117] A woman whose genitalia were not 'actively aroused' to lubricity would in his view experience acute discomfort in intercourse, while a man 'sufficiently coarse-grained to be satisfied with the woman's submission' committed an act of torture.[118] It followed that, far from being responsible for the 'Invention of the Frigid Woman', Ellis set out to dispel the myth that women were 'peculiarly liable to sexual anaesthesia'.[119] Frigidity where diagnosed he regarded as 'no defect on [the woman's] part' but due instead to the 'defective skill' and insensitive behaviour of the male partner who 'reserves to himself the indulgence of sex feeling'. There is correspondingly little reason to doubt the feminist intent behind Ellis' advocacy of women's 'erotic rights'.[120]

The contrasting sexual ideals of mutualists and radical feminists derived from a long-standing dispute within feminism over whether sex entailed pleasure or peril for women. Mutualists were heirs to a predominantly socialist feminist tradition extolling the 'mutual enjoyment' obtained in heterosexual intercourse. The Owenite William Thompson, in common with his early nineteenth-century contemporaries Robert Dale Owen and Richard Carlile, believed that penetrative sex lent an added 'glow' to the 'esteem and confidence existing between equals'.[121] These thinkers perceived four impediments to sexual bliss. Male selfishness and female inhibition were two, a third being what Percy Bysshe Shelley called the 'monkish and evangelical superstition' of chastity.[122] The other was the absence of effective birth control techniques, a problem addressed by a succession of best-selling if often illicit manuals detailing the use of sponges, douches and caps.

After Carlile's *Every Woman's Book* of 1826 there came George Drysdale's seminal *Elements of Social Science* (1855, revised 1857) and, most famously of all, Annie Besant's and Charles Bradlaugh's 1877 reissue of the American Charles Knowlton's *Fruits of Philosophy*.

Radical feminists drew upon the rival purity tradition of Mary Wollstonecraft and her husband William Godwin, who equated sex with disorder. Lust nullified love; passion addled reason; the conjoining of bodies produced no equivalent 'intercourse of minds'. The chastity abjured by their future son-in-law Shelley they wished 'more universally [to] prevail'.[123] And whereas William Thompson thought women men's equals in desire, Wollstonecraft applauded them for being much less 'under the influence of their appetites'. Practicality as much as primness made her fear men's 'unbridled indulgence' at a time when women's every handicap was attributed to their childbearing capacity, when conception was a lottery and when childbirth claimed the lives of many thousands of women, herself among them.[124]

Though the purity campaign expanded over the succeeding century to include opposition to all public displays of lewdness, radical feminists added only further doses of righteous indignation to Wollstonecraft's and Godwin's basic critique of heterosexuality. They considered it man's 'misfortune' that his sexuality was simply inferior to woman's. Her 'psychically developed' sensibility put his 'crude and sensuous' proclivities to shame.[125] If left unchecked, the 'foul imaginations and actions of men' subjected woman to rough usage and the risk of contracting venereal disease: problems that would grow were contraception to prevent pregnancy but incite promiscuity. And man himself did not escape unscathed, the libertine's 'enfeebled frame, his diseased tissues, his weak will, his gibbering idiocy, his raving insanity, and hideous criminality' testifying to the wages of sins of the flesh.[126] While Frances Swiney abhorred carnality and pronounced semen to be toxic, the comparatively moderate purity campaigner Ellice Hopkins accepted the possibility of mutual enjoyment in the act of conception.[127] All radical feminists nonetheless agreed that women were not to heed mutualist schemes for their sexual enlightenment. Whether induced by 'nature or... training... [or] past subjection', their 'mastery of self and sex' represented their most inimitable virtue. It was essential that they retained their purity, remaining celibate if necessary, to force men to become as 'pure and moral' as themselves.[128]

Such ideas were anathema to the antis, who endorsed the commonplace Victorian sentiment that male and female sexuality existed on 'quite different planes.' They believed man's sole aim to be the 'indulgence of masculine lust', an emotionless act bearing the imprint of his primitive will to conquer the female. Its 'urgent and pressing' nature required periodic release or, to put it more crudely, a double standard allowing men 'greater latitude'.[129] Woman possessed no semblance of desire and viewed intercourse as 'nothing more than . . . a means of ensuring maternity'.[130] But impregnation aside, 'submission to intimate conjugal relations' was a simple wifely obligation. The more 'distasteful' it was for her, the more 'merit' there was in her 'self-sacrifice', according to the perverted logic of Catholic physiologist St George Mivart, since 'no love is worthy of the name, or possesses any real value, unless it is consecrated by the idea of duty'. Sexual intimacy was inconceivable between partners seeking such divergent ends.[131]

Rutting in the manner envisaged by anti-suffragists struck mutualists like Havelock Ellis as 'unnatural and repressive' in the extreme. He feared that the unstinting exercise of male passions enforced the 'subservience of women as physically the weaker and sexually the more passive' sex: which, of course, was precisely what the antis planned.[132] Mutualists also refused to believe men to be so debased or women so elevated as the radical feminists made out. For men to possess a strong sex drive was not a matter of 'fault or defeat' on their part. Their 'excesses and errors in conjugality' were due to ignorance rather than the 'reckless sensuality' attributed to them in purity horror-stories about child-trafficking and VD.[133] In any case, argued writer and social reformer Louise Creighton, to dwell on the 'weakness and wickedness' of men hindered cross-sex cooperation against vice. Her jibe against purity campaigners' 'innocence [born] of ignorance' reflected mutualist suspicions of their sexual predilections.[134] Havelock Ellis alone identified lesbianism within the women's movement and his allegations have only recently received some historical corroboration from Martin Pugh's research into the relationship between Emmeline Pankhurst and composer Ethel Smythe.[135] More typical was the suggestion that 'incorruptible purity' came a little too easily to the 'desexualised' spinsters associated with radical feminism. 'A woman who has no sex instincts will speak and think of men as though, because they have, there is something low and animal in their nature,' Maude Royden complained. In this, if in little else, did she share common ground with birth control campaigner Stella Browne, who criticized those 'cold women' whose 'perfect mania for Prohibition' stemmed from their sexual inexperience. For woman to enjoy all that sex could offer, she had to surrender her 'martyr's crown.'[136]

From Sex War to Great War

Mutualists envisaged the relationship between the sexes becoming 'much more harmonious, much more humane, much more cooperative in the best sense, much more mental, much more spiritual, much more monogamous, and in every way much more equal than it is today.' Their model derived coherence from the manner in which each of its interlocking elements addressed discord under separate spheres. Segregation was intrinsically divisive, marriage was marred by 'fatal reticence' and sexual incompatibility stemmed from the misapprehension that love was to woman what lust was to man. Sex antagonism was equated with 'sex misunderstanding', with each sex's 'profound ignorance' of the other guaranteeing friction.[137] Mutualist solutions accordingly represented tiers of a larger whole, with mixing supporting marriage and marriage, sex. Boys and girls raised together would enter marriage well matched. A coeducated wife supported her husband's career 'without losing an atom of her womanliness' while the man knew better than to be a chauvinist 'hog'.[138] Joyful wedlock and sexual harmony in turn brought each other to a pitch of perfection, a 'nobler sexual love' forming the natural concomitant to a 'nobler conception of marriage' in which 'the body is equally honoured with the spirit'.[139]

Yet, however appealing the mutualists' model of loving interdependence and however inventive their solutions to sex antagonism, the rancour surrounding suffragette militancy threatened to drown them out in the years immediately preceding World War One. 'War is declared,' announced Christabel Pankhurst following the physical and sexual assault of suffragettes by policemen on the 'Black Friday' of 18 November 1910 and, though calling a ceasefire in response to the Asquith government's Conciliation Bill on suffrage, her mother decided upon 'unrelenting warfare' in the wake of its collapse in November 1911. An arson campaign launched in January 1913 turned the WSPU into a fully-fledged guerrilla movement, its firebrands becoming outlaws as railways stations, country houses and a packed Dublin theatre were put to the torch.[140]

As the WSPU's 'battle of righteousness' intensified, their target broadened to include not only 'all anti-suffrage forces, but . . . all neutral and non-active forces' as well. This effectively meant all men, the entire sex being held responsible for the 'political disfranchisement, the industrial robbery, and the sex exploitation of women'.[141] Although a man 'prepared to be actively a friend' nominally escaped censure, it was hard to see how he might establish his bona fides once the WSPU severed contact with male sympathizers in 1913. 'This is a women's movement and can only be conducted by women,' Christabel Pankhurst announced.[142] Also ostracized were women members uncomfortable with the WPSU's hardline stance. Emmeline Pethwick-Lawrence and husband Frederick left in the autumn of 1912, taking with them fellow spirit Elizabeth Robins and their tarnished conviction that suffragism was 'not directed in any sense *against* men'. In 1914 Christabel Pankhurst expelled sister Sylvia's East London Federation for its ties to the male labour movement.[143]

Antis responded in kind to escalating militancy. They became more organized, the single-sex anti-suffrage bodies for men and women established in 1908 merging into a unified National League for Opposing Woman Suffrage in 1911. While this remained a respectable organization, barracking and violence by antis made it next to impossible for suffragettes to hold any public meetings after 1912.[144] And as anti-suffragist rowdies answered suffragettes blow for blow, so did their propagandists match radical feminist vituperation in such works as E. Belfort Bax's *The Fraud of Feminism* and Sir Almroth Wright's *The Unexpurgated Case Against Woman Suffrage* (both issued in 1913). No quarter could be granted to what Wright considered to be 'sexually embittered' militants in whom all had 'turned into gall and bitterness of heart and hatred of men.'[145]

'Never had the relations of men and women been so uneasy as they were in the opening days of 1914,' wrote H.G. Wells. But when World War One erupted that same year, the diminution of sex antagonism seemed sudden and dramatic. Christabel Pankhurst's first reaction to the outbreak of war was to welcome the providential destruction of a 'man-made civilisation, hideous and cruel': 'This great war...is Nature's vengeance – is God's vengeance upon the people who held women in subjection...[and] for generations past sacrifice[d] women and the race to their lusts'.[146] Yet days later, her mother announced a formal truce in the 'war of women against men'. Following the declaration of a government amnesty, suffragettes became Britannias and transferred their wrath from man to Germans. In November 1914, Emmeline Pankhurst credited the war for reminding her how much 'nobility' resided in man's breast 'in addition to the other thing which we all deplore.' And by war's end, Christabel Pankhurst stressed that her short-lived Women's Party was in no sense 'actuated by sex antagonism.'[147]

No longer confronted by 'wild women' apparently intent on emasculating men, anti-suffragists found it impossible to sustain support for their own brand of sex war.[148] The end of militancy allowed moderate antis like Asquith to stage an otherwise awkward U-turn concerning suffrage and left diehards isolated when clause four of the Representation of the People Bill came up for debate. June 1917 was an inopportune moment for anti MPs to rehearse arguments about the 'hysterical and sentimental...nature of women' and claim that 'woman's weakness is her real strength' given that women were performing heavy labour alongside men in state-run armament factories. Far more appropriate were the sentiments expressed by Leicester MP, sometime secretary to the Fellowship of the New Life and future prime minister Ramsay MacDonald:

> there must be some bond of respect between the two [sexes], and there can be no such thing as a really effective respect between one who is conscious of his own superiority and who regards the other as something over which he must exercise the right of protection.

Soundly beaten, the National League for Opposing Woman Suffrage wound itself up in April 1918.[149]

For their part, mutualists shared the ambivalence identified by historian Susan Grayzel among other wartime commentators on sexual politics.[150] Gloomiest was their large contingent of pacifists. Helena Swanwick lamented the appeal of 'gross and immediate' sexual satisfaction among men and women segregated by the call-up and, for all his enthusiasm for a single sexual standard, Bertrand Russell declared the 'heavy' price of women's presumed promiscuity to be that of making 'almost all sex relations rather frivolous.' Indulgence and ordered progress did not mix.[151] Yet experimentation of a more acceptable sort was in evidence in the coeducational Little Commonwealth and in the British Society for the Study of Sex Psychology, established immediately before the war with the unmistakably mutualist vision of 'men and women thinking and working together for a common understanding...in matters which vitally concern both sexes alike.'[152] Together, the two signalled the emergence of a sex radical strain of mutuality, much as Marie Stopes' blockbuster of a marriage manual *Married Love* (1918) prefigured interwar efforts to divorce the sexual teachings of Edward Carpenter and Havelock Ellis from their utopian vision of 'far-reaching social reform' (see chapter two). Furthermore, the misgivings of Swanwick and Russell were eclipsed in most mutualists' minds by the wartime enfranchisement of women aged thirty and above, however partial and overdue. The abatement of sex antagonism struck Victor Gollancz as one of wartime's 'few happy results'.[153]

Mutuality, then, had a good war on the whole. Its adversaries had been largely silenced, H.G. Wells noting that the women's contribution to the war effort exploded anti-suffragists' every prejudice and that the burgeoning 'friendliness between people of opposite sexes' promised to destroy both chauvinistic 'gallantry' and the suffragettes' 'hostile distaste' for men.[154] War work and hospital visiting removed the vestiges of chaperonage, prompting Vera Brittain to declare it 'quite thrilling to be an unprotected female' in 1915. Women's enfranchisement dispelled the most manifestly unjust divide between the sexes. And, with the relations between men and women in public life finally resolved to general satisfaction, attention transferred from the political to the personal and to how emancipation might be accommodated in everyday interactions between women and men. Before the war, such questions had attracted starkly divergent solutions from radical feminists, anti-suffragists and mutualists. But the weakening of the sex antagonists by the combined forces of war and women's enfranchisement left the way clear for mutuality to become the new common-sense concerning private life. There remained the small matter of making the ideal real.[155]

2

The Great Experiment

Mutualists and Malcontents, c. 1918–45

The Great War and the 'great experiment' of female enfranchisement lent sexual politics what novelist Naomi Mitchison termed their 'curious, transitional' air after 1918.[1] A flurry of laws that dealt with the remaining political business of emancipation culminated in 1928 with the granting of universal suffrage to women, amid hopes of forging 'truer comradeship and closer cooperation'. The old practice of 'trying to divide mankind into sexes' lay at the root of 'so many of our troubles', remarked the first woman to sit in the Commons, Nancy Astor, and it was this division and its attendant sex antagonism that prime minister Stanley Baldwin promised emancipation would heal. The 'ground and justification' for feminist agitation and anti-feminist reaction had in his view been removed, the former being satisfied and the latter discredited. Political equality would bring about something he was sure all longed to see: the 'rational companionship' of men and women 'working together for the regeneration of their country and for the regeneration of the world.'[2]

The political emancipation of women left unresolved the hard task of finding the 'right use of this freedom', as Baldwin put it. This was the revised Woman Question: not whether or not women should be equal, but what equality meant. Uncertainty affected every aspect of women's status. In politics, the apparently emancipatory intent of a welter of egalitarian legislation was contradicted by a public sector ban on employing married women. In education, an official report on curricular differences between the sexes contained a riot of conflicting objectives.[3] In economics, writer Sylvia Anthony discerned no 'accepted code' regulating the relations of the sexes. In biology, such was the ambivalence over the capacities of women that Havelock Ellis displayed a new circumspection in the revised edition of his authoritative *Man and Woman*.[4] And in personal relationships, contemporaries thought emancipation to have wrought the greatest transformation. 'Equality before the law, careers for women, universal suffrage are as nothing,' argued Christian author A.G. Pite, 'compared with the changes that are taking place in the attitude of men and women to one another, modifying every habit of courtship, marriage and family life'. The outcome struck otherwise sober observers as potentially 'far more significant for the race ... than either the Reformation or the discovery of America.'[5]

One thing at least seemed certain: that the sex antagonism so prevalent before the war had all but dissipated after it. The great showdown between the 'feminine principle' and its masculine counterpart appeared to many commentators to have been dispelled by suffrage and the war which, as with any 'violent storm', had magically 'cleared the air' thereafter.[6] What remained of the anti-feminist cause was divested of its anti-suffragism: once its focus, now a dead force. Radical feminism shrunk to the point of almost total invisibility, only the odd splenetic book reprising the prewar fury of the purity campaigners and the suffragettes.[7] Though the deaths and disabilities suffered by men in the First World War threatened to exacerbate the 'surplus woman' problem, such anxieties abated in the 1930s as the marriage rate recovered.[8] Now that the sex war was over, argued H.G. Wells, men and women were rediscovering their 'inexorable need of each other', their attentions focused on matters of 'mutual adjustment'.[9]

The resolution of the suffrage question, the attenuation of sex antagonism and the confusion surrounding emancipation's impact on private life made the years after 1918 singularly propitious ones for the cause of mutuality. To begin with, mutualists were in the happy position of having been allied to suffragism but neither limited to it nor tainted by militancy. Mutuality offered what those tired of sex antagonism most wanted to hear: that coming to terms with equality would be a painless, even pleasurable, process. 'Man need not fear the competition of women,' stated popular writer Elsie Lang, for the 'true woman does not want to compete but to cooperate', her very nature making collaboration 'inevitable' in the opinion of poet and translator Willa Muir.[10] Moreover, with the 'Woman Problem' rapidly dissolving into an 'almost infinite series of variations of the problem of association between men and women', mutualists provided unusually clear and plausible solutions. They had long maintained that women's suffrage was only one element of a much broader revolution, its achievement a necessary preliminary to the larger task of improving personal relationships between the sexes. It was simple for them to present their ready-made programme for mixing, companionate marriage and sexual compatibility as the natural next step in achieving a rapprochement between men and women.[11]

The ease with which mutuality was yoked to the cause of women's wider emancipation accounted for its intellectual ascendancy after 1918. Its popularity among the intelligentsia was registered in the platform of the Federation of Progressive Societies and Individuals (or FPSI), a thirties curio which included among its officials the cream of forward-looking intellectuals: C.E.M. Joad, Harold Nicolson, Allan Young and Oliver Baldwin from the abortive New Party, feminists Vera Brittain and Rebecca West, sex reformer Janet Chance, psychologist Cyril Burt, psychoanalyst J.C. Flügel, cartoonist David Low, journalist Kingsley Martin, social scientist Barbara Wootton, scientist Julian Huxley and his novelist brother Aldous, plus Bertrand Russell, H.G. Wells and Leonard Woolf.[12] Accompanying the FPSI's proposals for disarmament and world government was an unmistakably mutualist platform concerning personal relationships. As a proponent of mixing and the 'interdependence of educational reform and sexual reform', the FPSI backed coeducation and affiliated the Woodcraft Folk, a sort of unisex Scouts for the *Manchester Guardian*-reading classes. As a sponsor of marriage reform, it pronounced the 'savage and absurd' nature of the existing laws to be obvious to all of its members and created a Marriage Law Reform Committee just after the Second World War. And as a supporter of sexual enlightenment, it fostered the Abortion Law Reform Society and liaised with the World League for Sexual Reform. Such institutional backing lent weight to the sweeping claim of communist and eugenicist Eden Paul that 'Intelligent persons, today, are sexual reformers.'[13]

Mutuality's appeal extended beyond the drawing rooms of Bloomsbury to the adjacent universities as ranking academics gave its doctrines the imprimatur of received wisdom. Anthropologists Bronislaw Malinowski and Edward Westermarck put their weight behind companionate marriage.[14] Educationalist J.J. Findlay cited the eradication of patriarchy and sex rivalry, and the advancement of democracy and a 'sense of comradeship', as compelling arguments in favour of coeducation, his partiality being almost unanimously shared by a 1946 sample of teachers.[15] Moral philosopher (and future idol of Tony Blair's) John Macmurray called for the sex act to become a 'means of communion' created through an 'essentially mutual' self-giving. Psychologist Ian Suttie's influential theory of a 'Taboo on Tenderness' pathologized the irrational and 'intensely anti-feminist' desire of males to segregate themselves from females, urging them instead to become less stand-offish as adolescents, more nurturing as fathers and altogether better 'comrades' to their womenfolk. What had once been the rhetoric of utopian politics was being translated into an argot of expertise.[16]

If anything signalled mutuality's burgeoning respectability, it was its endorsement by the Church of England at the Lambeth Conference of 1930. In contrast to the reactionary tone of the 1920 gathering, the Conference's 1930 report on marriage and sex finally acknowledged that women were no longer 'chattels' subject to 'hide-bound tradition'. In true mutualist fashion, it envisaged women's emancipation less in terms of independence than as an opportunity to forge a 'true partnership between man and woman in all the concerns of life'. This it welcomed although, adopting that tone of muddy compromise subsequently so characteristic of Anglicanism, it was quick to warn of its possible 'exaggerations' in marriage. The Church's stance on sex carried similar provisos. While applauding the 'clear atmosphere of candour, honesty and truth' in which sexuality could now be considered, and appreciating that married love promised to transport intercourse from an 'animal' baseness to a 'higher spiritual' plane, it denounced abortion in thunderous terms. Yet, however tentatively, the bishops gave their blessing to artificial methods of birth control under certain circumstances. Mutuality had gained a major convert.[17]

Revolution or Reform?

As the reach of the mutual ideal broadened after 1918, so two strains of mutuality emerged: what I term the sex radicals and the Christian mutualists. The sex radicals were the apostolic successors to the prewar mutualists and included in their number the educationalist A.S. Neill, the gynaecologist Norman Haire and the philosopher Bertrand Russell together with his wife Dora Russell, the bohemian novelist Ethel Mannin and the still-active Havelock Ellis. Christian mutualists were comparative latecomers to the mutualist cause. Before the war, clerics had divided over suffragism and provided succour to all sides of the argument. After it, although 'Mad' Dean Inge held out against women's emancipation and the Bishop of Salisbury refused to countenance sexual reform, something of a consensus emerged among liberal Christians that mutuality offered the best hope of reconciliation in the aftermath of the suffrage campaign. Among Christian mutualists might be counted such prominent Protestants as the King's chaplain G.E. Newsom, his personal physician Lord Dawson of Penn, theologian W.F. Lofthouse, social reformer Claud Mullins and birth control campaigner Marie Stopes, whose idiosyncratic brand of Quakerism granted her visions of God.[18]

The two schools of thought clashed head-on over religion. Sex radicals continued the free-thinking tradition of contempt for Christianity's degradation of women and 'condemnation of sexuality'.[19] The Russells considered the Church to be a malign institution. It had forced women to conform to a 'stupid ideal' through venerating the sexless Mary and demonizing the oversexed Eve. It had initially scorned marriage in favour of monasticism and then 'brutalised' it into a patriarchal institution. Worst of all, it had 'maligned, suppressed, abused and distorted' the sexual instinct.[20] Dora Russell was duly sardonic: 'Christianity, it is true, enjoins that the "twain become one flesh"; it has need to enjoin and enforce it, since all the rest of its teaching goes to prevent so miraculous a consummation. Yet supreme unions exist: they exist in spite, not because, of orthodox Christian doctrine.'[21] Though sex radicals chose 'modern knowledge' over faith, their gospel of pleasure contained its own mystical elements. Bertrand Russell went so far as to call for a new 'religion' through which lovers merged into a global consciousness.[22]

The sacrilegious nature of sex radicalism at once offended Christian mutualists and pricked them into disowning the more antediluvian aspects of their religion. Theologian Kenneth Ingram confessed 'orthodox Christian sex-morality' to be a 'sex-obsessed' creed too reactionary to survive in a 'progressively-minded age'.[23] Yet rather than exchange one muddled faith for the 'Unreasonableness of Anti-Christianity', like-minded thinkers devoted themselves instead to Biblical exegesis of a profoundly revisionist nature. They contrasted the patriarchal doctrines of the Hebrew Bible with the purportedly more enlightened ideas of the New Testament and distinguished between Christ's teachings on personal relationships and the 'dogmatic laws laid down by his followers.'[24] Writers variously 'repudiate[d]' Pauline teachings on marriage, condemned the 'perversion' of monastic celibacy and admitted to the over-representation of 'religious people' among the ranks of the repressed. This fusion of piety and progressivism allowed Christian mutualists to advance their agenda as if it were a holy cause.[25]

The contrasting ideological underpinnings of sex radicalism and Christian mutuality translated into respectively revolutionary and evolutionary approaches to the reformation of personal relationships. Sex radicals relished innovation and were consequently unfazed, indeed excited, by the manner in which women's emancipation had shattered 'all the old concepts of morality'. The 'feeble folk' who fretted about the instability of contemporary marriage were in Havelock Ellis' opinion pitting themselves against an ineluctable progress best met with a 'serene mind'.[26] Sex radicals had little time for incremental reform. 'Society exists for the life of personal relationship. Personal life does not exist for society,' stated John Macmurray, meaning that institutions had to cede to interpersonal desires rather than the other way around. Certain that change was inevitable in the wake of women's emancipation, eager to ditch the 'accumulated litter of customs and taboos' and confident of their 'complete scientific objectivity', sex radicals set out to restructure relations between men and women from scratch.[27]

Christian mutualists trod a more cautious line. They shared sex radicals' enthusiasm that the 'separation of the sexes' had been 'finally and utterly rejected', but were acutely conscious of manifold 'Difficulties of Transition' including marital strife, hedonism, heightened sex-consciousness, the ambition of some women to pursue unsuitably masculine occupations and the resistance of a few 'old fogeys' wishing to maintain a 'purely masculine life'.[28] Moreover, they slammed those sex radicals audacious enough to believe in 'no hard and fast line between masculinity and femininity'. The 'enormous far-reaching differences between the sexes' had in their view to be respected, for to do otherwise was to invite the proliferation of butch women and fey men.[29] The 'duty of examining and revising Victorian traditions' imposed on Christian mutualists by women's emancipation entailed disciplined progress, not foolhardy experimentation. Whereas sex radicals started from first principles and sought to build new relationships around them, they saw in mutuality a means of effecting a 'drastic reform' of existing societal arrangements stopping short of 'anarchic revolution'.[30]

The sex radical and Christian mutualist blueprints for mixing, marriage and sexuality contrasted accordingly. Sex radicals demonstrated their commitment to coeducation by founding a new wave of independent progressive schools including the Russells' Beacon Hill (1927), the Elmhirsts' Dartington Hall (1926) and A.S. Neill's Summerhill (1924), proclaimed by him to be 'the happiest school in the world'.[31] These establishments pursued the standard coeducational aim of eliminating 'conscious ignorance and…unconscious antagonisms' through more radical means than their prewar predecessors, including routine nudity, unabashed sex education and even mixed toilets some seventy years before *Ally McBeal*.[32] Christian mutualist coeducationalists opted for less libertarian methods. Whereas A.S. Neill encouraged his pupils to be 'actively heterosexual', the Quaker couple running Wennington was willing to teach adolescents all about sex provided they did not engage in it. 'Flirting', let alone fornication, was regarded as an 'unwise spoiling of a good thing' by ordained minister and sex manual author Leslie Weatherhead.[33] Christian mutualists hoped that a 'happy and bracing fellowship' of a socially sanctioned kind would diminish the appeal of 'undesirable' mixed free-for-alls and with it the 'strain of conscious sexual desire'.[34]

Marriage put sex radicals in the mood to experiment. Its 'old form' seemed to them wholly obsolescent and the demand for 'mutual liberty' made change inevitable if as yet undefined. Various alternatives surfaced: trial marriages of the kind espoused by the American Ben B. Lindsey and endorsed by Ellis and the Russells; the free love favoured by John Macmurray, Irene Clephane and Ethel Mannin; the loose, non-cohabiting arrangement preferred by Vera Brittain; and J.D. Unwin's futuristic 'Hopousian' scheme permitting a choice between continent 'Alpha' and contractual 'Beta' couplings.[35] Common to all was a hankering for 'something more adventurous, more fearless, more bold' than conventional marriage, plus a commitment to pluralism. 'Every kind of matrimonial arrangement should be allowed, provided there is no compulsion', maintained Dora Russell, the rider indicating the necessity of divorce reform.[36] Christian mutualists more straightforwardly favoured a new companionate form of marriage (see chapter four). They blanched at the prospect that women's emancipation would bring about the 'destruction of the family and an era of unlimited sexual freedom', regarding it instead as a chance to shunt marriage away from a 'stiff sort of legalism' towards a much closer 'comradeship'.[37] Divorce was accepted, if at all, as a necessary evil: a sentiment more in keeping with the 1923 and 1937 legal reforms than that easy route to 'happy marriages' spoken of by sex radicals. With the institution of wedlock retained but its patriarchal aspects removed, the 'true basis for the family' might be restored: 'the mutuality or reciprocity of duty and respect…between husband and wife.'[38]

Starker still were their differences over sex. Christian mutuality had strong roots in the moderate purity movement. From its less sex antagonistic wing came preacher Maude Royden and Alison Neilans, long-time editor of *The Shield: A Review of Moral and Social Hygiene*, while marriage reformers Edward Griffith and Herbert Gray were both involved with the British Social Hygiene Council. Seeking to steer a path between the 'rake' and the 'prude', Christian mutualists made great play of the distinction between wrong-headed repression and righteous self-control. Repression when externally enforced removed moral choice, and when internally imposed denied true expression of an individual's 'sex instinct'.[39] Self-control was in contrast a matter of 'Healthy-mindedness' which contained the 'overplus' of sexual energy without inducing either the 'evasion' of excessive guilt or the 'obsession' of over-indulgence.[40] Sex radicals thought little of continence and even less of purity conventionally defined. 'So-called purity' was so much 'sexual correctness' valued only by those who mistook 'outward formality' for an inner rectitude.[41] They instead advocated an 'innate purity' obtained not through self-control but a 'wholesome attitude of mind'. The 'deep intimacy and the intense companionship of happy mutual love' overrode the claims of orthodox morality and social sanction.[42]

Christian mutualists and sex radicals consequently possessed opposing visions of a single sexual standard. Both accepted that holding women to stricter standards than men was iniquitous in theory and ruinous in practice. At issue was whether men should henceforth aspire to achieve women's degree of continence, or whether women should be free to descend to men's lower level. Christian mutualists maintained that the 'Christian standard of purity' was 'equally binding on both sexes'. Casual sex they condemned on the grounds that, since intercourse was the 'most perfect form of union that human beings know', its highest purpose could only be honoured within the sanctified setting of a loving marriage.[43] Were sex to be governed by this single and higher standard, they believed that the 'grosser temptations' of lust and 'selfish gratification' would be vanquished, prostitution would disappear and the unmarried would sublimate their drives in physical exertion and civic duty.[44]

These arguments exasperated the sex radicals. Janet Chance credited dissolute men for 'seeking a positive good' under the double standard, albeit at a 'great cost to others'. Female virtue had in Bertrand Russell's opinion been based upon a 'fear of hell-fire and...pregnancy' now rendered irrelevant by secularization and contraception. 'To impose upon men the moral fetters which hitherto had only been endured by women' was therefore unfair on men and undesired by women.[45] It made more sense to conceive of sexual expression in terms of equal opportunities, so that 'if men are allowed pre-nuptial intercourse (as in fact they are), women must be allowed it also.' Since such undeniable ills as prostitution and venereal disease were the result of 'thwarting natural instincts' rather than licence, a relaxation of controls promised to reduce sex's uglier aspects.[46] As for adultery, its main problem was less the act itself than the irrational possessiveness it inspired in cuckolds, and as such was neither adequate grounds for divorce nor even cause for jealousy: 'The ready acceptance of new loves, new loyalties in the life of husband, wife or lover is an essential part of a revised sex ethic.'[47]

The two schools also differed over birth control, a pressing concern to mutualists following the establishment of Marie Stopes' first clinic in 1921. Without some sort of family planning, they agreed that couples' desire for 'common work and companionship' was liable to degenerate into 'complete demoralisation and mutual antagonism'. With it, spouses could avoid the twin evils of 'excessive child-bearing' and enforced abstinence.[48] Disputes arose over how far contraception should facilitate pleasure rather than simply space out births. Christian mutualists opposed the use of contraceptives for reasons of 'selfishness, luxury or mere convenience'. Preventing all births for pleasure's sake was an 'abomination', most especially when employing abortion, whereas the responsible use of family planning methods by spouses 'joined in the fearless and tender love of true marriage' redounded to the 'glory of God'.[49] But to sex radicals, artificial birth control signalled 'Man's Coming of Age', not to mention woman's. 'Knowledge of contraception has placed the woman on an equality with the man,' argued writer Irene Clephane, her enthusiasm for the potentialities of being a sexual 'free agent' illustrating exactly what the Christian mutualists were anxious to avoid.[50]

Sex, then, exemplified the measured progressivism of the Christian mutualists and the devil-may-care daring of the sex radicals. The former likened sex to electricity in its ability to perform 'miracles of light and warmth' when 'harnessed to social needs' but possessed of a 'lightning power of sudden destruction' when unleashed. To them, sex radicals appeared to be 'Decadents' out to debase the sacrament of sex due to their 'total inability to distinguish between pleasure and happiness'.[51] Yet sex radicals viewed their mission in no less moralistic terms. In pressing for a sexual enlightenment extending beyond the scope of bourgeois ethics, they too aimed at building a whole new society founded on heterosexual harmony. 'The struggle will go on,' promised Charles Edward Hempstead in his banned sex manual:

> surely one day we shall stand whence we may see the Eastern Sea, and look into the sunrise breaking across a world where men are lovely in their hopes and fearless in their thoughts and in their speech, where all things may be understood and all things spoken, where men and women may come together with straight eyes.

For all their differences, the two strains of mutuality therefore complemented each other. The sex radicals devised a libertarian agenda for the reform of personal relationships that would later come to be called permissiveness. While they were the prophets, Christian mutualists acted as popularizers when converting sex radicals' ideas into a more moderate and family-friendly form. What the first thought today, the second adopted tomorrow, rendering respectable what had once seemed unacceptable and gradually transforming the *avant garde* into the *de rigeur*.[52]

Dissent

So what opposition remained to mutuality? For a start, a few muted protests from what might be termed feminist irreconcilables. They were not on the whole the same radical feminists of old. Suffragettes were the victims of what one historian has described as their 'ironic constitutionalism' in believing the franchise to be the ultimate prize.[53] Their mission accomplished, Emmeline and Christabel Pankhurst opened an 'English Tea-Shop of Good Hope' on the French Riviera while their followers pursued welfarist agendas, relieved that they had 'not got to trouble with things of that sort any more'.[54] Equally pronounced was the demise of the radical feminist purity crusade. This was not a result of an anti-feminist backlash, as historians Susan Kingsley Kent and Sheila Jeffreys have contended.[55] On the contrary, purity was viewed by self-styled sexual progressives to have been an inextricable element of an outmoded patriarchal system, successively imposed by men on women and then on men by women in a pointless struggle to gain the moral upper hand. The old maid engrossed in 'purity campaigns and societies for the suppression of vice' remained as unloved a figure as ever.[56] But mutualists liked to think that succeeding her was a new generation of 'younger feminists' averse to elevating the spiritual above the carnal. 'Modern feminists are no longer so anxious as the feminists of thirty years ago to curtail the "vices" of men,' thought Bertrand Russell: 'they ask rather that what is permitted to men shall be permitted also to them. Their predecessors sought equality in moral slavery, whereas they seek equality in moral freedom.'[57]

Feminist opposition to mutuality consequently never cohered into a movement in this period. It is better characterized as a sense of unease concerning the 'cant about . . . comradeship' raised in the minds of feminists as a whole, even those like Maude Royden ordinarily well-disposed to mutuality. As such, it was not readily reducible to any 'old'–'new' feminist divide and only occasionally found full expression in the work of such oddballs as writer Dorothy Abb, etiquette expert Doris Langley Moore and the would-be woman Thomas Baty (aka Irene Clyde). These irreconcilables refused to bury the hatchet of the sex war. Power was a zero-sum game; woman's 'advances' were at man's 'expense': so naturally he tried to fob her off with the amiable fiction that the sexes had to 'advance together' and that 'feminism has been replaced by humanism'.[58] Equally fatuous was the idea of men and women being 'equal and opposite', all talk of 'two nicely balanced clans' serving to sanction inequality. As for the promise of shared sexual pleasure, irreconcilables warned women not to 'listen too deferentially to man' on the subject of their own desires. Expecting ardour instead of coldness from women was just another male trick designed to pacify the compliant and stigmatize the deviant.[59]

Nor were the irreconcilables impressed by the reality behind the rhetoric. They considered mixing to be admirable in theory but flawed in practice due to the resistance of men and the deference of women. Vera Brittain's experience of mixed organizations was that men asserted control, a disposition traced back by her fellow writer and housemate Winifred Holtby to their 'active, dominating' sex instinct.[60] Maude Royden thought it 'hardly possible for a convinced feminist to doubt that coeducation is the ideal education', yet worried that it was impractical given the prevalence of inequality outside the school setting. Mixed schools paid and promoted men more than women, while unassertive schoolgirls were 'apt to resign initiative and leadership to boys'. Royden reflected fondly upon the single-sex activities of the suffrage campaign in which women had gained self-confidence in the absence of men.[61]

Companionate marriage appeared impossible to Baty so long as the mutualist rhetoric of complementarity disguised the truth that man's 'active, superior and imperative' role made him master of a woman taught to be 'passive, inferior and submissive':

> It is obvious that marriage, as an institution, must inevitably, so long as this unnatural and fiendish distortion of character persists, be the cause of unhappiness, restlessness and discord. People say that 'each sex finds its completeness in marriage': but it is a shabby completeness...

All talk of spouses' '"equal but different" share in their marital duties' was in his view so much 'sentimentalist' guff.[62] Two lines of attack presented themselves to feminist irreconcilables opposed to mutualist conceptions of shared sexual pleasure. Baty held intercourse to be an act of 'seizure...subjection and control' in which the man used the woman as he chose. Though now prettified by 'protestations of equality, mutuality and affection', the 'naked reality' of its animal brutality could not ultimately be denied.[63] A contrasting argument was advanced by Doris Langley Moore, who regarded the notion of complementary sex instincts to be one more variation on a tired Victorian theme. Men were not 'essentially ardent and dominating'. Nor were women 'essentially passive, coy, retiring', but had instead been forced to hide their 'polygamous hankerings' under a veil of monogamy and maternal love due to social mores and multiple pregnancies. Women would turn promiscuous if men ever dared let them.[64]

Scepticism about the practical effects of political emancipation, awareness of the contrast between egalitarian intentions and iniquitous outcomes, a keen understanding of the power differences inherent in heterosexual relationships and a preference for 'feminism' over 'femininity': here were the germs of that demolition of the mutual ideal undertaken a generation later by the women's liberation movement. Yet irreconcilable opposition was handicapped in two major respects. The first was its marginality. Its few forthright advocates were obscure in the extreme, with the best-known among them, Baty, holed up in Japan and circulating his views through a privately printed journal distributed to 250 sympathizers.[65] The second problem was mutuality's kinship with feminism. Mutualists supported female enfranchisement and presented their ideas as the natural corollary of women's civic emancipation. Moreover, their message of harmony chimed with the desire noted by Susan Kingsley Kent for interwar feminists to eschew the 'slightest hint of sex war.'[66] To this strong pull even irreconcilables were not entirely immune, with Baty favouring coeducation and Abb entreating feminists to relinquish their 'old...anti-man attitude' in return for men's acceptance of women's equality. Then, she hoped, both might 'work together freely instead of dissipating their energies over civil war.' Perhaps the gulf between the mutualists and the irreconcilables was not altogether unbridgeable.[67]

A more full-throated challenge to mutuality came from anti-feminists including the modernists D.H. Lawrence and Wyndham Lewis, conservative moralists Dean Inge and C.K. Munro and such self-deprecatory women as teacher Charlotte Cowdroy and doctor and novelist Arabella Kenealey. Their undisputed leader was Anthony M. Ludovici, the cultivated, cat-loving and by all accounts charming erstwhile secretary to Rodin: a champion of aristocracy, enemy of democracy and writer of no fewer than eight anti-feminist works.[68] In common with mutualists and in contrast to feminist irreconcilables, anti-feminists believed in a complementarity of sorts between the sexes. The 'most excellent previsions and provisions of Nature' made men and women 'naturally dependent upon each other in every human relation,' Kenealey claimed: 'a dispensation which engenders reciprocal trust, affection and comradeship.' The catch was that an anti-feminist conception of complementarity entailed not equality but a hierarchy between master and servant. Man was without question 'the senior of the two sexes' and derived 'immense advantages' from his superior physical and mental powers.[69] Woman was a complex of disabilities, her innate flaws 'so essential a part of her vital equipment' that to tamper with them was to jeopardize her femininity and with it the future of the race. 'Nature has tied woman down to the earth by the leg and there she stays,' anti-feminists stated, to breed and rear and obey.[70] What did men render to women in return? Sustenance, semen, protection from other men, a chivalry confirming female inferiority and a mastery so enforced that women found it a 'joy to obey and no indignity, no hardship to serve.' It was a far cry from the sort of interdependence that mutualists had in mind.[71]

This savage creed, premised as it was on the inconceivability of true intimacy and equality between men and women, made antis reject every aspect of mutualists' plans for mixing, marriage and sex. Segregation was the customary condition of males and females according to anti-feminist lore, universally upheld by taboos and moderated only through limited contact in sex and marriage.[72] Man was happiest with his fellows and freed from the tedium and 'crushing responsibilities' of

51

domestic life. The need for same-sex friendship was weaker in women due to their family responsibilities and presumed cattiness, but those unfortunates without husband and children were best served by the 'medieval system of respectable and honourable sequestration for old maids'.[73] Anti-feminists consequently regarded the 'hugger-mugger of the sexes' so evident between the wars to be an artificial and unwelcome novelty. 'The House of Commons, the County Court, the hunting field, the playing field, the billiard room': nowhere now remained barred to women.[74] Androgyny seemed certain to follow. The recessive masculine traits of women became dominant if over-exposed to men, which in turn served to enervate and even emasculate vulnerable males.[75] Echoing the arguments employed by the boys' club leaders discussed in chapter three, antis argued that mixing was especially hazardous during childhood. Given that the 'whole everything' concerning males and females rested on 'otherness', D.H. Lawrence urged that boys and girls be kept apart. Familiarity in adolescence stripped them of their 'vital sex polarity' and substituted a 'sterilising' uniformity, a 'nice clean intimacy': the comradeship of 'neuters'.[76]

Antis thought that the mutualist model of marriage took insufficient account of the divergent interests of man and wife. Woman's principal concern was not marriage but maternity, her husband being viewed as an 'instrument' to support her brood. As such, she offered 'no reciprocity in the [marital] relationship' and could '*never* be a companion' in the 'modern', mutualist sense.[77] The true man, meanwhile, was an undomesticated animal, ever anxious to 'get away from his family, and from women altogether, and foregather in the communion of men.' The subordination of marriage to brotherhood meant that fatherhood assumed a 'relatively small part' in his life.[78] The ideal marriage was accordingly one in which spouses did not 'expect so much'. Give a man a 'comforting but innocuous' wife who did not cramp his freedom and he would be content.[79] A woman asked for nothing but that her provider 'behaves with average decency and earns a comfortable living'. The best partnerships were low-maintenance affairs in which 'she worked in her sphere; he in his.'[80]

This 'utilitarian' arrangement, less relationship than institution, was in the antis' view upset by the 'higher and less natural demands' made upon it by the companionate ideal. Victorian marriages in which the wife had 'obeyed the master without questioning his authority' had been placid affairs, but friction was almost inevitable when a 'modern woman has a distinct personality of her own' unless both partners displayed a high sense of duty.[81] Furthermore, 'too much association ... [and] too incessant exploration of each other's minds' by husband and wife proved counterproductive. A woman, convinced that she needed a 'trustworthy companion' with identical interests rather than a eugenically suitable mate, inclined towards marrying a passionless bore.[82] A man eager to enter into a total intimacy risked being left with '*no* sphere of activity' to call his own. Neither acknowledged the dispiriting reality that 'companionship' between any man and woman was nigh on 'impossible' due to their radically dissimilar natures. Marriage detached from its patriarchal foundations stood no chance of survival.[83]

There was no single anti-feminist line on sexuality. Most were regular moralists who disputed mutualist claims that the advance of civilization impelled the end of repression, since 'real social progress' had 'very little to do with sex'. But they also included among their ranks some of the most committed anti-puritans of their day including Anthony Ludovici, contemptuous of 'body-despising values' of modern Western society, and that decidedly ambivalent anti-feminist D.H. Lawrence, with his paeans to the sanctity of sex.[84] What united them was their opposition to the 'modern teaching that the sex-instinct is identical in men and women'. While mutualists maintained that men and women possessed equal if different desires, anti-feminists contended that each sex carried strong inheritances from their primal state in which the 'male sex-instinct was one of tyranny and subjugation' and the female's an attitude of 'surrender... engendered by fear'.[85]

The gulf between men's and women's sexual natures commended the double sexual standard to most anti-feminists. However 'ignorant, boring and uncompanionable' their husbands, wives would never consider adultery when preoccupied with maternal duties. Yet, however devoted he was to his wife, a husband's 'ever vagrant' eyes roamed free. Ludovici thought the solution obvious: that a young bachelor slaked his desires and a married man took a mistress 'wherever possible'.[86] The fact that a woman's instincts 'differ[ed] wholly from that of the male' also made it unrealistic for mutualists to imagine that the sexes achieved sexual harmony. Anti-feminists acknowledged the power of heterosexual desire, but contended that its very force rendered platonic relationships unworkable and further deepened the divide between women and men. In intercourse, the sexes met as strangers, their 'sexual cycle' touching only at 'one point, and that the briefest in its course'.[87]

Anti-feminists staged a more concerted challenge to mutuality than that offered by feminist irreconcilables, but their influence is best not overdrawn. Their dearest cause went out with a whimper when, despite the best efforts of Lord Rothermere's *Daily Mail* to 'Stop The Flapper Vote Folly', only ten MPs voted against extending the franchise to all women in 1928. Resistance was considered 'useless' in the face of a Tory Home Secretary who slotted women's suffrage into the 'long trend' of Whiggish political reform and a prime minister who pronounced anti-feminists' pessimism to be a 'complete fallacy' and their resistance entirely without 'heart'.[88] Anti-feminism thereafter found its clearest political voice within such peripheral arenas as the breakaway National Association of Schoolmasters and, curiously enough, the pin-up magazine *Men Only*. Although women still suffered from discrimination, most especially in employment law, victories over 'education, enfranchisement, and legal equality' convinced moderate feminists such as Ray Strachey that 'the main fight is over, and the main victory is won.'[89]

Political defeat when paired to their conviction that 'almost everybody today is an unconscious feminist' made anti-feminists style themselves the last of the chauvinists, upholding standards alien to their own time and place.[90] They searched abroad for havens of anti-feminism preferable to Britain's advanced case of 'Effemination': in the Orient, where men had no qualms about 'locking up their women'; and the Continent, where classicist G.W. Harris hoped that fascist Germany and Italy would reverse the 'Mutterdom of Man' through erecting a 'Concentration Camp for Women'.[91] They sought solace in the glories of patriarchies past when defending the now 'abused Victorian age [of] special peace and happiness in the relations of man to woman' and embracing an uncompromisingly anti-modernist agenda. Ludovici proposed that democracy and industry be abolished, towns levelled, spectacles and false teeth outlawed, craftsmanship revived and applied science replaced by the old arts of clairvoyance, telepathy and spiritual healing.[92] They dreamed, too, of some future 'Masculine Renaissance' in an era in which it would 'no longer be decent to be a Feminist'. This yearning for deliverance from modern-day Britain to anywhere and anytime less hostile to their ideals testified to their painful sense of isolation.[93]

Principles into Practice

The embittered obscurantism of anti-feminists and entrenched isolation of feminist irreconcilables showed the extent to which mutualists won the battle of ideas after 1918. The 'young intelligentsia' of Ethel Mannin's acquaintance considered the 'great figures of the time' to be not Anthony Ludovici or Thomas Baty but Sigmund Freud and the mutualist champions A.S. Neill, Bertrand Russell, Marie Stopes and Norman Haire.[94] But for all mutualists' campaigning, for all the pamphlets they wrote and manuals they sold, Britain did not appear to be a very mutualist place in the twenties and thirties. Three-quarters of state-funded secondary schools, a still higher proportion of private establishments and practically all youth clubs remained single-sex. The popularity of the all-female Townswomen's Guilds, the Women's Institute and the Women's League of Health and Beauty had its male-only counterpart in the pervasive 'clubbability' examined by historian Ross McKibbin.[95] Christian mutualist Eustace Chesser wrote off four-fifths of marriages as 'failures' and, for every 'sexually enlightened person...well versed in his Freud, his Havelock Ellis and his Hirschfeld', sex radical Norman Haire identified many more unfortunates oblivious to 'what a happy normal sex life should be.'[96] Indeed, the only people who could truly be said to be living the mutualist life between the wars were the sex radicals themselves, those 'progressive pioneers of the higher sexual purpose' who explored various forms of companionship, fornicated as they saw fit, established their own coeducational schools and enrolled their children in the Woodcraft Folk.[97] Pity consumed Dora Russell when contemplating the 'gulf' between the 'ignorant and intolerant' mass and her own circle's pursuit of 'ideals in human relations and...women's emancipation', however much 'conflict and even tragedy' ensued.[98]

World War Two seemed if anything to add to the obstacles confronting mutualists in their quest to create harmony between the sexes. It was not that they faced significant intellectual opposition. The association of Nazism with male chauvinism shut up all but the most knuckleheaded of anti-feminists and, with onetime sex warrior Cicely Hamilton enlisted by the British Council to catalogue the steady progress of women's rights and Maude Royden dismissing the 'idea of a cleavage between the interests of men and women' as sheer 'imbecility', the nay-saying of feminist malcontents proved weak and ineffective.[99] Nor did wartime mobilization produce much discernible sex antagonism. One government survey conducted in 1943 discovered that only 4 per cent of women workers perceived ill-will between male colleagues and themselves.[100] The problems mutualists detected were instead of a more private kind. Sex radicals and Christian mutualists agreed on the existence if not the nature of sexual tensions: the former lamenting the 'sex starvation' of troops separated from their womenfolk and the latter identifying 'indiscriminate sex relationships, premarital and extramarital relationships, abortion [and] venereal disease' on the home front. To this sex crisis Christian mutualists paired a marriage crisis 'terrifying in its bigness' and manifesting itself in the exponential rise of divorce during and just after the war.[101]

At the same time, the Second World War provided mutualists with new institutional means of tackling these problems. Total war, as marriage reformer Edward Griffith remarked, made 'personal behaviour...no longer our own affair...[but] also the concern of society'. That social concern invited state intervention. One government initiative, the establishment of Youth Recreation Centres, gave mutualist girls' club leaders the opportunity to create a mixed club movement which eclipsed its single-sex predecessor, as we shall see in chapter three. Another, the attempt to check a runaway divorce rate through 'wise counsel' and 'medical advice', gave marriage reformers their opportunity to expand into counselling, the subject of chapter four.[102] Just before the war, a solitary marriage guidance office had been founded in what counsellor David Mace took to be an atmosphere of widespread complacency. Immediately after it, he noted that 'marital maladjustment has become a social issue', leading to the creation of a National Marriage Guidance Council incorporating a hundred or more offices in receipt of state aid.[103]

The state had not become mutualist. These were minor policies dictated more by practical than ideological considerations, while politicians of all parties remained decidedly non-committal over such matters as coeducation and divorce.[104] Equally, mutualist thinkers did not turn into state functionaries and abandon their long-standing campaigning through the written word (or images, in the case of the soft-core pornographers discussed in chapter five). Social experiments of this sort nonetheless made mutualists engage more directly with those they sought to convert. Proselytizers became practitioners. Marriage counsellors faced distraught couples. Youth club leaders dealt with hormonally charged adolescents. Even pornographers eventually had to confront the concerns of women devoid of airbrushing and staples. The results confounded mutualists' expectations and tested their ideals to breaking point.

II
MUTUALITY TESTED

3

All Mixed Up
Boys, Girls and Youth Clubs

Ping-pong, orange squash, vinyl couches and linoleum floors: there was something deceptively mundane about youth clubs in mid twentieth-century Britain. They saw little of the grand ceremonials laid on by the uniformed youth organizations, with no flag-waving, bugle-blowing or badge-wearing on show.[1] They seemed staid in comparison to commercial youth culture, their fashion shows tame and their discos no substitute for the real thing.[2] And when set against postwar youth subcultures, they appeared utterly reactionary in their attempts to return the 'unattached' to adult supervision.[3] Awkward in-between affairs, neither purely recreational nor educational in character, youth clubs resembled holding pens for adolescents too old to be endearing and too conformist to be challenging to adult society.

What injected drama into this otherwise humdrum world was the introduction of mixing. Before the Second World War, youth clubs offered closely regulated, sexually segregated, separate and unequal provision to their adolescent working-class clientele.[4] During the war, a new sort of club emerged, casual in method and mixed in membership. After it, the mixed clubs flourished, girls' clubs vanished and boys' clubs began their gradual but irrevocable decline.[5] The rise of mixing involved a classic confrontation between proponents of mutuality and separate spheres. Enthusiasts portrayed mixing as creating concord between boys and girls in anticipation of marriage, a strategy rejected by boys' club leaders at the cost of their reputation among youth workers, state officials and, most crucially, adolescents themselves. Once considered natural, segregation appeared to be artificial for the new breed of teenagers.

The social impact of mixing stemmed from the sheer scale of youth club attendance in mid twentieth-century Britain. Government research conducted in 1969 found that 69 per cent of male and 71 per cent of female twenty-year-olds either were or had once been members of a 'youth club' as they understood the term.[6] The same survey indicated that a little over a quarter of all fourteen- to twenty-years-olds were youth club members at any one time (several times the teenage membership of the uniformed organizations) and, of these, some three-fifths attended once a week or more.[7] The growing expectation that boys and girls would grow up relating to, rather than secluded from, one another accordingly affected most people born since the Slump. Three-quarters of former members credited their mixed club with having contributed to the happiness of their subsequent married lives.[8]

What follows is primarily a tale of two organizations: the National Association of Boys' Clubs (or NABC, founded in 1925) and the National Organisation of Girls' Clubs (1911) and its successors, the National Council of Girls' Clubs (1926), the National Association of Girls' Clubs (1942), the National Association of Girls' Clubs and Mixed Clubs (1944), the National Association of Mixed Clubs and Girls' Clubs (1953) and the National Association of Youth Clubs (1961), whose name changes summarize the story in themselves (for simplicity's sake, I refer to the body as the 'NCGC' before 1945 and as the 'NAYC' thereafter). These confederal organizations served all the non-uniformed, non-church-based youth clubs in the United Kingdom outside Scotland: not directly administering them, but rather issuing guidance about how they might best be run and monitoring how local leaders actually ran them.[9] Supplementing their printed literature and archived minutes, therefore, is material drawn from regional club federations in London and Liverpool, cities whose proud philanthropic traditions spawned two of the strongest club cultures in Britain; from the central government, which adopted an increasingly interventionist role in youth work during this period; and from the multifarious club leaders, social commentators and concerned parties who debated the nature and direction of organized youth work. It should be noted that these are all 'adult' sources, the young leaving behind no self-generated records save for the odd club newsletter. Yet, although mediated through adult authorities, the thought and behaviour of adolescents emerge clearly enough through surveys and, in mirror image, through the actions of club leaders by turns appeasing and resisting their many and varied demands.

Boys' Clubs and Girls' Clubs

The boys' club movement was born out of that quintessential mix of altruism and anxiety, social reform and social control characteristic of middle-class philanthropy in the late nineteenth and early twentieth centuries. Anxiety stemmed from the condition of working-class boys thought to be physically deficient and morally suspect, unsupervised and overpaid, a disgrace and a menace to the society that had fostered them. Delinquency necessitated discipline, prompting turn-of-the-century boys' clubs to vow to curb their members' 'dangerous freedom' by inculcating a 'willing and cheerful submission to an authority outside themselves.' Historians Harry Hendrick and Victor Bailey have noted that the movement's founding fathers were accordingly also pioneers in the field of juvenile justice: Alexander Paterson, Borstal founder and 'the "Beveridge" of the penal system'; Charles Russell, Chief Inspector of Reformatory and Industrial Schools; and campaigning London magistrate Basil Henriques.[10]

But boys' clubs were founded on more than fear alone. Indeed, in their very miscreancy, club leaders detected glimpses of what boys might ideally become. What was vice but energy misspent? Was not criminality simply misdirected initiative? What, by this logic, were gangs if not embryonic clubs? Thus was the 'boy labour' question translated to leisure pursuits. Within the 'herd instinct', Henriques discerned the germ of 'loyalty and unselfishness for the service of society'. The 'games instinct', for all its 'perils of destruction and greed', contained the 'ideals of justice, courage and usefulness', while the dark potentialities of the 'sex instinct' were not to obscure the 'nobility of its ultimate purpose'.[11]

The optimism of club leaders like Basil Henriques derived from their faith in the universal, innate and ultimately redemptory quality of 'boy nature', whose characteristics agreed in their essentials with the storm and stress model of adolescence formulated by American psychologist G. Stanley Hall.[12] Boy nature was thought to consist of such moral qualities as 'keenness, sportsmanship, fair play, friendship' and expressed itself in a boisterousness containing the seeds of that manliness whose attainment was every boy's ultimate goal. Its fate, and that of the boys themselves, was decided between the years of fourteen and eighteen, which were considered to be as critical to boyhood as those of 1914–18 had been to the nation, with the 'same sudden break with the past, the same sense of restlessness, of struggle with strange conditions'.[13] Released from school, independent of maternal control and flitting from one job to the next, adolescent boys were at their most plastic and impressionable precisely when most exposed to the corrosive effects of poverty and vice. Neglect them then and they would sink to unfathomable 'depths of worthlessness and depravity.' But befriend them, nurture them and 'put to good purpose the virility that is bubbling within' them and it was possible to 'build upon the raw foundations of boy nature the structure of firm and vigorous manhood.'[14]

The function of the boys' club was to act as a greenhouse: a sheltered state of nature separated from the polluted surrounds of modern urban life in which a boy's character could be cultivated into full manhood. Naturalness formed the 'basic principle' of a distinctive club method. Clubs shunned the rituals and uniforms of the Boy Scouts. There was no place for membership rites and formal discipline was kept to a minimum (at least in theory). Boys were instead expected to conduct themselves without a 'trace of self-consciousness' and club activities were accordingly those undertaken without compunction: sport, games, more sport.[15] Such pursuits were themselves secondary to the instincts they fostered. The 'instinct for play' brought out in boys that reputedly masculine combination of teamwork and competition, affection and rivalry. Boys' 'instinct for comradeship', meanwhile, developed both among themselves and with their club leader, whose role was not simply to supervise but to teach by example how to be a man. He was expected to be an authority figure and a friend, a model of maturity and a boy at heart, bridging divisions of age and class with his loving tutelage.[16]

In performing their moral alchemy upon the individual boy, boys' clubs promised to act as the safety-net of society, creating the workers, fathers and citizens of the future from layabouts and roughs. They patriotically pledged to 'build up a finer race, a nation of fit men, fit to play its part in the Empire and the world.' They also reminded potential donors, in the wake of universal suffrage and the General Strike of 1926, that prime ministers, hitherto recruited from Eton, would henceforth be drawn from the elementary schools.[17] What better remedy, they suggested, than to form out of fraternity a 'great national team where boys of all classes and conditions are bound together by mutual sympathy and loyalty'. This disciplined yet informal, paternalistic and patriarchal approach to youth work won boys' clubs a 'considerable measure of national recognition' between the wars.[18]

Did boys' clubs live up to the ambitions of their founders? Not according to historian David Fowler, who in his *The First Teenagers* (1995) perceives a 'general malaise in lads' club work' in the interwar period. Faced with increasingly demanding adolescents, clubs alternatively retained their principles and lost their members, or else retained their members and lost their principles through crowd-pleasing appeals. Either way, he claims, the old mission of the boys' clubs went awry.[19] However, there is compelling evidence to the contrary. It is easy to mistake the relaxed methods of the boys' clubs for a relaxation in standards themselves. Club leaders were the first to argue that character building had nothing to do with dourness, drill and formal discipline, and the *New Survey of London Life and Labour* (1935) identified the prime virtue of the club method to be its lightly worn mission and unabashed appeal to the spirit of play.[20] Fowler's contention that boys' clubs were abandoning any 'clearly defined aims' in the interwar period also fails to account for the emergence and success of the National Association of Boys' Clubs. The NABC, founded in 1925 to give the boys' club movement a renewed purpose and a national profile, required its members to subscribe to a set of 'Principles and Aims' expressly designed to stiffen rather than abandon standards in boys' work. Its exaltation of boy nature and its programme for 'training in responsibility for the privileges and duties of manhood' should, by Fowler's reckoning, have had few takers in an age witnessing the birth of the proto-teenager. In fact, the NABC outgrew all other major youth organizations in the thirties, the number of affiliated clubs increasing over fivefold from its foundation to the outbreak of World War Two.[21] Participating clubs appeared to take its exacting ideals seriously, leading one outside observer to contrast the 'entirely ineffectual' church-based clubs in which boys 'just meet and play games' with the 'magnificent' clubs of the NABC and its affiliate, the London Federation of Boys' Clubs.[22] Before the First World War, even the champions of boys' clubs were prepared to concede that most were 'little more than pleasant, somewhat noisy lounging-places'. But by the 1930s, club leaders boasted that, whereas clubs once had 'little method in their system, and lack of vision as to their goal', the boys' club movement now knew 'what it wants to do... [and] how to do it.' With grand aims, a high public profile and a distinctive pedagogy and developmental psychology, boys' clubs were much more than a form of organized loitering.[23]

Girls' clubs were initially less ambitious affairs. While boys' clubs sought to sculpt their members' rough-hewn masculinity, they saw their mission as that of protecting a femininity fully formed. Their founding creed was purity, that of keeping girls 'innocent and pure' amid the manifold 'Perils in the City', and as such strove 'simply to provide an efficient counter-attraction to the streets'.[24] The dwindling of the purity crusade after the First World War (see chapter two) deprived girls' club leaders of even this spartan rationale. Some clubs stultified and stood accused of choking the 'independent spirit' of interwar girls by offering them protection alone. Yet many club leaders were happy to jettison the dry moralizing tone of the old girls' clubs and concentrate on making girls' lives a little less constraining and dull. Charity worker Margaret Simey recalled her fellow girls' club leaders in Liverpool as 'pioneers of applied emancipation' who 'wreaked havoc in the marriage market' by raising their members' education above that of local boys.[25] Clubs tended to bodies as well as minds through Scandinavian country dancing and an innovative 'keep fit' campaign. Though professedly 'modern and progressive' in outlook and tinged with a moderate sort of feminism (they received support from MPs Margaret Bondfield, Ellen Wilkinson and Thelma Cazalet), theirs was a practical programme devoid of any female equivalent to boy nature.[26]

If girls' clubs possessed little of the same sense of mission that drove the boys' clubs, so did they lack the wherewithal to fund their comparatively modest aims. Individual clubs were poorer, smaller and met less frequently than their male counterparts. Their umbrella organization, the National Council of Girls' Clubs, had half the membership and a third of the assets of the NABC immediately before World War Two. Their minor standing stemmed from the fact that women could 'contribute shillings where men contribute guineas' and that people saw less need for girls' clubs thanks to female adolescence being thought a smoother affair. Neither driven by fears of delinquency nor inspired by visions of human perfection, their pledge to make home life less of 'a struggle and a muddle' seemed almost trifling.[27]

Basil Henriques was wrong to think that 'there were no mixed clubs' before the Second World War, but his oversight testified to their tentative and sketchy beginnings. Mixed socials had existed to some extent since the inception of the youth club movement and many of the more adventurous boys' and girls' clubs staged periodic 'open evenings' prior to 1914.[28] The first fully mixed clubs emerged at around the same time as coeducational progressive schools and for similarly mutualist motives. The Barnsbury Club was founded in 1910 on the basis that 'boys and girls were meant to be mutual helps, not hindrances; that each possessed something the other lacked' and that mixing would dispel the sense of mystery surrounding the other sex. On a less elevated level, Miss Sharpley of the Acland Mixed Club (established in 1893) thought it 'very desirable that boys and girls should do things in common'.[29]

These were exceptions to the rule at a time when most respectable observers associated unadulterated mixing with the degeneracy of the unrespectable urban poor. 'In the street... [boys and girls] mix freely enough,' observed social reformer E.J. Urwick, dismayed by their 'incessant interchange of coarse and meaningless chaff'. For the boy, an enthusiasm to mix smacked of a 'disagreeable precocity' otherwise exhibited through smoking and reading 'bloods'.[30] For the girl, it was considered a still more dangerous enterprise, her 'morbid passion' for adventure and romance leading her to frequent seedy dance-halls and contract hasty, dysgenic marriages. Not only did most leaders proscribe mixing in their clubs, but Maude Stanley of the Soho Club hoped to dissuade her charges from mixing at all: 'The girl who has her club will not need the idle companionship of lads. She will not want them, for she will have her girl friends, her interests, her occupations for leisure hours in her club'.[31]

World War One gave club leaders reason to change their minds. Adolescent boys were at their most troublesome in wartime, leading to a disquieting upsurge in juvenile crime, while their enlisted older brothers found themselves idle between spells of active duty. Equally unsettled were the female munitions workers transplanted to new areas, upon whom soldiers were held to have an 'exciting, unsteadying effect'.[32] Acknowledging the impossibility of outlawing all such liaisons, the Women's Patrol Committee sought instead to supervise factory girls within suitably orderly mixed clubs. Crystal Palace hosted the first such venture in the autumn of 1914 and several more followed, often with governmental assistance and designed to promote a 'friendly intercourse' that stopped short of 'silly flirtation'.[33]

Such initiatives proved to be something of a false dawn for mixing. To be sure, they transformed it from 'unattainable ideal' to practical proposition. The twenties and thirties witnessed a proliferation of mixed evenings within single-sex clubs as well the emergence of such middle-class mixed youth organizations as the Woodcraft Folk and the far larger Youth Hostels Association.[34] Yet wartime expedients failed to make mixing the norm for working-class adolescents. Mixed ventures disappeared soon after 1918 other than in Manchester and, although there existed a National Association of Mixed Clubs, it left scant trace of its activities and did not 'appear to be of much consequence'.[35]

These faltering steps towards mixing elicited contrasting reactions from boys' and girls' club leaders between the wars. Segregation in boys' clubs was no incidental aspect of their programme, nor merely a device to exclude females, but was rather testament to their leaders' determination to keep the sexes 'definitely different'. Henriques wished to make males 'as manly as possible', females 'as womanly as possible' and considered segregation essential for the 'fullest development of those qualities which have ennobled each sex.'[36] At no time was this truer than adolescence, when the sexes were thought under normal circumstances to 'drift apart almost entirely.' The rapidly maturing girl had marriage in mind by her mid teens, an age at which any healthy-minded boy was 'not interested in girls and would regard their presence in his club as an intrusion.' Until seventeen or so, or at the very earliest sixteen and a half, boys were best left to pursue their boyish enthusiasms among their own kind.[37] To allow otherwise risked stimulating unnatural interests damaging to boys' healthy maturation as well as the club ethos. Such was the matter with the 'dance-hall type' of boy who, having been corrupted by '"bunny-hugging"... with scantily-clothed girls', arrived at the club brandishing rubber johnnies and boycotted gymnastics for fear of creasing his trousers.[38] Worse still, girls might use their sirenic powers to lure boys away from the clubs altogether. No wonder that boys' club leaders were inclined to think that 'the less the boys "bother with girls", the better club members they are'.[39]

Scottish boys' club luminary Stanley Nairne was not so oblivious to the interwar mutualist climate as to dispute that 'in these days, it is more and more necessary for Boys' Clubs to provide an opportunity for the boys bringing their girl friends to the Club.' But the NABC was adamant that mixing be confined to monthly socials for the older members, while its plans for 'training... the right attitude towards the other sex' were chauvinistic in the extreme.[40] Rather than encouraging easy-going social intercourse, the standard text for club leaders instructed them to use mixed events as object lessons in discriminating between 'what is and what is not a decent type of girl':

> The leader should talk to the boys quite frankly about the girls who come to the mixed activities. He must point out the unnaturalness of the painted lips, the plucked eyebrows and the over-powdered face. He must express his views on the loud type of girl who displays all the vulgarities of her sex. He must create a public opinion on the decencies and indecencies of female conduct, so that the boys gradually get to perceive the difference. In one club an Elsie Vee (L.C.V. meaning 'low, common, vulgar') has by tradition come to be recognised as the type of girl not wanted at a club dance. This is a tremendous step forward...

The concessions made towards mixing by the boys' clubs between the wars could prove not so much token as downright insulting to the girls admitted.[41]

In contrast, most (though not all) girls' club leaders of the interwar period advocated some measure of mixing for reasons at once practical and ideological. Practically speaking, less money, less influence and fewer members provided them with sound incentives for seeking an alliance with the boys' clubs. The track-record of mixed clubs as an effective alternative to 'pavement flirtations' during the First World War convinced many of them that well-supervised mixing could be both palatable to themselves and attractive to girls.[42] The appeal of mixing appeared all the stronger among the interwar generation of girls, whose exposure to 'new consumerism' equipped them with a cheap glamour designed to attract boys and whose excursions to the cinema, the seaside and the *palais de danse* provided opportunities for doing so. The result was that 'every year' the NCGC recorded a yet 'stronger demand' from their members for mixed activities, a demand that if left unsatisfied would, they believed, lead girls to abandon the clubs' country dancing in search of romance.[43]

Their mild feminism also made girls' club leaders receptive to mutualist arguments for mixing. Towards the close of the suffrage campaign, Louise Creighton, NCGC president and scourge of Christabel Pankhurst (see chapter one), had characterized feminism as the conviction that there were a 'great many [things] which can be best done when men and women work together.' Girls' club literature similarly presented the partial enfranchisement of women in 1918 as evidence of a new form of chivalric 'comradeship' superseding men's old-fashioned condescension. And as mutualist ideas became increasingly influential after the First World War, club leaders contemplated how best to align their movement to the 'growing belief that young people of the two sexes should meet freely in a healthy atmosphere of fellowship'.[44] Mixing satisfied all these ambitions. Echoing the mutualist pioneers of the previous generation, its advocates spoke of the separation of the sexes causing adolescents to overlook the commonalities between the sexes in favour of 'clumping people into a mass marked "Women" and into another mass marked "Men"'. Segregation was held to produce either excessive sex-consciousness or an indifference to 'male society' among girl members injurious to their marriage prospects.[45] It therefore seemed imperative that boys and girls met on terms of 'friendship and equality' within mixed clubs. For society's benefit, it would teach them the nature of 'true comradeship between men and women'. For their own, boys might become less prone to 'hardness and harshness' and girls a touch less 'hypersensitive'.[46]

Such hopes remained pipe-dreams as long as single-sex provision was institutionally entrenched. Not one of the eleven founder members of the Standing Conference of National Voluntary Youth Organisations in 1936 was mixed.[47] The obvious route to more mixing appeared to be cooperation between the NCGC and the NABC but, despite courteous exchanges and fully four years of negotiations, their doctrinal differences stymied formal agreement. Heavily chaperoned evenings arranged on an *ad hoc* basis were about as far as mixing went before 1939.[48]

The Upheaval of War

It took war and the combined effects of youth pressure, state intervention and girls' club opportunism to inaugurate a fully-fledged mixed club movement in Britain. The young took up mixed leisure activities with enthusiasm during World War Two. In pubs, the proportion of female customers doubled as women took advantage of wartime wages and loosened social constraints to drink with men in uniform.[49] And in clubs, observers identified a new precocity among the wartime generation associated with a wish to mix. Girls' club leaders wrote repeatedly of an 'earlier maturity' among the young in wartime manifesting itself in a 'far greater demand for mixed clubs'. The same phenomenon, given a negative spin, was noted by the NABC's Basil Henriques, who complained in 1942 that 'jitter-bugging noises', 'sensuous' cinema and 'cheap, glamorous literature' had made adolescent boys inordinately interested in girls.[50]

Statistics corroborated such impressions. A 1945 survey conducted in Liverpool found mixing to be welcomed by all but a 'small minority', as did a nationwide study of fourteen- to twenty-year-olds involved in youth organizations undertaken the previous year. More than two-thirds of the boys liked the idea of mixed youth centres 'very much' compared to only a quarter who felt similarly about single-sex clubs. Conversely, only 8 per cent actively disliked youth centres, a figure rising to 57 per cent when asked the same about boys' clubs. The contrast was even greater among girls. Fully three-quarters enthused about youth centres and a similar proportion scorned single-sex clubs. From a list of thirteen leisure pursuits, going to mixed youth centres was the activity these girls most fancied doing and going to girls' clubs what they expected to like least of all.[51]

For the young to wish to mix was one thing; to be allowed to, another matter entirely. The response of the state, increasingly involved in youth work following the 'Service of Youth' circular of November 1939, was at first complicated by its inability to decide whether to treat wartime youth as an asset or a liability.[52] Ideally, policy-makers wished to channel adolescents' 'spirit of adventure' into the war effort and to train them as the nation's first reserve. This called for the reestablishment of such pre-service organizations as the Army Cadets. These bodies had fallen out of favour with government and the young alike in the anti-militaristic interwar period, but were now reformed, their resources replenished and recruits gathered in by the tens of thousands following the mandatory registration of sixteen- to eighteen-year-old boys introduced in January 1942.[53]

Patronage of pre-service organizations left two major problems unresolved. The first was that the young were manifestly not as idealistic as ministers and civil servants wished them to be. In wartime the ill-disciplined among them took advantage of parental absence, evacuation and the blackout to embark on a spectacular delinquency spree. After a severe dip in the first months of war, convictions of male youths rose in the following two years to a rate 30 per cent higher than the prewar figure before levelling off thereafter. Female juvenile delinquency, though 'fortunately much smaller' in scale, had almost doubled by 1943. This crime wave attracted public concern as magistrates routinely condemned the high wartime wages of boys and the press tut-tutted over girls' lax behaviour. Though government officials doubtless wished otherwise, they acknowledged that the 'undisciplined youth of the streets' was beyond the grasp of 'the "respectable" club or centre', let alone the pre-service organizations.[54]

The second issue concerned what to do with the girls, a question no one in government was particularly keen to address. When, after much prevarication, the state assumed responsibility for the girls' pre-service organizations in January 1942, it did so on an informal basis, with the organizations given no resources and under the supervision not of the military but of the Board of Education.[55] However inclined they were to treat girls as an afterthought, officials still accepted that they deserved, indeed required, some state-funded leisure activities. Historian Penny Tinkler notes that state ventures paired an ambition to supervise girls' budding sexuality with the more positive purpose of turning them into citizens.[56] Citizenship implied some measure of equality and governmental bodies were accordingly concerned that organized leisure provision was 'less adequate' for girls than for boys. Hence the objection of the Board of Education to the County Badge scheme mooted by Gordonstoun founder Kurt Hahn on the grounds that it was presented '*entirely* from the boy's angle.' Any government initiative had in its view to be 'so planned as to apply to both sexes.'[57] A determination to enrol girls enabled them to benefit disproportionately from the wartime recruitment drive. In Nottinghamshire, boys outnumbered girls two to one in youth organizations in 1942; two years later, the ratio was more like five to four.[58]

Officials turned to mixed clubs as the least worst solution to the twin challenges posed by delinquents and girls. Their appeal to girls was such that one local report considered it to be a 'necessary accompaniment of large-scale organised provision' for them. It was also widely thought that if girls were not provided with wholesome (that is, regulated) mixed leisure activities in wartime, then they would be sure to mix in a cruder manner, invoking the spectre of teen pregnancy. As for potential delinquents, mixing formed part of a package of attractions intended to draw them into youth clubs in the most expeditious way possible. This necessitated dispensing with the niceties of character training and giving the young roughly what they wanted rather than what they were thought to need – mixing included.[59]

Seeking by turns to conciliate and control the young, state-funded bodies consequently became 'obsessed with the need for promoting mixed clubs and youth centres' in the eyes of their critics. One initiative was a club network for unmarried and displaced soldiers and war-workers aged between twenty and thirty-five.[60] Far more controversial were the so-called 'In and Out Clubs', often nothing more than glorified bomb shelters, with no dues, a drop-in membership, little leadership, an informal approach and, almost invariably, mixing. Then there were the standard-issue Youth Recreation Centres, an example of which was Paddington's Clarendon Youth Centre. Established in 1940 to quell 'loafing, horseplaying and gambling', it set out to attract the sort of member that the other clubs did not reach. This meant no 'high-flown aims' and also no sexual segregation, since west London was not a 'club area' in which adolescents had been 'brought up to [expect] it'.[61]

The National Association of Boys' Clubs and the National Council of Girls' Clubs reacted in opposite ways to the transformed climate for youth work. From the outset, boys' club leaders were alert to the danger that the 'urgent need of keeping boys and girls off the darkened streets will lead to proposals to start organizations under the name of clubs for mixed dancing and similar activities without membership or subscription.' The rapid emergence of Youth Recreation Centres and their like gave form to their misgivings. The centres' crowd-pleasing programme represented the very 'travesty of that of a good boys' club' from their exacting perspective.[62] Their age range was 'impossibly wide', their educational value non-existent, their undemanding activities an opportunity for 'merely messing away the time in... the most irritating and boring manner.' They hoped that Youth Recreation Centres were simply wartime expedients that might form the 'nucleus of a good Boys' and/or Girls' Club' once peace came. But they feared – rightly, as it turned out – that such clubs posed a direct challenge to boys' clubs and the values they upheld.[63]

What really exercised boys' club leaders about the Youth Recreation Centres was the fact that they were almost without exception mixed. 'They're at it again,' complained an anonymous boys' club leader in 1939, presumably recalling the First World War: 'They're telling us... we must have mixed clubs, we must have dancing or else the boys will get into mischief.' To him, this raised the prospect of boys being 'drugged into feebleness to the strain of crooners' were segregation to be abandoned in a 'panic surrender of ideals and standards'.[64] Such sentiments were reiterated by a host of wartime club leaders fearful of mixing's eroticizing and androgynizing effects. Whereas the normal boy naturally affected to be a 'woman-hater' during adolescence, one immersed in female company fell victim to their influence before his manliness was fully formed. The example of girls introduced too much 'refinement and gentility' into his temperament, making him 'a spectator rather than a player of boys' games' and encouraging him to dance rather than box.[65] These club leaders regarded it as immaterial 'whether Mixed Clubs are popular or not' because they knew what was best for boys better than the boys themselves. Since there was self-evidently 'something radically wrong' with adolescent boys dissatisfied with the company of their own sex, it was the duty of boys' clubs to help them change their ways.[66]

The NCGC was in contrast 'only too delighted' to throw in its lot with the state during wartime. Supportive to the point of sycophancy, it passed votes of thanks to the Board of Education and may have used the fact that its chairwoman, Katharine Elliot, was married to the Conservative politician Walter Elliot to facilitate a cosy lunch with a high-ranking minister.[67] What really earned it a reputation for being 'go-ahead and open-minded and cooperative' within government circles, however, was its can-do spirit and genuine enthusiasm for state intervention. This was to some degree a matter of necessity. Girls' clubs were hit even harder than boys' clubs by bombing, the blackout and the commandeering of club premises, though were perhaps somewhat less affected by the call-up of club leaders. In November 1940, the Blitz had shut down well over 90 per cent of London's girls' clubs, compared to the three-quarters of boys' clubs still claiming to remain open for business. Were girls' clubs to continue to operate, substantial resources had to be forthcoming from the state.[68]

Practicalities aside, girls' club leaders found themselves in fundamental sympathy with the aims and objectives of the Youth Recreation Centres. The doctrinal laxity of the Centres matched their own pragmatic perspective and gave them leave to abandon 'revoltingly dull' techniques based on one-to-one bonding between leader and member in favour of a group-centred, environmental approach in which 'young adults' used club facilities as they wished.[69] Furthermore, the unisex basis of the Youth Recreation Centres realized the long-cherished aspirations of many girls' club leaders to institute wholesale mixing. Their ambitions went well beyond the 'guest nights' before the war, retrospectively dismissed as stilted occasions where boys were vetted by a 'forbidding band of spinster helpers' and girls were invited to boys' clubs to perform the cleaning chores. Nor were they willing to settle for 'twin clubs' with separate sections for boys and girls, since they seemed 'at best makeshifts' compared to the real thing. The new clubs promoted by the NCGC were to be properly mixed affairs with joint male and female leaders and a club committee composed of equal numbers of either sex. Single-sex pursuits were to be relegated to side-rooms or occasional events, much like the mixed evenings of old.[70]

Enthusiasts for mixing adapted familiar mutualist arguments for progress and citizenship to the conditions of war. They commended mixed clubs as 'miniature democratic societies' suitable to a nation fighting for freedom, and appealed to wartime collectivism in their portrayal of boys and girls learning to 'carry joint responsibility by a fair division of labour and to trust and work with each other.'[71] The chairwoman of the NCGC presented mixing as being as modern as utility wear. 'Are you a Victorian?' Katharine Elliot asked: 'Are we going to return to the Victorian or Edwardian age and segregate the sexes?'[72] She left it to others in the organization to counter the various practical objections to mixing. They claimed the differential between boys' and girls' maturation rates to be no obstacle to the mixing of older adolescents and accepted that sexual dalliances were a normal part of growing up. Besides, their obsessive aspects could be remedied if mixed clubs taught sweethearts that 'love consists less in gazing at each other than in looking forward together in the same direction.'[73] The NCGC's education officer, Josephine Macalister Brew, derided all opponents, whether 'avowed man-haters' running old-fashioned girls' clubs or 'men's men' using boys' clubs as a refuge against all things female. The age of clubs acting as 'bombproof shelter[s] from the opposite sex' had passed. That of mixing had in her view arrived.[74]

Despite their conflicting attitudes to mixing, it was not immediately apparent that the NABC and NCGC were incapable of jointly administering wartime mixed clubs. Boys' club leaders conceded that mixed activities were 'more important under present abnormal conditions' and even, in the singular case of Basil Henriques, could momentarily be persuaded that mixed clubs were 'the youth organisations of the future'. They accordingly signalled their willingness to help run twin clubs or, at a stretch, mixed clubs with distinct boys' sections.[75] For their part, girls' clubs had been in the shadow of the boys' clubs too long to act unilaterally.[76] The discussions about mixing abandoned inconclusively before the war therefore resumed in 1942, only to founder once again on the two organizations' incompatible views on the roles and relations of the sexes. The NABC retained faith in separate spheres and would countenance mixing only if there existed sufficient segregated activities to stimulate the 'full development of all that is virile in the boy, and all that is graceful and delicate and feminine in the girl'. The NCGC conversely stressed the overlapping interests of the sexes and the importance of allowing club girls 'the same privileges, and ... responsibilities as their brothers.'[77] Disagreement centred upon whether adolescent boys in mixed clubs should be treated as boys first and adolescents second, or the other way around. The NABC insisted upon the former, offering to accept a limited measure of mixing provided that boys' sections within mixed clubs (affiliated to itself) nurtured 'qualities of manliness' through 'hard games', camaraderie and the example of a male leader. The NCGC replied that if adolescents instinctively segregated themselves, so be it, but in fact most regarded mixing as 'natural' and 'enjoyed themselves best, in their limited free hours, when in the company of each other.'[78]

Such 'irreconcilable ... differences of opinion' torpedoed negotiations between the two bodies at the local as well as the national level. In Leeds, mixing was regarded by boys' clubs as a 'temporary and wartime development' but by girls' clubs as an intrinsic good, and an attempt by the London boys' and girls' club federations to form a joint mixed club committee collapsed when mixed club leaders engineered a complete merger with the girls' organization immediately after the war.[79] Central and local government officials blamed the breakdown in talks on the intransigence of the boys' clubs, which soon discovered that any settlement would have served them better than none at all. With agreement, mixing might have been contained within acceptable bounds at a time when they were comfortably the larger and more powerful movement. Without it, the NABC petulantly abandoned all mixed work save in small villages, leaving the NCGC free to establish itself as the sole coordinator of secular mixed club work in 1944. The gravity of its mistake began to dawn on the NABC in 1946:

> there is a large number of boys in mixed youth clubs or centres affiliated to the NAGC&MC, or affiliated to no organisation, who are not in Boys' Sections as defined by the NABC...As a consequence the NABC not only cannot grant affiliation or associate membership to such centres, but also has no entrée into them... Furthermore many new Youth Centres and mixed clubs looked to the NAGC&MC for affiliation and completely ignored the NABC...

Boys' clubs were on their way towards becoming peripheral to youth leisure provision.[80]

The effects of war had been as paradoxical as they were profound. Of the two sorts of government youth work launched in the Second World War – the segregated pre-service organizations and the mixed Youth Recreation Centres – it was the latter, less favoured kind that proved to be much the more permanent. Though the popularity of the pre-service organizations was a wartime phenomenon only, the hastily improvised and somewhat shambolic Youth Centres formed the blueprint for the postwar Youth Service. There was also an unexpected winner among the youth organizations. Whereas the NABC recorded a respectable 20 per cent increase in membership during the war, the NCGC ballooned to twice its prewar size. The reason was obvious enough. Boys' clubs chose tradition and girls' clubs, innovation. The doctrinal rigidity of boys' club leaders had made them wary of government intervention and unwilling to modify their approach for the sake of winning favour with officials and adolescents alike. In contrast, girls' club leaders had worked in tandem with the government and the young to accomplish their shared ambition (albeit one inspired by different motives) of creating genuinely mixed clubs. Once complementary, the two organizations were now competitors offering rival models of how best to regulate the relations between boys and girls.

The Impact of Mixing

The boys' club movement entered the postwar period with its faith in boy nature intact. 'I have sometimes heard it said that the boy of today is entirely different from the boy of pre-war years, but I have always doubted it,' declared NABC chairman Lord Aberdare in 1950. Boys were *'still boys'*, he believed, their 'essential natures' untouched by their 'tougher, more cynical or more sophisticated...veneer'.[81] Since boys were 'exactly as they were', their needs were decreed 'the same as they used to be', so sparing club leaders the awkward task of updating their club method. Segregation was to be retained regardless of the wishes of club members themselves, as Aberdare made plain in 1948:

> We are sometimes accused of being reactionary and out of touch with reality because of our views on this particular subject. In this connection there is, I think, an unfortunate tendency to assume that what young people say they want is that same thing that they in fact need...The subjective opinions of boys and girls are notoriously unreliable...[82]

Opposition to mixing came to define the NABC over the following decades, its successive policy pronouncements revealing it to be an organization obsessed. A 1948 policy document commended segregation as the best environment in which to foster 'friendship, responsibility, physical vigour, adventure and...craftsmanship'. In 1954, the manner was tetchier, the language more strident. And in 1975, by which point even the Scouts were advocating some mixing for the over-sixteens, the NABC's ideas for 'The Way Ahead' boiled down to a defence of single-sex provision.[83]

The determination of postwar boys' clubs to 'resist pressures to compromise', though nothing if not principled, was also suicidal. The NABC's membership peaked in 1949 at 210,000 following a concerted expansion drive initiated by returning POWs and supported by such heavyweights as Field-Marshal Montgomery and prime minister Clement Attlee, only to drop in the following five years to their prewar level of around 160,000.[84] At first, it insisted that it was undergoing 'consolidation', not 'stagnation', then pinned its hopes on capturing baby-boomers, then blamed a dearth of leaders but, as its membership barely sustained itself over the following two decades, its aim became one of cornering a niche market. In 1953, NABC vice-president Waldo McGillicuddy Eagar suggested that 'the way to "more Clubs and better Clubs" might lie through fewer Clubs which do not pander to the weakness of youth but challenge the moral splendour of boyhood.' A decade later, NABC publications openly conceded the 'distinct' if 'deplorable' possibility of the 'eventual disappearance of Boys' Clubs'. So it transpired: at this point already smaller than the NAYC, the organization was half as large by the beginning of the seventies and a mere quarter its size a decade on.[85]

With stagnant membership came institutional and intellectual isolation. The NABC's strained relations with government bodies in the Second World War worsened thereafter. Civil servants despaired over the NABC as much for its anti-statist gentlemanly amateurism and archaic 'boy mystique' as for what they perceived to be its strange belief that mixed clubs were 'hotbeds of immorality'. Moreover, for boys' club leaders to lambast state-run 'Temples of Youth' that crushed 'the simple, the natural ... the unpretentious' instincts of boyhood was an unwise policy when paired to an inflated sense of entitlement.[86] Privileged access to the New Towns, use of air raid shelters, assistance from the emergency services, induction classes for National Servicemen: some strange hubris impelled the NABC to bombard officials and politicians with requests for favours in the immediate postwar years. The Ministry of Education delivered successive rebuffs, the most momentous being its refusal to support the NABC's vastly ambitious 'Bridge-Builders' recruitment drive because it omitted girls.[87]

Although boys' clubs suffered no direct financial penalty from being considered 'one of the less deserving' youth organizations by Whitehall, they paid for their opposition to mixing on a local level. The NABC complained that some local authorities refused to support boys' clubs or, more typically, used funding to 'bring persuasion to bear' on them to mix.[88] In Northumberland, the local education authority obliged boys' clubs to establish girls' sections in order to receive grant aid; in London, the 'strong bias' of local officials against segregation reputedly influenced many boys' clubs to admit girls; and nationwide, the NABC found 'more and more' local authorities making support to boys' clubs conditional upon their providing facilities for girls.[89] The organization got nowhere appealing to the Ministry. 'LEAs cannot be bludgeoned into supporting boys' clubs,' memoed a departmental official, particularly when boys' clubs gave such a 'bad impression' through their stubborn isolationism. Senior NABC figures were right to regard state aid as a Trojan horse.[90]

The growth of mixing throughout postwar society (see chapter six) further marginalized boys' clubs. Their heyday had seen them part of a network of mutually interweaving and self-supporting segregated institutions. Leaders and an ethos had come from private boys' schools and their members from the state-funded variety. Boys' club leaders had also drawn comfort from the conviction that 'any normally sexed and intelligent psychologist, medical man, schoolmaster or mistress' naturally favoured segregation.[91] The postwar period detached boys' clubs from these supports. The decline of segregated secondary education forced the NABC to switch from arguing that single-sex clubs corresponded to pedagogical orthodoxy to the opposite claim that they formed a necessary bulwark against an otherwise uniform heterosociality. 'Can't the poor boys be allowed a few hours on their own in companionship which helps them to grow to manly vigour?' pleaded Eagar in 1950.[92] Such arguments found little favour with a new generation of experts on adolescence who overturned the NABC's developmental models, decried the 'undesirability of any segregation based on sex' and accused boys' clubs of 'deceiv[ing] themselves' when seeking to 'preserve their boys from feminine advances'.[93] The Tavistock's A.T.M. Wilson argued that single-sex clubs hindered the development of 'mature and responsible relations with the other sex' and fellow psychologist Gwilym Roberts cited 'experimental research and clinical experience' in support of his view that homosexuality and a 'flabby, narcissistic, dreamy romanticism' threatened any boy deprived of female company.[94]

Spurned by the state and stung by new orthodoxies, boys' club leaders rejected a society that appeared to be rejecting them. The NABC could not identify a postwar trend without denouncing it. Secularization, family breakdown, the work ethic, bureaucracy, contraceptives in slot machines and the 'indifferent materialism... opportunistic pleasure and sexual indiscipline' of postwar society all attracted censure. Boys' club leaders had reason to fear for the standing of 'decency [and] manliness' and some tacitly acknowledged their creed to be a 'declining asset' and their methods to be 'out of date'. Even so, the NABC's predominantly antediluvian tone compared unfavourably with the NAYC's avowed progressivism and gratuitously alienated potential recruits, thereby compounding its sense of isolation and courting death by generation gap.[95]

Boys' club leaders could resist change, but they could not ultimately escape its impact. Their reluctance to credit postwar adolescents with a greater maturity led to their attracting an ever-younger cohort of boys. In comparison to the NAYC's claim in 1964 to recruit three-quarters of its membership from the over-sixteens, the NABC discovered four years later that half its clubs contained a majority of schoolboys, compelling it to lower its official age of entry to just eleven in the mid 1970s.[96] A club programme thought suitable for adolescents before the war appealed largely to pre-pubescents after it. Necessity also dictated the increase in weekly dance nights at boys' clubs in order to pacify their members and extract dues from their female guests, despite the hatred that many leaders harboured towards dancing for being at once Americanized, commercialized and heterosocial.[97] Determined that mixing would not infiltrate the organization by stealth, the NABC sought to tighten its conditions for membership in 1950 and again in 1963. On each occasion, however, it had to rescind its policy after pressure from individual clubs and county federations prepared to tolerate a measure of mixing in order to remain attractive to the young and eligible for local authority aid. By the late 1960s, the NABC routinely awarded associate membership to mixed clubs and only the largest and oldest boys' clubs still refused to make any provision for girls. As segregationism slowly, painfully dwindled away, traditionalist boys' club leaders were left bereft: politically, intellectually and culturally isolated, cursing the fact that boys would no longer be boys.[98]

The NAYC set out to be everything that the NABC was not after the Second World War and, in terms of membership, succeeded handsomely. Following wartime gains, its numbers remained at a steady three-quarters of the NABC's in the first decade after the war. Then in the mid fifties the NAYC began to grow and did not stop for the next quarter century. In 1958, it overtook the NABC for the first time. Half a dozen years later, it was larger by a third and another half dozen years after that its boys alone outnumbered those in the NABC. Boasting 320,000 members in 1970 (a figure that was to double during the seventies), the NAYC was twice the size of the NABC. The simultaneous extinction of girls' clubs went unlamented. NAYC members in 1946 split almost exactly three ways between girls in girls' clubs, girls in mixed clubs and boys. But the first five years after the Second World

War halved the number of girls' clubs affiliated to the organization and in the fifties their numbers nosedived. By the mid sixties only four hundred girls remained in the once-thriving single-sex clubs of Liverpool and the NAYC no longer bothered to collect statistics for girls' clubs' membership.[99] The sad fact that girls' clubs lacked a rationale to continue made their passing remarkable only for its rapidity. Those that had survived through the Second World War were often 'little more than sewing circles', conspicuously amateurish, dowdy and under-resourced compared to the spanking new youth centres. Since commentators assumed (and surveys confirmed) that girls much preferred to be with boys, since boys pressurized girls' clubs to let them in and since not a single girls' club leader seems to have opposed mixing publicly in the 1950s and 1960s, the case for girls' clubs either to fold or to mix appeared unanswerable.[100]

Mixed clubs became mainstream and single-sex clubs marginal not just numerically but politically, institutionally and intellectually. State support for mixing was never official policy, remaining as in wartime largely a matter of practicality. The goal of central and local government to provide leisure facilities on a voluntary basis with finite resources presented sound economic reasons to found and fund a unisex club instead of one apiece for boys and girls. More idealistically, the seminal 1960 Albemarle Report on youth leisure provision took pains to 'emphasise the value of mixed activities' as one of 'the most important contributions which the Youth Service can make.' It considered mixing to be preferable due to adolescent demand, the rise of coeducation, the need to attract boys of National Service age and the manner in which the 'happy and healthy relationships ... between boy and girl' formed in mixed clubs could serve as a 'better preparation for life and for marriage.'[101] The NAYC found it correspondingly easy to consolidate its reputation in Whitehall as being 'probably the best [organization] in the youth field'. It always appeared (fairly or otherwise) to be the accommodating party in its negotiations with the NABC and, when requested to submit information on experimental projects in 1965, elicited replies from every one of its federations in contrast to the NABC's perfunctory response.[102] The mixed club movement also enjoyed privileged status on a local level. Some local authorities simply 'believed in mixed clubs' and warned the NABC not to encroach upon their work, while education inspectors were left in no doubt that 'the Department was all for it [i.e. mixing]' and were known to act accordingly.[103]

Mixed clubs benefited from coeducation and revised psychological models of adolescence. New mixed schools commonly established their own mixed clubs and postwar psychologists endorsed mixing as 'one of the best possible ways of establishing objective courtship contacts and of eliminating "love madness"'. The NAYC returned the compliment by endorsing coeducation and sponsoring its own social scientific studies. Boys' clubs drew inspiration from 'Greek thought, Roman strength and Christian faith'; mixed club theorists cited the fashionable American anthropologist Margaret Mead.[104] The birth of the teenager likewise held no perils for the mixed club movement. Whereas the NABC took until the mid seventies to adopt the new lexicon of 'teenagers' and 'young adults', the NAYC made reference to 'Teen-age' culture fully a quarter of a century earlier.[105] And while boys' club leaders blamed 'spiritual and moral hunger' for the teenager's inclination to behave 'prematurely like an adult', mixed club leaders responded with alacrity to adolescents' budding 'social' and 'mental' maturity.[106] A fourteen-year-old had been treated as a 'mere child' in interwar girls' clubs, but her postwar equivalent received the status of an adolescent with corresponding rights and duties. The NAYC's general secretary announced in 1964 that traditional club work was no longer appropriate for the over-sixteens.[107]

Strong growth, abundant optimism and a meeting of minds with experts and policy-makers provided the context for the creation of a new mixed club method. So unaccustomed was Britain to organized mixing for adolescents that mixed club leaders effectively had to start from scratch. There existed no 'experience and tradition' to guide them, no 'communicable techniques' for club leadership, indeed 'no standards recognised for specifically mixed work.'[108] Expediency aside, two principles underpinned mixed clubs. The first was to be up to date. Against the NABC's quest for continuity, NAYC leaders since the Second World War had accepted that the 'modern Jack and Jill' were 'breezy, casual...harder, cooler' in comparison to their parents and needed a new sort of club to match. They distanced themselves from the organization's own restrictive beginnings when 'surplus [sexual] energy' had been sublimated into physical jerks, and embraced the modern 'scientific' techniques pioneered by the wartime Youth Recreation Centres.[109] An *avant garde* of mixed club leaders experimented with 'youth coffee bar[s]' and even 'undercover' clubs unbeholden to 'the formal, the authoritarian and the verbally pious' methods of old. Most controversially of all, Ray Gosling set up a leaderless, riotous club for unclubbables in Leicester that he ill-advisedly described as a hangout for 'thieves and murderers' where 'virgins may be raped.' Other mixed clubs were primmer affairs, albeit less adult-led, more youth-driven, less evangelizing and more matter-of-fact than either contemporaneous boys' clubs or the girls' clubs of old.[110]

The clubs' second aim was the mutualist one of drawing boys and girls 'happily into companionship in the doing of pleasant and useful things together'. Convinced of the wrong-headedness of 'war between the sexes', club leaders conceived of mixing as exemplary of a 'civilised society' in which men and women 'walk side by side'.[111] Ambitions of this kind inspired endeavours to promote intimacy and equality in club life. Intimacy between boys and girls was to be achieved through their 'concentration on a common interest' in activities and social intercourse. Such 'shared social training' would gradually replace the 'false notions and misplaced conventions which obscure men and women in each other's eyes' with a 'bond of common humanity... stronger than the divisions of sex'.[112] Equality in mixed clubs was enshrined in their constitution's insistence on 'equal rights, duties and opportunities' for both sexes. Mixing, claimed the writer on girls Pearl Jephcott, 'inevitably raises questions relating to equal responsibilities in connection with running the society at all its levels, from the canteen upwards. Joint committees and joint duties and privileges bring home fairly forcibly the case for equality, as distinct from identity, of the sexes.'[113]

Jephcott's distinction between equality and identity indicated that boys and girls were expected to 'respect each other's identities' as distinct sexes. Both were to make their quintessential contribution to club life, the boys providing 'order and achievement' and the girls a splash of 'colour'.[114] Club leaders regarded each sex to be 'the best civiliser of the other'. Boys learnt from girls a modicum of manners, while girls in turn became 'less tomboyish and more feminine' by competing for the attention of boys. The ultimate aim was to prepare the young for married life. Clubs leaders provided formal instruction on the subject using the classic texts of the marriage reform movement examined in chapter four.[115] It was through everyday interactions, however, that they hoped to replace the 'petty friction, misunderstanding, disappointment and boredom' afflicting poor matches with the 'harmonious personal relationships based upon mutual understanding' of which mixed club members were capable.[116]

Sex in mixed clubs was a touchy subject. Sensitive to allegations that their movement was a 'thinly disguised matrimonial agency' and not above a certain priggishness themselves, club leaders publicly underplayed the incidence of hanky-panky and privately expelled some caught petting.[117] However, their mutualist outlook ensured that their condemnation of 'cheap' sexual encounters was counterbalanced by a disdain for 'Victorian prudery'.[118] What was needed, they thought, was for the young to pair the notion that 'love is not sinful' with a corresponding 'sense of responsibility', so that physicality was divorced from promiscuity and married to long-lasting relationships based on 'warmth, comradeship and mutual interests'.[119]

Such was the theory of the mixed club method, one in which cheap and cheerful leisure activities contributed to the higher aim of cultivating good relations between the sexes. Meeting on the 'firm common ground of membership with no taint of superiority or inferiority', boys and girls were to learn everything from 'the art of receiving or giving a cup of tea without awkwardness' to that of 'choosing a partner for life', never hectored but always gently 'guided towards an intelligent choice of companions' from which to select the perfect future spouse.[120] Yet the actual dynamics of mixed clubs were a good deal messier and less mutualist than the ideologues anticipated or desired. To begin with, the hands-off approach of the mixed club method militated against the club leaders' more didactic aims. Adolescents exploited the freedom granted to them in postwar mixed clubs to the extent of insisting that the club was 'either theirs or else they will have none of it'.[121] This left club leaders in a quandary. Attempting to impose order invited disaffection and defection, but 'total capitulation' threatened to turn clubs into teenage hops, as social commentator T.R. Fyvel observed:

> My own composite impression left from visits to many London youth clubs is of strenuous activity in a gym; of rather dressed-up youths playing billiards or ping-pong; of rather self-conscious teenage girls; of a frequent undertone of defiance contrasting with the middle-class voices of club leaders and student helpers; and, nearly always, the picture of one particular room where a gramophone was turned on to top volume and scores of younger boys and girls crowded on the floor, a few jiving, the majority just standing and listening to the appalling blare.[122]

The unforeseen difficulties of translating theory into practice also compromised the mutualist ambitions of mixed clubs. The most basic problem lay in maintaining a proper balance between the sexes. Considering that many boys enjoyed a choice between mixed and single-sex provision while the demise of girls' clubs left girls with the option of mixing or nothing, mixed club membership might have been expected to be predominantly female. The opposite happened. Boys formed a majority, sometimes an overwhelming one, of mixed club members from the outset. A national survey of mixed clubs undertaken in 1948 counted considerably more boys in most cases and a 1950 south London case study found 'extremely small' numbers of girls. The NAYC membership statistics confirm that boys constituted a steady 55 per cent or so of mixed club members in the quarter century after the war.[123]

Retention not recruitment accounted for low female numbers. Girls were every bit as likely to join mixed clubs and indeed appear to have formed a slight majority of the incoming cohort of fourteen-year-olds, yet left in droves once they reached seventeen or so and from eighteen onwards were outnumbered in the clubs by a factor of two or three to one. Many explanations arose – 'going steady', household responsibilities, the rival attractions of dance-halls, the wish to dissociate themselves from younger girls and immature and rowdy boys – but almost all revolved around the rapid maturation of teenage girls as soon as they left school. This begged a question: if club girls considered boys of the same age 'childish, silly [and] too young', then were not boys' club leaders right to argue that different maturation rates made the two sexes incompatible during adolescence? Mixed club theorists countered by pointing to the 'overlapping' developmental patterns of the sexes and arguing that, though club girls preferred to date older boys, the age difference was usually too small to matter. Their supporting research was, however, methodologically flawed in that it failed to sample the girls who left clubs, only those who stayed.[124] Despite their best efforts to finesse the problem, club leaders knew all too well that younger boys displayed a 'strong anti-girl feeling' while older girls 'desperately [wanted] contact with men' and considered club boys as too young to interest them. The result was an escalating imbalance in membership, one hapless northern club leader reporting that 'as each batch of boys joined up . . . a similar knot of girls quietly disappear[ed]'.[125]

Mixed clubs lacked enough female leaders as well as members. Mutualist logic suggested that there should be a man and woman in charge of each club so as to provide same-sex and opposite-sex role models for their charges. Such a balance could be engineered in the top echelons of the NAYC (which briefly appointed dual presidents and general secretaries of either sex), but not at the grassroots, where the professionalization of youth work favoured men. The philanthropic spinsters who had dominated the girls' club movement and pioneered mixing were gradually pensioned off and in their place arrived mostly male salaried youth workers. Men in 1950 already comprised 70 per cent of club leaders in non-metropolitan mixed clubs and by the late seventies they outnumbered women nationally five to one. Although women were better represented among the ranks of club assistants, the predominance of male leaders reinforced the marginality of girls. 'Men leaders are not expected to relate to girl members, other than in the most superficial manner', it was found, while those who did otherwise risked being thought over-familiar.[126]

The extent to which boys and girls actually mixed in mixed clubs was also open to question. Support for the principle of mixing was not the problem. All the girls and 90 per cent of the boys in a 1958 school survey considered mixing an essential feature of any ideal club and other research indicated that most members of single-sex organizations also preferred mixed clubs if given the choice.[127] Boys in mixed clubs expressed a preference for mixing over segregation in every activity save outdoor sport, while many girls were even keen to join in the boys' football.[128] Words were not matched by actions, however, for in mixed clubs boys 'remained aloof' and girls in turn 'kept themselves separate'.[129] This disparity between thought and behaviour may be explained in part by the apparently universal tensions evident in encounters between adolescents unused to mixed company. The doyenne of feminist psychology Eleanor Maccoby argues that the manner in which children segregate themselves into single-sex peer groups from the ages of about three to eleven creates difficulties in group interactions between the sexes lasting through adolescence and beyond.[130] Mixed youth club members belonged to the age group most prone to problems in this regard, since the pubescent sexuality that drew most of them to the other sex (and thereby into the clubs) pulled against pre-pubescent homosocial bonds. From this perspective, the curious spectacle of gaggles of each sex 'circl[ing] round each other like nervous animals' signified not indifference but ambivalence. Tangential contact allowed boys and girls to balance the risk of cross-sex association with the security of segregation.[131]

Yet awkwardness all too often bled into antagonism. Boys tended to view any non-sexual contact with girls as compromising their masculinity. Cooperating with girls over running the canteen made a boy a 'sissie', while competing with them in sports and games introduced the appalling possibility of defeat at the hands of the weaker sex. Rather than risk being thought so soppy as to enjoy female company, it seemed safer for boys to 'frighten the girls, especially the quiet ones, by pulling them onto their knees or lifting up their skirts', so sacrificing friendship for crude sexual display.[132] While boys often despised girls for what they were – that is, for not being boys – girls resented boys for what they did. The complaints they relayed to Julia Hanmer in 1964 covered all bases:

> they don't know how to treat girls, think girls are around mainly for their benefit, don't ask them to dance, stare at them as if they came from outer space, are rude, without manners, stupid, scatty, conceited, too unintelligent to converse with. Girls say boys are inclined to stick together, sit in small groups all the evening, think they own the place, think they show off their manhood by swearing and talking big. They try to boss the club, try to show girls up, ignore girls, take the mickey; they look down on girls and they are only nice if they have to be.

Distress over boys' behaviour did not make girls separatists. On the contrary, Hanmer's London survey found them almost unanimously wanting to be 'more friendly with boys', while a 1949 Mass-Observation study found that almost twice as many teenage girls in general preferred to spend their leisure time in mixed groups than with a girlfriend or, for that matter, their boyfriend.[133] A profound asymmetry resulted as female overtures went 'unreciprocated' from boys who had better things to do than bother with girls. 'The girls wanted to be with the boys,' observed one bemused club leader, but the boys 'preferred a stag party'.[134]

Such was the glum lesson of mixed club dances. Dancing was far and away girls' favourite activity for its dreamy mix of glamour, romance and physical release. Unfortunately, it took two to tango and boys ranked dances a lowly fourth among their preferred youth club activities. For many, they were a recreation of last resort, 'something you do to pass the night'; for others, their presence in youth clubs was 'as intolerable as offensive weapons.'[135] Boys often preferred to 'just stand around' rather than ask girls to dance or, when coaxed or otherwise corralled onto the dance floor, were manifestly reluctant to be Fred Astaires to the girls' Ginger Rogers. Some would simply shuffle about as if 'standing around at a football match'. Others approached the activity in a purely narcissistic manner, 'with their heads to one side, seeming not so much interested in their partners as intent on displaying their skill as dancers or their newest suits.' In this potentially most mutual of youth club activities, boys tended to tread on girls' toes and their feelings to boot.[136]

Leaders of mixed clubs were of two minds about the indifference and antipathy existing between club boys and girls. Outright feuding was condemned, yet club theorists were no different from most of their contemporaries in believing that 'certain invariable sex distinctions' engendered divergent, if complementary, male and female interests. Following the lead of Margaret Mead, they spoke of girls' childbearing capacity making them more 'passive and self-contained' in contrast to boys' compensatory 'need for *active* achievement' and accordingly laid on many single-sex activities.[137] Girls' expressed interest in 'fashion, hair-styling, cosmetics, and the opposite sex' inspired any number of courses in Beauty Culture, Cookery and Homecraft, Child Welfare and Happy Hostess, Happy Home. Boys conversely received quaint etiquette advice on the virtue of walking curbside of their girlfriends plus woodworking, biking and sports galore in order to refute boys' clubs' allegations of mixing's effeminizing effects.[138] From one perspective, segregated pursuits taught each sex there were 'limits beyond which none can go and barriers which none should try to break down.' From another, they somewhat paradoxically brought the sexes together. Boys used their 'prowess in games' to impress the girls, while girls mastered the womanly arts in preparation for marriage.[139]

The pleasing symmetry of segregated activities disguised the extent to which they advantaged boys, alienated girls and compromised mixed clubs' mutualist objectives. Boys were offered much the more attractive things to do, in part because they seemed easier to please, in part because they were more 'demanding' and 'noisy'. Facilities fees, sporting equipment and craft-making materials mainly or exclusively benefiting boys seem to have accounted for the greater part of most mixed clubs' discretionary spending.[140] And when separate and superior activities were not provided on their behalf, boys tended to monopolize the best club facilities, charging about the place and barring the girls from the billiards table and the gym. Table-tennis rooms proved a particularly choice battleground, with boys variously discovered hiding the balls from the girls, refusing to play with any who beat them and laying siege to those foolhardy enough to play on their own.[141]

Girls were comparatively disadvantaged. Their interests were the last to be catered for and the first to be cut. 'Many a club will provide equipment for woodwork for the boys,' the NAYC shamefacedly admitted, but 'will not think of taking out a year's subscription for... [girls'] "glossy magazines"'. Such 'meanness' was matched by an opportunistic tendency to channel girls' enthusiasms into utilitarian ends by training 'tomorrow's housewife' through that day's club chores.[142] Even so, many club leaders viewed girls to be not neglected so much as neglectful of the opportunities available to them. The girls milled about on the margins of the clubs, chatting conspiratorially, diffident to organized activities and impervious to admonitions that they find something constructive to do. No 'great enthusiasm' greeted the segregated activities provided for them. And while leaders were 'willing, even eager' to offer girls-only nights to balance those commonly provided for boys, attempts to do so attracted as few as a fifth of those normally attending. Faced with such apparent apathy, obduracy and thorough perversity, club leaders were known to let their 'impatience' and 'despair' get the better of them by treating girls 'either as if they are boys, or as if it were a pity they are not boys, or as if they could be boys if they tried!'[143]

It was strange and somewhat unjust that boys were viewed as normative and girls as deviant in postwar youth clubs. Girls were, after all, the more natural recruits to the cause of mutuality. It was they who most wished to mix and who more readily associated adolescent interaction with preparation for marriage. Indeed, Julia Hanmer thought that it was for this very reason that they disliked the girlie pastimes on offer:

Activities that teach role-content, such as home-making, and role behaviour, such as manners, are not themselves a training in cooperative relationships. Activities that teach girls to be sexually attractive are also no substitute...It is almost like saying 'We expect you to marry and have children and are prepared to teach you the content of the roles of housewife and Mum, but we are not going to give you any help with the most crucial aspect of all – finding a suitable man.'[144]

Boys were torn between their conflicting desires to mix and to retain the exclusive privileges of masculinity. They commonly achieved the best of both worlds by securing segregated facilities for themselves while controlling the nature and extent of their contact with girls. Their success was mutuality's failure, as nominally mixed clubs became male-dominated domains. Mixing brought girls and boys together in a circumscribed fashion and on unequal terms.

By the sixties and early seventies, mixing was as commonplace as segregation had been only a generation before. The NAYC claimed victory, its former leader Katharine Elliot content that youth clubs had taken their place as part of a 'mixed society' and its supporters rejoicing that it had created 'opportunities for wholesome friendships with members of the opposite sex' unknown to previous generations.[145] The NABC, meanwhile, all but admitted defeat. From its perspective, to mix meant surrender, but not to mix meant stomaching that 'the role of Boys' Clubs is bound to be a minority one.' Asked to choose between sacrificing its convictions and its members, it fudged the issue, remaining officially opposed to mixing while turning a blind eye to its proliferation in ostensibly single-sex clubs. So continued the slow death of the boys' club and its treasured ideals.[146]

Seen in this light, the inexorable rise of mixed youth clubs in mid twentieth-century Britain has all the appeal of a morality tale. Institutionally, girls' clubs were rewarded for responding positively to the expressed desire of boys and girls to be together whereas boys' clubs were punished for their rearguard opposition by being consigned to the margins of youth leisure provision. Intellectually, mixing formed part of an avowedly progressive basket of ideas about youth and relations between the sexes that, having been pioneered by turn-of-the-century suffragists, coeducationalists and other assorted nonconformists, enjoyed mass support by World War Two. Conversely, a prescriptive and proscriptive model of masculinity survived in boys' clubs only as part of a bleak anti-modernism testifying to their isolation. And socially, youth pressure persuaded the government, the girls' clubs and, fifty years later, even the boys' clubs to accept their right to mix.[147] Without the groundswell of adolescent opinion in favour of mixing, the state would not have created unisex Youth Recreation Centres in wartime, the girls' clubs would not have thrown themselves into mixing, and mixed clubs would not have predominated after the Second World War.

Yet there remains much to cast doubt on any triumphalist account. Though theoretically rival outfits, postwar mixed clubs and boys' clubs exhibited disquieting similarities. In mixed clubs, girls were officially included but effectively sidelined; in boys' clubs, they were formally excluded but actually admitted. The net effect was roughly the same:

mixing combined with the marginalization of girls. Muddying things further were the internal contradictions of a mutuality at once uncompromising in its attacks on the artificiality of segregation and female subjugation but unquestioning of the naturalness of customary sex roles. Mixed club leaders reflected such confusions when preaching intimacy while proving all too eager to get girls under the hair-dryers and boys on the lathes. Most apparently thought they had struck a balance between joint and separate activities sensitive to the similarities and differences between the sexes. To believe that, however, was to overlook the ability of boys to gain better segregated facilities and either dominate mixed activities or avoid them altogether.

This pointed to the final irony: that the young were at once most responsible for mixing and for subverting its best intentions. Boys were mutualist enough to want to mix but often insufficiently so to treat their sisters as comrades and equals. Their sins were ones of commission: commandeering the best facilities, terrorizing the girls, being inconsiderate and puerile and chauvinistic. If boys were too macho to be true mutualists, girls were generally too unassertive to challenge them. Too often they took the back seat in club committees, prevaricated over whether it was ladylike to beat boys at games and chose to be wallflowers sooner than ask boys to dance.[148] Their sins, though of omission, were scarcely less damaging to mutuality than the boorishness of boys. By failing to claim their fair share of resources, by lacking the confidence to approach boys as equals and by largely deserting the clubs in later adolescence, they allowed the boys to make mixed clubs their own. Clubs designed to bring boys and girls closer together witnessed endless skirmishes in what was the pettiest of sex wars. Mutuality of a kind had triumphed, but any ambitions to usher in a new age of harmonious cooperation between the sexes remained sadly unfulfilled.

4

Marriage for Moderns
Problems of Patriarchy and Companionship

What is the secret of a happy marriage? Is it the attraction of opposites, the charm and mystery of another sex ... each treading a separate path? Or is it a sense of equal partnership, community of interests and mutual understanding, and a sharing together of the common tasks which go into the making of the family home?[1]

These questions, posed by feminist Barbara Drake during the Second World War, had been the subject of intense dispute fifty years before and remain debatable over fifty years later; but for most of her contemporaries there was but one answer. The former option stood for the discredited patriarchal model of marriage and its hermetically separate spheres. The latter, with its emphasis upon equality, intimacy, sharing and communication, contained the essence of a companionate ideal advocated by marriage reformers in mid twentieth-century Britain.

Marriage reform may be defined as a school of thought in favour of a measured revision of matrimonial law, enlightened sexual attitudes and a radical restructuring of marital roles in the wake of women's emancipation. Its most prominent adherents were A. Herbert Gray, David R. Mace and Edward F. Griffith. In 1946, the trio founded the National Marriage Guidance Council (or NMGC, today known as Relate), the single most influential body concerned with marriage in this period. And they, together with such fellow Christians as Eustace Chesser, Leslie Weatherhead, Helena Wright, Barbara Cartland, Mary Macaulay and Marie Stopes, exercised a virtual monopoly over marriage and sex manuals in the half century following the First World War.[2] Marriage reformers were broadly supported in their ambitions by such social scientists as Edward Westermarck and Ronald Fletcher and, to a lesser extent, by sex radicals like Havelock Ellis and Bertrand Russell. They attracted postwar governmental support for their counselling activities and prepared the way for the permissive legislation concerning abortion and divorce introduced in the 1960s.[3]

Marriage reformers cast themselves as the witnesses and agents of the evolution of marriage to a higher and happier state. They believed that a patriarchal arrangement in which the husband exercised brutal dominion over his 'helpless' wife was fit only for the 'lower stages of civilisation'. Conversely, emancipation and companionate marriage were meant to go together like a horse and carriage for a generation of women no longer willing to accept the 'simultaneous duties of a kept mistress and a household drudge.'[4] However, a companionship intended to be a panacea to the ills of patriarchy in fact created a whole new order of marital problems. What exactly was equality? Was closeness compatible with the sexual division of labour? Was men's task simply to cede power? Did women have a right to orgasms? Could the great hopes invested in marriage reform be realized? All was uncertain once patriarchal dictates no longer held. Such dilemmas were not merely the abstract concerns of marriage reformers, but were confronted by innumerable couples coming to terms with marital change.

This chapter has a double purpose: to analyse the marriage reformers' conception of patriarchy and companionship in mid twentieth-century Britain and to examine how the two models operated in problem marriages. There are three main reasons to explore marriages through their problems. The first is the purely practical one that, while happy families leave behind holiday snaps, those unhappy enough to seek help had their travails recorded in unrivalled detail by sundry counselling organizations. The second lies in their presumed abnormality. Marriages cannot be considered problematic without recourse to norms, and marriage counselling required some yardstick of success. The diagnosis and treatment of marriage problems accordingly smokes out the assumptions of couples and counsellors about what marriage should and should not be. This raises a third rationale: that troubled marriages need not be typical to reveal the dynamics of family life. The pioneering family historian Lawrence Stone once likened marital breakdown to political upheaval in the manner in which each exposes underlying structures:

> Like a revolution in the polity, a bitterly disputed marital separation provides us with a unique and privileged view into otherwise hidden areas of thought and behaviour... [including] such matters as marital fidelity, marital cruelty, sexuality, patriarchal authority, individual

autonomy, the expected roles of the two genders, and the rival responsibilities and claims of husband and wife for child custody, care and maintenance.[5]

A comparative study of the problems within patriarchal and companionate marriages in mid twentieth-century Britain allows the intrinsic strengths and stresses of the two rival systems to be revealed. Every marriage has its own peculiarities, but the types of problems it encounters and the manner in which they are addressed depend largely upon social mores.

Marriage Reform

Patriarchy was little theorized but much criticized by mid twentieth-century marriage reformers on egalitarian grounds. They believed that a patriarch appointed himself the 'official head of the house, [who] has the power of final veto and must be obeyed'. The wife was in turn 'patient, submissive, home-centred and self-effacing'.[6] Inequality bred distance in reformers' eyes. Man and woman inhabited their own separate spheres and expected the other to provide services instead of affection, thereby reducing a potentially 'intimate and beautiful association' to a mere 'commercial partnership'. The wife served as a skivvy in return for subsistence, while the 'bad tempered, bullying husband' who used his home as a hotel deprived himself of close contact with his family. Sex was considered particularly prone to suffer under patriarchy. 'Bring together an ignorant, dominating, passionate man and an innocent, apprehensive girl,' warned the NMGC's Hugh Lyon, 'and the stage is set for tragedy.'[7]

Marriage reformers were happy to report that patriarchy had had its day, its ancient foundations 'finally collapsing in a heap of ruins' in the new 'atomic age'.[8] Many factors contributed to the perceived eclipse of patriarchal marriage: 'increased economic stress on family institutions, new status of woman, scientific approach to sex, decline in religion and social upheaval and disorder on world-wide scale'. Of these, the most decisive was held to be women's emancipation:

> In a former age, matrimony was an infinitely simpler state than it is today. The savage female had been well broken in, she was content to obey her husband, and happy in her obedience. Today the wife has acquired more personality of her own... She seeks to become the

partner and comrade of her husband, and the modern husband would no longer be satisfied with a Victorian wife.[9]

Marriage reformers were of two minds about the consequences, at once rejoicing that emancipation created a 'fuller and finer' relationship and fearing its impact upon marital stability. Freedom was all well and good, but if wrongly interpreted could make women shun marriage or claim an identity of marital roles that obscured the 'functional differences' between the sexes. 'The nature of the male is essentially dominant, the female submissive,' argued David Mace, adding that 'any undue interference with these roles will produce disaster in a marriage relationship.'[10] But whatever his reservations, Mace accepted that the 'old patriarchal stuff just won't do for today'. A 'new kind' of family was needed, he thought, one based not on 'authority and obedience' but on equality and cooperation. Emancipation had created the greatest opportunity 'in the whole of human history to make family life what it was meant to be.'[11]

'Modern Democratic Marriage' went by many names – partnership marriage, symmetrical marriage, loose-knit, joint-conjugal marriage – but all meant one thing: companionship.[12] The roots of companionate marriage have been subject to any number of competing and contradictory claims. Its beginnings have been dated to the 1950s, the 1920s, the nineteenth century, the eighteenth century, even the Middle Ages.[13] And, indeed, a companionate ideal of being 'united by the bonds of affection, congeniality and common interests' evidently existed in the higher-class Georgian and Victorian couples studied by Lawrence Stone, Randolph Trumbach, Amanda Vickery, Jeanne Peterson, Leonore Davidoff and Catherine Hall. These husbands and wives saw marriage as being less an institution than a relationship intended to serve as their primary arena for emotional expression and satisfaction.[14] What distinguished twentieth-century companionship was its emphasis on equality. Whereas loving devotion between spouses had once been thought perfectly consistent with husbandly authority, marriage reformers saw the two as utterly incompatible. In their view 'equal partnership' represented the 'only basis for mutual respect and mutual affection.'[15]

The keywords of companionship were intimacy and equality. Intimacy was at once achieved and expressed through privacy, closeness, communication, sharing, understanding and friendship. Privacy was vital, from the keeping of confidences to the 'absolute privacy' essential for good sex. Allied to it was closeness, that intense interdependence which united couples on 'every plane of [their] existence'.[16] This entailed perfect communication and 'complete mutual trust' as well as shared interests. Spouses were encouraged to shop together, exercise together, collect stamps together and become so synchronized in their 'opinions, customs and emotions' as always to wish for 'the same thing at the same time.'[17] Out of closeness and communication came that meeting of minds through which couples discovered that love was but 'another word for "understanding".'[18] Intimacy also involved a friendship that ideally preceded passion and invariably outlasted it, providing a 'steady warmth' once desire's 'raging forest fire' had died down. Companionship meant the 'marriage of good friends'.[19]

Equality neatly complemented intimacy in being another kind of sharing, a 'sharing of mutual esteem'. As we have already seen, marriage reformers believed that marital equality accompanied women's wider emancipation, being essential to entice them into wedlock and to keep them there. But the democratization of marriage was much more than a begrudging acceptance of the inevitable. 'Again and again' couples wrote to economist and sometime marriage reformer William Beveridge about the 'better companionship of husband and wife' wrought by equality. Some reformers even believed that marriage offered women a degree of liberty surpassing that in public life, since within it, 'cooperation based on equality is attainable *now*'.[20]

Equality did not mean identity to the marriage reformers. To belabour the differences between the sexes was the besetting sin of patriarchy, yet to expect the other sex to 'feel, think and behave' exactly like oneself invited only 'antagonism'. Since husband and wife were equal precisely because they were different, what they required was an 'equality of status and not of function' entailing the revision rather than the abolition of the existing household division of labour.[21] This meant that all decisions had to be arrived at by 'mutual discussion and agreement.' It was no longer acceptable for a paterfamilias to lay down the law. The wife additionally deserved a measure of economic independence, most often conceived in terms of guaranteeing her an income other than her weekly housekeeping allowance. The more daring of marriage reformers called for the state endowment of housewives, which in the opinion of advice columnist Leonora Eyles would enable a woman to 'beautify the home, train her mind to befitting motherhood, have a little time to play, and be a pal as well as a safety-valve to her man': true companionship indeed.[22]

Wives were also thought to need some sort of life beyond housework. Marriage reformers were second to none in attacking the 'purposeless and unsatisfied life' of the 'Woman in the Little House'. The drudge was prone to 'suburban neurosis' and a very poor partner to boot: 'She is tired, dispirited, disinterested [sic], and unable to respond to her husband's overtures.'[23] Yet because marriage reformers seldom doubted that 'homemaking is mainly the wife's sphere', the only remedy seemed to be one of alleviating her burden through domestic appliances, husbandly help, family limitation and the outlet of paid employment. Part-time work was deemed good for the woman, who gained confidence and expertise without sacrificing one jot of her 'feminine appeal'. And it was good for the marriage, since the 'wife's experiences in the workaday world should tend to make her a more interesting companion.'[24]

The 'domestication of husbands' followed naturally from the emancipation of wives. Marriage reformers warned that without some sharing of housework the wife felt 'unfairly put upon' and the husband found himself at a 'loose end'. Though excused from the most conventionally feminine tasks, men were expected to help 'setting fires, cleaning grates, carrying coals, making beds, washing dishes, cooking, scrubbing floors, cleaning brass and silver, etc., etc.'[25] Reformers also urged them to take a more active role in the upbringing of their children. The 'heavy father' of yore had acted only as a distant disciplinarian to his children. In contrast, Marie Stopes credited the 'modern young man' with an 'intense desire for fatherhood...very remarkable in its extent and its beauty'. He was primed to read bedtime stories, dandle the children on his knees and, on occasion, push the pram. Most of all, he was to act as a role model, being the sort of man whom his daughters would wish to marry and his sons to become.[26] Fatherhood taught a man the pleasures of loving duty and brought him closer to his children and wife. In return for a little childcare, housework and shopping, he exchanged an 'unpaid domestic servant' for an 'intelligent, independent companion' in a marriage brimful of 'lasting love and mutual respect'.[27]

'I believe in the rightness and beauty of natural sex expression as the framework of love,' went The Creed of the Happy Wife: 'I believe that any sexual gesture, play or craving of my husband or myself is natural, provided only that it demands the participation and seeks the happiness of the mate as well as the self.' Yet her inhibitions were many. Her sheltered upbringing forbade her that 'frankness of desire' enjoyed by men and instilled in her a blushing 'maidenly reserve'. Communication with her husband on sexual matters was correspondingly tricky, but anything could be overcome by 'frank discussion' and by conquering inhibitions. In intercourse, she was not to be 'so naive as to suppose that I can give adequate outlet to my own primal urge, to the highest joy to my mate, by playing only a passive role in our love-making.' The 'new code of adult sex expression' taught her to 'join my partner in the sexual union just as wholeheartedly as I step with my dancing partner on the ballroom floor.' Only in this manner would she experience the 'supreme joy' of sex: that 'intensity of tenderness' between her husband and herself that came from their 'perfect adjustment' to each other.[28]

This catechism, contained in a mass-market marriage manual of the 1930s, captured the centrality of sex to companionship as the 'consummation of mutual adoration'. Its enemy, as the Happy Wife indicated, was thought to be ignorance and reticence. 'Not one husband in twelve knows enough of the technique of love to enable him to impart and receive half the pleasure which should be derived from sexual union ... The overwhelming majority of wives *never* know the supreme joy which the sex act can yield to the ideally mated,' calculated consultant psychologist Eustace Chesser.[29] Ignorance took much of the blame for the behaviour of those husbands who treated sex as a 'cruel, repellent, clumsy assault'. Reformers instructed such men not only to elicit consent but to display consideration to his wife's singular sexual requirements: to view foreplay as more than a chore; to delay his orgasm and foster hers; to become a sensitive lover exercising the 'utmost gentleness and restraint'.[30]

Women's ignorance was held to take the opposite form of prim inhibition. 'Most well brought-up girls' believed that 'sexual illiteracy is a mark of respectability and moral rectitude', according to clinicians Kenneth Walker and Peter Fletcher. The major culprit was the 'miseducation' in prudery of such unfortunates as the Happy Wife; as late as the 1950s the NMGC felt obliged to inform women how to pronounce '*va-jie-ner*'.[31] But a woman's modesty was also attributed in part to the natural latency and diffuseness of female sexuality. Whereas the average man felt an urgent stirring in his loins from adolescence onwards, the 'typical healthy unwedded girl ... rarely experiences any definite sexual desire'. She accordingly had to be sexually 'awakened' under the tender tutelage of her husband and '*taught*, gradually, how to enjoy love on its physical side.'[32]

What women like the Happy Wife needed to learn was what

historian Ross McKibbin has called the 'most subversive doctrine' of the new sex teaching: that woman's libido was the equal of man's. The sexes possessed 'rather similar sex desires', stated the NMGC, so that a 'satisfactory sex life is just as necessary for a woman as for a man.' It added that women were 'so made' that intercourse should induce in them 'what is called an "orgasm",' though what an orgasm was was regrettably 'difficult to describe.'[33] Whatever their nature, regular and preferably multiple orgasms for women were held by marriage reformers to be desirable if not essential to every happy companionate marriage. One particularly bizarre diagram in *The Encyclopaedia of Sex Practice* (1951) indicated that through simultaneous climax alone could couples experience 'voluptuous sensations' sufficient to make spheres ascend pyramids and flowers kiss.[34]

Woman's right to the 'satisfaction of her sexual needs' made it incumbent upon both parties to 'ensure that in actual practice she receives it'.[35] The husband was 'duty bound to assist his wife to achieve orgasm', while any outstanding fears of sex on the part of the wife received short shrift. Guilt was 'untenable', coldness 'unnaturally' induced, fear of pregnancy a 'false attitude' and purity so much 'useless . . . self-pity'.[36] Wives were even encouraged to have intercourse when not particularly disposed to do so. Though they considered 'conjugal rights' to be simply a 'species of rape', reformers thought it detrimental to marriage for a woman to spurn her husband's every advance. They cautioned a sexless woman against marrying and a married woman to 'give herself gladly' should her husband not abide her refusal. Historians Sheila Jeffreys and Margaret Jackson rightly contend that the expectation placed on women to enjoy sex constituted a coercive new sexual norm. As norms went, however, it was one that provided wives with greater opportunities for pleasure and fewer possibilities of pain than the valorization of women's sexlessness which it strove to replace.[37]

Supplementary to woman's 'love right' to equal pleasure was recognition that 'her sex needs are different from those of a man.' Male desire was 'complete within itself', unattached to a paternal instinct or even to a particular partner, an 'urgent' itch as quickly sated as it was provoked.[38] In contrast, a woman's sexuality was thought to be more emotional, variable, cyclical and individual, 'less easily aroused, more deeply stirred and [taking] much longer to settle down afterwards.' Failure to acknowledge the 'fundamental difference' between male and female sexual needs, marriage reformers warned, 'probably [does] more than anything else to cloud the marital horizon and to spoil the harmony of countless marriages.'[39] This emphasis on sexual difference proved distinctly double-edged. It performed a real service to women in loudly trumpeting their equal if different needs (the NMGC's Edward Griffith instructing husbands to remain erect for upwards of half an hour to allow women time to climax). Yet it also required that men remain on top. 'The basic role of the husband in the sex relationship is an active one,' stated his colleague David Mace: 'He is the initiator.'[40] A certain assertiveness, even aggression, was considered to be imperative for the man to attain an erection and orchestrate the proceedings; those who customarily failed to take the dominant role were 'not strictly speaking normal' and prone to impotency. The woman in turn was warned not to confuse equality with 'identity of feeling'. She was to be the 'responsive' or 'receptive' partner: neither passive and inert nor exactly active in the sense of being assertive – that was the man's task – but rather displaying an active passivity, an eager receptivity to her husband's thrusting desire.[41]

Such was the companionate ideal, commended by marriage reformers as an altogether 'more difficult though more rewarding' arrangement than patriarchy, as William Beveridge explained:

The man [formerly] rode in front and held the reins; his wife sat behind firmly strapped to him . . . All very simple and satisfactory – to our fathers. Today's marriage isn't like that . . . [but] more like two people riding abreast on the same horse, doing a rather difficult balancing feat and each holding one rein. It's more companionable than the old way, but it's more complicated, and must at times be rather confusing to the horse. How do married couples decide which way they're going when they disagree now that each has an equal voice?[42]

The rewards came from the closeness of a marriage of true equals. As with any form of tyranny, patriarchy brought but mean privileges for the oppressors and misery for the oppressed, whereas couples pursuing the companionate ideal stood to attain a love 'wider and deeper' than anything previously imaginable.[43] These, then, were the models of patriarchy and companionship current in the marriage literature of mid twentieth-century Britain: the one characterized, in a manner less descriptive than denunciatory, as unequal, distant and sexually divisive; the other championed as the solution to marriage's manifold problems in its equality, intimacy and sexual harmony. But how did theory correspond to actuality? Was patriarchy so bad and companionship so sublime as the marriage reformers made out? How did husbands and wives actually relate to each other in the two sorts of marriages? For answers, we must shift from prescription to practice and consider how the two systems shaped everyday encounters between warring husbands and wives.

Poor Marriages

The problems of patriarchal marriages in mid twentieth-century Britain are best sought among the unreconstructed working class, adjudged by marriage reformers to have been those least affected by their doctrines. The 'brain-worker' was credited with seeking 'companionacy and mental compatibility' in his partner. The unskilled labourer was conversely thought to view a wife as 'a thing to tend the house, bear children and minister to physical appetites'.[44] And for such lower-working-class marriages, there exists no better source than the case-notes of the Family Welfare Association (FWA).[45] Founded in 1869 as The Society for Organising Charitable Relief and Repressing Mendacity and known until 1946 as the Charity Organisation Society, the FWA served primarily as a conduit channelling money from philanthropic bodies to the poorest of the 'deserving' poor. Its investigative role serves historians doubly well, firstly because its role as a mediating body between claimants and charities necessitated keeping information on file. Files were retrieved and reopened each time a family applied for help, so that its misfortunes might be catalogued over a period of decades, with updates provided whenever trouble recurred. Secondly, the FWA's pioneering case-work methods entailed regular meetings between case-worker and client accompanied by record-keeping of quite extraordinary detail. No source is free from bias and the occasional comments of case-workers betray the strange blend of philanthropy and psychoanalysis informing their interview technique.[46] Yet the opinions of the case-workers are for the most part clearly distinguishable from those of their interviewees and the hundreds of pages of near-verbatim testimony are as close as historians are likely to come to an accurate and immediate account of lower-working-class family life. Unlike much contemporaneous commentary on poor families, these records are largely devoid of middle-class moralizing; unlike the working-class autobiographies and oral history interviews favoured by most family historians, they are untainted by hindsight and selective memory.[47]

Although marriage problems did not officially become a primary concern of the FWA until 1959, it had long offered guidance when it encountered them. As it happened, it did so very regularly indeed, with case-workers estimating the proportion of clients experiencing such difficulties to be anything between 30 and 90 per cent.[48] The higher figure tallies more closely with the cases examined here, which were selected to give a broad geographical and chronological spread as well as on the basis of their size: the bulkier, the better. Of the 132 files consulted, covering the period from 1929 to 1965 (when the archive ends), only a seventh gave no indication of marriage problems and of these, one in three concerned widows. Some sixty-eight provided detailed evidence of marital strife. The case-notes of these families form the core evidence for this section. Their names and identifying details have all been changed or omitted entirely where frequent use of the same case might allow identification through cross-referencing.[49]

Besides being too few in number to be amenable to much statistical analysis, the FWA records are limited in several other respects. To begin with, the sample is almost uniformly drawn from those 'rough' working-class families in sufficiently serious difficulties to need charitable help. Furthermore, the clients come solely from London, from Hammersmith in the west to Tower Hamlets in the east. Given the wide variety of family structures identified in historical research on other regions and subsections of the working class, it may be that the findings relate solely to the 'unrespectable' metropolitan poor.[50] The records also convey little sense of change over time. The Slump put some out of work, the Second World War took more off to fight, postwar affluence gave husbands more security and wives more opportunity to work and consume. Yet none of these events had much discernible effect on the marital problems presented to the FWA, either because such conflicts were so intractable as to be impervious to external developments, or because the sample size is too small to reveal their impact.[51]

Then there is the fact that practically all FWA interviews were conducted with wives. Men tended to be at work when case-workers visited and, though habitually interviewed at some early stage in the cases, were known to object to 'unwarrantable interference in [their] domestic privacy' by case-workers apparently trying to 'pry and break up the family'. But if husbands were hostile to case-workers, the case-workers (mostly middle-class spinsters) generally did not reciprocate, one future general secretary of the FWA charitably concluding that husbands bore their 'fair share of the burden of family life'.[52] Case-workers also frequently sought to corroborate a wife's testimony with relatives, neighbours, vicars, schools or other charities with which the family had had dealings. So although the FWA cases afford us a wife's-eye view of marriage problems, they are by no means hopelessly partial in their perspective when used alongside contemporaneous social scientific studies. With these provisos in mind, it is possible to reconstruct the power dynamics of troubled marriages in mid twentieth-century London: why these men and women married, what spousal roles they performed, how their interests diverged, who controlled whom and whether separation benefited either party when conflict could no longer be contained.

Most marriages encountered by the FWA were made not in heaven but out of bleak necessity. Almost all the mid twentieth-century generation married and on the whole married young, with marriage rates climbing and the mean age at first marriage falling to unprecedented levels after the Second World War.[53] For women in particular marriage represented a means of graduating to adulthood and slipping free from unhappy family ties. Mrs Burbage wedded to 'escape' her family's wrath over her pregnancy; Mrs Morrison 'just did it after pressure from him and to spite parents'. Marriage represented a security precious to a woman like Mrs Lancaster, who had been 'young and had nobody to turn to.' Cohabitation afforded no similar protection, as Mrs Ibstock found to her cost: 'She emphasised that she would not again set up house with a man without being married, as she has learned her lesson.' Courtship could be 'lovey-dovey', though some women remembered having been badgered into submission. Working-class women could not afford to be choosy or to delay their decision lest they be left on the shelf. 'It was different for girls who had a good home, they could consider more whom they married,' explained Mrs Silesby, 'but when you had nothing, you did not think much.' In any case, protracted romances were liable to be cut short by accidental pregnancies and the subsequent shotgun weddings, an unwelcome contingency that a man wishing to 'get on, and...have more behind him before he got married' tended to blame on the carelessness or calculation of his partner.

Expectations of marriage were low on both sides. The psychiatrists Eliot Slater and Moya Woodside identified a predominantly

101

instrumental attitude among the lower-class London couples they interviewed in the 1940s, marriage being considered to be 'less *to* someone than *for* something'.[54] Men's motivations remain obscure in the FWA cases though, judging by their complaints, they looked first of all for a good housekeeper and complaisant sexual partner, as indicated by Mr Birstall's gripes over his wife's '"laziness" in the home' and 'refusal of sex relations.' The more extensive evidence on wives reveals their realistically modest aspirations. Their overriding concern was to find a good provider. A 'very decent chap...who would make a very good husband' was one who 'would bring his money home on Friday night and give it to her, and not be erratic'. Besides cash, a man was also expected to provide his wife with children, exposing one impotent, child-hating fellow to ridicule for failing to be a 'normal husband'. Otherwise, wives mainly defined goodness as being the absence of negative traits: not drinking, not gambling, not straying unaccountably from home, the type who 'never asked' for untoward amounts of intercourse and 'never complained' should he be refused.[55]

Upon marrying, these men and women assumed full adult responsibilities in a savagely capricious environment. Their lives were bounded by poverty and ill-health. Mental or physical illness was a constant threat to the normal functioning of families; unemployment another. Sickness put many out of work, but the Slump chose its victims more indiscriminately. A fit man seldom found himself jobless during the postwar boom except through fecklessness or sheer perversity, a distressingly common condition among FWA claimants. A fair number of them were also criminals, which at once hindered them in obtaining regular employment and removed the need to do so. To poverty and precarious health were added parlous housing conditions calculated to strain any marriage. Living in a hut on wasteland without heat or water was responsible for 'a lot of the trouble between them' according to one battered wife, while sharing a room with their daughter forced another couple to abstain from intercourse with attendant distress. But at least these couples managed to ''ave a house [of] their own', as was expected of nuclear families in mid twentieth-century Britain. Those unfortunate newlyweds forced to lodge with their in-laws inevitably encountered difficulties, a typical case involving the maternal mother-in-law antagonizing the husband and sowing dissension between him and her daughter.

How did people cope in the face of such adversity? Through the strength of kin and community networks, according to an influential school of social commentators in the 1950s. Two seminal works issued by the Institute of Community Studies in 1957, Peter Townsend's *The Family Life of Old People* and Peter Willmott's and Michael Young's *Family and Kinship in East London,* drew attention to the power of the extended family in creating 'ties of blood, duty, affection, common interests and daily acquaintance' essential to the well-being of its members. That same year, Richard Hoggart famously paid tribute to the manner in which common moral standards and the kindness of neighbours underpinned family security during his childhood in Leeds.[56] Unfortunately for the FWA families, the social supports of church, neighbours and kin were in their case often ineffective or decidedly counterproductive. Religion was a weak force in these people's lives, despite a number of them being Irish Catholics. At the margins, it made people like Mrs Birstall and Mr O'Neill guilty about sex or unwilling to separate. But those who did turn to the church for guidance may well have regretted it. One woman who heeded her priest's injunctions against divorce was repaid by his accusing her of being a 'very weak person' for allowing her child to be christened by a rival denomination.

Another mainstay for put-upon women, the neighbours, appear in these records to have been far from supportive. Neighbourly gossip did not create here that network of female solidarity described in Melanie Tebbutt's history of the subject.[57] Rather, it served as a career hierarchy for housewives, its verdicts determining the standing of every woman on the street. Female neighbours were quick to judge, readily informing on other wives who appeared to go out too much at the expense of their children. And they were slow to forgive. Mrs Braunstone found herself ostracized years after she had quit drinking, leading the case-worker to conclude that 'the women in her neighbourhood have been sterner in their judgements upon her than the men.' As a method of shaming bad husbands, female gossip appears to have been largely ineffective, since the worst knew no shame and in any case inhabited a parallel world of workmates and drinking partners. As a means of further isolating women in troubled families, however, it proved all too effective. Mrs Shepshed confessed that 'she can't go anywhere because she tells people that they are "getting on nicely"... and hates telling lies', while another woman was forced to open the door to her abusive husband 'because of what the neighbours would say'.[58]

Relatives played a more active role in marriages than did neighbours or the church. The time had passed when parents chose their children's spouses but, when displeased, they were sure to make their feelings known. Her son had 'never looked at a member of the opposite sex!' exclaimed the possessive Mrs Dixon senior, until he wedded a woman of doubtful virtue who 'cannot cook even a rice pudding' and had altogether 'dragged her boy down.' Yet the partiality of parents limited their power, as did the value attached to privacy in mid-century marriages. Spouses deeply resented interference from in-laws. Wives tended to view their mothers-in-law as competitors for their husbands' affections and as unwarranted intruders into their housewifely realm, whereas husbands liked to keep arguments within the immediate family, where they were in control. When his wife informed her mother of his profligate gambling habits, Mr Barwell was accordingly 'very annoyed indeed, telling her there were some secrets between husband and wife that no one else ought to know about.' Wives were accordingly reluctant to reveal their husbands' mistreatment of them and expressed anguish if they did. Deprived of effective external supports and commonly with 'no social life and no companionship' to speak of, such women were left to cope alone.

While poverty and isolation determined these families' lowly position within society, their sex governed each individual's place within the family. Men expected and got the 'best of everything', reported sociologist Ferdynand Zweig in his 1950s study of working-class households, their privileged position accepted by their wives as a simple 'matter of fact'.[59] Power was grounded in the sexual division of labour. It began with knowledge: husbands generally knew more about their wives than their wives knew about them. They were effectively their wives' employers, paying their wages and supervising their work. At the same time, men tended to keep their lives hidden from their wives' prying eyes. Mrs Houghton had no knowledge of where her husband worked or went since he 'never speaks of his activities' and ate elsewhere, while another woman confessed her total ignorance of her husband's movements: 'No dear, he goes out all day – and don't ask me where he goes, because I don't know.'

Men's superior earning capacity established their authority as an incontestable economic truth. Working-class London households operated the 'pocket money' system whereby a husband gave his wife a fixed weekly amount for housekeeping expenses and retained the remainder of his wages for outgoings and various little luxuries. The FWA records accordingly had two columns for income, 'earns' and 'gives': the disparity between the two figures varying widely. A typical working man in the 1940s earning five pounds gross and four pounds ten shillings after tax apportioned three pounds to the house and spent the remainder on fares, clothes and lunches as well as drink, bets and cigarettes.[60] But a bad husband withheld anything up to half his wages and claimed any further income – a military pension, even the child allowance – as his own.

Wives often worked outside the home – it was a mark of these families' lack of respectability that they did so – but employment provided them with neither a truly independent earning capacity nor the same sense of authority as a male breadwinner. Granted, they occasionally derived some scraps of autonomy from their jobs. A wife recalled how she had gained 'a bit of independence' in paid work before an unplanned pregnancy beached her back home, and it was that same 'feeling of independence' which one hapless woman identified as the main attraction of work, allowing her to 'get away from her family a bit, and be able to eat a meal without being surrounded by an audience'. Yet that was as far as freedom went. These women's wages remained pitifully low in this period, perhaps half what their husbands earned, and most worked simply because needs must, due to an ill, absent, underpaid or exceptionally stingy husband.

Severely disadvantaged by the customary division of income, wives were relatively powerless to confront their husbands over money matters. Most did not know how much their husbands earned and, wrote sociologist Peter Townsend, 'many did not think they had a right to know.'[61] In any case, the meanest men were not telling. Mr Barwell kept his financial affairs a 'closed book' and Mr Gartree allegedly earned half as much again as he was prepared to admit. Those wives determined to press their claim for a greater share of the income found their husbands liable to brook no argument on the matter. One found her husband 'quite unsympathetic to any plea' to increase his pitiable allowance for their seven children despite 'always seem[ing] to have wads of one pound notes'. Another was informed by her man that 'so long as he had his money for cigarettes and beer he could not care about the rest.' The first was forced to take on paid work for which she had insufficient time and energy. The second, driven into debt, found herself being propositioned by a shop assistant promising to 'pay up himself if she would be his "fancy woman".' The wages of men's sin truly fell upon the wives.[62]

Men's licensed profligacy if taken to excess could bankrupt whole families. Zweig reckoned the shortfall of necessities among forties London households to be caused solely by the 'excessive pocket money of the husband which he spends on his indulgences . . . the bad habits of betting, drinking and smoking.'[63] Wives were improvident as well (it was the commonest complaint levelled against them), though commonly out of foolish as opposed to selfish reasons. The margin of error when managing low wages was perilously slight, with a single incautious purchase threatening to produce insurmountable arrears. Yet young wives, sometimes without prior experience of managing a household, could be utterly unworldly in their budgeting. 'She hasn't a clue how to handle money,' moaned Mr Ashby: 'She is unable to draw the line between what she wants and what she has to buy it with.' Such wifely folly was ultimately the husband's problem. Law and custom combined to hold him responsible for all his wife's debts: one of the few penalties of patriarchal power.

If economic power over his wife did not suffice, a husband's ultimate advantage lay in his fists. 'Knocking the wife about' was so routine as to be almost acceptable when practised in moderation, so that the courts granted wives separation orders for cruelty only if the assaults were persistent and 'exceptionally violent' as opposed to an 'ordinary scuffle'. Of my sample of sixty-eight FWA cases involving serious marital difficulties, some eighteen detailed wife-beating.[64] Violence was in some cases nothing more systematic than the unforeseen outcome of a particularly nasty quarrel. Mrs Ashby put her husband's belligerence down to their intolerable living conditions, while Mrs Bassett found her husband usually 'quite normal', only turning nasty during one of his inexplicable 'moods'. It was not unknown for wives to defend themselves, giving the proceedings a certain Punch and Judy quality: 'Well, when he hits the baby, I hit him and then he hits me back'. In other marriages, wife-beating bore all the hallmarks of an instrument of control. Two men used death threats to keep their wives faithful and a third beat his partner when she refused sex. The regular batterer augmented his cruelty with a certain guile. One husband chose to attack his wife when she was holding the baby, making sure to strike her around the head so as to leave no marks. Men of this sort were aggressive in other aspects of their lives. Violence for them was habitual, acceptable, effective. The greater his physical superiority over his wife, the easier it was for a battering husband to remain in control.

Husbands and wives interviewed by the FWA tended to approach sex from opposing sides. It remained a commonplace in these communities that women could – or should – not enjoy intercourse. 'Sex is duty, and women are not trained to expect any particular pleasure,' found Slater and Woodside in their wartime study of lower-class London couples: 'Responsiveness in...wives was hardly expected'. Ignorance played its part. It was an 'almost universal complaint' among the impoverished women served by the Family Service Units that 'they had been told nothing about the facts of life by their mothers'.[65] That one woman somehow managed to remain clueless about the mechanics of sex until the very delivery of her first child went some way towards explaining why she 'regard[ed] any intimacy as a wifely duty and nothing more'. But even otherwise compliant wives were likely to be put off sex by their husbands' brutal technique. Men's primal pleasure sometimes divorced sex from emotion. One disturbed husband bore a 'horror of kissing' ('He likes intercourse or nothing'), whereas his wife much preferred to be gently caressed. Such men took little account of their wives' desires.

If the act of intercourse did not itself repel women, the prospect of continual pregnancy often did. 'The girls' interest in sex dies...when the glamour of marriage wears off and they find that sex means babies,' reported sociologist Madeleine Kerr in her study of disadvantaged Liverpudlians: 'In every case where the woman has admitted a pleasure in sexual intercourse, the number of her children has been small.'[66] To 'fall' pregnant, as the phrase bleakly suggested, was dangerous and cumbersome and, for all their desire for children, women eventually forswore having too much of a good thing. One wife admitted that her excessive fecundity made her 'scared stiff' of intercourse and another's revulsion towards sex was surely connected to the agonies she had endured during labour: 'She now shakes all over with terror if a friend even says to her she is expecting a baby.'

Contraception was available but widely unpopular. It was expensive for the poorest families and unreliable when used by the unpractised. One wife complained that she first tried using a Dutch cap 'but it didn't make any difference, she couldn't trust it, and eventually threw it away'. Switching to condoms had only made matters 'worse still' because 'he didn't much care for it, and it had hurt her'. Abortion was seldom mentioned and, before the Pill, it seems that wives believed sterilization to be their best safeguard. Yet abstinence and withdrawal still appear to have been the most widely used forms of family planning among these couples, leaving wives dependent upon their husbands to control both the frequency of intercourse and the chance of conception within it. Needless to say, husbands often proved wilfully inconsiderate. After having nearly died from one of many miscarriages, Mrs Ratcliffe understandably 'lost all interest in intercourse, which became fearful and repugnant to her, and her husband with it.' Her protestations being in vain, she fell pregnant once again, for the tenth time in eight exhausting years.[67]

Husbands consequently desired sex much more than wives were willing to submit to it. Men were 'usually more...oversexed' than women, thought one wife; 'a woman...doesn't mind if she doesn't have it any more, but it's different for a man,' commented another. Ideally, couples reached some sort of accommodation, as an elderly Eastender explained to Peter Townsend:

> Well, the woman don't want too much of it. Any decent woman at all, well, my wife she never says anything to me because she knows that I never touch her, not for three or four months at a time, then when I do she don't say nothing because she knows I've been waiting all that time.

The London wives interviewed by Slater and Woodside deemed husbands to be good or otherwise according to the frequency of their sexual demands: 'he's a thorough gentleman' and 'he's very thoughtful' being some of the accolades bestowed upon 'considerate' men.[68] Mrs Fleckney duly considered her husband 'good' and 'fair' because he was moderate in his demands. Another wife calculated sex 'about once every three weeks' to be 'all right' and 'nothing excessive'. Men judged women on the opposite principle that a 'good' wife acquiesced without demur. One woman accordingly chided herself for denying her husband for fear of pregnancy since 'she thought it wasn't really fair on the man', and Mrs Fleckney repaid her husband's kindness by doing her best not to 'refuse him'. But a few did refuse. Whether disgusted by their experience of intercourse, appalled by the prospect of further pregnancies or determined to punish husbands for their philandering, they exercised their only effective control over the sexual relationship. Some husbands considered the denial of their conjugal rights to be grounds for desertion. Others took physical reprisals. 'Is he like this to me because I have refused him since baby was born?', one battered wife 'naively' asked her case-worker, while in the Barton household the husband made 'persistent sexual demands, and would hit her if she refused.'

Men enjoyed alternative outlets thanks to the double standard. Mr Lambert repaid his wife's fidelity during his absence in wartime by regularly frequenting prostitutes and Mr Merrick convinced his wife to accept him living with her 'when he feels like it' while seeing another woman 'in between'. Wifely adultery was curtailed by strict policing from possessive husbands terrified of being cuckolded. 'He won't let her out without him and is always extremely jealous if she goes with any men, if only for a friendly chat,' complained Mrs Loseby, while Mrs Gaddesby found her husband 'very suspicious if she goes out alone and threatens if she ever left him he would kill her.' Those wives inclined to commit adultery generally did so when safely out of men's supervisory power. Mrs Clarendon, Mrs Banks and Mrs Beecham found lovers when their husbands were respectively away at war, in hospital and in prison, the last vowing to murder her upon his release.

Lower-class husbands and wives experiencing marriage problems therefore lived largely separate lives in households where spousal affection was secondary both to subsistence and to the privileges exercised by men. Under such circumstances, it was understandable that many wed more to become mothers than wives. 'It was kids she wanted really, not a husband,' one woman admitted: 'She thought some women were like that. It was really children they wanted, and a husband (by implication) only a means to that end.' For all the pain and inconvenience of pregnancy and the subsequent exhausting years of child-rearing, almost all wives were thrilled by motherhood. Mrs Gartree felt 'at her best when...carrying a child' and another wife could not believe her fortune when her baby arrived. She had longed for a daughter for years and thought 'that it couldn't be, she never got what she wanted'. Women without children were frequently desperate to have them. A post-menopausal wife felt guilty about her childlessness and, when the barren Mrs Bartram was told by an adoption agency that no suitable children were available, she 'broke down completely and said that she would have to go home to her husband and leave him and have a Children's Home of her own.'[69]

Their parental longings frequently went unreciprocated by their husbands. 'She had wanted children, but he "didn't care",' was a tension running through several of the marriages encountered by the FWA. Mr Frith wished to postpone things until they had better housing, but his wife 'wanted to have a baby at once'. When she unexpectedly conceived, his initial ambivalence turned to indifference. Pregnancy under these conditions was a tense affair. Men became distinctly tetchy over their wives' self-absorption and the customary embargo on intercourse. Expecting wives, on the other hand, were unusually sensitive to their husbands' behaviour, so that one woman fled to her mother's house after being punched in the stomach when heavy with child.

Growing families brought great costs and few benefits to cash-strapped husbands and introduced a yet greater 'separation of interest' between themselves and their wives, noted the Fabian Maud Pember Reeves in her classic *Round About a Pound a Week* (1913).[70] It was therefore not unknown for men to wish to rid themselves of any unwanted additions, as when Mr Granby persuaded his wife to foster her 'little companion' so as not to disrupt his career. And, if finding themselves lumped with children, fathers could react poorly to their increasing marginalization. The mentally ill Mr Silesby exacted revenge by denying his children every pleasure imaginable and another man allowed his behaviour to deteriorate precipitously soon after the last child was born, neglecting his wife for women and beer.

The opposing interests of men and women in patriarchal marriages over money, sex and children gave them plenty to row about. And row they did: 'husbands and wives fall out often, and any conflict between them is overt,' reported B. M. Spinley in her psychological study of impoverished west Londoners. Marital disputes were, however, characterized by a strange forbearance on the part of wives. Such women were hardly doormats ('loud, aggressive, obscene' was Spinley's description of them), yet in Zweig's opinion working-class women displayed a 'great reluctance to complain about their husband's behaviour, even if . . . shocking. There was always an understatement of their case'.[71] A factor in women's otherwise inexplicable loyalty was that their primary identification as mothers led them to expect less, and endure more, from men. One woman was married to the worst of husbands, yet she considered that she 'had really got what she wanted out of life' on account of her children. Another reason was the enduring power of love. 'Yes, whatever he does to me I still love him,' declared Mrs Gaddesby when confessing that she would take her husband back after his latest assault upon herself and her children. But behind most wives' forbearance lay a singular lack of choice. The main complaint of those experiencing marriage problems concerned their husbands' abuse of a patriarchal power which, by its very definition, they were in no position to challenge. The only relief available to many was to leave the marriage altogether, yet the one thing worse than being miserably married was not being married at all. For a woman who wanted a 'normal married life [of] looking after [her husband] and having her children home', separation removed what little stability she possessed and easily led to the loss of respectability, income, even children. Divorce meant ostracism, Zweig noting the standing of such women to be 'even lower than that of a single girl.' Poverty followed, due to the erratic and nugatory nature of maintenance payments and employers' aversion to 'the *divorcée* type'.[72] Remarriage and renewed economic dependency represented the least worst option in the circumstances, but divorced women with children were damaged goods unlikely to attract another man. There was wisdom in Mrs Harcourt's unwillingness to leave her irritable and abusive common-law husband. 'She has not been happy during the years she has been with him,' she confessed, 'but the plain fact is that he is the only form of security in her life and she is afraid to abandon it.'

Husbands found it somewhat simpler to desert. They generally had the wherewithal to do so and, when remote from their children, felt fewer ties. The withdrawal of their earning power devastated the families they left behind: 'Now, with no husband, no money, another baby on the way and eviction in two days' time, she felt overwhelmed and hopeless about being able to cope with or provide for the children.' But a man who had no new woman to look after him also risked entering a spiral of decline. The wayward Mr Newarke took to 'drinking very heavily, and [had] been involved in street fights when he is said to have gone "completely mad"' after his wife refused finally to take him back.

Despite the many obstacles in the way of individuals wishing to walk out, separations were commonplace and if messy brought hitherto private wars under the purview of the legal system, a wilful and remote institution in the eyes of the London poor.[73] Theoretically, family law was sympathetic to women, its provisions on cruelty and maintenance orders in particular being designed for their benefit. But the *de jure* advantages granted to wives were far outweighed by the *de facto* disadvantages created by their economic dependency. The legal responsibilities imposed upon men could be turned to their own advantage, with two absent husbands keeping control of the rent book out of sheer vindictiveness. Poor women also found that it was one thing to obtain justice and another to enact it. Mrs Kibworth lacked the necessary cash to enforce an eviction order against her husband and the sorely used Mrs Gower, wanting nothing more than a solicitor's letter telling her husband to 'behave himself', decided to do without when informed that the fee was three guineas. The same applied to maintenance orders which, even when paid, were derisorily small. Hence custody rights over the children, though a privilege wives enjoyed over their estranged husbands, could become as much a burden as a blessing. Nor did the principles of 'innocence' and 'guilt' upon which matrimonial law was founded translate into effective justice. Injured parties with insufficient evidence were left disappointed, such as the wife unable to prove her husband's infidelity and having 'little to show' for her alleged beatings on account of her failure to bruise. She and other unhappy spouses whose partners did not demonstrably commit the three cardinal sins of desertion, adultery or cruelty found themselves effectively trapped. Were they simply to walk out, they were automatically the 'guilty' one. If male, they could be sued for maintenance; if female, they risked finding themselves penniless.

When insufficient grounds existed to seek recourse in law or when partners were otherwise unwilling to separate, marriages degenerated into empty shells. 'Both say they want to be happily married but that the marriage is hopeless; they stay together,' was the grim arrangement under which many couples lived, with each spouse confined to their own 'little private cell of misery'. In the absence of alternatives, these moribund relationships could last indefinitely: 'The marriage never seems to have got off the ground yet they have stayed together for eighteen years.' There they were left bemoaning their fate and thinking, like Mrs Lancaster, that marriage was 'one big mistake'.

Trouble and Strife

The stereotype of the brutal working-class husband domineering over his wife, propagated as it was by generations of middle-class social investigators and marriage reformers, has fallen out of favour with historians of the family.[74] Some draw attention to the advantages wives derived from the sexual division of labour. The women described by Elizabeth Roberts, Joanna Bourke and Ross McKibbin took pride in housekeeping, enjoyed warm relationships with Gran and kids and would countenance no husbandly interference in either.[75] Others identify a working-class version of companionship. Diana Gittins sees shared housework, childcare, decision-making and leisure activities to have been common in marriages of two wage-earners, while Trevor Lummis finds evidence of spousal cooperation and affection even in East Anglian fishing communities where wives remained at home.[76]

Men appear in these historical accounts to have been anything but overbearing masters of the house. 'For every negative, distant husband or father, there were dozens of warm working-class domestic men,' states Bourke: men like Lummis's homebodies and McKibbin's hobbyists pottering about the garden shed.[77] Husbands who attempted to exert patriarchal power are considered by Jerry White, Ellen Ross and Carl Chinn to have found it difficult to do so. Insecurity over employment, intimidation by mothers-in-law and isolation from household management made men's authority in these historians' view at most a 'wobbly fixture' and often no more than a 'façade' over a 'hidden matriarchy'.[78] Wives, meanwhile, are portrayed as having given as good as they got, whether through what Bourke terms the 'risk-averse' methods of 'placid sabotage', the 'open insubordination' of fists and rows or the enlistment of their neighbours, mothers and children to their side.[79]

The dismal testimony contained in the FWA archives indicates, however, that the figure of the working-class patriarch cannot altogether be laid to rest. Recent historical writing has ably demonstrated the manner in which women sought to confront and circumvent male power. Yet by no means all husbands were sufficiently amiable, pliable or vulnerable as to accede to their wives' demands. Whereas Gittins and Roberts find patriarchal marriages to have been somewhat unusual, their iniquities contrasting with the power-sharing 'normative' among other working-class couples, the FWA records suggest that patriarchy was the default state to which impoverished families reverted when men were unwilling, and women unable, to moderate husbands' inherent financial and physical advantages.[80] It is to their credit that historians have recently been able to unearth many examples of dutiful family men who did not exploit their position, but since the 'implied bargain of role-segregation' outlined by McKibbin involved husbands having to 'efface' themselves to the extent that they were undermined by matricentrism, excluded from domestic decision-making and frustrated in their sexual desires, the temptation always existed for them to assert their authority even at the risk of destabilizing their marriages.[81]

Nor do the FWA case-notes support the notion that lower working-class wives could hit back in the event of conflict. Husbands so minded could ordinarily impose their will through a series of negative sanctions ultimately destructive of family life. They enjoyed an unequal share of the family income and reserved the power to withhold support from their wives, whether retaining the housekeeping money or simply clearing off. They could control women though supervision and, if deemed necessary, through sexual coercion and violence. Matriarchal authority was not strictly comparable to its patriarchal counterpart. A working-class woman exercised control as a mother by rights, but whatever power she possessed as a wife was not intrinsic to her wifely role but contingent upon favourable extraneous conditions. The first of these was the existence of strong kin and neighbourhood ties, the second was the goodwill of the husband. The marriage problems encountered by the FWA show how easily and how devastatingly these happy circumstances could be stripped away from women, with external support often conspicuous by its absence and husbandly magnanimity seldom to be seen. In such situations, limited employment opportunities, low pay, the inaccessibility of legal redress and the dependency enforced by pregnancy and child-rearing diminished wives' capacity to resist.

Marriage reformers were therefore wrong to identify male domination within the generality of the working class but not to condemn the structural inequality existing between husbands and wives. Separate spheres formed a lopsided arrangement, the successful functioning of which required that husbands moderate their powers. Those who refused to do so transformed a sexual division of labour intended to stabilize working-class marriage into an instrument of tyranny and destruction. Patriarchal power at once produced most marital strife among the London poor and tilted its outcome in favour of men.

Companionship and Its Discontents

The companionate ideal had not penetrated the consciousness of the typical couple coming to the Family Welfare Association. The two axes around which their marriage revolved – the husband's domination of his wife and the mother's monopolization of her children – militated against the intimate equality which companionship ideally entailed. Yet in the late 1950s and early 1960s, the FWA occasionally came across a very different type of client. One man's ideal marriage was that of a 'perfect companionship' based on the 'sharing of mutual interests' in which neither partner wanted to be apart from the other. Another thought that 'to be a good husband and father' meant not breadwinning but an intense involvement in domestic affairs. A third, when asked whether 'a husband should order his wife's life', replied that, on the contrary, 'marriage should be a partnership.' It was not just men who expressed emancipated sentiments. Mrs Eyres wished to be a 'person in her own right' with time to herself away from her housewifely responsibilities while, after years of counselling women who submitted to sex as a wifely chore, case-workers could not have anticipated Mrs Linwood's outspoken demands: 'She said how much she wanted her husband to kiss and cuddle her, she wanted her husband to love her for herself and she felt in intercourse he was only getting his own pleasure and using her as a body and she just wasn't a participant at all.'

That a wife would dare to chastise her husband's sexual technique indicated a key aspect of these cases: that spousal roles were less clear-cut than in the patriarchal working-class marriages more commonly seen by the FWA. These men frequently washed nappies and helped their children with homework, and not only expected women to play an 'active part' in intercourse but also preferred on occasion to 'take the passive role' themselves. There were even instances of genuine role reversal. In the Monsell family, it was the wife who had the affairs, devoted herself to paid work, abstained from housework and left her husband holding the baby when she walked out. With the overlapping of roles came a greater degree of equality between spouses, the assertiveness of Mrs Monsell and Mrs Linwood indicating how the standing of husband and wife rested less on masculine privilege than on the power of personality. Spousal relations were not just more equitable but more unstable and prone to flux. Consider the case of Mr and Mrs Eyres, which at first appeared to involve an unequal match between an assured husband and an insecure wife. She had been shy and virginal when they met and allowed him to tutor her in sexual matters and much else besides. Yet as the counselling sessions wore on, and particularly after the arrival of children, she became somewhat more confident at the same time as his anxieties over masculine identity began to surface. Once very much the dominant partner, he eventually felt himself to be the weaker one and regarded women to be 'on a pedestal looking down on him'.

Heightened expectations, new standards of sexual satisfaction, indistinct spousal roles, shifting power relations: these were a different order of complaints from those ordinarily presented to the FWA. But precisely what distinguished these couples from run-of-the-mill FWA marriages made them similar to the clients of other counselling organizations established immediately after the Second World War. The similarities began with class composition. The fact that these clients were upper working- or lower middle-class (the husbands included a clerk, a postgraduate student, an upwardly mobile taxi-driver and a downwardly mobile white-collar criminal) gave them less in common with other FWA clients than those attending its offshoot, the Family Discussion Bureau (founded in 1948). The FDB drew under a fifth of its clients from the ranks of the semi-skilled and unskilled, inviting accusations that it neglected material marriage problems in favour of psychological ones, but in this it was not alone.[82] The National Marriage Guidance Council attracted a similar class of client and the Tavistock Clinic's Marital Unit (established in 1949) selected a 'relatively sophisticated' clientele on the grounds that 'less intelligent and socio-economically favoured' couples lacked the 'verbal and educational resources' to benefit from its techniques.[83] And, while the psychotherapeutic approach of the Marital Unit and the FDB (itself absorbed into the Tavistock Institute in 1956) differed from that of an NMGC rooted in marriage reform, these three organizations uniformly discounted the impact of 'environmental pressure' in the making and breaking of marriages.[84]

Their marital difficulties as well as their class made these FWA couples all too typical of those encountered by these postwar counselling organizations. Their unrealized goals of sharing and sexual pleasure tallied with the inflated 'standards and expectations of marital satisfaction' considered by the FDB to be not just distinctive of contemporary marriages in general but responsible for their 'apparent failure'. The sexual problems of the Linwoods bore parallels to the 'anxiety and alarm' identified by the Tavistock's Henry Dicks in reaction to the 'subversion of old decencies'. And the FDB's Lily Pincus found the blurred spousal roles exhibited by the Monsells and the Eyreses to be a common condition. Whereas traditional societies established 'clearly differentiated' roles for the sexes, she argued that modern individuals faced the task of 'developing their masculinity and femininity' without fixed societal standards.[85]

These cases suggested that something had gone wrong with companionship. Here was evidence that expectations of emancipation, sexual satisfaction and the revision of orthodox husbandly and wifely roles served to accentuate rather than eliminate marital strife. Here were couples apparently injured by the very ideals to which they aspired. Such was the message of the writings of marriage counsellors (a term I take to include all practitioners in the field, from psychoanalysts and NMGC volunteers to doctors and advice columnists) which, in the absence of any Marital Unit, FDB or NMGC archives comparable to those of the FWA, provide some of the best available evidence on companionate marriage problems.[86] The strange testimony of clients like Mr Three and Mrs Grumble, whose multifarious pseudonyms indicate the variety of texts used, offers a privileged insight into how ideals of intimacy, equality and shared sexual pleasure at once revolutionized and problematized married life.

Aspirant companionate couples found intimacy difficult to accomplish and hard to cope with. The first obstacle to its attainment was the sexual division of labour, according to social scientists investigating the relationship between work and family life. 'Men's work has been structured as though men did not have families,' reported Rhona and Robert Rapoport, causing husbands to display a split commitment between family and career.[87] Though the 'spread of the ideal of a close, companionate type of marriage' made the situation 'increasingly unacceptable' to women, some husbands nonetheless held their wives at bay. Full-time housewives consigned to the other side of the work divide consequently found it difficult to get close to their partners. 'He can share the housework as much as one likes, but he still walks out into a different world at half past nine every day,' one woman told Hannah Gavron in her study of 'captive wives'.[88]

A possible counterweight to the sexual division of labour was for men to help around the house, yet sociological studies indicated that their modest efforts in this regard did not significantly alter women's lot. Even two-career families thought it natural and inevitable that women bore the 'main brunt' of domestic tasks.[89] Moreover, husbandly participation incited conflict when, as doctor Mary Macaulay noted, the 'confusion of roles' prompted tactless men to tell women how to do the housework. Mr Thirteen's idea of 'role-sharing' was to present his wife with lists of chores and Mr Two considered his instructions on how Mrs Two 'should run the house and ... spend any money' to be 'kindly, magnanimous, and reasonably democratic' in intention.[90] But if men could be high-handed, women could be prickly over controlling their own little realm. 'I have heard many wives say they would love to have a husband who could cook,' commented NMGC training officer J.H. Wallis, 'yet nevertheless complain bitterly if he starts to do it.'[91]

The manner in which parenthood accentuated the sexual division of labour had the potential to divide companionate couples every bit as profoundly as their patriarchal counterparts. Whereas spouses were able to live 'almost identical lives' before they had children, any resulting intimacy came under pressure from the 'inescapable differentiation between the two sexes once there is a child'.[92] Take the case of the Carters. After giving birth, Mrs Carter found herself 'tied to domesticity', ignored by her husband and dependent by default upon the support of her female relatives. Mr Carter had enjoyed the 'companionship' of their childless days, but felt distanced from his wife once they became parents and, like her, turned to the company of his own sex. Though in the Carters' case it was the wife who feared that her partner would form an exclusive bond with the baby, more problem marriages contained husbands distraught over their wives' absorption in motherhood. Once again, wives deprived of control over other aspects of their lives sought solace in a jealously guarded domesticity.[93]

The mutual incomprehension of forthcoming wives and withholding husbands further checked intimacy. While women generally valued dialogue, men tended to resist 'discussing the minutiae of married life'. Herbert Gray reported that husbands remained 'quite uninterested in their wives' lives' and what they termed 'women's rubbish'.[94] Such insensitivity seemed a matter of level-headedness to the husbands concerned. Mr Price refused his wife's 'quite silly' requests for reassurance on the grounds that he 'couldn't be that sloppy', while the 'devastating rationality' of Mr Four made him so disdain his wife's 'sloppy sentiment' that he employed equal measures of condescension and sarcasm in order to teach her 'sense'.[95] Incompatibility erupted into hostility when women charged men with being unforgivably unemotional and men erected defences against their wives' apparent invasiveness and bogus intuition. The NMGC warned that a 'strong, silent man' provoked ever more desperate attempts by the woman to elicit a reaction, a vicious cycle illustrated by Mrs Four's 'hysterical tempers' making Mr Four withdraw in silence, which in turn drove her into yet deeper despair.[96]

If achieving intimacy proved deeply problematic, its attainment could itself produce major problems. 'The more you are together, the more you will discover about each other,' promised science writer Roger Pilkington, before adding that not all revelations would be pleasant and some might be downright infuriating. The Bruces derived 'enchantment' from the distance between them in their courtship, only to find their love 'almost obliterated' in the pressure-cooker of marriage. Similarly, the determination of Michael and his wife to be 'completely intimate and honest with each other' involved admitting the uncomfortable truth that their sex life was 'not as exciting as it was.'[97] Some couples took the quest for closeness so far as to upset the complementarity extolled by marriage reformers. Accustomed to 'work together and play together' in their single lives, they found it hard to adjust to 'playing a very different role' as man and wife. Such was the case with the Coopers, her concern that her femininity distanced her from her husband matched by his anxiety that a womanly wife would force him to become a real man. However hard it was to accept sex difference, counsellors thought it still harder to maintain a pretence of sameness. One paradox of intimacy was that it was best accomplished by couples who observed its limits.[98]

Intimacy also verged dangerously upon claustrophobia. An 'invasion of...privacy' was at once advocated by marriage reformers in the name of disclosure and feared for its 'terrifying closeness'. They warned that mutual dependence undermined each spouse's autonomy and produced harmony only through 'narrowing and impoverishing the joint and individual experience.'[99] Counsellors reported the intensity of companionship to be 'particularly threatening' to men's sense of self. Those who equated masculinity with independence feared that 'identifying too closely' with their wives would compromise their assigned role. And, expected as men to 'control their feelings much more than women', they dared not expose their sensitive side to their wives lest they lose control.[100] Such husbands simply clammed up, Mr Phillips stating that he 'just hadn't got any emotions' and Mr Cooper doing his best to project a 'Colonel Nasser'-type invulnerability in order to avoid seeming 'weak and exposed'. For them, as for some other men in counselling, intimacy proved a mixed blessing, even a curse.[101]

The egalitarian aspects of companionate marriage introduced dilemmas peculiar to each sex. The problems of wives were brilliantly dissected by the American sociologist Talcott Parsons in the 1940s and 1950s. Parsons believed that companionship made spouses equal by treating each as a 'fully responsible "partner"'. For husbands to assume the 'instrumental' role and wives the 'expressive' one offered them an equality of status while preventing rivalry between them. Yet Parsons saw that this model of marriage played havoc with femininity. On the one hand, women unused to the responsibilities of equality harboured 'dependency cravings' out of kilter with the 'genuine independence' they now enjoyed. On the other, they balked at the lingering tendency to 'define the feminine role psychologically as one strongly marked by elements of dependency'. There was nothing inherently inferior about being a housewife, but it was still commonly regarded as such, to the distress and resentment of housewives themselves.[102]

The two great concerns identified by Parsons – the wish for security and the indignity of feminine inferiority – suffused the testimony of unhappy wives in mid twentieth-century Britain. One class of wife was unwilling to surrender the apparent security of a dependent existence. Divorce lawyer Edward Kaufmann despaired over how many women chose to 'renounce their aspirations toward intellectual and economic independence' by quitting their jobs upon marriage. Even when allowing for the external pressures militating against wives' employment, he could only conclude that there was a psychological imperative behind their self-imposed subordination verging upon the masochistic.[103] It was a charge, however extreme, which received some support from case histories supplied by the head of the Tavistock's Marital Unit, Henry Dicks. Mrs Twenty-Eight wanted 'someone to belong to', Mrs Six wished to surrender herself to a man and Mrs Twenty-Four displayed 'spaniel-like' tendencies towards her husband.[104] There were also numerous cases of wives disappointed by insufficiently dominant husbands. 'I like a man who is rough and dominates,' sighed Mrs One, forlorn at having married someone 'soppy and sentimental.'[105]

The opposite problem concerned wives who equated femininity with degradation. These women often reacted against their upbringing. Mrs Carter had sabotaged her mother's attempts to make her into a 'little lady' by turning all tomboyish and Mrs Three defined herself against her mother by refusing to be a 'doormat'.[106] To these early experiences were added what counsellors identified as a specifically feminist indictment of the subordination of women. Mrs Three was adamant that there should be 'no exploitation of woman by man' and assailed her unreconstructed husband with demands for 'equality and independence'.[107] Likewise, 'bristling feminist' Mrs Two despised her husband's paternalism and 'fervent feminist' Mrs Robinson could not rest easy with the 'social and sexual humiliations' inflicted upon women in Asia.[108] The great frequency of 'masculinized' women in marriage counselling literature may in part be explained by the psychoanalytical inclinations of some marriage counsellors, always on the lookout for Adlerian 'masculine protest'. But, given the uncertainty surrounding the position of newly enfranchised women (see chapter two), they also indicated the awkwardness of squaring difference with equality.[109]

Such women could not reconcile themselves to the sexual division of labour. Mrs Three displayed an unhousewifely 'lack of responsibility and maternal feeling', while Mrs Robinson found it 'impossible to comply and say "Yes, dear" like other women'. A distaste for house-wifery sometimes translated into jealousy of a husband's job, as when

Mrs Twenty-Seven complained of being '"only the Head's wife" at everybody's beck and call'.[110] Career women often found wifehood particularly trying. Their independent careers appeared to deprive marriage of its symmetry and the husband of his unique identity, his potential loss of 'pride' being commensurate to her gain in 'self-respect'. The opposite problem faced any recently wed woman who gave up work due to motherhood, the marriage bar or personal preference. Having enjoyed 'freedom and financial independence' when single and employed, marriage might not seem the 'best means of entry into a fuller life' but rather a 'sacrifice of such status as she has won, and a life of isolation, restricted interests and renewed dependence'.[111] 'What would it feel like to be quite dependent on the husband – materially, physically, emotionally?' wondered Mrs Cooper. Her desire to be a 'lady of leisure' conflicted with her misgivings at becoming more reliant upon another than at any time since infancy. These concerns were shared by career women Mrs Clarke and Mrs F., who associated housewifery with indolence and 'thinking silly feminine thoughts'.[112] Though Mrs Cooper and Mrs F. overcame their doubts over leaving paid employment by flinging themselves headlong into femininity, Mrs Clarke's worst fears about the housewife's lot came true. Being 'only a woman' offered her little satisfaction, she complained. Whereas she had once outearned her husband, she now felt weak and powerless: 'Everything is upside down. I am now totally incompetent; I can't take any responsibilities.' Failing to do more than tinker with the sexual division of labour, companionship offered women like Mrs Clarke no simple solutions.[113]

Post-patriarchal husbands had lost their imperiousness but had not yet found a role, according to NMGC co-founder Herbert Gray: 'The Victorian husband was not troubled. His way was made plain for him by custom and tradition . . . But his grandsons are troubled – very much troubled.' They, no less than their wives, were confused by the consequences of women's emancipation. Intellectually, many were quite willing to 'concede the equal status of their wives', argued Eustace Chesser, but emotionally they recoiled from its effects. He ascribed their reservations to a reluctance to surrender their 'dominant status'. Yet selfishness did not account for the genuine bafflement expressed by many husbands over their allotted role. As one nonplussed client of the Family Discussion Bureau remarked, 'It must have been easy to be a man if you were a knight in shining armour and your princess was just waiting for you to rescue her.'[114]

Like their wives, men in counselling divided (and were internally divided) over the competing claims of emancipation and tradition. Counsellors discovered traditional husbands to be so exercised by the issue of 'who wears the trousers' as to regard marriage to an 'emancipated, energetic and ambitious' woman to be tantamount to emasculation: hence the anguish of Mr Phillips over being a 'mere workman' in comparison to his white-collar wife.[115] Other men forestalled such a contingency by being 'fanatically opposed' to their wives undertaking paid employment, an attitude encountered by Maggie when her partner interpreted her wish to work as a 'slight against him as a husband' and a slur on his breadwinning capacities.[116] Though traditional men wanted traditional wives, they found to their cost that emancipation emboldened women to resist clumsy assertions of authority. Hugh was an archetypal 'dominating, overbearing male who does not regard his wife as an equal partner, but only requires her passive submission.' For years, he bullied his wife Joan, only to be flabbergasted when she 'finally rebelled and asked him to set her free.' These sudden reversals of power relations perplexed the unfortunate Mr Phillips, who wanted to know why 'women were always saying that they wanted you to be "manly" but when you were they did not like it and were hurt, or jeered at you.'[117]

Ostensibly emancipated husbands were not the godsends they promised to be. Their progressivism proved in some cases to be an unstable affair, as when a man apparently content with a 'partner-wife' suddenly revealed an 'urge to dominate'.[118] The Twenty-Fours' marriage began as an 'all-in-all' arrangement complete with a common value system, a 'very good sexual relation' and 'mutual support in their parallel and often shared careers', but soon changed out of all recognition due to the husband's 'uncontrollable tempers and fitful violence'. Mrs Three was convinced that she had found an ideal partner who mirrored her beliefs on 'sexual equality, shared values, no exploitation of woman by man'. Upon marrying, however, he turned reactionary and refused to accede to her egalitarian demands.[119] Other husbands set out to achieve a little emancipation of their own by trying to 'off-load' responsibilities onto their overburdened wives. Mr Thirteen was one of this breed, a 'passive' man eager to shirk the customarily male tasks of 'finance, child discipline, external relations [and] major decision-making'. Mr Clarke proved equally unwilling to assume his duties. His professed desire to become a 'good and responsible husband' did not quell his fear that settling down represented a 'complete and final surrender' and his corresponding penchant for 'breaking out' into reckless behaviour.[120] The scale and variety of arguments concerning the respective roles of husband and wife made J.H. Wallis believe that couples simply needed something to row about. 'Experience of counselling,' he wrote, 'convinces me that these envies, complaints and arguments are not socially determined and will never disappear no matter what social utopia is provided for us'.[121]

Sexual problems in companionate marriage were a mixture of the old and the new. Depressingly familiar was the large proportion of wives who found no satisfaction in sex and husbands who divorced sex from emotion. 'Many wives are afraid to take an active part in intercourse because of some lingering fear that it would not be "womanly",' reported J. H. Wallis: women like Mrs Milton, who could not decide whether sex was a good or a bad thing; Mrs Twenty-One, who viewed intercourse as a 'purely selfish' act on the part of the man; and Mrs Phillips, whose acute sense of shame made her unable to undress in view of her husband or even herself.[122] Such wives differed from their patriarchal counterparts not in their reticence but in their reactions to it. So strong was the 'current doctrine that [women] should enjoy sexual satisfaction' that the inhibited commonly felt themselves to be failures. Mrs Robinson was one such woman, worried that she had 'no sexual feelings' not on her own account (she confessed that she 'would gladly do without intercourse altogether') but because 'she had read somewhere that a woman should "want sex at certain periods when the seed detached itself".' Some blamed their husbands while others blamed themselves, leading to the 'ironic' situation that women experienced guilt 'because they do not manifest *sufficient* sexuality'.[123]

The new types of sex problem, like those of companionship more generally, stemmed from the contradictions inherent in the ideal. Women's dilemmas lay in reconciling their twin desires of sexual pleasure and emancipation. Certain wives were emancipated enough to expect enjoyment but insufficiently so as to take the initiative. Mrs Gordon, Mrs Colindale and Mrs Lawrence were all married to inadequate husbands who seldom satisfied them. But Mrs Gordon found it too humiliating to suggest having sex, and Mrs Colindale believed that trying to appear 'more inviting' smacked of 'acting like a prostitute'.[124] For her part, Mrs Lawrence refused to have any truck with 'permissive nonsense' and expressed her faith in 'old-fashioned virtues'. In consequence, although 'physically it was agony for her to go to bed wanting sex and have him give her a chaste goodnight kiss', she nonetheless felt unable to take command. 'He would certainly think her "not nice" if she tried to initiate intercourse,' she explained, 'and anyway that was the man's job, wasn't it?'[125] Such attitudes occasionally translated into wives' seeking sexual fulfilment through total surrender to a stronger force. Mrs Donovan, for one, got her kicks from a husband who refused to kiss or caress her, used his penis like a 'dagger' and forbade contraception. Counsellors believed that submission more commonly served to remove a woman's guilt, for example interpreting Mrs Eighteen's dreams about being overpowered by gangsters with guns as serving to assuage her terror of penetration.[126]

Fantasies of this kind were the stuff of nightmares for those women who equated sex with being 'mastered', 'overmanned' and forced to surrender to the 'subordinate role' of womanhood.[127] From their opposite perspective, they too rejected the marriage reformers' notion of an active passivity as a contradiction in terms. Mrs Cooper preferred her husband to be 'stronger in every way' outside the bedroom, but confessed that 'in bed I cannot bear it' since she regarded intercourse as 'humiliating to a woman', understandably so given her husband's callous technique. Another wife feared 'losing control of her body' to her sexually aggressive husband, a reaction shared by Mrs Robinson:

> she felt it would be dreadful if she let herself lose control; her husband would then be in control of her... to enjoy sexual intercourse and to have feelings as a woman was tantamount to 'going mad', to losing her intelligence and judgement – in short, losing everything she valued and called 'I'.[128]

Marriage counsellors considered wives who 'deeply resent[ed] what seems to them a subservient role' in sex to be the principal victims of 'non-responsiveness', to give frigidity its newly sanitized name. A 'refusal to be a woman' led to a wife 'refusing to relate to a man' while envying men their supposedly superior position.[129] Under the prompting of analysts looking for signs of 'penis envy', non-responsive wives readily confessed to all manner of butch longings. Mrs Eighteen fantasized about being Superman, Mrs Ten identified with tough guys in Westerns and Mrs Twenty was diagnosed as 'another phallic Amazon'.[130] Counsellors saw it as their duty to transform any 'Miss Tomboy' they encountered into a 'Mrs Goodlover', fully accepting of her womanliness. The simple assurance that she need not simply submit in sex provided a degree of reassurance to a woman like Mrs Philips, but resistance could be considerable from those who related sex to the injustice of living in a 'man's world'.[131] However, once wives accepted their ascribed role in intercourse, they reportedly became more at ease with their womanliness, dressing in a 'more feminine fashion' and even 'enjoy[ing] the household chores'.[132]

At the other extreme to women who associated female sexuality with passivity were those who demanded an active part in intercourse. David Mace related how he had witnessed a three-stage evolution of sexual attitudes during his long career as a counsellor. Originally wives complained about their husbands' unwelcome advances. Then husbands began to demand that their wives 'function properly' and show a little something of that equal desire they had heard so much about. But by the sixties and seventies the tables had been turned. It was wives who now expressed indignation that their partners were so 'clumsy and inept' as to deny them 'the orgasm to which they are entitled!'[133] Marriage reformers regarded these wives' insistence upon the 'Necessity for Orgasm' as a gross misinterpretation of sexual equality. It injured their concept of sex as a loving exchange, in which nothing should be demanded and nothing involuntarily given. The value of intercourse was to be judged by the degree to which it deepened the bond between husband and wife, so that the 'mere presence or absence of orgasm' (in women) constituted an entirely insufficient 'criterion of successful intimacy.' An overly selfish attitude replaced what was good about women's sexuality, namely their interweaving of sex with love, with an attitude as crude and mechanistic as men's.[134]

Such concerns focused upon the clitoris which – long before the attention devoted to clitoral orgasms in the 1960s – was acknowledged by most marriage reformers to be more sensitive than the vagina. Their problem lay in reconciling this fact to their ideals of complementarity. The clitoris's resemblance to a vestigial penis led them to regard it as the locus of women's 'more masculine side' as opposed to the vagina's distinctly feminine 'receptive creativity'. A woman's failure to acknowledge her vagina as the centre of her sexual satisfaction therefore indicated resistance to the 'joining together of opposites' and a rebuff to her partner's masculinity, since 'she will neither flow to a man emotionally nor fully accept his sexuality'.[135] Marriage counsellors accordingly underplayed the importance of clitoral orgasms, contending either that the diffuse quality of women's sexuality rendered the precise physical location of orgasm irrelevant or else that vaginal orgasms were much the superior sort. The NMGC declared 'every couple' to be duty bound to strive for the 'ideal' in which the wife gradually became accustomed to vaginal stimulation 'until in the end she no longer needs excitement of the clitoris as well.'[136]

The grand confusion surrounding what constituted sexual emancipation for women created any number of potential difficulties for men. A wife's outright inertness in intercourse caused profound distress. Mr Jackson resented his wife's conception of sex as 'just something you have to put up with' and Mr Cooper, though he acted all uncaring, complained that the 'cold and stiff' demeanour of his wife during intercourse made it 'just like raping her.'[137] Equally problematic were those passive wives who expected their husbands to be masterful seducers. 'I wish you had been stronger and had beaten all this stupidity out of me,' Mrs Eighteen told her sexually unassertive husband. If only he had 'overcome my tears and fighting' when the subject of sex was first broached, then things would have been 'all right', she complained: 'Now that he has to wait for my consent it will never come.'[138] Still greater problems arose from women's demands for an equal share in sexual pleasure. 'The dictum that the woman has as much right as the man to experience orgasm has been interpreted by the man to mean that he is responsible for her achieving the experience,' claimed popular sex writer Robert Chartham. The man accordingly considered it a 'terrible blow to his sexual self-respect' were his wife not to achieve climax. 'I love my girl and it's awful to see her left in that state and to know I'm responsible,' was Mr Jenkins' response to being informed by his wife that he came too quickly. He read sex manuals galore for tips on foreplay, but they did not improve matters and seem to have reinforced his conviction that he was obliged to provide his wife with regular doses of exhilaration.[139]

Two factors undermined husbands' ability to perform their prescribed sexual role. Those unfamiliar with 'concern[ing] themselves with the values of the other person' in intercourse were apt to manifest terror at any suggestion of intimacy. One chronic example was that of Mr Cooper, able to have intercourse only on his own 'omnipotent terms':

> he used her to prove himself a man and became quite unaware of her as a person. She became 'any woman to me, almost as if she were a prostitute', and he became 'just any man'. To him it is just as if he had split off sex from the rest of their relationship . . . [140]

The new sex teaching sometimes unwittingly encouraged such men's instrumental approach. J.H. Wallis lamented how manuals devalued 'spontaneity and naturalness' and encouraged 'technique-hungry' husbands to experiment upon their 'disconsolate or exasperated' wives.[141] The sexual revolution represented to them an opportunity to explore 'new types of stimulation' and they took badly to their wives' often 'reticent' response: hence the anguish of Hans when his wife refused to wear a miniskirt for fear of appearing tarty.[142]

The second, related problem was that women's proclaimed right to equal pleasure ran counter to some men's ingrained association of sex with power. David Mace claimed that husbands who were content with the 'non-responding woman of the past' found it hard to perform once they were expected to satisfy their wives.[143] Case histories supported his arguments. Mr Gordon plunged into a 'state of panic' when his wife initiated sex and Mr Colindale, having long been accustomed to 'pleasing himself' in intercourse, took the new-found assertion of his wife to be a threat to his masculinity. He could not cope with her insistence that they have sex more than once a fortnight and retreated into a miserable impotency.[144] In finding husbands to be far more 'vulnerable to a sense of personal failure', counsellors exposed the myth that men regarded sex as an impersonal act. Much less supportive of the goals of marriage reform was the implication that many men could not successfully orchestrate intercourse, let alone tutor their wives. If the woman was naturally inhibited and 'sexual anxiety' formed an 'essential part of a husband's make-up', how could sex become the crowning glory of companionate marriage?[145]

Explaining Discord

If counsellors were to be believed, a chasm existed between the ideal and the reality of companionship among couples who were at once confounded by and resistant to the quest for intimacy, equality and shared sexual satisfaction. Intimacy at its best deepened the relationship between husband and wife. But with it came introspection, noted anthropologist Edmund Leach, as well as 'narrow privacy' and 'tawdry secrets' and an 'intensification of emotional stress'. Many in counselling, husbands especially, failed to subsume their identity into a partnership of intimates. This was partly a matter of necessity, with jobs competing with the family for men's loyalty and commitment, yet it also represented a revolt of sorts against the marriage bond, a predicament unforgettably dramatized in John Osborne's Look Back in Anger (1956).[146]

127

Expectations of equality created difficulties within marriage unknown in the simpler, more iniquitous state of patriarchy. Patriarchal marriage prescribed rights and responsibilities for husbands and wives, the infringement of which provided grounds for conflict. In contrast, problems in companionate marriages often derived from the sheer absence of clear rules and roles. With 'power-relations of the traditional order' no longer in operation, husbands and wives found it hard to strike that necessary balance between similarity and difference enjoined upon them by marriage reformers. Some clung to anachronistic models of masculinity and femininity, while others aspired towards an androgyny at odds with complementarity. The greatest strife occurred when partners failed to agree on how egalitarian they wished to be, as when the independent-minded Mrs Rivaux berated and assaulted her husband for presuming 'that he was the master and that she had to do as he wanted.' Women's emancipation was meant to produce amity, not shouts and blows.[147]

Counsellors also found that sex was scarcely the unifying force marriage reformers imagined it to be. 'All the incidents and attitudes that cause misunderstanding and friction in married life ... are of little importance if husband and wife know that basically they are all-in-all to one another and that sexual union will restore harmony,' opined Mary Macaulay. But sex often brought to a head all other conflicts and uncertainties concerning spousal roles, turning what was meant to be an exquisite union into a 'struggle for intra-marital ascendancy and submission'.[148] Furthermore, if good sex constituted what Barbara Cartland termed the 'be-all and end-all of marriage', then bad sex represented a sound reason to separate. 'I'm mostly left all strung up – can't get to sleep,' complained Mrs Jenkins after another unsatisfactory bout of intercourse: 'He tries to help me get there with his hands – like they said you should – but it's no good – makes me feel worse – and when he falls asleep I could scream! – Honestly, Mrs A., I shall leave him if we can't get it right.' As sociologist Martin Richards has noted, the great weight placed upon sexual pleasure made monogamy more important but adultery more likely.[149]

So what accounted for such a disjuncture between marriage reformers' hopes for companionship and the experiences of it recorded in counselling literature? Three explanations present themselves, focusing respectively on who was counselled, who counselled them and what they actually encountered. The simplest is that these problem marriages were by definition atypical. Two questionnaires distributed in the late 1940s and early 1950s – one by Mass-Observation to its (middle-class and liberal) National Panel members, the other by Eustace Chesser to nearly 4,000 wives – reported around one twentieth of respondents expressing overall dissatisfaction with their marriages.[150] These figures put the extent of marital problems into perspective, but should not be taken to indicate the success of companionate marriage. After all, Peter Willmott and Michael Young came across many contented East End marriages wholly untouched by the companionate ideal. Polls are also snapshots. One spouse in twenty may have been unhappy at any time, but a considerably higher proportion experienced difficulties during the course of their marriages. The American sociologists Richard A. Mackey and Bernard A. O'Brien discovered as much in a recent survey of marriages that had lasted over twenty years. Of these couples, 12 per cent recalled major conflicts soon after marrying, rising to 29 per cent in the child-rearing years, before falling to 7 per cent once their children left home. Another American study, based on longitudinal data collected by the University of California at Berkeley, suggests that the problems thrown up by companionship in Britain mirrored those elsewhere. The 'hopes and disappointments' identified by historian Jessica Weiss among these normal Californian couples in their 'Quest for Togetherness' would have been familiar to many a British husband and wife undergoing counselling.[151]

Difficulties coexisted with general expressions of contentment in mid twentieth-century marriages. This was apparent in the Mass-Observation survey, which indicated that one in five wives considered her husband to be insensitive in bed, the same number never or rarely achieved orgasms, and one in seven wished that she and her partner were 'physically more co-operative and passionate during love-making' – yet only one in twenty pronounced herself 'generally dissatisfied' with her marriage.[152] Sociologist Hannah Gavron recorded a comparable 4 per cent of 'positively unhappy' wives among her sixties sample of forty-eight young, middle-class mothers. Two-thirds of them expressed the quintessentially mutualist sentiment that their marriages were more egalitarian than their mothers', and almost all the couples interviewed by social anthropologist Elizabeth Bott in the fifties believed that 'the modern family was better than the Victorian family.'[153] Yet 'conflict and stress' afflicted Gavron's interviewees, while the most companionate wives in Bott's sample were precisely those most prone to complain of 'isolation, boredom and fatigue'. These problems did not translate into overt marital dissatisfaction because they were attributed to factors other than the marriage itself. Gavron's subjects blamed motherhood and Bott's the 'social situation' for their plight, leaving their husbands in the clear. It is therefore likely that couples in counselling, while evidently not representative of most marriages most of the time, represented the extreme end of a spectrum of discontent affecting many other marriages on a sporadic basis.[154]

Another potential bias concerning counselling was that much of it was performed by psychotherapists critical of the theory and methods of marriage reform. Psychotherapists (by which I mean psychoanalysts, psychiatrists, psychiatric social workers and clinically trained sex therapists) did not object to companionship as such. On the contrary, they supported complementarity and equality between spouses. 'That wives as well as husbands have rights for sexual satisfaction, that spouses must be trusted companions as well as legal marital partners, and that the difficulties as well as the enjoyments of life must be equally shared' represented, to the psychotherapeutic FDB as much as to critic of psychotherapy David Mace, the pathway towards unprecedented 'possibilities of achieving satisfaction in marriage'.[155] At the same time, their distinct intellectual tradition led psychotherapists to doubt the ease with which this might be achieved. Mutuality was in a sense an Enlightenment project. Its enemies were ignorance and spent custom; its remedies knowledge and reform. Marriage reformers accordingly believed that 'matrimonial discord is a psychological problem that can be solved' by teaching couples the rational way to conduct their relationships. To think otherwise was to deprive marriage guidance and advice manuals of their very rationale.[156] Psychotherapists held a more troubling outlook on human nature. The outmoded ideas obstructing companionship were not in their view simply the remnants of a patriarchal society. They were those of the individual, the neurotic obsessions bequeathed by the traumas of early childhood.

Psychotherapists also lacked the faith shown by marriage reformers in commonsensical explanations for marital problems, let alone cures. They delighted in the counterintuitive and viewed the behaviours preoccupying marriage reformers to be no more than the visible portion of underlying afflictions. Advice columnist Mayo Wingate attributed 90 per cent of marital discord to sexual maladjustment requiring straightforward correction. Psychiatrist Henry Dicks, however, maintained that 'sexual disturbance is never a diagnosis but always a symptom of conflict in the person about libidinal object-relations': an altogether more complex matter.[157] Although Wingate believed that 'a little knowledge of each other's characters' would bring spouses together, Dicks argued that unconscious 'defence mechanisms' including denial, repression, displacement and projection prevented individuals from making rational assessments of their partners and themselves. What marriage reformers mistook for ignorance was evidence of resistance, to be overcome by years of patient and circuitous analysis.[158]

These debates were about more than methodology. They were concerned with whether marriages were susceptible to simple reform. Did correct technique produce the 'Perfect Sex-Act'? Was love really the 'One Solution' to any and every ill? Psychotherapists very much doubted it. 'There is no such thing, outside the realms of imagination, as a marriage that is free from conflict,' stated the Tavistock's A.G. Thompson. Dicks concurred, portraying love and hate, concord and discord as being what made a marriage 'live'. While marriage reformers made happiness their ultimate goal, he placed 'happiness' within inverted commas.[159] Psychiatric social worker E.M. Goldberg cast further doubt on the mutualist orthodoxy that 'good and happy marriage is based on a close partnership in which interests are shared, problems discussed, and roles flexible and interchangeable.' He maintained that couples with any manner of 'unconventional role assignments' could prosper provided that they satisfied each other's peculiar needs, while the 'clearly distinguishable' marital roles of segregated marriage made it easier for a child to identify with the same-sex parent.[160] The same problem of 'role confusion' concerned Dicks, who saw women's emancipation as having introduced ambivalence among husbands and wives over their respective roles. The FDB for its part referred to the harm inflicted by sex manuals, their 'dogmatic standards about "normality"' creating fears of being '"abnormal" or inferior' among the insecure.[161]

Psychotherapists' jaundiced attitudes towards companionship when combined with their belief in an inherently conflicted psyche go some way towards explaining the disconcerting portrait of marriage in counselling literature. For Dicks to interpret one woman's sexual non-responsiveness in terms of her 'armour of hate masked by seductiveness against the devastated males who threatened her phallic pride' may have revealed more about him than her. Moreover, the influence of psychotherapy extended beyond the Tavistock, the FDB and the Institute of Psychosexual Medicine into that redoubt of marriage reform, the NMGC. Its co-founder Edward Griffith became a Jungian, its training officer J.H. Wallis underwent analysis by Alfred Adler, one of its textbooks devoted a chapter to the unconscious, and psychiatrists were on hand to advise each of its more than one hundred branches.[162]

But can the contrast between upbeat marriage manuals and downbeat counselling records be attributed solely to the victory of psychotherapy over marriage reform? Not all marriage reformers were won over to psychotherapeutic techniques. Mary Macaulay's belief that 'most married couples will sort out their own problems if they can be patient and learn to listen to one another' made her reject psychoanalysis. David Mace, meanwhile, denounced aspects of Freudianism as immoral mumbo-jumbo, prompting Henry Dicks to class him a cliché-ridden amateur. Moreover, psychotherapists were hardly alone in identifying a downside to companionship. That their findings were reiterated in large part by gynaecologists and advice columnists, sociologists and sexologists, divorce lawyers and matchmakers, undermines the idea that psychotherapists' case histories merely represented projections, as it were, of their own pet concerns.[163]

This brings us to the possibility that companionship was indeed failing to deliver the goods for many couples. Such was the glum conclusion of marriage reformers-cum-counsellors who, by the late 1960s and early 1970s, had begun to comprehend the paradox of companionship: that its virtues were its vices, that what had been presented as remedies to the ill-effects of patriarchy produced a variety of unwanted side-effects. The idea that equality would make marriages run 'sweetly and smoothly' had been exposed as a fallacy, admitted David and Vera Mace, as the rival claims of husbands and wives created an 'endless series of disagreements.' Agony aunt Mary Grant accepted that true togetherness, besides being 'unattainable', was not the 'sole answer to all our emotional needs'. And the very complexity of sexual problems suggested that a dab of technique and a whole lot of understanding would not do. 'Experience of counselling has taught me to be sceptical of the claim, so widely made a few years ago, that most sexual difficulties arise from ignorance,' stated J.H. Wallis. He, like his clients, had discovered that ills once perceived to be transitional in nature had become permanent fixtures of modern marriage.[164]

Marriage reformers of the late sixties and early seventies accordingly disowned the idea of marriage as a 'warm steam-bath of mutual affection' in favour of avowedly 'more realistic' aims, methods and pronouncements. They had once touted companionship as the solution to the problem of patriarchy. Now it was companionship's failings that most exercised their minds.[165] Their principal counselling organization,

the NMGC, had originally been envisaged as a 'hospital for sick...
marriages' that would dispense advice of a largely sexual nature. A
quarter of a century later, it downplayed its didactic role by offering
'counselling' rather than 'guidance', detected sexual difficulties in under
a third of cases and shied away from its earlier claim of being able to
cure 'the large majority' of marital complaints. And marriage reformers'
main mouthpiece, the advice manual, attested to a disillusionment
verging on despair. As the classic texts finally went out of print, a new
breed of manuals emerged targeting not newlyweds eager to be initiated
into *The Art of Lasting Happiness* but such less romantic markets as
The Woman on the Verge of Divorce.[166]

The latter title, by the NMGC's long-time house-writer Angela Reed,
caught the new mood in its unsparing comparison between
companionate 'Expectations' and dispiriting 'Reality'. Equality had
failed to produce the expected dividends in marital contentment: 'In
theory, ideal marriage today is an equal partnership. The phrase has
stuck but is it, or can it ever be? Do people really want to be equal in
an intensely personal relationship? And what does being equal mean?'
In practice, patriarchy had been replaced by a 'wavering balance'
between traditional and emancipated sex roles unsatisfactory to both
partners and responsible for a 'whole new series of marriage difficulties
caused by confusion of male and female roles.' She characterized the
quest for closeness as involving as much pain as pleasure since couples
who did everything together often ended up 'choking each other.'
Moreover, the belief that spouses should share an identity of interests
courted disappointment in the event that their wishes clashed. Nor were
the increased expectations of sexual enjoyment the great boon that they
were meant to be. Wives in particular retained some of their inhibitions
and felt inadequate when told that 'sex is there at the drop of a hat'.[167]
Reed's was a powerful critique of companionship and its discontents,
yet she could think of no better alternative. For all her warnings about
the suffocating and alienating aspects of intimacy, she still insisted that
couples should strive towards 'total communication at all levels',
including the sexual. Companionship, it seemed, was the worst of all
possible arrangements – except for all the other ones.[168]

5

Porn Free

Men's Sexuality and Women's Emancipation

If sex in Britain 'began / In nineteen-sixty-three ... Between the end of the *Chatterley* ban / and the Beatles' first LP,' then the first recognizably modern pornography appeared the year after that. 1964 saw the launch of *King* and the *Pirelli Calendar*, followed by *Penthouse* in 1965 (for its first four years an exclusively British publication), *Mayfair* in 1966, the *Penthouse* offshoots *Forum* and *Lords* in 1968 and Paul Raymond's revamped *Men Only* and *Club International* in 1971 and 1972. The new pornography announced itself with an unprecedented audacity. 'We like sex,' proclaimed Raymond in the first issue of *King*: 'sex can be fun ... Good entertainment, wherever it is found, demands the recognition of sex ... there is nothing moral in hiding sex, or in pretending that the sight of a pretty girl undressed can corrupt any man, young or old.' Bolder still was *Penthouse*, launched upon a million mailshots to such publicity that it provoked parliamentary questions and whose debut cover-girl broke with pin-up, and *Playboy*, convention not only by removing her clothes but by spreading her legs and turning the cheerful cheesecake smile into a look of lust.[1]

The new magazines were the products of a permissive society whose every facet, from fashion to abortion, they sought to capture within their pages. Pornography fed as well as fed off permissive culture, influencing everything from advertising to high art and deserving consideration alongside popular music and television comedy as one of Britain's most significant contributions to the sixties scene. The cultural centrality of pornography reveals permissiveness to have been not just a series of liberalizing laws but also a popular movement supported by the legions of male masturbators who bought soft-core porn. These men's importance was not underestimated at the time, when their demand for increasingly salacious material made a nonsense of the obscenity laws and pornography succeeded prostitution as the principal symbol of sexual malaise.[2]

Sixties pornography was also mutuality's bastard son. It was born out of a like-minded attempt to rescue sexuality from the 'prudy-prudy swamps of Victorianism'. It echoed the sex radicals' ambition to create a 'new morality' based upon an ultra-modern 'rational, humanistic and responsible sex ethic'. It spoke their language of women's sexual emancipation and shared something of their hope that the sexes were coming closer together upon the basis of mutual desire. Within these magazines appeared a utopian vision of a sexualized society populated by two sexes undergoing parallel emancipations, with women freed of their sexual inhibitions and men from their breadwinning burdens into a consumeristic, individualistic lifestyle. Yet, like the married couples and mixed club leaders studied in the previous two chapters, pornographers found mutuality easier to imagine than to achieve. What were passed off as descriptions of women's sexual awakening were often prescriptions for how things should be and, when sexual emancipation gave way to women's liberation at the turn of the seventies, the magazines vilified those feminists who punctured their dreams.[3]

The small print: pornography is defined in this chapter as material whose principal intention is to arouse sexual feeling. Gay porn is excluded from consideration since it does not much touch upon relations between the sexes and has in any case been well covered elsewhere. Omitted also is hard-core (in the restrictive British sense of depictions of penetrative sex), being less popular and, since illegal, less widely produced domestically. My subject-matter is accordingly soft-core magazines considered in the round, their photospreads examined alongside their profiles of models, consumer columns, editorials and sexology. The reasons are that a word can be worth a thousand pictures; that this is how they were intended to be read; that articles assumed an unprecedented importance in soft-core during this period; and because only by comparing and contrasting the various elements of the magazines can the full scope of the pornographic project for masculinity and femininity be revealed.[4]

The Pornography of Alibis

Pornography was a pariah in pre-permissive Britain. It had no legal standing and few public defenders, being condemned as morally warped and aesthetically debased by conservative moralists and leftist intellectuals alike: hence George Orwell's inclusion of 'Pornsec', the pornography-producing division of the Ministry of Truth, at the centre of The Party's efforts to pacify the Proles and 'distort and dirty' the sex instinct.[5] It was further damned for its association with masturbation, whose medical threat had receded but whose stigma remained in a society that believed in sex serving an instrumental end: if no longer solely for the purposes of procreation, then to cement companionship.[6]

Censure and censorship could not kill pornography, but warped its market and stunted its development. Explicit, illicit material was by its very nature difficult and expensive to obtain. Legal material survived in submerged forms as a lust that dared not speak its name. It clothed itself in what historian Thomas Waugh has termed alibis, fronts behind which the erotic might hide. Straight pornography employed three alibis – the naturist, the artistic and the pin-up – each representing a distinct genre with its own publications and stylistic protocols, the maintenance of which proved to be a highly effective form of self-censorship.[7]

Since the 1930s, naturist magazines enjoyed the indulgence of censors customarily reserved for eccentrics and became famous for their photographs of women glancing across their shoulders with come-hither eyes or crouching catlike with predatory expressions. Yet these pictures' juxtaposition to classical studies of women comporting themselves like vestal virgins and distinctly unenticing shots of men and women mowing lawns and strumming guitars revealed the conflicting and conflicted aims of the publications. While catering to a sex-hungry readership, the foremost naturist journal, *Health and Efficiency*, was run by bona fide enthusiasts who presented nudity as natural, sensual not sexual, no more impure than 'having a hot bath'. They resented notoriety, feared censorship, disowned explicit Continental publications and refused requests to print 'integral' (unairbrushed) nudes.[8]

The artistic alibi, which derived from the use of nude photographs as aids for portraiture in the nineteenth century, was revived in the late 1930s by three established photographers – Walter Bird, John Everard and Horace Narbeth (alias 'Roye') – who found a ready market in the new general interest magazines *Men Only* and *Lilliput* (launched in 1935 and 1937 respectively).[9] The artistic nude proved unsuitable as a pornographic medium to the extent that its alibi had to be protected. Art was not meant to come cheaply and volumes might cost a hefty one or two pounds. Furthermore, for their alibis to be credible, photographers had to demonstrate some technical proficiency and be conversant with artistic conventions, severely limiting the number of practitioners. It was a problem circumvented to some degree in the postwar period with the rise of such magazines as *Amateur Photographer*, but their nude portraits were still dressed up as artistic endeavours and accompanied by a sufficient number of yacht and kitten pictures, not to mention hundreds of pages of tedious technical details, to deter all but the most dedicated of masturbators. The artistic alibi also dictated how the nude might be shown, suppressing the very hint of sexual invitation and conforming to painterly conventions of a hundred years before. This meant not naming the models, limiting their expressions to the pensive or the joyous and generally having them avert their eyes, as if entirely unconscious of being photographed. Pouting was most definitely prohibited. Even the most daring of the artistic nude publications – Roye's *Unique Editions* (1958), which was unsuccessfully prosecuted for showing unairbrushed full frontals – appeared in an exquisite subscribers-only edition, kept the models anonymous, adhered to the alibis of beauty and verisimilitude and not once confessed to any improper motives.[10]

Pin-ups were trapped in innuendo. Their more transparent sexual intent imposed stricter limits upon what they could show, meaning that they had to do as much as possible with rather little in the way of flesh. The model's lips were therefore fuller, her legs longer, her breasts larger and her figure more callipygous than anything seen in naturist or artistic nudes. While the latter denied all that they revealed, the cheesecakes implied all that they were forced to conceal. Yet, however fine the line between suggestiveness and outright lewdness, it was one that had to be maintained. Pin-ups might 'provoke' and even 'beguile us into adventurous daydreams' but were on no account permitted to 'excite': their 'contained [and] carefully channelled' mode of arousal resembling the look-but-don't-touch 'parasexuality' to which Peter Bailey refers in his study of Victorian barmaids.[11] They were also expected to be fit for family viewing. Britain's very own sex bomb, Diana Dors, supported the notion that pin-ups appealing exclusively to men were somehow improper when claiming that, while a portion of her fan mail came from schoolboys or 'cranks', fully 90 per cent of it was written by 'middle-aged housewives and spinsters'. Married men, she insisted, were careful not to send off for her photograph for fear that their wives would have 'something to say.'[12] *Parade* accordingly advertised itself as 'The Man's Magazine which Women Love to Read', *Lilliput* paired its women with comic photographs and even an aggressively masculine magazine like *Men Only* ensured that its number of nudes remained at a 'strictly limited' level.[13]

Not only did the pornography of alibis perform the work of the censors on their behalf, it also shared many attitudes with the respectable society that shunned it. While the one expressed what the other sought to repress, pornographers and their persecutors alike found it hard to conceive of a place for sexuality in society. In 1961, the leading men's magazine *Men Only* remained unsure whether chastity was out of date and counselled bachelors to let their desires 'subside': '"Repression" never follows sexual disappointment and has absolutely nothing to do with the conscious suppression of feelings which a mature man exercises when he wants to control his behaviour.'[14] Such attitudes translated in visual terms into an escapism that removed eroticism from everyday life, whether in naturist arcadias, the 'glamour' world of the pin-ups or the studio settings of the artistic alibi, which rested upon the dichotomy between art and life. Any intrusion of reality could only deflate the fantasy.[15]

Pornographers were also wedded to the pre-mutualist notion that normal women were uninterested in or downright hostile to sex. *Men Only*'s cartoons depicted two sorts of woman: the dream woman being that unattainable blonde in the street; the sobering truth, the frumpy wife pulling at your arm. Hence the popularity of the voyeuristic conceit, which suggested that women were ordinarily so resistant to men's attentions that you had to catch them unawares. In naturist photographs, women were consumed by an inexplicable gaiety as they innocently frolicked in sylvan glades. Artistic studies offered privileged access to the painter's studio, where the model indicated no awareness that her body was on view to any but the artist alone. Pin-ups would, for their part, show a model casually undressing or a tantalizing glimpse of undies as she ascended a step-ladder. In involving no reciprocal desire on the part of women and presenting male arousal as an unexpected occurrence to be grasped when available, voyeurism suggested that sex was customarily kept under wraps. Apparently unable to conceive of female desire as ordinary and natural, pornographers depicted women of an extraordinary and artificial kind, moving social commentator Richard Hoggart to object that cheesecakes had been 'pasteurised' out of their very corporeality.[16]

A partial exception to this rule were the new pin-up magazines of the late 1950s, which broke some of the existing conventions of soft-core pornography. Beginning with Harrison Marks' *Kamera* in 1958, a host of interchangeable publications with uniformly naff titles (*Glimpse*, *Skirt*, *Teasy*, *Woww*) combined frontal nudity with unambiguously sexual motives. But while eschewing the old standards of seemliness, these shared many of the conceptual limitations of the pornography of alibis. They promised glamour, a scarce commodity in the likes of Leicester and Oadby, where they were produced. What they in fact delivered was a sorry package of what appeared to be prostitutes pawing themselves in unattractive suburban settings. They were as escapist as their predecessors, merely exchanging woods and studios for claustrophobic interiors, oases of eroticism in a barren world. And they were similarly incapable of imagining a healthy female carnality. Whereas women had been purified in the artistic and naturist nudes and sanitized in the pin-ups, here they were defiled. Save for the well-designed *Kamera* itself, these were sordid rags, small and tawdry, cheaply produced and dishonestly packaged, the pictorial equivalent of a bit of rough.[17]

Neither these conceptual obstacles nor being ostracized and officially outlawed stopped pornography from becoming ubiquitous by the 1950s. 'Sex in shiny packets' was available for most tastes, according to Richard Hoggart, from the moralizing salacity of the *News of the World* and the ribaldry of the seaside postcards to the sadomasochism of the gangster novelettes. Pin-ups in particular 'assaulted' him from every direction: the sub-Varga drawings in the working-class papers, the 'Technicolor cheesecakes' in their lower middle-class counterparts and the rafts of dirty pictures in the 'spicy magazines'. But Hoggart was right to point out what a perplexing impression of sex they conveyed. The figures were 'strangely ersatz', he noted, and bore no obvious relation to intercourse. This was soon to change.[18]

Permissiveness and the New Pornography

The 'permissive moment' in Britain almost exactly spanned the sixties. From the Obscene Publications Act of 1959 to the relaxation of divorce laws a decade later, a succession of ambiguously liberal laws sought to deregulate personal (mainly sexual) behaviour while removing it to the private sphere. In defiance of this attempted privatization of sexuality, however, was that massive publicization of sexuality in sixties culture that linked Profumo to the Rolling Stones to the Gay Liberation Front. The reason lay in those popular forces for permissiveness – the proliferation of betting, abortions, marital breakdowns and 'overt' homosexuals – that at once forced politicians to act and confounded their intentions, so that each effort to expel private life from public view only accentuated the escalation of hitherto impermissible activities.[19]

The unintended consequences of permissive legislation and the power of popular permissiveness were exemplified in the new pornography appearing in the mid 1960s. These magazines looked different from anything previously produced in Britain. They epitomized sixties style, their colour spreads and upmarket articles outclassing the fraudulent covers, blurry black and white photographs and illiterate captioning of most pin-up magazines. Size also mattered, the new titles being quadruple the dimensions of the usual pornographic publications and designed to grace any bachelor's coffee table, not to be secreted within an inside pocket. The novelty of these publications went beyond mere matters of presentation, however, as they signalled their arrival by overturning every convention observed by pre-permissive pornography. Alibis were the first thing to go, with Sunday supplements ridiculed for their surreptitious displays of nudity and *Amateur Photographer* lampooned as 'Amateur Pornographer'.[20] Also to end was that pusillanimous accommodation with censorship encapsulated in alibis as *Penthouse* tested the very limits of legality by displaying pubic hair from 1970 onwards, so precipitating the 'Pubic Wars' that made soft-core much less soft than before.[21]

No legislative change made this possible. The Obscene Publications Act had been designed to stop smut of this sort and in 1964, the very year when the first of the new magazines appeared, Parliament was tightening up the provisions against porn. But the obscenity laws were rendered effectively unenforceable against soft-core by the workings of the permissive society. The 1959 Act had been founded upon the principle of control through classification: distinguishing between art and obscenity, between different media, different consumers (effectively incorruptible intellectuals versus 'wives and servants') and different producers (the 'serious artist' who exercised 'artistic restraint' as against 'the other man ... who sits down and thinks "I want to make my readers as randy as I can, as often as I can"').[22] Yet 1959 proved an inauspicious time to establish such distinctions. The following decade was characterized by the elision of cultural boundaries, a reaction against the paternalistic protection of women and children and an intelligentsia practically guaranteed to behave in an unrestrained and irresponsible manner. The new pornographers duly championed cultural cross-fertilization, exploited every inconsistency in the obscenity law and bought a patina of respectability in the form of literary contributions from such eminent sex radicals as scientist Sir Julian Huxley and lawyer John Mortimer.

Pornographers could also count upon the support of an immoral majority that wanted their product and supported their libertarian goals; at no time before or since has there been such tolerance towards soft-core porn. And as men's magazines moved from under the counter to the top shelf, existing publications either adapted (like *Men Only*) or folded. The number of general interest 'adult' titles increased from three to fifty in a decade and sales ballooned (see table 1). According to one mid 1970s survey, four-fifths of men and half that number of women enjoyed looking at 'sexy pictures'. The magazines were effectively too large to prosecute, the audience too large to persecute.[23]

Table 1: Monthly circulation of major British pornographic magazines, 1966–76

	1966	*1971*	*1976*
Penthouse	150,000	218,000	429,000
Mayfair	n/a	164,000	461,000
Men Only	n/a	150,000	434,000
Club International	–	–	324,000

Sources: *Penthouse*; 'Periodicals and the Alternative Press', *Royal Commission on the Press* (London, 1977), 46.

Permissiveness changed not only what could be shown but also what could be thought. Following *Playboy*'s lead, the new pornography refused to divorce its readers' sexuality from their other interests in the manner of pre-permissive porn, instead presenting an integrated package of features and pictorials structured around a sexual theme. It injected sex into such conventional elements of men's magazines as motoring and clothing sections and added new features to explain the bewildering proliferation of sexual possibilities now on display.[24] *Mayfair* carried an editorial column, 'Scene', devoted to nothing but the chronicling of the progressive revelation of sexuality in the public sphere. It began one year, 1969, by predicting a 'nude new year' and applauding the first advertisements baring all in the broadsheets. By July, it heralded women's revolt against underpants and bras. August's 'Scene' speculated on the imminent possibility of 'TV toplessness' now that *Top of the Pops* featured 'micro-skirted, tight-pantied, hip-grinding dancers'. The October edition drew attention to see-through fashions and in November 'Scene' marvelled at how, in one short year, public nudity had become so widely acceptable. The year ended on a cultural note, with a report of a Frankfurt art exhibition at which a naked woman stood within an outsized frame.[25]

The sexualization of society emboldened the new pornography to reject the cultural isolation of the pornography of alibis in favour of an enthusiastic interaction with other aspects of sixties culture. From fashion, the new pornography gained glimpses of masculine and feminine emancipation and in turn won plaudits from fashion designers like Mary Quant who saw similarities between pornographic images of women and their own. Advertising and pornography borrowed so freely from each other that, in the *Pirelli Calendar,* they fused into one.[26] Pornographers and the counterculture enjoyed a fertile if tetchy relationship, with some shared interests in the sixties giving way to outright antagonism in the seventies as the more right-on publications belatedly embraced the women's movement. Sexologists, who had for decades disavowed any connection with pornography, were now recruited by the dozen to chart the new frontiers of sexuality. What they received in return was permission to let their hair down: to become more populist and experiential and to move away from matters of sexual function and conjugal relations towards those issues of pleasure and diversity best illustrated in Alex Comfort's *The Joy of Sex* (1972).[27]

Most striking was the reversed relationship between pornography and art. No longer interested in maintaining the alibi that pornography was really art, pornographers now dared to suggest that most art was really pornographic, leading *King* and *Club International* to reconstruct the erotic paintings of Manet and Beardsley. The only difference between 'pornographic and pure art', claimed *Penthouse*, was simply a 'matter of time'.[28] With the pornographers subjecting all claims of artistic purity to questioning and mockery, it was the art world itself that sounded disingenuous when denying any titillatory intent: the subject of jokes from Monty Python (as a critic discoursed on 'the place of the nude in the history of tart') and despair from critics ('everything is now tainted or coloured by the debate...over pornography and censorship,' complained the curator of an erotic art exhibition in 1971). In this manner, the new pornography became central to an emerging post-modern culture based upon the transgression of cultural distinctions.[29]

The permissive society also allowed the new pornography to repudiate escapism in its photospreads. The pornography of alibis had created alternative universes in which male sexual desire was satisfied. But with sex now saturating everything from soap ads to high politics

(Christine Keeler was *King*'s first pin-up), pornographers announced that there was no need to seek sanctuary in unreality. The pictorials' settings were less realistic than aspirational: stylish, certainly, yet not so fantastic as to constitute escapism. The same could be said for the models, who were pitched somewhere between the earthy women of *Spick* and the impossibly distant and unattainable Californian beauties of *Playboy*. They were nineteen-year-old Chelsea girls almost to a woman and exuded the borough's posh bohemianism. Their career plans were likewise uncommon but not unreal: top-flight secretaries, aspirant actresses and vets.[30]

Another indication of the new pornographers' wish to abandon the otherworldly settings of old was their constant promotion of Britain as a sexual Shangri-La. This must have been a revelatory concept to a generation of men who had hitherto relied on America for its sex pulps, Scandinavia for its blue photographs and France's Olympia Press for its hard-core literature, and whose pin-up magazines in the fifties had confirmed the dispiriting contrast between Continental glamour and native wholesomeness.[31] Yet now the British 'bird' was proclaimed to be 'suddenly the most attractive, the most desirable, the most startling girl in the world', with *Mayfair* insisting upon a home-grown 'Dolly of the Month' for its first three dozen issues. For their part, foreign models were presented as *ingénues* drawn inexorably to the sexual magnet that was swinging London, enchanted by its nightlife and enraptured by the superior sexual technique of British men (another favourite theme of the sixties magazines). In overturning Britain's reputation as the land of cold fish, the new pornography suggested that escapism was futile when sex was present everywhere in the here and now.[32]

The new pornographers of the 1960s presented themselves as the beneficiaries, mirrors and sponsors of the permissive society. They began by insisting upon a place for porn free from dissembling and untrammelled by censorship. They continued by forming close links with other sexual discourses. Their final role in relation to the permissive society was as guide and sponsor, interpreting the meaning of permissiveness and attempting to mould society according to their desires. To this end, magazines employed a whole host of missionizing techniques. The sexology assumed an air of impartiality while promoting very definite models of sexual behaviour. The consumer columns urged male readers to become sexual beings pursuing permissive lifestyles. Pictorials displaying pornographers' feminine ideal sat alongside spurious personality profiles detailing how they wished women to behave.

It was unclear, however, how far the new pornography's vision of masculinity and femininity corresponded to the lives of men and women in the 1960s. Pornographers insisted that theirs was not an 'unreal world of fantasy women and masturbatory images', maintaining that 'pictures provide contact with reality'. They promoted an aspirational lifestyle at the cusp of the real and the ideal: attractive yet still attainable given sufficient will.[33] Above all, it was the contention of the new pornographers that permissiveness made possible what had once been fantastic, that fantasy and reality were converging. *Mayfair* found its dreams realized in the 'fabulous girl on Platform Four, the zoom-away girl in the souped-up Mini'. It was in this optimistic belief that a 'new age' of 'intellectual enlightenment' was being born that the sixties pornographers set about reforming masculinity and femininity alike.[34]

Tomorrow's Men

The new pornography promoted an ideal of masculinity that covered everything from what to wear to how to make love. Its archetypal man was an ingenious blend of the traditional and the modern, the manly and the unisex. As such, he retained his customary authority as the 'King' or 'Lord' of the magazines' titles, a point reinforced by the *Penthouse* models' unanimous preference for 'completely masculine' men: 'A man should be a man: good strong shoulders, decisive in his views and opinions, willing to take command of a situation.' Here the model was the Victorian patriarch whom women 'pampered and pleased at the drop of a whim.'[35] At the same time, the Victorian gentleman had been weighed down by the 'burden of breadwinning' and the requirement to be 'strong, brave, dry-eyed, decisive'. His authoritative air had been maintained only at the cost of rejecting 'anything smacking of femininity, familiarity with the arts, overt domesticity, fashionable trivia, and sartorial pretensions.' Far better, the new pornographers thought, to be an 'emancipated man' who, if lacking the some of the power of his patriarchal forefathers, was nonetheless more expressive, stylish and relaxed.[36]

'Tomorrow's Man' was well groomed, wore smart clothes, dug jazz and drove a fast, 'phallic' car, much like his archetype, James Bond. He likewise chose a sexual lifestyle, constructing his identity around his desires. Hence the pictorials provided women to be attracted to, the consumer columns told men how to attract them and the sexology coached them in matters of attitude and technique. The accent on aspiration was reflected in the columns' titles: 'View from the Top' for *Penthouse*'s editorials, 'Groom at the Top' for its toiletries section.[37] Individualism was somehow aligned to male bonding. The magazines were obsessed with the idea of clubs, from their titles (*Club*) through 'book societies' down to the promotion of *King* as bestowing a sort of honorary membership of Soho's Raymond Revuebar. Clubbability involved fraternity, but it also implied exclusivity and as such corresponded to the new pornographers' ambition of creating a 'select group' of emancipated men.[38]

Unfortunately for the pornographers, theirs was a hopelessly ambitious and increasingly unsustainable model of masculinity problematic in two major respects: first, whether the ideal bore any relation to reality; and second, whether emancipation compromised men's traditional authority. The first problem derived from the fact that their subscribers were no James Bonds, and to pretend otherwise required an immense amount of wishful thinking: that they lived in 'Penthouses' in 'Mayfair'; that they were actually desired by the models in the magazines. Occasionally realism won out and the magazines conceded, however reluctantly and covertly, the limits of men's emancipation. While supposed to be sexual sophisticates, the readers were in fact addressed as enthusiastic amateurs and given 'dictionary supplements' to mug up on the meaning of terms like 'lesbianism' and 'sodomy'. The pornographers also worked hard to overcome men's sexual 'guilt and self-condemnation' by assuaging their every insecurity. The readership was assured that masturbation was a 'perfectly normal' matter and that a 'liking for breasts' indicated not immaturity but rather a 'civilised and sophisticated sexual personality.' What was not said was every bit as important as what was. *Mayfair*'s interest in 'female sexual response' tactfully did not extend to their preferences regarding men's physical appearance, sexual technique and penile size.[39]

Hopes for a masculine fraternity were similarly illusory. Sex provided inadequate grounds for solidarity since it involved denying what the men really had in common (a penchant for masturbation) while pretending that there was a single heterosexuality around which all could bond. The something-for-everyone approach of sixties soft-core – consecutive covers of 1969's *Mayfair* portrayed a dominatrix, a retro woman in antique drawers, a spot of bondage, the Continental charms of Brigitte Bardot and a model on a tiger skin resplendent in an Oriental head-dress – could not last. The following decade spawned speciality magazines which cut into the market share of the soft-core generalists.[40]

Fragmentation also occurred along class lines, a subject provoking no little confusion in the new pornography. *Mayfair* portrayed itself as 'classless' while at the same time boasting that three-quarters of its readers were professionals or executives. Meanwhile, the very success of *Penthouse* detracted from its top-hole image. Consequently, its promise that the Penthouse Club (modelled on the Playboy Club in Mayfair) would admit only 'men of means and influence' had to be abandoned in favour of open membership in response to the volume of demand. Publisher Bob Guccione tried with *Lords* to create a still more exclusive version of *Penthouse*, but its high price tag, obsession with fashion and comparative lack of women made it just too exclusive to last longer than a year. What the market wanted was in fact the exact opposite: a low-class sex'n'fun replacement for the old-fashioned *Parade* and *Spick*. David Sullivan duly obliged in the 1970s with tawdry publications like *Whitehouse* that, together with Raymond's *Club International* and the *Sun*'s Page Three girls, revived working-class porn. With the seventies pornographic market split by class and sexual tastes, the idea of a male community of pornography readers became unsustainable.[41]

A further dilemma for the new pornography involved balancing emancipation with the maintenance of a traditional masculine authority. This was a key concern of their excursions into sexology, which superficially displayed the magazines at their most progressive. *Penthouse* possessed in Alan Hull Walton a sex radical of long standing, prepared to endorse a then-illegal homosexuality as being 'natural and as normal, and as much God-created and even God-desired as is the more usual heterosexual form of love.'[42] *Mayfair*, while confining itself to straight sex, presented its mission in mutualist terms:

> it has been an aspect of British life, from which we are now fortunately recovering, that men have been encouraged to think of women as incomprehensible, aloof creatures. Segregated schools and the residue of late nineteenth-century attitudes placed women in a totally unrealistic social position ... [But now] for the first time, men can listen and understand while women express emotions that, until now, have been suppressed.

Permissiveness thus made it at once possible and essential for men to cultivate a 'deep awareness of woman's physical and emotional needs'.[43]

Behind this progressive rhetoric, however, there lurked decidedly unemancipated views. It transpired that men were to attain a 'comprehensive knowledge' of women in order to exercise power over them. A man first needed to 'understand what kind of "hang-ups" are causing a particular girl to refuse him' for him to be able to 'seek out the knowledge necessary to overcome them.'[44] Understanding women's desires did not necessarily entail any greater consideration in that a man was to 'compromise and sympathise' with his partner only insofar as it did not interfere with his control of the relationship.[45] In any case, women were not thought to know their own minds. While they said they wanted '"kind" men', they actually responded to 'a very different kind of man...[the] decisive, dominant' type and enjoyed being 'ordered about, bossed and even bullied.' Men were expected to know better than to take women's assertiveness too seriously. Even the most headstrong woman was yearning to be dominated: 'faced with a man who has obviously a strong character, she quickly accepted the "humiliation" of sex with her knickers on and finished whimpering against his chest.'[46]

Female sexual assertion was a recurring concern in the new pornography's sexological columns. The first two issues of *Penthouse* contained articles by American sexologists explaining how 'sexual equality', however 'desirable in theory', produced 'confused and conflictual' encounters between emasculated men and masculinized women. 'Unmanning' their partners, women in turn came to 'despise the male who is no longer able to dominate' so that the problem spiralled, creating a society of 'anxious, impotent' husbands and 'terrified, sobbing, frigid' wives.[47] Pursuing the theme that women suffered when men surrendered to their overbearing demands, *Mayfair* contended that aggressive women sought not to challenge their partners' dominance so much as put it to the mettle. The manly response to such 'hysterical or antagonistic' behaviour was therefore a 'hard slap across the face'. In this manner a man might 'assert authority' in an arena where he had no 'fear of losing', while his woman would in turn feel 'grateful for the beatings [she] had received'. So was the new pornography able to reconcile a progressive attitude towards women's sexual emancipation with the retention of traditional patriarchal power.[48]

All the tensions between tradition and modernity, expectation and aspiration, and masculine emancipation and manly domination were encapsulated in the new pornography's treatment of menswear. The men's magazines of the sixties took fashion seriously and, with the demise of specialist publications like *The Outfitter*, *Men in Vogue* and the magazine *Town*, were among the most important organs for its coverage. Their reasons were commercial ('*Mayfair* readers spend more on their appearance than 95 per cent of the population,' it told its advertisers) but also ideological, since they perceived clothing to be an index of men's emancipation. Conventional male dress was thought to reflect the constriction of established masculine roles. For the past century, men had worn clothes to express status, not personality and to show less what they were than what they were not: neither a worker nor a homosexual nor a woman. The 'revolution in menswear' of the 1960s therefore involved a triple 'emancipation' from stereotypes of class, sexuality and manhood. As social divisions diminished, a man could discard his class uniform in favour of more individualistic attire. Once homosexuality had attained a degree of acceptance, 'colours and exaggerations men once avoided as stigmatizing became free for any man to adopt.'[49] And if men were still slightly ahead of women in matters of sexuality, in fashion it was they who had inhibitions to overcome. The flowering of male fashion in the sixties was presented as a welcome by-product of the decline of traditional manliness. 'Freed from dead convention' and with 'masculinity standards' no longer based on 'beer-swilling, rugger-playing and hearty pastimes', men might indulge in a spot of role-playing. A man could be a cowboy, a Victorian gentleman, a gangster (all subjects of early *Penthouse* fashion features) or, for that matter, 'an elegant fop, serious business man...and anything else he pleasures.' Men were also at liberty not only to be 'vain' but also, like women, 'to allure, to intrigue, to beguile, to dazzle'.[50]

These were radical proposals, much more so than the controlled release of sartorial expression countenanced by Burton's and the 'heterosexualisation of display' in *Town* that have been studied by Frank Mort, Peter Thompson and Sean Nixon.[51] As outlandish were the clothes themselves. In addition to suits and ties, there were caftans and smocks, flowery shirts and briefs of every colour. But did this new wardrobe correspond to any accepted notion of masculinity? Could a real man been seen in a cravat? The fashion writers insisted so, since the Peacock Male was showy by nature and since overtly butch attire was a sign of sexual insecurity: 'only the non-man needs sartorial camouflage to establish exactly what he is'. The pictorials also did their best to masculinize fashion by showing women worshipping men for their sophistication and taste. The camper the costume, the more manly the model used, so that an unimpeachably rugged figure like the actor

Edward Woodward could get away with wearing a caftan, a jumpsuit with a silk scarf and a gold 'camel driver's robe' decorated with blue and white flowers.[52]

But by the beginning of the 1970s, the magazines' attempt to 'emancipate male fashions' was clearly faltering. *Lords*, which had contained as many pictures of clothed men as of naked women, died in 1969. *Mayfair* and *Penthouse* dropped their fashion coverage entirely in 1972 and 1973 respectively.[53] For their part, *Men Only* and *Club International*, in line with their publisher's disgust that the phallus had been so 'publicly derided and ridiculed' in underpants ads, adopted an illiberal line on male display. *Cosmopolitan*'s male centrefold was consequently parodied in a centrefold of a hairy, obese castrate, indicating that men should not be depicted like women, while the photospreads showed men adopting ludicrously macho postures or else exposing themselves on hillsides to demonstrate the merits of raincoats as 'flasher' gear.[54]

Fashion exemplified the failed ambitions of the new pornography for the reformation of masculinity. Here the pornographers' plans for a consumerist, sexualized and emancipated lifestyle were at their most apparent. Men were meant to dress to impress and for success: to express their new-found individuality, leisure and style. Yet the magazines could not reconcile masculinity as it was to masculinity as they wished it to be. Men were not sufficiently interested in clothes to justify extensive fashion coverage and the men's magazines of the early seventies returned to the old staples of cars and girls. For all the reassurance that unisex fashions were so 'intensely masculine' that 'any self-respecting wrestler would wear [them] to his wedding', it was immensely difficult to square emancipation with domination. Dressing hunky models in the most *outré* of outfits and surrounding them by adoring females was less a blending of the manly and the modern than a doomed attempt to reconcile the irreconcilable. Reality tugged at fantasy, pulling it down.[55]

Sexual Emancipation and Women's Liberation

In contrast to pre-permissive pornography, whose interest in women had begun and ended with their vital statistics, the new pornography was absolutely fascinated by all things feminine. Believing real women to be uninterested in intercourse, the pornography of alibis had been uninterested in real women. Conversely, sixties pornography was so curious about women because of the hopes it placed in their sexual emancipation. At the same time as American sexologists Masters and Johnson were discovering that women had an orgasmic capacity superior to men's, it began to depict women who were as desiring as they were desirable. There was no sign yet of the pluralistic and 'problematized' sexuality detected by cultural critic Linda Williams in hard-core films, simply a celebration that women seemed disposed to respond favourably to men's clamant passions.[56]

Such was the message of the photospreads of the *Penthouse* 'Pets' and *Mayfair* 'Dollies', which portrayed women in a manner inconceivable in the pornography of alibis. Every effort was made to present female desire as normal. In contrast to their pin-up predecessors, the models looked as though they actually wanted sex, their complicity signalled by their trademark look of 'collusion' in an imaginary sexual act.[57] And when not watching us watching them, the models had a habit of 'constantly examining themselves, as if preoccupied with their own sexuality'. Such poses once again sanctioned the male gaze while also suggesting that women nursed the same desires as men, even to the point of thirsting after their own bodies.[58] The new look represented a sort of pornographic Reformation, stripping away the flummery of ritual and the arcane conventions observed by the pornography of alibis in favour of a direct relationship between viewer and viewed. Impediments to intercourse – whether actual, like lingerie, or conceptual, like innuendo and the pin-ups' whole symbolic language of coyness, cheekiness, cheerfulness – were all removed. The emphasis was upon the natural, with make-up kept to a minimum and the repertoire of poses reduced to a refined casualness. The pictures were at first no more brazen than those in magazines such as *Kamera*, yet the contrast lay in the models' demeanour. They were not grimly baring all, but were nubile, affluent, sophisticated. They defied the dichotomy between madonna and whore. These were nice girls who did.

The wish to present women as willing sexual partners rendered inappropriate the debasement, objectification and violence that some feminist theorists claim to be characteristic of all pornographic images of women. Sexualized violence was conspicuous by its absence in sixties soft-core, save arguably for some bondage shots. Partly this was for reasons of legality, but any hint of coercion would also have contravened the conviction of the new pornographers that women wanted sex as much as men.[59] The same could be said for objectification, which like voyeurism was only necessary for pornographic purposes if a woman's personality was likely to detract from her sexual appeal. This had been the case in the pre-permissive era, when ordinary women were assumed to lack sexual desire. But the new pornography generally refrained from presenting women as depersonalized sex objects. So, instead of the single shots of anonymous nymphs favoured by the pornography of alibis, it printed whole series of photographs of the same model supplemented by a lengthy profile.[60]

These fabricated personality profiles provided a composite portrait of the new pornography's feminine ideal. Like her male counterpart, the perfect woman blended emancipated attitudes and behaviours with traditional womanly traits: a new, more 'masculinized' femininity with an older, girlier form. They endorsed the pictures' message that women's sexuality was now similar to men's. 'We have as much interest in sex as men do,' declared Pet Amber Dean-Smith, while Paula Francis denounced the double standard as 'totally absurd' and explained that as a 'woman and . . . a sensual being' she had the 'same sexual feelings as a man and [was] entitled to express them with the same kind of freedom that a man does.'[61] The Pets also enthused about the masculine interests and activities promoted elsewhere in the magazines. Linda Richie enjoyed action programmes like *Z Cars* and *The Avengers* and Lilyan Howe enthused about motor racing, 'adventure and danger' and 'old barrelhouse jazz'.[62] At the same time, the models betrayed an essentially feminine sensibility. Howe envied men their 'freedom' but remained 'female through and through', while Denise Johns would be doing 'daring, unfeminine things' like playing football one minute before her 'Victorian, romantic' temperament inspired her to write a love poem the next.[63]

Two favourite personae embodied other balancing acts that women were expected to perform. The first was that of the redeemed tomboy, which softened the fairly assertive poses struck by the models by exposing their inner womanliness. *Mayfair*'s Sally had childhood ambitions of becoming a WREN until she 'suddenly realised I was a woman. I was interested in feminine things, I was interested in boys, and the thought of wodging [*sic*] my new soft breasts into a tight serge uniform lost its attraction very quickly.' Angela Lester likewise thought herself 'doomed to be a life-long tomboy' before she gladly embraced the 'world of utter femininity'.[64] The second was that of the 'child-woman', a delicious mixture of innocence and experience also evident in the pictorials. Mia Martin's 'young and defenceless' appearance belied her 'woman's voice and ways'. Conversely, Cindy McDee was all brassiness on the surface ('I don't take shit from men') but, with clanging cliché, was 'baby-soft' beneath her 'tough and cynical exterior': 'She closes her eyes. She's a little girl now, lost momentarily in a daydream. Then, mysteriously, she opens them wide [and becomes]... an almost ageless... *woman*'. The ideal woman of the Pet profiles was thus both modern and traditional, womanly and childish, partially masculinized yet feminine to the core.[65]

Articles matched the pictorials and profiles in their enthusiasm for the blossoming of the female libido. 'Natural woman has a sexual desire which is the match of that of her mate,' argued *Penthouse*; 'girls today... are more demanding, physically and mentally... [they] recognise themselves as sexual equals, and should be approached as such,' *Mayfair* confirmed.[66] The magazines searched for signs of women's sexual blossoming in their everyday lives. *King* found its proof in the 'new-found frankness of the ladies magazines' on show in *Nova*, *Queen* and *She*. *Mayfair*, meanwhile, doggedly followed the progress of the 'non-pantie revolution' in its quest for visible confirmation that young women were ready and willing for sex: 'Girls are feeling for the first time what it is like to be free of restricting, uncomfortable undergarments and it is becoming acceptable – indeed almost obligatory – for them to display as much leg, or as much breast, or as much of anything else as they want to.'[67] The magazine urged women onwards towards complete nudity and the ditching of knickers, bras and slips. It had greater reservations about the decline of stockings, neatly framing as they did the thighs and genitalia, but accepted their impracticability for the non-pantie-wearing woman and seldom featured them in its photospreads. Provided that women abandoned underpants, men were prepared to forgo their devotion to stockings and accept, 'albeit grudgingly', the merits of tights.[68]

The magazines' enthusiasm for women's sexual emancipation made them ultra-permissive. They routinely condemned the double standard as 'unjust' and 'archaic'. They were also unrivalled advocates of women's contraceptive rights, carrying earnest symposia on abortion reform and laudatory articles on 'Women Who Made Birth Control Respectable'.[69] 'The Final Inequality', declared a *Penthouse* contributor in 1968, was the 'denial by convention to woman to the right to ordain her own sexual destiny.' *Penthouse* accordingly deemed the 1967 Abortion Act to be 'well-meaning but insufficient' on the grounds (later advanced by women's liberationists) that doctors exercised too much control over women's reproductive freedom.[70] Their motives were as self-evident as they were self-serving. There was something immensely attractive about the idea of girls who just couldn't say no, while the mass availability of birth control promised to divorce pleasure from procreation and forestall any unintended consequences of women's newly casual attitude towards sex. Besides, 'men *cannot* be permissive if there is nobody for them to be permissive with.' But it was the fond belief of the new pornographers that women were the agents of their own emancipation. *Mayfair*'s first cover story described a 'new breed' of 'sexual suffragettes' eager to 'claim a privilege long denied them by men: to go to bed with whom they want, whenever they want'.[71]

Sex gave men a stake in women's emancipation by allowing them to feel involved and assuring them that there was something in it for them. As such, the freeing of women's sexuality was advanced in the new pornography as the best reason for men to accept women's wider gains. A generation before, following an earlier wave of women's emancipation, *Men Only* had encouraged its readers to bed then sack their female secretaries and ran an employer's explanation of why he wanted 'No More Women in My Office, Thank You!' after having dismissed his entire female staff.[72] Yet now *Mayfair* enjoined men to 'broaden [their] outlooks' concerning working women, reasoning that something resembling an equality of opportunity introduced wonderful new possibilities for office sex: 'When a dolly is earning slightly less than a junior executive, the business barrier between them cannot stand fast for long.' To view every 'secretary-bird' as a potential lay sanctioned sexual harassment and eroticizing women's freedom certainly belittled their accomplishments. But equally, the promise of sexual availability sweetened the pill (not to mention the Pill) of women's burgeoning independence. 'The text for the sixties,' *Mayfair* declared, 'is that girls are good to look at, and enjoy being looked at.' Sixties woman had suddenly discovered the joy of sex.[73]

Such were the hopes invested in women's sexual flowering and, had women indeed been emancipating themselves in the manner proposed, all would have been well – at least from the pornographers' point of view. As it was, doubts always existed in their minds over the nature and direction of women's emancipation. Had it gone far enough, they wondered? Had it gone too far? Had it careered completely out of the control of men? Ambivalence over female emancipation was present from the very birth of the new pornography. *King* was inconsistent on the matter of power relations in the bedroom, with one issue enjoining husbands to dictate everything from 'mastery of the lights' to the 'early morning tea routine' and its successor condemning the 'man-made myth that still consigns women to the role of passive partners'. And while *Mayfair* never once expressed doubts about women's rights in the first three years of its existence, *Penthouse* could be found denouncing misogyny in one breath and 'masculinized' women in the next.[74]

Out of the mouths of babes, or rather Pets, came confirmation that too much equality could be a bad thing. Money Turner was apparently looking for 'a man who knows how to dominate me' and Amber Dean-Smith wanted her 'strong man' to wear the trousers and make the decisions after having 'taken the girl's feelings and desires into consideration'.[75] One 1965 Pet, Bambi Lynn-Davies, spoke for all in her happy acceptance of her own inferiority:

> I could never think of myself as being equal to men. A girl naturally hasn't the rights that a man has and wouldn't be happy if she did. A man earns his place in the world and his aggressiveness and responsibilities put him into a different category altogether. I think the emancipation of woman and the false equality we seem to enjoy had [sic] done more damage to our relationships with men than anything else I can think of.[76]

With the launch of *Lords* late in 1968, these undertones of disquiet turned into overtones of panic. From the chipped lettering of its masthead through the archaisms of its house-style to its corseted models, the magazine's designer chauvinism wryly lamented the decay of male power:

> Emancipated woman has emerged, along with the unnatural notion of equality and other subtle underminings of her lord's pre-eminence. With the citadels of masculine privilege crumbing on all sides, *Lords* now stands forth on behalf of the emancipation of man. While commerce and politicians and audience-seekers of all kinds curry the favours of the newly affluent and influential female, *Lords–The Gentleman's Companion* hastens to the support of the beleaguered male ... in unashamed defiance of the women's world we live in.[77]

Lest *Lords* be thought an isolated jest, the same celebration of patriarchy past appeared in the Penthouse Club launched in October 1969. Its 'traditional attitude' dictated that Pets were to don abbreviated maid's outfits and curtsey aplenty in recognition that 'the male remains the master and the females are there to please him'. Such reactionary sentiments, however facetious, would have been out of place amidst the jubilant contemporaneity of three or four years before.[78]

At about the same time as *Lords* and the Penthouse Club were jokily trying to reverse a century of women's rights, *Mayfair* began to have doubts about whether emancipation had gone far enough. Characteristically for the magazine, its concern centred on women's fashion. The miniskirt was to *Mayfair* 'Britain's major contribution to the twentieth century' and its prime symbol of the sexual revolution. Once maxis threatened to envelop women's legs at the turn of the decade, the magazine immediately went into denial and refused to believe that women would 'surrender' the 'freedom' to titillate men. There was 'no danger' that minis were on the way out, claimed *Mayfair* (a trifle optimistically) at the end of 1970 and, even if women were to abandon them, it vowed that it was 'certainly not giving them up': defiance indeed.[79] *Mayfair*'s worst fears were confirmed by its 1969 survey of erotic dressing. Its women interviewees were found to 'prefer elegant feminine clothes to the briefer garments that men find most attractive' – long gowns and demure drawers instead of minis and briefs – and, far from wanting to reveal all, were actually 'reserved and anxious about displaying their bodies very much.'[80] The further *Mayfair* probed, the more it uncovered differences amounting to a complete 'dichotomy between male and female attitudes towards sexual attractiveness.' Women's attitudes to underwear were 'utterly different' to those of men. They seldom dressed sexily without their partners' encouragement. They were incapable of 'divorcing sexuality from their entire love function in nearly the same way that men are', being put off by 'any blatant suggestion of sex.' And when pornographic images were thrust under their noses in an attempt to 'bridge the gap between male and female feelings on erotica', the magazine discovered that women had a greater need for 'personal love'. Women did not seem so emancipated after all.[81]

But up to 1970, the new pornography's fears concerning women's emancipation were outweighed by its high hopes of their sexual awakening. *Mayfair*'s doubts about women's sartorial emancipation ran concurrently with its breathless announcement that 'bare female bodies ... were appearing everywhere in the greatest rash of down to the skin promotion since the Rape of the Sabine Women'.[82] Fears were also as yet unfocused and diffuse. *Penthouse*'s sexologists found emancipated women too 'masculine', yet their counterparts in *Mayfair* were complaining that women remained disappointingly 'feminine' in their attitudes to clothes and casual sex.[83] There was also little sign before the seventies that the pornographers wished to fight any battle of the sexes. Sexual warfare was a 'maiming way of life' conducted by 'impotent males and frigid females' soured by their own 'personal handicaps and unfortunate experiences with the opposite sex,' argued a *Penthouse* article in 1965. *Mayfair* reminded its readers that 'Satisfied Women Aren't Bitter' and its model, Kitty Randall, advanced the quintessentially mutualist argument that there could be no 'war between the sexes...when both sides are provided with such complementary devices'.[84] Feminism was mentioned only twice before 1970, with Pet profiles characterizing it in an almost Edwardian manner as 'blue stocking' and 'anti-men'.[85]

The advent of women's liberation at once escalated and focused pornographers' fears of a misdirected emancipation as ambivalence hardened into a pornography of backlash. Anti-feminism was admittedly more pronounced in some magazines than in others in the early 1970s. Fretting about women's fashion was about as close as *Mayfair* got to acknowledging the changing sexual climate. Instead, it retreated into an escapism not dissimilar to that of pre-permissive pornography. In its editorial line, this took the form of its quaint defence of miniskirts, 'stocking tributes' and an anachronistic use of language: 'dishy dolly birds' was hardly the lingo of 1970. In its pictures, it led to an increasing use of nature scenes wholly divorced from contemporary society. The models were also less sassy than their sixties equivalents: the 'true girl of 1970' being 'reserved and sentimental.' It was as if women's liberation had never happened.[86]

Penthouse mirrored *Mayfair* in its shift towards natural settings in the early 1970s. The Chelsea milieu was replaced by the likes of 'Beaume Idyll...a rural fantasy land...[where girls] beset by the tensions of urban living [are] retreating from metropolitan routine.'[87] Escapism was evident in the introduction of 'lesbian' spreads that, together with the first hints of fetishism, signalled a newly fantastic and artificial element to the pictorials. The Pets were more feminine in appearance and less boyish in their interests, the motor racing enthusiasts of old being replaced by horsy girls, cooks and collectors of Victoriana.[88] They were also positively Stepfordy in their desire to be dominated: not a new theme, but one now reiterated in every fictional profile. Polly Anne Pendleton was the first of a succession of doormat women who signified a disillusionment with the course of women's emancipation. She was a 'genuine old-fashioned girl' who bucked the *Zeitgeist* of 'rebellious youth and permissive morality and generation gaps' in her longing for separate spheres: 'I think it was a happier life when the father was really the head of the household and the mother was busy bringing up five or six youngsters. It takes a lot of the stress out of living when people know their own role, doesn't it?'[89] In the next three years, there followed a litany of submissiveness from *Penthouse* Pets:

I'm a quiet girl who enjoys being dominated.

I think that exploitation is only undesirable when you don't like being exploited. I enjoy being ordered around by men; the more I'm bossed the better I like it ...

I don't want to be equal to the man I love. He's just got to be the boss.

The chronology was significant. The Pendleton spread appeared in July 1970, five months after the inaugural Women's Liberation Conference at Ruskin College and, not fortuitously, the first issue of *Penthouse* to acknowledge the existence of the women's movement. And once women's liberationists began issuing manifestos in 1971, the magazine immediately had its Pets respond like so many living dolls.[90]

The Pets' supposed objections to second-wave feminism were sixfold. The first was that sexual emancipation had already liberated women. 'What do we have to be liberated from?' asked one Pet. 'Liberation for women is what I am doing now – posing like this for *Penthouse*,' explained another: 'It would never have been possible in my mother's youth. She would have been condemned, instead of admired, for showing off all her beauty.'[91] Second, it followed that feminists must be women whose plainness had made them miss out on the pleasures of the sexual revolution. According to Judy Jones, 'militancy in the women's lib movement increases in direct proportion to a woman's lack of desirability,' while Lesley Burrows could think of no possible reason for feminists to 'behav[e] as they do, except to compensate for their personal lack of attractiveness'.[92]

Third, women had no wish to be liberated. Pets enjoyed the perks of femininity, Beth Alison Williams being careful not to be 'aggressively permissive' because 'I like to play the dainty lady ... I like a man to open the door to me'. In turn, they felt it proper that men exercised their 'supremacy'. Women's liberation would be disadvantageous for both sexes, since women would be deprived of the 'chivalry and good manners' that they so enjoyed, while men's sex-appeal would diminish as their true masculinity was 'suppressed'.[93] Fourth, even if women desired liberation, their essential femininity prevented them from attaining it. Judy Jones' intention to master men lost out to her impulse 'to be the one that is dominated', while Lynette Asquith discovered that 'A man only has to say, "Do this" and I do it', cooking and cleaning on demand.[94]

The Pets' fifth objection was the inimitably mutualist one that the women's movement threatened the rapprochement already achieved between women and men. Women's liberationists 'missed the whole point' of heterosexuality, thought Lesley Burrows, namely that the sexes were 'so much better *together*'. Radical feminism's advocacy of lesbianism, despite playing into a favourite male fantasy, was thus deemed ridiculous on the grounds that men had 'too much to offer'.[95] The sixth reason was perhaps the most intriguing: that women had nothing to envy in men, since the 'respectable Establishment male image' created so much stress and so severely checked men's expressiveness that any woman would find it 'absolutely intolerable.' Feminists' wish to overturn sex differences was thus as unwelcome as it was impracticable: 'Men and women are just as badly – or as well – off as each other, so what's the point in changing one routine for another?'[96]

Penthouse's articles and editorials answered the four demands of the women's liberation movement – for universal access to contraception and nursery provision, and equal pay and educational opportunities – point by point. Contraception was fine, but nurseries superfluous since 'A mother, whatever Women's Lib...may say, usually wants to stay home'. Equal pay was by turns unnecessary (having already been achieved by middle-class women), unjust (as husbands and fathers needed to earn a family wage) and counterproductive (as women would be sacked). As for equal opportunities, they were wasted upon women governed by their maternal instinct and menstrual cycle, for whom the idea of competing with men 'never crossed their minds.' What feminists attributed to discrimination, *Penthouse* put down to male superiority. It was 'high time [women] recognised their inferiority... and quietly went about their business.' Equality was feminism's 'big lie'.[97]

This critique of women's liberation expanded into an entire agenda of men's rights, from allegations of reverse discrimination ('You hear . . . nothing about equal pensions, or two-way alimony') to the defence of accused rapists: 'Rape Requires Consent... it is virtually impossible for a woman to be sexually penetrated *against her will* by a single, unaided man.'[98] Men were the 'put-down' sex, uncomplainingly labouring at their often 'miserable, unfulfilled' careers under a 'manifestly unjust' legal system.[99] Here lay an irony: for in refuting the allegations of oppression by highlighting the plight of men, *Penthouse* effectively conceded that its vision of masculine emancipation was utterly fantastic. The ideal was the leisured man liberated from social conventions; the reality that of the careworn breadwinner subject to a conditioning process far more 'fraught' than that endured by women. The women's movement revealed in every sense how unemancipated was the *Penthouse* man.[100]

More misogynistic still than *Penthouse* was *Men Only*, which after Paul Raymond's take-over rose to become the best-selling men's magazine. Raymond used the relaunch issue of March 1971 (the month of the first Women's Liberation Movement rally) to promote his own 'manifesto for the restoration of male dominance'. His thesis was that women's emancipation emasculated men. Women had demanded economic equality only to monopolize the consumer marketplace, had muscled into male fraternities while conceding no privileges of their own and had subjected men to all manner of humiliations. And all the time, men had accepted women's emancipation in return for the promise of sexual reward. First, they allowed women to control the family finances on the understanding that they would control the love-making. Men then abolished the double standard in the hope that women would put out more. Finally, they devoted their intellectual ingenuity to the provision of contraceptives and sex aids in order to encourage women to become active sexual partners. All this, only to be traduced: 'The great cheat at the moment is the attempt to persuade him that the more emancipated and available women become, the better his chances will be. Nothing, of course, could be further from the truth. As woman's public sensuality blossoms and spreads, so man's correspondingly withers and shrivels.' By equipping women with vibrators and artificial insemination that separated intercourse from both orgasmic pleasure and reproduction, men had rendered themselves 'redundant'. The Amazonian autonomy and affectless promiscuity of the 'Pill-taking dolly bird... removed [men's] masculinity as neatly as a vet castrating a sheep' and drove them into a terrified homosexuality. Women now ruled men throughout their lives: from infant dependency through the agonies of 'spotty and tender' adolescence to marriage, when men surrendered their incomes to their wives and committed themselves to a monogamy that women might at any moment break.[101]

Raymond's flippant solution was to form a 'Gentleman's Liberation Movement'. A self-respecting man could no longer allow himself to be a 'lib-lab uni-sexed ambidextrous devotee of gay this and gay that'. He had to reassert his dominance and, most importantly, inoculate himself against women's sexual wiles since 'a man who is continually bombarded with female symbols and female shapes is whittling away his sexual intensity.' His plans for women essentially involved rewriting the marriage contract in men's favour. To guarantee that the housework was done, equal pay would be withdrawn and a man permitted to marry as many women as were necessary for his domestic requirements, divorcing those who failed to pull their weight. A woman could not vote or take the Pill without her husband's consent. Finally, 'we must teach our girls modesty. Special places can be set aside where there can be considerable titillation for males ... Hence my Revuebar!'[102] There was, of course, much comic intent in Raymond's prescriptions, but much less so in his basic analysis. His fear of the objectification of men reappeared in *Club International*'s attack on *Cosmopolitan*, while his homophobia corresponded with the many *Men Only* cartoons lampooning gays. His arguments also made sense of the pictorials in the revamped *Men Only*, which attained new levels of fetishization and objectification and contained the first depiction of sadism in a soft-core magazine.[103]

Seven years separated Raymond's ebullient launch of *King* in 1964 and his diatribe against women's liberation in the relaunched *Men Only*. In the former, his talk was all of 'progress'; in the latter, it was full of 'defeat' and 'atrophy' and the 'so-called permissive society.' And whereas he had once promised 'laughing haystack and sunshine girls, not grimacing plastic mac and whiplash girls', what he delivered in 1971 was flogging galore and a lewd food cover in which a woman, her head obscured, had a lobster placed over her genitals and a candlestick positioned upon one breast: stripped of personality, oiled and served up as food for impure thought.[104]

Between the gaiety of *King* and the sordidness of the new *Men Only* lay a raft of sundered expectations. The first had been a product of permissiveness, the second a reaction to women's liberation, which represented to the new pornographers contrasting periods in which everything went right and everything went wrong. The permissive society transformed the very premises of pornography, revealing the 'shame which covers everything' in the pornography of alibis to have stemmed as much from conceptual as from legal limitations. Pre-permissive pornographers had found it difficult to imagine the open expression of sexuality or a reciprocal female desire, resulting in escapist and voyeuristic fantasies. The seepage of sex into sixties culture, however, permitted the new pornographers to relocate their fantasies into the contemporary, proximate setting of swinging London and to become at once gleeful spectators of, and active participants in, the sexual revolution.[105]

Whereas a 'female emancipation' that expanded sexual opportunity was dandy, a 'women's liberation' revolting against sexual exploitation was anything but. Second-wave feminism exploded the new pornographers' vision of a convergence between the real and the ideal. The result was that the various components of the new pornography split apart. Notions of masculine emancipation were abruptly abandoned; the pictorials provided escapist fantasies of emancipated-but-not-liberated girls to counterbalance a hatred of autonomous women; and the new pornographers were left, like Hugh Hefner, clinging to an outdated permissive ideal of 'the non-girdle look, the bikini, the miniskirt, the openness to nudity' while railing against the 'extreme form of new feminism' that was 'unalterably opposed to the romantic boy-girl society that *Playboy* promotes.'[106]

Pornography and Mutuality

It was remarkable that sixties pornographers had sought to adapt mutuality to their own ends. Remarkable, but somehow wrong. To begin with, the emergence of mutualist pornography as late as the 1960s testified to the residual influence of a sexual culture unwilling or unable to conceive of women's desire as the equal of men's. The promotion of women's sexual awakening in mid-century marriage manuals and sex advice literature found no echo in the pages of pre-permissive pornographic magazines. Although the birth of the new pornography signalled a victory for mutuality all the more significant for being unexpected, pornography had rejected reciprocity in sexuality for many decades before.

Mutuality in pornography was not only overdue but deformed. It had been a key tenet of mutualist doctrine that sex should not be divorced from love and that marriage formed the best – even the only – setting for intercourse. In contrast, the new pornography, while less explicit than *Playboy* in its promotion of a specifically bachelor lifestyle, said little about love and nothing about marriage in relation to sex. In this, of course, it was hardly peculiar. Pornography typically represents male sexuality devoid of sentimentality – active, explicit, promiscuous, goal-driven – and, as with prostitution, exploits the fact that men's partners are averse to fully satisfying such desires. As such, there was something inherently paradoxical in pornographic magazines promoting a vision of sexual convergence between men and women when they owed their existence to the opposite. It involved simultaneously affirming male heterosexuality and diverting it from intercourse into solitary outlets. Moreover, it required imagining a necessarily *ersatz* female sexuality for, had sixties women been behaving in the manner the new pornographers portrayed, the magazines would have gone out of business. In the absence of actual female participation, they staged a mock dialogue between the sexes, acting as ventriloquists on behalf of models made to say what their male readership wanted to hear. Mutuality's idealism was subordinated to the purposes of turning men on.[107]

The new pornography was also profoundly ambivalent about the egalitarian aspects of mutuality. Still associating masculinity with authority, its fashion pages and sexological columns alike suggested that men could not easily emancipate themselves without jeopardizing their right to rule. The magazines' fears about women's unbridled emancipation likewise produced contradictory noises about their role even before the onset of second-wave feminism. It was no surprise, then, that pornographers' flirtation with mutuality proved to be so short-lived. Their loss of faith in women's sexual emancipation in the early seventies was as dramatic as had been their conversion half a dozen years earlier and provides the best evidence we have to support the arguments of Andrea Dworkin and others that pornography staged a backlash against women's liberation. But far from corroborating their further contention that all pornography demonstrates men's 'unchanging faith' of misogyny, it was only due to their blind romance with women's sexual liberation in the sixties that the new pornographers responded to second-wave feminism with all the jealous loathing of a lover spurned.[108]

There is a certain poignancy, then, in the trajectory of pornography in mid twentieth-century Britain. It emerged from a pitiful, hypocritical existence before permissiveness to flower briefly in the sixties only then to succumb in the seventies to men's latent fears.[109] Yet, however hyperbolic their reaction, it was not irrational for pornographers to view the women's liberation movement as antithetical to mutuality.

Overturning any cosy assumption that sexual pleasure could be accommodated within existing power relations, second-wave feminists denied the existence of a concordance between a masculine and a feminine emancipation. Like a canary down a mine, the sudden death of mutuality in pornography gave early warning of the challenge that women's liberation posed to the whole ideal.

III

MUTUALITY ECLIPSED

1. Edward Carpenter, pioneer of mutuality, 1905 (Corbis)

2. Havelock Ellis, sex radical, 1929 (Mary Evans)

3. The great marriage debate, 1891 (*Illustrated Police News*,
4 April 1891)

4. The suffragette challenge: purity versus indecency, 1913
(*The Suffragette*, 17 October 1913)

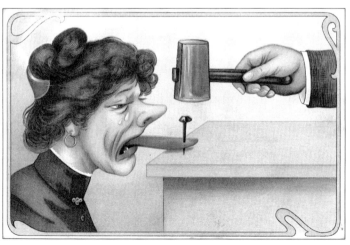

5. The anti-suffragist backlash: silencing female protest, 1913
(Mary Evans)

6. Manly pursuits in a boys' club, 1949 (Hulton)

7. Boys watch girls dance in a mixed club, *c.*1970 (Hulton)

8. Spicing up marriage, 1954 (Hulton)

9. The spousal division of labour, 1948 (Hulton)

10. Pre-permissive pornography: a Soho bookshop, 1956 (Hulton)

11. The pornography of permissiveness: *Penthouse* publisher
Bob Guccione, *c.*1970 (Corbis)

12. Germaine Greer, champion of female autonomy, 1965 (Hulton)

13. Countercultural couple Richard and Louise Neville, 1968 (Corbis)

14. The face of the future?: Renée Zellweger as the singleton
Bridget Jones, 2001 (Rex)

Fallout

The Challenge of Second-Wave
Feminism, c. 1945–90

Mutuality reached its zenith in the quarter century after the Second World War. That war, much like the First, quelled its critics. The number of anti-feminist tracts published after 1945 represented a fraction of those issued between the wars, while the 'reasonable feminism' of the postwar period foresaw an end to the 'ancient antagonism' between masculinity and femininity.[1] Christian mutualists shared such enthusiasm for the 'accelerating progress in partnership between the sexes' evident in companionate marriage and the 'mutual fellowship' of mixing, while prominent sex radical Alex Comfort declared his 'ideal of sensible enjoyment' in sex to be 'within reach' in 1963.[2] When influential Quakers and the Bishop of Woolwich chose the same year to propose a 'New Morality' bearing unmistakable similarities to sex radicalism, a merger between the two strains of mutuality seemed possible at last.[3]

Impressive also was the degree to which mutuality was put into practice after 1945, effecting the transition from ideal to actuality that had largely eluded it between the wars. Mixed leisure became the rule and segregation the exception thanks to the decline of established single-sex pursuits. Though the Women's Institutes held their own, mothers' meetings lost members and single women ventured into mixed espresso bars and pubs.[4] Gentleman's clubs dwindled into a tatty obsolescence when faced with the 'pressures of democracy and women' while, at the other end of the social scale, the football terraces were emptying. Attendance figures more than halved in the 1950s and England's World Cup victory in 1966 only temporarily arrested long-term losses. Mutuality and the family television set worked hand in hand to keep couples together at home.[5]

Evidence of mixing was even more pronounced among the young. Accompanying the spread of mixed youth clubs was the sudden expansion of mixed secondary schools that, despite receiving little encouragement from central government, outnumbered their single-sex counterparts two to one by the 1970s. Coeducation appealed to educationalists who perceived it to be the natural extension of comprehensive schooling, while the coeducated overwhelmingly credited their schools for having 'helped them in everyday relations with the opposite sex ... [and in] making a happy marriage'.[6] Slower to mix were the independent schools and the ancient universities, where the pressure to reform started from below. The fact that boy boarders in single-sex schools were twice as likely to feel shy towards the opposite sex than their coeducational equivalents, coupled with their anxiety that segregation 'activated homosexual instincts', made them complain that they saw 'too little of the other sex and wanted more contact with girls.'[7] For their part, student radicals focused their campaign for mixed colleges and dorms on the right to fornicate: 'Complete sexual freedom is a number one demand for any student movement. All forms of sexual repression and of puritan "discipline" should be abolished.' Coeducation first appeared in top-notch public schools towards the end of the sixties in response to falling rolls and as a means of consolidating other liberalizing measures. Only in the early seventies did Oxbridge begin to mix in order to attract the best undergraduates and mollify them when *in situ*. But once a few male colleges went mixed, student demand saw to it that the rest followed suit.[8]

Marriage in the sixties became nigh on universal (96 per cent of women marrying before the age of 45) and also apparently companionate. The twin housing and baby booms created privatized nuclear families of the sort favoured by marriage reformers and surveys indicated that couples had attitudes to match. Whereas the toiling wives encountered by Ferdynand Zweig at the beginning of the fifties accepted men's privileges without demur, the affluent working-class husbands he interviewed a decade later had turned into dutiful 'home-bird[s]' who endorsed the 'absolute or near equality' of their wives by a margin of three to one.[9] Fellow social scientist Ronald Fletcher depicted a glorious future for companionship when writing of the 'complete eclipse' of Victorian patriarchy by partnerships founded upon 'personal freedom, equality of status and mutuality of consideration'.[10]

Sex was perhaps the last element of mutuality to fall into place, but research undertaken by Mass-Observation in 1949 and Geoffrey Gorer in 1950 revealed considerable public support for Christian mutualist precepts. Sex 'for its own sake' or that undertaken without sufficient 'self-control' was duly condemned, but its performance as part of a loving marriage seemed 'very important' to a majority and 'fairly important' to most of the remainder. Nearly two-thirds of those polled approved of birth control, nine-tenths endorsed a single sexual standard and a majority condemned pre-marital sex, the women being more likely to practise what they preached. Most significant was that the great majority (of men in particular) believed women to 'enjoy the physical side of sex just as much as men'.[11] When Gorer repeated his survey in 1969 among a somewhat younger sample, the proportion thinking women to be uninterested in intercourse was smaller still and a disparity between male and female attitudes to the matter was no longer evident. In the interim, the introduction of the Pill in 1961 and the legalization of abortion in 1967 had begun to transform women's sexual behaviour, the media had hyped sex to the rafters, a *New Society* readers' poll had listed a 'healthier attitude to sex' as the second greatest postwar social change, Parliament had carried a sex radical agenda of marital and sexual reform and even pornographic magazines had been won over, if only temporarily, to the mutualist aim of uniting men and women on the basis of shared sexual desire.[12]

Social Change

Yet mutuality's dominance after 1945 was not as total as it appeared, first of all on account of class. Mutuality had originated as a higher-class critique of the archetypally higher-class phenomena of public school, paterfamilias and sexual prudery and it was telling that the most ambitious postwar effort to implement its ideals occurred within the London counterculture: a metropolitan, bohemian milieu reminiscent of the Fellowship of the New Life all those decades before. To be sure, mutualists had universalizing ambitions, but the proselytizing efforts of marriage reformers and mixed club leaders made a limited impact on the lower reaches of the British class system. As we have seen, working-class adolescents in mixed clubs turned the mutualist sentiments of their elders and betters to their own, often subversive ends. Equally troubling was the imperviousness to companionate doctrines of lower working-class couples, such as those examined in chapter four. Mutualists placed their faith in the 'Principle of Stratified Diffusion' whereby the 'egalitarian tendency' already apparent within middle-class marriages would percolate downwards in due course, but surveys indicated just how far that process had to go. Whereas Mass-Observation found that the educated members of its National Panel considered marriage a 'personal arrangement, at its best productive of much happiness and stability, but necessitating caution, co-operation and mutual adjustment', it reported that the 'man in the street' viewed the matter in less 'moral', more 'mundane' terms. And while over half of the former had read sex manuals by the likes of Havelock Ellis and Marie Stopes, only a twelfth of the latter could claim to have done the same. The social reach of mutuality extended nothing like as far as its champions desired.[13]

Postwar immigration provided mutualists with fresh opportunities to missionize, though with equally disheartening results. From a Western perspective, South Asian customs represented a throwback to separate spheres in their strict segregation of adolescents, 'close chaperoning' of girls and hostility to such 'romantic notions' as companionate marriage. A husband who expected his wife to 'serve, satisfy his sexual desires and bear his children' brought to mind the very worst sort of Victorian patriarch.[14] White commentators conversely regarded West Indian families to be 'functionally matriarchal', albeit 'idealistically patriarchal'. Blame fell upon errant males, who were reputedly too busy venting their sexual drive to embrace marriage and monogamy.[15] Highlighting how immigrants' relationships lacked the 'sense of companionship which is such an important factor in western marriages' could simply serve to bolster feelings of white superiority. A more well-meaning, yet no less complacent, approach was to treat immigration as a prime opportunity to introduce other races to the blessings of mutuality.[16] South Asians were expected to benefit from exposure to Britain's permissive attitude towards the 'mixing of sexes' and 'recognition of the body'. West Indian men, being considered too permissive for their own good, were instead encouraged to grow up and settle down with women who had learnt from their white sisters that 'English wives do not allow their husbands to dominate the home, but ... expect at least to be equal partners'.[17]

Immigrants viewed matters differently. Mutuality to many South Asians represented an assault on tradition and community cohesion. Mixing sullied their daughters' reputations, love matches threatened arranged marriages, spousal companionship marginalized kin networks and sexual permissiveness spelt immorality.[18] Loyalty to their own mores made them scornful of British ones, one straw poll revealing near unanimity among South Asians that white marriages were unstable and adulterous and white women 'oversexed'.[19] Those dissidents, such as the Sikh Bhola Singh, who saw merit in 'the Western concept of love and compatibility' were likely to encounter spousal resistance. Bhola's wife was 'flustered' by his 'romantic or affectionate' overtures and continued to regard sex as 'necessary only for procreation'. And those foolhardy enough to marry out, though reportedly appreciative of the 'intimacy and . . . companionship' attainable with white women, were customarily ostracized by their own community even more than by whites.[20]

West Indians had fewer qualms about mutuality in principle and, to a degree unacknowledged by whites, embraced it in practice. White commentators tended to portray the 'Anglo-American ideal of love and marriage' as either making little headway among most Afro-Caribbean immigrants or else destabilizing already dysfunctional relationships. Psychiatrist Ari Kiev diagnosed a 'vicious circle of increasing conflict between the sexes' as men's opposition to marital equality pushed wives to claim still greater independence.[21] Yet West Indian writers, while acknowledging that the tensions between men and women manifest in the colonial Caribbean had not disappeared in Britain, nonetheless felt guardedly optimistic. 'In the West Indies it is rare to see a man doing housework or minding children,' reported black social worker Katrin Fitzherbert, whereas in Britain 'most men help their wives with cooking and cleaning and take an active part in bringing up their children.'[22] West Indian men generally disowned their reputation for having 'abnormal and excessive' sexual appetites and treated white paranoia about interracial sex with a bemusement bordering on outrage. As these men discovered every time they were turned away from a dance-hall, whatever enthusiasm whites had for mixing of the sexes was undercut by their fears over mixing of the races. Mutualist ideals once again fell victim to extrinsic social concerns.[23]

Another problem faced by mutuality was that, as with any intellectual orthodoxy in a rapidly modernizing society, it began to seem a trifle stale. The shopworn quality of mixing was sorely evident in the independent progressive schools which, having pioneered coeducation before the Second World War, seemed far from progressive thereafter. Mounting sexual activity among their charges prompted disciplinary action from school authorities concerned to maintain the wholesomeness of social intercourse. Yet puritanical rules and regular diatribes against the 'sophistication' of sixties girls and the 'Beatle hair' of the boys alienated their pupils and confirmed their unworldliness among radical educationalists. One observer likened the schools to 'beleaguered garrisons, viewing the outside world as hostile and predatory.'[24]

Three postwar trends raised unresolved questions over the mutualist conception of marriage. The first was that the lifting of prohibitions against married women workers and the demand for part-time employees persuaded almost half of all wives to undertake paid work by the end of the 1960s. Most commentators applauded the 'liberating effect' of this profound social change and no more considered it a threat to marriage than did the women concerned.[25] The working wives questioned by Viola Klein never mentioned 'feminist egalitarianism' as a reason for undertaking employment and believed by a ratio of twelve to one that their jobs enhanced rather than damaged their marriages. They regarded their paid work as both complementary and secondary to that of their husbands, with even educated career women generally being prepared to reduce their hours sooner than disrupt their married life.[26] Yet women who entered the workplace lacking a spirit of independence commonly acquired one over time. Historical sociologist Janet Saltzman Chafetz has argued that single working women had cause to delay and even reject the path of marriage and motherhood when it hindered career development. Wives, meanwhile, could feel simultaneously empowered and cheated in employment, the confidence they derived from their new skills and income paired to resentment over the 'relative deprivation and unbalanced exchange with their husbands' caused by their double burden.[27]

The second issue was male participation in childcare, the need for which increased in line with wives' new earning responsibilities. Mutualists did their best to talk up a 'massive change' in fatherly roles, but indifference, inertia and the inflexibility of full-time work severely curtailed paternal involvement.[28] The vogue for maternal attachment theory worsened matters by consigning fathers to an 'indirect' parental role. So obsessed was psychiatrist D.W. Winnicott with motherly influence that he could think of nothing for fathers to do other than 'stay alive during the children's early years.'[29] The spectre of maternal deprivation induced guilt in mothers who worked outside the home and 'excruciating boredom' in many who didn't, placing yet further pressure on marriage.[30]

Third came divorce. Interwar marriage reformers had hoped that 'true and lasting comradeship' would ultimately reduce the incidence of marital breakdown but, following a surge in divorces after the war, a royal commission on the subject expressed the opposite view that 'equal partnership' subjected marriages to 'new strains'. Sex radicals contended that divorce was a price worth paying for 'higher standards and expectations of marriage' and challenged the divided Anglicans to do the same: 'if the Church maintains with such rigour that true marriage should be founded only on mutual love, how can it possibly maintain with equal rigour that marriage should be perpetuated when that same love has ceased?'[31] The Church of England held out until the mid sixties, after which its change of heart made possible the introduction of divorce by mutual consent for England and Wales in 1969. Yet, as divorces doubled and redoubled in the sixties and seventies, critics of liberalization received some belated vindication. They had reason to claim that 'every time one makes divorce easier, one makes marriage cheaper', so eroding the very bedrock of mutuality between men and women. They also drew attention to the failure of marriage reform to make women economically independent. 'The changes which have taken place in personal relationships inside the home,' noted wives' champion Edith Summerskill, 'have not been accompanied by any improvement in the financial status of the wife.' Companionship appeared unable to stem divorce or alleviate its consequences.[32]

The sexual revolution at once realized and rendered obsolete mutualist dreams of sexual harmony. Abortion allowed an otherwise overburdened woman to become a 'better wife and mother' but also her unmarried sister to evade the consequences of casual sex and thereby any lasting commitments. The Pill furthered women's emancipation at the risk of spoiling sex for almost half of young men who, according to one survey, considered it a 'threat to [their] dominant role.'[33] And the parallel relaxation of the double standard bore out long-standing concerns among Christian mutualists that women were sloughing off the 'patriarch's ideal of womanhood' only to 'conform to the lecher's instead.' That the dissident Christians Eustace Chesser and the Bishop of Woolwich preached tolerance of pre-marital intercourse simply compounded moral unease.[34] Yet even most sex radicals shared Christian mutualists' distaste for the popular permissiveness exemplified by sixties porn. Their delusion that smut would perish when exposed to sexual enlightenment made the arrival of the new pornography as unanticipated as it was unwelcome. The commodification of sexuality when paired to women's apparently imitative quest for the 'satisfaction of a purely physical appetite' caused the disillusioned Dora Russell to lament that the sixties had spawned 'a very great deal more sex ... [but a] decrease in the volume of love.'[35]

Youth Revolt

Still more troubling were indications among the young that mutuality had failed in its essential aim of dispelling hostility between the sexes. The first signs came from the anti-mutualist attitudes struck in much postwar male youth culture. Playwright John Osborne implored men to find 'passion and identity' in fraternity, not marriage, and his fellow 'Angry Young Men' Kingsley Amis, John Braine and Stan Barstow included in their novels a trusted sidekick whom the male protagonist trusted more than any woman.[36] Brotherhood also appeared in gang customs observed by the bohemian Colin MacInnes, with Teddy Boys engaging in 'exclusive masculine communion' as their girlfriends straggled along ten feet behind.[37] Gangs tended to view girls either as appendages or as threats to male solidarity, the resultant 'sex-hostility' prompting concerned mutualists to plead for the creation of mixed gangs instead.[38] Disenchantment with marriage accompanied antipathy to mixing among some fashionable young men of the 1950s and 1960s. They scorned the narrowed horizons and subsiding passions of a man serving a 'life sentence' under the thumb of a shrewish and adulterous wife. Better to remain single or, if married, patriarchal and uncowed: 'My wife'll have to look after any kids I fill her with, keep the house spotless.'[39] Sex was likewise divorced from intimacy in the Angries' book lest they succumb to the suffocating desire of a wife who 'devour[ed] one whole every time'. The best sex was to be had outside marriage with worldly adulterers or a 'nice willin' little virgin', a winning technique being to satisfy women's desire to be beaten 'black and blue.' Such sub-Lawrentian sentiments ran contrary to the tender affection enjoined on men by marriage reformers.[40]

For all their eloquence and power, these diatribes probably represented a minority protest against prevailing mutualist attitudes. The machismo of gang culture rejected rather than reflected the 'conventional notion of the healthy masculine life', as epitomized by that bulk of Manchester's male undergraduates who expressed 'no sympathy for the Angry Young Men'.[41] Nor did opposition to mutuality command assent within male popular culture. For every Mick Jagger singing the praises of misogyny, there was a 'family man' like Marty Wilde censuring the Angries for being 'vulgar exhibitionists' or, for that matter, a John Lennon practising his own transcendental brand of mutuality. Postwar youth culture raised serious questions, however crudely, about the drawbacks of mutuality for men. But more pertinently, perhaps, it gained prominence through its ability to shock – and few things were more shocking to fifties and sixties sensibilities than the suggestion that men were breaking their side of the mutualist compact.[42]

Women's rebellion against mutuality proved to be an incomparably more serious affair. Its immediate origins lay in the counterculture of late 1960s London, which represented the final flourishing of sex radicalism in its ambition to pioneer a 'different sort of sexual/social behaviour'. Mixing of the most uninhibited kind was one of the hallmarks of the underground. 'Girls are everywhere,' crowed *Oz* editor Richard Neville: 'at sit-ins, be-ins, loot-ins – "equi-sexual with ease"'.[43] Countercultural marriages pushed companionship to its limit so that the institution was nothing and the relationship everything between partners determined 'to share everything, to be together all the time.' And, with permissiveness overcoming inhibitions and the Pill guarding against untoward accidents, sex was to Neville the ultimate expression of heterosexual bonding:

> When boy meets girl, within minutes of drifting off to a comfortable location, boy can be happily splashing about in girl's cunt, both of them up each other's arses, sucking and fucking with compassionate enthusiasm. No more tedious 'will she or won't she by Saturday?' but a total tactile information exchange ... [44]

Countercultural women resembled 1920s flappers in regarding emancipation as a prize available to anyone 'young enough, energetic enough and bloody-minded enough' to seize their chance.[45] The childless among them could compete for an array of glamorous jobs in a near full-employment society and, thanks to contraception and the abolition of the marriage bar, could keep them for as long as they chose. The D.H. Lawrence and Havelock Ellis volumes they hoarded under their pillows as teenagers taught them that sex could be an 'incredible physical experience' rather than a 'guilt-ridden surrender in sordid circumstances'.[46] Emancipation was also very much on the agenda of countercultural men. The modish androgyny of male pop stars and actors snubbed its nose at the 'masculinity cult' and its attendant burdens of respectability and responsibility, while the profusion of female nudes in underground periodicals signified a liberation of sorts of men's puerile desires.[47]

But women in the underground, expecting the most of mutuality, instead experienced the full scale of its shortcomings at first hand. The ideal of mixing was undercut by the casual chauvinism of male counterculturalists who planned the revolution while their womenfolk made the coffee. Women suffered any number of indignities in the offices of underground magazines: being assigned menial 'chick work' out of public view, receiving authorial credit by first name only, seeing their impassioned articles about sexual politics printed over expanses of female flesh. The same happened in political campaigns. 'Very largely we complement the men,' complained the left-wing journalist Sheila Rowbotham: 'we hold small groups together, we send out reminders, we type out leaflets, we administer rather than initiate.' Women's expectations of equality chafed against men's easy assumption of authority.[48]

No less frustrating for countercultural women were their individual entanglements with men. Monogamous relationships replicated the established domestic division of labour to the point of parody in those cases where the woman was expected to be on hand 'cooking, answering the phone and rolling her master's joints.' Free love came harder to women than men, who proved on the whole less troubled by bonds of affection and more enamoured with libertarian ideals. 'There was a lot of misery,' remembered 'hippy chick' Nicola Lane: 'There was supposed to be no jealousy, no possessiveness. What it meant was that men fucked around.'[49] Such problems played out in Michelene Wandor's ill-starred marriage to Ed Victor, the future publisher of *Ink*. They had intended to be the perfect companionate couple, sharing their souls and the housework with it. But Wandor found that 'reality crashes in' once parenthood consigned them to the traditional roles of out-at-work husband and stay-at-home wife. She stewed indoors, aggrieved over forfeiting her career and envious of the carefree teenage girls of the London 'scene'. Her loss was his opportunity as he reportedly deserted her in order to 'screw women around the clock.' She became a natural recruit to women's liberation.[50]

The abundant sexual opportunities of the counterculture, while not exactly a negative experience, bestowed on women fewer benefits and greater costs. The then fashionable equation of sexual with personal freedom convinced some to engage in guilt-free, conception-free, no-strings-attached sex only to find themselves feeling empty and unfulfilled. Orgasms were faked and high expectations 'more often than not...disappointed'.[51] Being able to say yes made it harder to say no and insecurities arose over whether others were 'more turned on, having more fun, or simply better at it.'[52] Disturbing too was the ubiquity of naked women in underground magazines. The notorious *Oz* cartoon of a priapic Rupert Bear 'violated' one woman's sensibilities and sadomasochistic chic convinced another that 'sexual liberation was turning into a kind of ghastly celebration of sexual violence'.[53] The true meaning of liberation plagued Sheila Rowbotham as she weighed her yearning to be 'overwhelmed sexually' against her 'equally strong wish to be independent'. Was promiscuity indeed 'emancipation', she wondered, or simply an 'inversion of male attitudes'?[54]

So long as the petty slights, wrecked relationships and sexual humiliations experienced by women in the underground were conceived of in apolitical terms, they remained a series of seemingly insoluble personal problems: a woman's unassertiveness in mixed company; her awkward choices regarding marriage and motherhood; her inability to decide what she wanted from men in bed; her nagging feeling that 'the sixties were really happening just over there'.[55] The callousness of some men in the underground left Sheila Rowbotham distraught, but she found herself 'floundering around' in a morass of self-pity in the absence of any available ideological or institutional means of protest.[56] Yet the counterculture did not just dash women's expectations. It revolutionized them. Its wild idealism encouraged women to stop accepting their lot as being 'how things happen' and start considering how they were 'supposed to happen'. Its giddy curiosity made novelist Angela Carter ask questions about 'the nature of reality' that inexorably led to her 'questioning the nature of [her] reality as a woman.' These women's expanded sense of the possible made their hurt all the rawer, their feelings of injustice the greater and their willingness to tolerate unsatisfactory personal relationships far less pronounced. The gap between hope and experience formed the grounds for revolt.[57]

As countercultural women in Britain began to translate their personal pain into political protest, new feminist ideas filtering across the Atlantic in the late 1960s simply escalated a process already well underway. What they received from their counterparts in the American new left – and what acted as the catalyst for the British women's liberation movement – was a conceptual and organizational framework. Organization came in the form of the all-female consciousness-raising (or C-R) group. A typical session involved a circle of women each explaining in turn 'why she was with her particular sexual partner' in order to extrapolate from their medley of personal experiences an overarching theory of the female condition.[58] C-R provided its participants with an intoxicating mix of selfhood and togetherness. Here a woman gained, 'sometimes for the first time in [her life], an identity independent of a man's.' She got the chance to speak openly about her experiences knowing that she would not be laughed at or criticized, but instead respected and loved and treated as if she mattered. She was no longer merely a 'wife, mother and sex object' but an individual of 'social worth', instantly qualified as such by her womanhood alone.[59] Meeting together was thrilling in itself for a generation of women who 'primarily related to men', according to feminist theorist Juliet Mitchell. She was 'surprised that it was "all right" talking just to women', and the initiation of domestic violence activist Erin Pizzey into the women's movement represented the first occasion in a decade that she had gone out unaccompanied by her husband.[60] In discussions within the 'warmth and comradeship of the small group', a woman's subjectivity – her every personal hang-up and hurt and aspiration – chimed with another woman's experience, and another's, and another's, until it formed part of a collective consciousness that extended from her through the group to the whole of womankind. The 'sense of revelation and exhilaration' was positively electric.[61]

Consciousness-raising groups proved the ideal forum for British women to grapple with the second great innovation of American feminism. This was the idea that 'the personal is political': that the wellsprings of discontent tapped by women in the counterculture were not their own fault nor sheer hard luck but due to the systemic societal oppression of women. 'Inner battles, to be fought for myself alone, became outer battles, to be fought alongside the whole female sex,' Jill Tweedie recalled. Women's low wages, their domestic responsibilities, their lack of self-confidence, their marital problems and sexual inhibitions and trying personal encounters with men: all spelt subjugation. This conceptual breakthrough struck fellow journalist Rosie Boycott as being spellbinding yet strangely obvious: 'How could she not have thought of all this before?'[62]

The emphasis on the private at the expense of the public estranged these self-styled 'second-wave' feminists from the 'first-wave' feminists of an older generation. Sheila Rowbotham considered established feminism to be a bluestocking creed, its adherents to be 'asexual' and its concern with 'external rights' to be narrow in comparison to the 'personal relationships which preoccupied' her mind. Her goal was an all-encompassing liberation, theirs but an emancipation removing women's legal disabilities.[63] Second-wave feminists charged that the ameliorative efforts of the past half century had not much altered women's lot. The vote made 'less difference' than had seemed conceivable to suffragists. Legal reforms brought 'superficial' improvements that left 'ingrained attitudes' untouched.[64] 'Superficial' also were the apparent convergence of sex roles and the impact of women entering the workplace. Even the employment legislation of 1969 meant little to the women's liberation movement formed that same year. 'Equal Pay Is Not Enough,' stated Rowbotham: 'We Want The Moon.'[65]

The breach with mutuality was more decisive still, though at first less self-evident. As historian Jane Lewis remarks, the fact that second-wave feminists 'focused primarily on the private sphere' gave them an affinity with sixties sex and marriage reformers that they lacked with first-wave feminists. The inseparability of the personal and the political was no news to mutualists long accustomed to insisting that equality began at home.[66] Moreover, the personal unhappiness experienced by many women in the counterculture could strengthen their resolve to make love work. Sue O'Sullivan noted a prevailing belief at the movement's first national conference in 1970 that 'women's liberation would create better relationships between men and women' while, as we shall see, mutualist thinkers made faintly amicable noises in reply.[67]

The similarities ended there. Whereas mutuality represented intellectual orthodoxy, Germaine Greer urged women to 'question the most basic assumptions about feminine normality'. The former's ambition to reform individual relationships rang hollow to those such as writer Lee Comer who saw 'no personal solutions' in an endemically discriminatory society. Equality in difference was for women's liberationists a contradiction in terms, as was any natural alliance between progressive men and women after their clashes in the underground.[68] Most tellingly of all, Comer rudely contradicted mutualist self-congratulation over having vanquished 'Victorian domestic tyrannies' when stating that 'we have not travelled so far from the Victorian era as we would like to think'. Mutualists found the same charges levelled against them as they had once made against separate spheres: of creating a simulacrum of equality; of confusing contentment with silent resentment; of expecting love to cure the ills of patriarchy; of situating men and women on what Comer perceived to be 'opposite poles' of society, separated by an 'enormous chasm of oppression, degradation and misunderstanding'. Suddenly modern love seemed not so modern as all that.[69]

From this perspective, women had been betrayed by a mutualist ideal long on rhetoric and short on delivery. They had been promised equality and harmony with men only to find their relationships inherently 'unequal and fraught with antagonism'. Expectations of 'great intimacy' had been confounded by the contrasting socialization of women and men.[70] And according to its sternest critic, the self-help writer Liz Hodgkinson, mutuality's every remedy had proved either ineffective or detrimental: coeducation effecting no 'lessening of hostilities', marriage failing to deliver 'perfect love, perfect companionship and perfect compatibility' and heterosexuality creating a baneful 'mutual dependence' between ideally self-sufficient individuals.[71] Against mutuality's ambitions to foster understanding between the sexes, second-wave feminists confessed to their 'lack of trust' in men and a corresponding suspicion that any premature reconciliation would leave patriarchy intact.[72] Convinced that as things stood relationships between men and women could not rise above 'the mutuality of whore and pimp', the women's liberation movement set about formulating a comprehensive critique of mutualist doctrines regarding mixing, marriage and sex.[73]

The Trouble with Mutuality

Second-wave feminists charged that mixing could not succeed whilst women remained so self-deprecatory and men so self-regarding. Germaine Greer identified something childish about the panoply of 'coin-collecting [and] old schoolism [and] half-hearted sporting activities', about the pubs and clubs and Masonic Lodges that, for all the postwar inroads of heterosociality, seemed to be so entrenched an aspect of men's lives.[74] At the same time, the manner in which men escaped to 'the bars and ... the Buff, the football' aroused no little envy from feminists stuck at home. They viewed male-only institutions as impediments to equality, enabling men to 'remove themselves from the possibility of knowing what women's real interests are': hence the pub occupations staged by early women's liberationists and Women Against Rape's storming of the Athenaeum club.[75]

Male bonding was contrasted with female backbiting in one mid-seventies liberationist manifesto. Taught from childhood to seek fulfilment through pleasing men, women were thought to regard each other either as rivals or else as 'more boring, more silly, somehow less whole' than the other sex.[76] One woman, Una, described the practical consequences of having 'only wanted to know men'. Around women, she was 'very insecure and touchy'. In the presence of any man, she felt 'very competitive' and invariably took his side. And with a chosen man, she became 'his' woman, moulding herself around his expectations.[77] Dependence when combined with men's detachment appeared to make mixing an unequal encounter. Men simply 'tend[ed] to dominate mixed groups', hogging the conversation and relishing the approbation of female sycophants. For their part, women in mixed company reported that 'inarticulacy, shyness' and an inferiority complex militated against self-assertion.[78]

Insights into the iniquities of heterosociality discredited that showcase of mixing, the coeducational school. Many women's liberationists considered mixed schools to be at best a grand irrelevance, at worst a misnomer due to the continuing separation of the sexes. No fewer than 98 per cent of them segregated certain subjects in the early seventies, the careerism nurtured in boys contrasting with girls' training for housewifery or the dilettantism of the ladies who lunch.[79] Feminist researchers found that boys colonized school facilities and treated girls as a 'negative reference group' to be subjected to taunts and the odd grope: humiliations that cowed girls were in no position to repel. From the perspective of writer Dale Spender, the mutualist hope that coeducation prepared children for adulthood was being realized in a cruel fashion:

it is undeniable that mixed-sex education is preparation for 'real life' (as is often asserted), for in real life it is men who dominate and control; but this is not equality of educational opportunity; it is indoctrination and practice in the art of domination and subordination ...[80]

The equality and intimacy held to characterize companionate marriage were condemned mainly on the grounds that they did not exist. 'What is meant by equality?', asked sociologist Ann Oakley. She perceived any 'equality of status and "mutuality" between husband and wife' as excusing the sexual division of labour and 'complementarity' as a euphemism for 'uncomfortable division and difference'. Whereas marriage reformers did their best to portray husbands' contribution to housework as admirably half-full, feminist theorists denounced it as pitifully half-empty. Mica Nava's response to men doing the dishes was to think 'Big deal!'[81] Women's liberationists declined to believe in happy housewives. Essayist Angela Hamblin maintained that hard labour ground women down in the 'isolation and silence of suburbia'. Nor could their paid work be anything more than 'pseudo-egalitarian' if husbands refused to split the chores. Subservience masqueraded as interdependence in relationships akin to those between master and maid.[82]

Marital intimacy struck feminist writers as being by turns mythical and counterproductive. A coincidence of husbands' and wives' 'social worlds' did not in Oakley's view nullify women's subordination. Paraphrasing American sociologist Jessie Bernard, she spoke of 'two marriages: "his" and "hers"', separate entities that no amount of verbiage about an indivisibility of interests could reduce into a single, simple whole. Margaret Elphinstone similarly found that perfect communication between partners remained an idle dream: 'I can be with a man, and perhaps there are moments when we see each other clearly... [and] sexism ceases to exist for us. Such moments can only be moments, because usually we live inside our cultural patterns'.[83] Hamblin believed such distance to be perpetuated by men fearful that to 'get really close and identify with women' compromised their autonomy. Wives were in contrast considered overly eager to pour themselves into their relationships, Comer remarking that their very selflessness threatened to leave them entirely 'without a self'. Romantic love made a wife believe in equality despite her dependency and aspire to intimacy regardless of husbandly resistance. It was as much for the false consciousness that it instilled in women as for the oppression it inflicted upon them that made marriage such a target of these writers' wrath. In their eyes, wifely contentment had to be challenged were women ever truly to be free.[84]

Feminist critics of heterosexuality such as Bea Campbell began by repudiating the notion of a 'necessary complementarity between men's and women's sexual (as against procreative) faculties'. The idea that female desire was a diffuse sensibility qualitatively different from the 'real, concrete, urgent, visible' male sex drive seemed to her so much 'magical mush'.[85] Women were not designed to be 'passive receptacles of sperm', nor were men naturally the thrusting *conquistadors* of the mutualists' imaginings. Instead, Irene Fick discerned 'no biological difference between the sexuality of the human female and the human male' and Ros Coward declared that sex was 'never instinctual' in human society.[86] Debunking the naturalistic fallacy rendered suspect any wider claims for sexual mutuality. Equality was inconceivable to

Greer so long as woman's alleged receptivity was 'synonymous with passivity' and her genitalia considered a 'mere hole' for the man to poke about in. Intimacy seemed equally improbable between timid women and selfish men. 'Approaching each other from their opposite poles, husbands and wives miss each other in the dark and clutch at phantoms,' she wrote. In intercourse, the sexes were 'never more incommunicative, never more alone'.[87]

The Solution of Autonomy

In place of mutuality, most second-wave feminists advocated autonomy so that, in the words of the Women's Liberation Workshop, 'women stopped being so dependent on men.' Mixing was to be substituted by a sisterhood best expressed in the consciousness-raising group. In the 'secure, accepting, positive' company of their fellows, women were encouraged to comprehend their common oppression and to feel whole in the absence of male partners. They discovered how to love each other and the necessity of 'putting women first'. They learned, in short, the benefits of 'transferring [their] allegiance' from the other sex to their own: to include women and exclude men.[88] It was natural that a movement which privileged sisterhood above relationships with men should attract those predisposed to its message: women like Bronwen, who vowed she would 'never trust another man'; 'Spitfire', agonizing over her partner's promiscuity; and Alison, for whom feminism absolved her from feeling 'guilty about not getting married and holding dogmatic views.'[89] Women who did not enter the movement ill-disposed to men found that discussions of male misbehaviour tended to render them so. Listening to other women's horror stories in C-R sessions made Debby Gregory 'so sensitive to the hatred of women' by male chauvinists that she nursed violent ambitions towards them. A technique that had begun primarily as a method for understanding male–female interactions became an alternative to them as women gained the courage to 'exit from miserable, oppressive relationships with men'.[90]

Sisterhood put paid to the efforts of prodigal male counterculturalists to make liberation a joint endeavour. As the 'first generation of males ... made to feel guilty about their chauvinism', men's liberationists emulated feminists in renouncing patriarchy and the malign aspects of their masculine role. Most fixed on androgyny as the surest means to achieve harmony with women and peace with themselves, prompting experiments with 'Radical Effeminism' and, in the case of gay liberationists, the 'shock drag' of pairing frocks with beards.[91] Men's liberationists won a hearing from sections of the women's movement in its early days. Some entered mixed consciousness-raising groups and communes, as in the case of one homosexual collective that pooled its members' clothing and all conventions to boot, so that women donned men's Y-fronts and men wore women's cardigans with casual abandon.[92]

Doubts soon arose in many feminists' minds over whether men and women could truly work in tandem. The equation made by men's liberationists between the restrictiveness of masculine and feminine norms smacked of sheer presumption, a denial of both male oppression and the uniqueness of female subjectivity. Worse still, men's presence threatened to divide women from each other and deprive the women's movement of its independent existence. As one Mancunian feminist perceived it, a feminist had to identify 'totally with women' and work 'exclusively for women' lest her affections and energies go into men. A slew of late sixties C-R groups accordingly expelled men after a handful of meetings and, after briefly allying with gays against their common heterosexist foe, lesbians left the Gay Liberation Front in 1972 upon discovering that 'there is just one kind of man': the 'phallocentric' kind.[93] Though the men's liberationist movement had vowed in 1973 not to become a 'rent-a-crèche organisation servicing the women's movement', this is precisely what it became by the end of the decade due to feminist disengagement. But even volunteers for 'Crèches Against Sexism' were still irredeemably male in the eyes of some women, to be greeted with an emphatic 'Ugh'. Sisterhood to them meant separatism.[94]

Autonomy in marriage involved at the very least more equality and less intimacy. Husbands had to shoulder fully half the housework and permit wives the independence to develop those 'factors of [their] personality... killed' by companionship. 'A woman needs time alone,' stated the Peckham Rye Women's Liberation group, including the 'right to sleep alone' and the right not to 'touch, caress, console' her husband and children upon demand.[95] In this spirit, Debby Gregory encouraged women to effect a 'fundamental separation of ourselves from all our relationships' conducive to 'emotional celibacy'. So might women learn like men to consider marriage as 'only a part of their life, instead of the whole'.[96]

Personal space failed to satisfy those second-wave feminists who regarded marriage as irredeemably oppressive and whose desire for 'being independent and... autonomous' translated into 'the idea of separate lives'.[97] Quite what this entailed remained unclear. Germaine Greer, Lee Comer and Ann Oakley wrote devastating screeds against the nuclear family but offered little in the way of solutions. Greer confessed the alternatives to be 'vague', Comer airily advocated 'fluid...expressions of love and affection' and Oakley was if anything more gnomic still in her wish that partners would form a 'close and freely perpetuated intimacy, in a space that allows each to breathe and find her or his own separate destiny.'[98] Further confusion arose over how autonomy was to be squared with parenting. For some, the quest for self-realization made family ties seem like so many encumbrances. Hence Sue Bruley's consciousness-raising group was overwhelmingly 'anti-children' and one of the original planks of the Women's Liberation Movement manifesto demanded that women be 'freed from children' through the establishment of round-the-clock nurseries.[99] Yet shared parenting or communal arrangements threatened to expand men's power over children at the expense of women's. Jo Sutton and Scarlet Friedman even speculated that new fatherhood was a patriarchal plot teaching boys how to 'ally with men...and protect male control'.[100] Was it not more sensible to make childcare an exclusively female concern? As early as 1969, second-wave feminists were championing single motherhood and four years later the seminal journal *Shrew* answered the question 'Are Fathers Really Necessary?' firmly in the negative. 'We know that a woman does not need to have a man. We know that a child does not need to have a father,' went one late seventies refrain. Autonomy increasingly came to mean not the freedom from looking after children but that of having them independently of men.[101]

It was also unclear exactly what was meant by 'sexual self-determination'. For some, the 'feminist dream of autonomy' involved a woman becoming an 'agent' rather than an 'object'. Whereas the sham emancipation of the 1960s had simply made women 'more readily available', Angela Hamblin argued the '*real* sexual liberation' made possible by second-wave feminism put them 'directly in touch with [their] own forceful sexual capacities'.[102] The (re)discovery of the clitoral orgasm by American feminist Anna Koedt at a stroke reduced its vaginal equivalent to the status of 'myth', endowed women with climactic powers 'far in excess' of men's and discredited the missionary position.[103] Germaine Greer suggested that men be 'relieved' of their directing role in intercourse and many feminists were reported to have sex only when they initiated it themselves. To achieve both power and pleasure, claimed Greer, 'The cunt must come into its own.'[104]

A more literal interpretation of autonomy involved dispensing with men altogether. Because male authority was thought to rest upon the containment of the female libido, because penetration implied subordination and because penises were deemed ill-equipped to stimulate the clitoris (a majority of feminists in one survey declaring penetrative sex to be 'irrelevant or obstructive to their orgasms'), some feminists opted for 'masturbation, lesbianism or celibacy.'[105] Masturbation was advanced as the surest means of attaining orgasm and as a process of self-discovery, occasioning ads for vibrators in feminist periodicals and novelist Jeanette Winterson's recommendation that manual stimulation be part of every women's 'general fitness programme'.[106] Abstinence represented a duller option, for all the efforts of one self-help guide for celibates to present it as 'the *most* emancipated way of life there is'. It nonetheless appealed to a woman like Loulou Brown, whose experience of abuse made her prefer a 'lonely life' to the 'nonsense of a heterosexual existence'.[107]

Homosexuality was a better bet for women wishing to combine sex and love. Two sorts of lesbianism existed in the women's movement, the first being the more conventionally sexual kind. Before the gay and women's liberation movements, lesbians had felt negated and isolated in the 'ring o' roses of the heterosexual whirl'. There were 'no women-only things' in the sixties, recalled Helen Liddy, save for the 'grotty, overcharged and mixed' pubs prepared to tolerate Sapphist patrons. Discriminated against, and attracted by all-female company, lesbians flocked to the feminist cause.[108] But the traffic between lesbianism and women's liberation was very much two-way as hundreds of formerly straight feminists became 'political lesbians' as a means of cutting loose from men. For women to seek 'comfort, warmth, closeness, intimacy and sexual pleasure [from] members of a social group whose interests directly and in every way conflicted with [their own]' made no sense to women like Tasmin Wilton.[109] It seemed much easier to ditch men and start afresh, so side-stepping the whole painful business of recasting existing relationships with men in a feminist mould. Besides, since sexual orientation was presumed to be as socially conditioned as sex roles themselves, there was every reason to experiment. So effectively did sisterhood blur the boundaries between platonic love and sexual longing that feminists routinely described their adoption of political lesbianism as an 'extension of the closeness that grows up between women working together'.[110]

The Campaign for Homosexual Equality claimed lesbianism to be

186

'essentially different' from heterosexuality: 'Love between women is not a relationship of subordination and domination, of activity and passivity – it is a love between complete equals which profits from each woman's knowledge of her own, and therefore her lover's body.' As lesbians, women no longer had to choose between their hearts and their heads, between passion and principle, between ecstasy and devotion, between exciting womanizers and dependable bores.[111] Though some saw the superior quantity and quality of orgasms to be the 'big thing' in favour of lesbianism, for most they were but optional extras to that unique understanding of woman by woman betokening a whole new lifestyle. Lesbianism seemed at once safer and more satisfying, politically sound, deliciously intimate, the very 'epitome of sisterhood'.[112]

Radical Feminism and Absolute Autonomy

The primary question facing feminism in the seventies was how far to push the autonomous ideal. How far had mutuality – and men with it – to be rejected in order for true liberation to be obtained? The shift towards separatism proceeded by degrees. It started with single-sex consciousness-raising groups, which evolved from being a short-term tactic to boost women's self-confidence into the most characteristic feature of the women's movement. Some of the first women's liberationists emphasized that the immediate need for women-only activities neither precluded men's eventual admittance nor 'in any way' indicated that men's and women's interests were ineluctably opposed. However, the influential theorist Juliet Mitchell told her sisters to 'forget the excuses' in 1971. Her justification of segregation on the 'obvious' grounds that 'we are...the oppressed people and around this we organise' rapidly became feminist orthodoxy.[113] The next step towards separatism occurred in the national conferences. Whereas the inaugural Ruskin College gathering of 1970 allowed some sixty men into its main meetings (but not to attend workshops or influence policy), the following year saw them ejected from the conference floor after the Maoist Harpul Brah physically intervened on behalf of his wife during one uproarious debate.[114] The following conference even barred them from the disco. In 1973, it was the turn of the London Women's Liberation Workshop to exclude men. Men continued to march in the International Women's Day demonstration, but their presence enraged so many feminists that after 1975 it ceased to be a unifying event.

By the mid seventies, men had been expelled from all the principal political activities of the women's movement. Its meetings were single-sex and most of its magazines were produced strictly by and for women. But what about feminists' private lives? Did they too have to be purged of masculine influence? Yes, according to radical feminists: those members of the women's movement whose 'preoccupation with male sexual behaviour and . . . the need for separatist strategies of liberation' pushed the condemnation of mutuality and the advocacy of autonomy to their logical extreme.[115] Radical feminism was associated with political lesbianism. Though not all radical feminists were political lesbians nor all political lesbians, radical feminists, the two groups overlapped and their organizational strength grew in tandem. Inspired by parallel American developments, radical feminists were first in evidence at the 1971 conference and issued a manifesto in 1972. They became a notable presence at the national conference held in Bristol in 1973 and an unavoidable one at Edinburgh in 1974. That same year, lesbians held their first national gathering and the *Women's Liberation Workshop Newsletter* began its controversial serialization of the inflammatory American CLIT Statement, with its message that 'Feminism means lesbianism'.[116]

From this point onwards, radical feminists strongly influenced national policy. Whereas the founding demands of the women's liberation movement in 1971 concerned practical matters, those added thereafter bore a radical feminist imprint. In 1975, they successfully inserted a pro-lesbian plank into the official platform and in 1978 achieved a Pyrrhic victory over two further demands concerning sexual coercion and violence, the ensuing 'polarisation and hostilities' between them and their critics being so severe that no one offered to host a national conference again.[117] The aftermath saw radical feminists consolidate their position within a women's movement which, though now without any semblance of a unified national organization, in all likelihood grew over the following half dozen years. Nationally, they dominated its two principle mouthpieces through controlling the *W.I.R.E.S.* editorial collective after 1978 and exercising increasing power over the more widely circulated *Spare Rib* from 1980 onwards.[118] And on a local level, Amanda Sebestyen noticed in 1979 how 'nowadays a lot of socialist feminists agree that radical feminists were right' and accepted their general line on reducing contact with men. 'Suddenly everyone was grappling with compulsory heterosexuality . . . political lesbianism [and] separatism' in the consciousness-raising groups of the late seventies.[119]

Radical feminists built upon existing feminist critiques when savaging the mutual ideal. Mixing was condemned as contaminating, 'every contact' with men being held responsible for 'dominat[ing] and pollut[ing]' a woman's everyday existence by Sheila Jeffreys, their chief ideologue. Jeffreys also contributed to *Political Lesbianism: The Case against Heterosexuality* (1979), which identified marriage as the 'basic unit of the political structure of male supremacy.' The same tract depicted heterosexuality as sheer violation, with rape, paedophilia, prostitution and 'ordinary' sex considered variations on the same ghastly theme. The radical feminist remedy was as uncompromising as the diagnosis. It meant absolute autonomy: total abstinence from all relationships with men. Women were not to mix, not to marry and most especially not to sleep with men, for 'a fucked woman is a woman under the control of men'.[120]

Initiation into radical feminism was portrayed by Amanda Sebestyen as a purging process in which no concessions to conventional femininity were to be allowed: 'We cut our hair very short and stopped wearing "women's" clothes, we stopped smiling and being "nice".' No men or male-related products escaped the separatists' embargo. They formed their own bands, ran their own shops, mended their own boilers and conducted any unavoidable business with men with an air of utter loathing. True believers like Nora Joanchild favoured aborting male foetuses:

When will, after the first seven female weeks,
We look upon the foetus formed with penis
AND STOP THERE
Stop cherishing these festering cores
Stop suckling WITH OUR LIVES
these future men
who will be so free to RAPE
MOLEST
MUTILATE
MURDER
OUR DAUGHTERS ... [121]

Although most radical feminists theoretically accepted that men could change, few believed they would. Their 'endless discussions on the evils of men' dwelt upon the defects 'inherent in maleness'. The one way of making men more sensitive, joked Jeffreys, was by 'attaching electrodes to their willies.'[122]

Put more positively, separatism offered an appealingly straight-forward solution to the seemingly intractable problem of feminists' relationships with men. 'It was all so wonderfully clear,' recalled lapsed convert Maggie Christie: 'Women's oppression was men's fault. It made sense for women to get out of heterosexual relationships and be lesbians. I'd been struggling with these ideas on my own and here were women who seemed to have them all worked out.' Women like her revelled in the unparalleled opportunities offered by separatism for 'really putting into practice what we've talked about for ages – *sisterhood*.'[123] Radical feminists accused women who juggled politics and their private lives with men of treating feminism as a 'hobby'. Separatism conversely allowed them to form the first militant cells of the women's revolution whose ultimate aim was 'killing and/or physically challenging male hatred of women'. In place of a mutualist vision of harmonious cooperation between the sexes appeared their equally utopian goal of an 'all-woman world' that, admitted ex-separatist Janet Dixon, was at best unrealistic and at worst genocidal.[124]

Political scientists Joni Lovenduski and Vicky Randall credit radical feminists for having 'set the terms of feminist debate' in the early 1980s. They also largely orchestrated the movement's two most spectacular manifestations in this period, the Greenham protest and the campaign against male sexual violence, which together signalled the scale of feminist disaffection with mutuality.[125] The Greenham Common Women's Peace Camp was an unlikely vehicle for radical feminism in that it was initiated in 1981 by an outspoken anti-separatist and attracted criticism from some radical feminists for detracting attention from routine male violence.[126] But although it originally contained not just heterosexual feminists but male sympathizers, the widespread conversion of the former and expulsion of the latter soon turned it into what was widely celebrated (and derided) as the 'most vigorous force for lesbian liberation in the world'.[127]

Greenham served as a laboratory for women to experiment with separatism in its purest form. 'We can do anything!' exclaimed Caroline Taylor, thrilled that the constraints of sexist society held no power amidst the mud and polythene of the peace camp. Sisterhood formed the basis of communal existence, with every woman respected and included by virtue of her sex alone. The campaign's strong mystical element worshipped womanliness as a religion, while its propaganda ridiculed men as boys with highly lethal toys.[128] Though Greenham militated against heterosexual relationships, the alternatives seldom seemed so attractive. Here more than anywhere else there existed 'practical support [for]...real non-monogamy' and lesbianism was so much the norm that one woman confessed that she 'forgot that women could be heterosexual.' A minority entered the camp as lesbians, but sociologist Sasha Roseneil finds that a majority ended up that way.[129] Strength in numbers gave these women the confidence to cast aside every aspect of the hated feminine norm, to spurn men and glory in their deviance:

Men call us names to be nasty and rude
Like lesbian, man-hater, witch and prostitute.
What a laugh, 'cause half of it's true.
The fragile docile image of our sex must die.
Through centuries of silence we are screaming into action.[130]

Less obviously separatist, and all the more successful for it, was the campaign against sexual violence. Here radical feminists channelled a medley of initially unrelated causes into their anti-male crusade. Issues such as domestic violence were initially championed by feminists opposed to the movement's radical wing.[131] Others including rape, pornography and sexual harassment first attained prominence in the United States.[132] Still more, most particularly child abuse, were not initially associated with feminism at all.[133] The police, the NSPCC, politicians, social workers, Fleet Street and, not least of all, criminals like Peter Sutcliffe shared with feminists the credit for creating a 'moral panic' that enveloped such seemingly disparate phenomena as snuff movies, child abuse in Cleveland and the haunting disappearance of Suzy Lamplugh.[134]

Radical feminists stood second to none, however, in the vehemence and coherence of their campaign against sexual violence. A single group, the London Revolutionary Feminists, established the first feminist anti-pornography organization, planned the first Reclaim the Night demonstration, orchestrated the first picketing of porn shops and collaborated with the London Rape Action Group in a campaign against sexist advertising. It was radical feminists from Leeds who, in the shadow of the Yorkshire Ripper case, hosted the groundbreaking Sexual Violence Against Women conference in 1980, and it was the radical feminists involved in Women Against Rape and Feminists Against Sexual Terrorism who together founded the umbrella organization Women Against Violence Against Women.[135] Radical

UNIVERSITY OF WINCHESTER LIBRARY

feminists were also prominent in the two major anti-pornography bodies of the 1980s, the Campaign against Pornography and the Campaign against Pornography and Censorship.[136]

The avowed intent of radical feminists was to transform an ostensibly uncontroversial cause whose impetus and popularity extended far beyond the organized women's movement into a full-scale assault upon personal relationships between women and men. Their methods were to erase the distinction between sexual violence and everyday interactions between the sexes, to broaden the blame from individual men to the whole sex and to create a more inclusive notion of female victimhood. Not ones for pedantic distinctions, radical feminists advanced a definition of sexual violence that did not distinguish between coercion and consent nor between physical and psychological harm. Rape they redefined to encompass 'all the sexual assaults, verbal and physical, that we all suffer in our daily contact with men' in addition to 'forcible penetration'.[137] As such, losing one's virginity, becoming a prostitute, being touched up or chatted up or subjected to sexual therapy were all considered forms of rape. By the same token, an expanded concept of male violence accommodated flashing, fashion, offensive language, pornography, psychiatry, gynaecology and mixed hospital wards, not to mention penetrative sex.[138]

No clear division existed in radical feminists' eyes between violent and non-violent men or normal and abnormal male sexuality. '*All* men are potential rapists' and '*all men* gain from incest', they iterated.[139] Wife-batterers and child-murderers formed the executive arm of a patriarchal society that 'could not function without the widespread prevalence of male sexual violence'.[140] Sadomasochistic pornography likewise represented the 'Authorised Version' of the male gaze, as a flyer distributed by the London Revolutionary Feminist Group explained:

Porn is the way men like to see women – submissive, obedient, helpless, naked, open and available, longing to be violated. It encourages men to see women as bodies which exist solely for their pleasure; bodies to be leered at, groped, assaulted and raped – used and thrown away...Do you know a man who has never looked at porn – your father, husband, son, brother, boyfriend, doctor, schoolteacher? How can they look at it and respect women? How can they look at it and respect you?[141]

Just as all men were thought to collude in sexual violence, so were all women deemed to be its casualties. Every woman was 'assaulted' by the countless pornographic images on public view. Every woman routinely experienced 'verbal and physical ... sexual assaults'. Every woman was a rape victim insofar as rape 'affected all of our lives'.[142] Radical feminists warned women to be aware of the continual threat of male sexual violence. At no time could they let down their guard when sexual harassment was an 'all-day, everyday occurrence'. Nowhere were they safe, not even 'in the place supposed to be women's haven, the home'. And no man could be trusted: 'Fathers, husbands, brothers, uncles, sons – none [is] exempt'.[143] With men identified as brutes and women as victims, the old slogans of sex antagonism were removed from their mothballs and reused for the first time in fifty years. Second-wave radical feminists consciously echoed those of the first when justifying 'anger and hate towards men' in reaction to men's prior aggression. And, just like their foremothers, they rejected compromise on 'male terms'. The purity campaign was reborn, sex war resumed, mutuality once more under severe attack.[144]

Mutuality Under Siege

Though attracting at its height perhaps no more than 10,000 activists, the women's liberation movement tore through mutuality's institutional and intellectual foundations. The value Germaine Greer placed on women's subjectivity emboldened her to take on the institutional power of the 'doctors, psychiatrists, health visitors, priests [and] marriage counsellors' who had done so much to advance the cause of mutuality in mid-century Britain (see chapters two and four). 'We have no need of experts,' agreed Debby Gregory, and other feminists joined her in denouncing the entire applied wing of mutuality for sanctioning women's subjugation.[145] Marriage guidance counsellors administered a 'dose of ideology' to supposedly 'problem' families. Gynaecologists doled out 'Medical Mystifications' teaching women to be sexually passive.[146] Psychologists presumed to 'fix' rebellious women and child guidance counsellors patched up the dysfunctional family unit. All were 'enemies' of feminism.[147]

Women's liberationists matched their words with actions by establishing alternative social institutions for women. Often this involved nothing more than creating single-sex versions of existing services. Well-woman clinics and women's therapy centres reduced women's reliance on male gynaecologists and analysts, while all-female drama groups produced agitprop and forged thespian sisterhood.

Mixed youth clubs, once the pride of mutualists (see chapter three), now attracted radical feminist youth workers intent on reversing the 'rundown of the girls' club movement'. Mixing had not in their view instituted equality so much as lowered female participation and brainwashed those who remained into becoming 'home-loving wives and mothers, willing to cook, clean, copulate and procreate on demand.'[148] The Girls' Work Movement accordingly strove to heighten 'female consciousness' through segregated activities within mixed clubs. These were not to be the usual make-up sessions and fashion shows, but such macho pursuits as motorcycling and martial arts. Films instructed girls about women mechanics, lesbianism and all-women communes.[149] Discussion groups introduced them to 'positive alternatives' to marriage and invited them to 'explore their sexuality' free of heterosexist assumptions. Girls might even get to play *Time of the Month*, the National Association of Youth Clubs' very own menstruation board game.[150] Mixed clubs continued to grow, but the charge that they were 'in reality boys' clubs...run by men' prompted a flurry of official investigations. Institutions once expressly intended to foster sexual equality now stood accused of systemic discrimination.[151]

Then there were the new feminist institutions designed to tackle the dark side of heterosexuality. The great mutualist bodies like the marriage guidance organizations and the independent progressive schools saw their purpose as being to create or restore harmony between the sexes. Women's liberationists operated on the contrary principle that conflict between men and women was neither abnormal nor remediable except by making women independent of men. The first refuge for battered women was established in 1972 and the English Collective of Prostitutes followed in 1975. The London Rape Crisis Centre and an Incest Crisis Line appeared in 1976 and 1978. Operations of this sort served the triple purpose of alleviating the harm men inflicted on women, exposing its extent and recruiting women to the feminist cause. They worked. Natalie St John discovered the women's movement 'in the same way many other women have': that is, by leaving a violent marriage for a women's refuge before undertaking a polytechnic social work course to aid women in the same plight. Grassroots activism and local authority patronage meant that by the mid eighties a medium-sized city like Newcastle possessed a women's centre, a women's refuge, a rape crisis centre, a lesbian line and a women's theatre company, while the Greater London Council supported over 500 women's projects thanks to the largesse of

Ken Livingstone. A movement unable to sustain its own national organization had nonetheless embedded itself in the very interstices of state-funded social provision.[152]

Second-wave feminism's intellectual challenge to mutuality focused on the concept of complementarity, the notion that men and women possessed different natures but identical interests. This single idea supported a whole array of ancillary teachings: that mixing was a natural condition at once enhancing and enhanced by the inherent differences between males and females; that married couples might best live a shared life by observing a sexual division of labour; that intercourse found men and women at their most different yet most united. Most women's liberationists argued the opposite proposition that the sexes possessed similar natures but conflicting interests. Drawing upon the latest anthropological and psychological evidence, they debunked the 'ideology of women's innate difference from men'. Biological essentialism was replaced in mainstream feminist thinking by a social constructionism according to which inborn male and female 'sex' characteristics had little influence upon the 'gender' roles imposed by patriarchal norms. Germaine Greer famously contended that masculinity signified power and femininity only 'castratedness': the 'female eunuch' being denuded of her true womanliness and with it her confidence, energy, sexuality and dignity, right down to her body hair.[153]

Their conviction that complementarity entailed a 'relation of domination and subordination' gave second-wave feminists both motive and method for attacking past leviathans of mutualist thinking. Socialist feminist Sheila Rowbotham upbraided Edward Carpenter for his belief in 'fixed feminine characteristics'. Radical feminist Margaret Jackson excoriated Havelock Ellis for having sired a 'Sexual Liberation' that ran counter to 'Women's Liberation'. And the credit that Marie Stopes, Stella Browne and Dora Russell received for the 'good intentions' of their interwar sex campaigns did not stop Bea Campbell from criticizing their declared preference for heterosexuality over lesbianism and the vagina over the clitoris.[154] Ire also fell upon sociologists of the family for their 'dewy-eyed' vision of companionship, with Ronald Fletcher accused of peddling a 'myth of equality of status in marriage'.[155] The determination to explore the 'underside of the ideal family or the happy couple' drove women's liberationists into the social sciences in the 1970s and 1980s, thereby transforming a discipline once supportive of mutuality into a powerhouse of feminist activism.[156]

Mutualist responses to the feminist challenge were most clearly articulated in sex guides and marriage manuals, genres still respectively dominated by sex radicals and marriage reformers.[157] Marriage manuals accepted much of the feminist critique of companionship. The backsliding that had begun in the sixties (see chapter four) proceeded apace thereafter as authors variously disowned the 'foolish expectation of perfection' and admitted that simultaneous orgasms were more trouble than they were worth. Marriage reformers agreed with women's liberationists that the 'low status of motherhood, housework and domesticity' made women 'dwindl[e] into wives', and chastised husbands for their insensitivity and obsession with breadwinning.[158] They also took on board the charge that marriage compromised a woman's autonomy, Family Welfare Association director Robert Morley characterizing women's liberation as a just protest against the 'sacrifice of self' required of conventional wives. The remedy proposed by Shirley Conran in her hit 'Superwoman' series was that a wife learnt to be 'sensibly selfish', reduced housework to a minimum and undertook activities '*for* herself and *by* herself'.[159]

Self-help books for husbands and fathers met feminist criticisms that men fulfilled no useful function within the family. The besweatered Gyles Brandreth welcomed the end of the 'smug and slippered' paterfamilias and urged his readers to accept 'the most demanding challenge that any man can face': that of becoming a 'Complete Husband'. Such a man was not only a wage-earner, a father and a 'gentle gentleman who remembers to say "I love you" before intercourse and "Thank you" after' but also a housewife, maid and all-purpose dogsbody.[160] Accompanying the 'Complete Husband' was the 'Essential Father', who likewise bucked the 'sexual stereotyping' of men. Advocates claimed new fatherhood to be a matter of equality and practicality in an age of working mothers, but presented greater male involvement above all in terms of a revised mutuality. Whereas segregated childcare detached fathers from their families and mothers from wider society, shared parenting promised to bridge the 'great divide between men and women'.[161]

Sex radicals were more accommodating still to a feminist movement they believed to be furthering the 'full realisation of mutual encountering and shared sexual enjoyment'. They vaunted their progressive credentials by proclaiming the supremacy of the clitoral orgasm and imploring men to accept that there was more to sex than penises and penetration. 'As to the Women's Lib,' stated Alex Comfort in *The Joy of Sex* (1972), 'nobody can possibly be a good lover – or a whole man – if he doesn't regard women as [a] people and [b] equals. That is really all there is to be said.'[162] The utopians G.L. Simons, James Hemming and Zena Maxwell went so far as to envisage feminists as their allies in creating a harmonious, androgynous world. The 'Completely Permissive Society' proposed by Simons minimized sex differences through artificial reproduction and supplemented marriage with casual sex and copious porn (he was also the author of *Pornography without Prejudice: A Reply to Objectors*), while Hemming's and Maxwell's hopes for a 'new kind of creative love between the sexes' encapsulated mutuality at its airiest.[163]

Conciliatory gestures of this kind could not disguise the alarm of mutualist intellectuals confronted by women's liberation. Although only peripheral figures like socialite Arianna Stassinopoulos unequivocally rejected feminist plans for personal relationships, ambivalence beset mutualist writers of every persuasion. The stock of marriage had fallen so low that authors of marriage manuals questioned their very function. Should an eighties manual promote marriage, asked relationships expert Claire Rayner, 'or discourage it...or merely report on its state...? And is there any point anyway when matrimonial mortality is...horrendous'?[164] Much like the pornographers examined in chapter five, some of Rayner's colleagues found renewed purpose in defending the 'mutual dignity achieved through the complementarity of the sexes' against the claims of an 'extreme...feminism' seeking 'total independence from men'. They criticized women's liberationists for disregarding the privileges of wifehood, the difference between patriarchal and companionate marriage and the 'biological... emotional and...intellectual' imperatives behind femininity.[165] But the rededication of marriage reformers to a companionship that had by their own admission 'failed to work in practice' altogether lacked conviction. Who would now believe David Mace's proclamation of a 'new kind of co-operative marriage in which husband and wife establish mutuality at all levels' when he had announced the same thing thirty years before? His was a postdated cheque on an overdrawn account.[166]

Ambitions to domesticate husbands and fathers were likewise undercut by ill-disguised anxiety over male reluctance and female resistance. The Complete Husband seemed something of a chimera in the light of Gyles Brandreth's expectation that men would dust furniture (instructions included) only when their wives were otherwise engaged. His admission that the contemporary husband was 'not entirely sure of his place' suggested that male domesticity remained more fond aspiration than accomplished fact.[167] The same could be said for the idea of new fatherhood that, despite occasional assurances that it was 'evident already', inspired little confidence even among its champions. *The Baby Book for Fathers* (1978) conceded that women's liberation had not enhanced the father's role so much as left him 'shifting uneasily about wondering...what he is for, whether, in fact, he is necessary at all.'[168] New fatherhood was consequently vital not for women, whose drive for autonomy threatened to make men redundant, but rather as a quid pro quo whereby mothers gained equality at work in exchange for 'relinquish[ing] some of the power they have over the world of home and family.'[169] Furthermore, the new father was conceived more as a complementary role model than a 'male auxiliary mother'. Fatherhood from this perspective took on a macho aspect, with Martin Francis' stress on its 'virile' and 'potent' aspects in *Fathering for Men* (1986) suggestive of overcompensation. Viewing women's liberation as opportunity and threat in equal measure, new fatherhood literature vacillated between accommodating feminism within a revised mutualist model and reconstituting male power. Like the marriage manuals, these works were bereft of old mutualist certainties while devoid of convincing alternatives.[170]

There was little exceptionable or, indeed, novel about the egalitarianism and hazy utopianism of sex radicals. Sex radicalism had consistently allied itself with feminism and had always attracted beautiful dreamers. The problem lay in how poorly its conception of liberation matched that of seventies feminists. The contrast began with sex radicals' apparent belief that women were already men's equals. Hemming and Maxwell pronounced the 'decline of masculine dominance' to have been underway well before the advent of women's liberation and, at least in the opinion of Stuart and Susan Holroyd, 'sexual equality' was a done deal.[171] Yet their claims of equality – however premature – did not quell apprehension over women's burgeoning sexual demands. Some feared that the 'lunatic fringe of women's lib' sought the maximum number of partners for the minimum emotional outlay. Such a 'multi-orgasmic monster', they warned, was 'strik[ing] at the very basis of the male–female relationship'.[172] Others took the opposite tack when portraying feminist critiques of sex to be evidence of inhibition. Supposedly liberated women were 'completely unaware' of their capability – their responsibility, even – to climax: 'You have hands, mouths, tongues and vaginas! For pity's sake, use them!'[173] Sex radicals' rhapsodies over the 'interest and delight and mutuality and passion' of heterosexual relationships squared poorly with feminist accounts. Their emphasis upon the 'innocent' and 'playful' nature of heterosexual role-playing indicated a reluctance to grapple with issues of power. And, oblivious to feminist demands for autonomy, they maintained that all women wanted was 'a society in which men and women team up to shape the future'. As such, sex radicalism represented something of a false start in the reformation of mutuality. Men and women had to do more than kiss and make up.[174]

Revisionism

Those outside the women's movement proved unable to reconcile the mutual and autonomous ideals. The reluctance of sex radicals and Christian mutualists to acknowledge the possibility of conflict between mutuality and feminism made them recoil from women's liberation with injured expressions of shock and denial. Men's liberationists, by turns apologetic over their complicity in patriarchy and abrasive in their demand for 'men's rights', were too confused in their aims and insignificant in their numbers to restore the old alliance between New Women and New Men. The first credible plans for a marriage between mutuality and feminism consequently emerged from within the women's movement itself, from those mostly socialist feminist revisionists – straight (Sheila Rowbotham, Lynne Segal, Ros Coward and Susie Orbach) and otherwise (Sue O'Sullivan and Lesbian Left) – who refused to choose between their politics and their personal relationships with men.[175]

Revisionism originated as a reaction against radical feminism and its promotion of lesbian separatism as the sole means for women to attain autonomy. The paradox of radical feminism was that of many freedom movements in that its struggle for collective liberation denied individuals their own independence. Its partisans told feminists whom not to sleep with: 'Men are the enemy. Heterosexual women are collaborators with the enemy.' They told them what not to wear, the sight of lesbians in leathers and chains so appalling those who equated sadomasochism with heterosexuality that they sought to ban them from the London Lesbian and Gay Centre in 1985.[176] They even stipulated a uniform: 'Baggy Dungarees; Floppy Shirts; Plimsolls; At least four suitable political badges' and definitely no skirts, according to their detractors. Under the new hard line expounded by Gail Chester, 'to be a feminist [was] no longer synonymous with being in the Women's

Liberation Movement': one had to be a card-carrying political lesbian and practising separatist as well. Radical feminism was the sternest of mistresses.[177]

Many women unaffiliated to radical feminism were prepared to abide such hectoring for the sake of the unity of a movement already fractured along lines of class and race. They appreciated that radical feminism's simple message of male oppression had as much potential to unite feminists as to divide them. The campaign against pornography and sexual violence in particular drew support from a wide spectrum of women incensed at misogyny and indifferent to or ignorant of the aims of its radical feminist instigators. Of those who disagreed, some straight women chose contrition over opposition at a time when 'heterosexuality was perceived as ideological suicide' while others simply withdrew from the women's movement, as was reportedly the effect of two separatist manifestos published in the movement's in-house journal *W.I.R.E.S.*[178]

Revisionists, however, were unwilling to placate or concede to what they perceived to be an anti-family, anti-sex, anti-men 'new feminist consensus'. These women were often veteran campaigners who recalled the beginnings of the women's liberation movement as an 'attempt to understand the ambiguity in relations between men and women'. They recollected how most feminists in the early seventies had wished to reform, not renounce, relationships with men. They remembered the calls in those first years for women's right to 'demand what they wanted' from men in bed. They reflected too upon the respect once granted to each and every woman's subjectivity, the emphasis upon emotional honesty and the insistence that theories corresponded to personal experience.[179]

By the late seventies and early eighties, revisionists found themselves scarcely able to recognize – or sympathize with – the movement they had founded. Radical feminists had in their view forsaken examining the 'complexities and confusion' of personal relationships in favour of a sloganeering that violated every founding principle of second-wave feminism. Privileging theory over experience, they failed in Sheila Rowbotham's eyes to ground their models in 'actual relationships between human beings'.[180] Denying female subjectivity, they refused straight feminists their '"right" to a "self-defined sexuality" which actively oppresses their lesbian sisters.' Opposing individual agency, they appeared to supplant 'compulsory heterosexuality' with their own 'set of "must-dos"' for women. And by choosing separatism, they gave up on that hard task of improving heterosexual relationships held by revisionists to be what feminism was 'ultimately... about.'[181]

Revisionists charged that, far from uniting women against a common male enemy, radical feminists divided the movement and brought it into disrepute. In Bea Campbell's opinion, separatism conflated economic with emotional dependency and autonomy with sequestration, thereby escalating a legitimate 'political separation for definite means and ends' into a pointless 'lived separation.'[182] The ironic outcome of this doctrinaire form of sisterhood was to set woman against woman. Conflict between radical feminists and their opponents split many a consciousness-raising group, scuppered national conferences, soured the 'sisterly spirit' at *Spare Rib*, turned London Women's Liberation Workshop meetings into 'rituals of entrenched and polarised animosity' and isolated those separatists who declined to visit laxer feminists lest they encountered rogue males.[183] Revisionists also considered a 'blanket feminist condemnation' of marriage to be short-sighted in the extreme. They felt obliged to point out that women fell in love, got married and had children 'because they *desire* to' and that their informed decisions merited more than contempt. Such stunts as launching a 'Don't Do It, Di' campaign to coincide with the 1981 royal wedding risked confirming the opinion of one woman interviewed by Suzanne Lowry that joining the women's movement would 'rob her of her children... her comfort... her husband'. Lowry worried that feminism had become an ideology of outcasts – 'divorced women, battered women, lonely women, single parents, lesbians' – condemning the married majority to a 'twilight world' where the lure of emancipation competed against women's aversion to sacrificing their every wifely satisfaction.[184]

Sexual matters found revisionists and radical feminists at their most opposed. Against the indiscriminate radical feminist attacks on heterosexuality, revisionists detected a 'complexity' in sexuality exemplified by the central role of fantasy and the fluidity of power relations between consenting partners.[185] Whereas such radical feminists as Maria Katyachild saw in porn pure 'hatred of women', revisionists mulled over the possibility of 'moral' pornography and the attractions of erotica for women.[186] The idea that 'all feminists [could] and should be political lesbians' offended revisionists of all sexual orientations. Bisexuals resented being thought 'chicken' for their pluralism and some lesbians argued that political lesbianism 'undermined lesbian sexuality' by being concerned less with desire between women than abstinence from men.[187] The 'rumblings of an uprising' were also apparent among straight women weary of being treated as feminism's 'guilty secret'. 'You fascist bullies,' exclaimed the unrepentant Debby Gregory: 'don't fucking tell me or another woman what to do.'[188]

What prevented the revisionist attack on radical feminism from becoming just another internecine struggle within the women's movement and broadened it into a concerted attempt to reconcile feminism and mutuality was that its critique fed into wider concerns among feminists about the practical difficulties of implementing the autonomous ideal. Autonomy, like mutuality, was not all sweetness and light. Sisterhood all too easily degenerated into a 'coercive consensus' that glossed over differences between women, yet to presume unity made conflict all the more jarring when it arose.[189] Jo Somerset entered her commune believing that sisterly love would 'go on forever' only for the 'unthinkable' to happen as fights occurred and factions formed, while Rosie Boycott likewise found that the 'romantic notion of sisterhood' left her ill-prepared for her bust-up with fellow *Spare Rib* editor, Marsha Rowe. Rueful experience made it 'very fashionable to rubbish the idea of sisterhood' by the early 1980s.[190]

Revisionists had cause to reconsider their attitude to marriage. Mary Ingham and her friends devoted their early adulthoods to exploring the opportunities open to single, liberated women in outright revolt against the 'soft options' of feminine domesticity. Settling down had seemed tantamount to giving up. As they matured, they grew tired of flat-sharing and hungry for affection. 'It wasn't that we wanted to capitulate into downtrodden, dependent little *hausfrau* [*sic*],' Ingham explained: 'we simply craved a loving, reciprocal relationship with a man'.[191] 'Growing up' also propelled Griselda Pollock into wedlock and out of organized feminism. Having inveighed against marriage throughout her twenties, she gradually came to appreciate its security against the 'distracting, disruptive' effect of casual affairs. Pollock's feminist circle proved hostile to her change of heart and, when forced to decide between the love of her sisters and that of one man, she chose marriage. She and Ingham returned to seeking individual rather than collective solutions to private dilemmas, much as women had done before second-wave feminism.[192]

Women also discovered for themselves that sexual autonomy was more easily imagined than implemented. For all the appeal of lesbianism, it was clearly not to everyone's taste. Some straight feminists remained wary of lesbians and resentful that newcomers to the movement were 'liable to be accused of being a lesbian before [they had] ever even thought about it.'[193] Others considered it unrealistic for feminists to change their sexual preferences to correspond to their politics. Lesbianism was a sexual orientation, thought Erin Pizzey, not a stance to be adopted at will. A third group was curious enough to try lesbian sex but insufficiently so to repeat the experience, Rosie Boycott describing her solitary same-sex affair as 'friendly rather than passionate'.[194] But what really disturbed feminists new to lesbian relationships was their discovery that 'jealousy, possessiveness and romantic obsessions' were not solely heterosexual afflictions. Fired by lesbian 'propaganda' telling her that 'it's so marvellous with a woman', Lisa exposed all her vulnerabilities to one female partner in the hope of achieving 'perfect communication'. The outcome was predictably disastrous and hurt her more than any of her straight relationships.[195] Her disappointment was unfortunately far from unique. When polygamous, as was sometimes compulsory in communes, some lesbians feared that they became as affectless as the most promiscuous of men.[196] But when monogamous, the majority of lesbian couples were adjudged by Sue Bruley to exhibit the 'worst features of coupledom' in their 'highly jealous and possessive' behaviour.[197]

Revisionist attacks and adverse experiences thinned the ranks of radical feminists as the eighties wore on. Those political lesbians with reason to regret their 'unrealistic expectations' returned to the heterosexual fold, some 'shamefacedly', others feeling better equipped to form satisfactory relationships with men.[198] Radical feminism also suffered from the forcible evictions at Greenham Common in 1984 and the cooption of the sexual violence crusade by such non-feminist organizations as Childline. The growing prominence of black feminism further questioned radical feminism's moral authority by encouraging a pluralism alien to its regimentation and undercutting white lesbians' claim to be patriarchy's worst victims: hence the farcical attempt of Wilmette Brown to seize command of the Greenham protest by virtue of being black.[199] By the end of the decade, the Leeds Revolutionary Feminist Group had vanished, the girls' unit of the NAYC had disbanded, the GLC's Women's Committee had been abolished and the remnants of lesbian activism within municipal feminism were pilloried as representing the worst excesses of the 'loony left'. The 'increasingly beleaguered' radical feminists lost their grip on what remained of the organized women's movement.[200]

Misgivings over radical feminism when combined with the practical difficulties of autonomy gave rise to the first plausible if sketchy efforts to fuse the autonomous and mutual ideals. Feminism from a revisionist perspective was not about separatism and sex war, but about reforming the relationships between men and women from within. Within mixed company, men might learn to value what Nira Yuval-Davis characterized as 'genuine friendship and intimacy on a roughly egalitarian basis.' Their 'justifiable fears' about separatism deserved better than 'derision' and their 'potentially sympathetic' stance more than a brusque rebuff.[201] Within a 'feminist marriage' in which men mucked in with the childcare and housework, couples might combat the structural inequality of 'marriage as an institution'. Onetime radical feminist Frankie Rickford returned to heterosexual relationships 'less frightened of [men], more sure of who I was and what I wanted' thanks to her time in the women's movement.[202] And within reconfigured partnerships, women might alter the conditions under which they were 'prepared to share sexuality with men.' The emphasis was upon tenderness and interchangeability. 'With a blurring of roles can come a new discovery of sexual potential,' counselled the writer Helen Franks: 'not for exploitation, but for shared and enriched experiences.'[203]

These ideas received their fullest exposition in the writings of Luise Eichenbaum and Susie Orbach, joint founders of the London Women's Therapy Centre and, in Orbach's case, future *confidante* to the Princess of Wales. Like Edward Carpenter a century earlier, they reasoned that the contrasting upbringing of boys and girls produced 'deep confusion and misunderstanding' later in life.[204] Yet, just as Carpenter once glimpsed a 'new order' amidst the wreckage of the old, so Eichenbaum and Orbach discerned precursors of a 'social revolution' promising to bridge the rift between the sexes.[205] They predicted that an equal division of paid work and parenting would gradually effect a beautiful change in the sexes, making men more gentle and women more assertive. Parents would jointly raise sons free of misogyny and daughters unafflicted by any painful ambivalence towards their mothers. Successive generations of men and women, each more androgynous than the last, would eventually achieve the balance between selfhood and unity, individuality and identity, autonomy and mutuality necessary for successful partnerships: 'In heterosexual relations we can foresee a coming together of a woman and a man on the basis of two separate and autonomous people seeking intimacy... With psychological separateness and economic independence, women and men can relate to one another on the basis of equal exchange'.[206]

If this all sounded like a return to mutuality, then, in a sense, it was.

After a decade of anti-mutualist iconoclasm, assorted feminists began to speak tentatively of 'mutual aid, interdependence, affection and love', of a 'mutuality of...needs', of the 'mutuality and relaxed affection' existing in the best relationships between men and women.[207] Yet revisionists envisaged no Hollywood-style reconciliation in which woman's every misgiving was to be to be banished by a single lingering kiss. Their proposed marriage of mutuality and autonomy carried with it very significant provisos. In place of complementarity, they proclaimed '*Vive la similarité!*' No more would discrimination be passed off as natural difference nor happy relationships be used to excuse the structural inequalities between men and women outside their personal lives.[208] Closeness was to be distrusted insofar as it risked a woman 'losing her separateness and being invaded by a man'. If mixing had its place, then so did sisterhood. The girls' night out, no less than the consciousness-raising group, was no longer to be regarded as a secondary and inferior activity. Marriage might be recuperated, but was to maintain a 'fine balance of independence and dependence' and take its place as one living arrangement among others, single motherhood included. Variety also applied to sexuality, with the missionary position considered just one of many, many options.[209] Nuanced and pluralistic, this was a model wedded to the promise but aware of the problems of mutuality. Behind it lay a century of troubled mutualist endeavour; ahead the hard road of cautious advance. Jaded, perhaps, wiser, certainly, men and women continued on their painful progress towards reconciling intimacy to equality: the holy grail of modern love.

Epilogue
Alone Together, c. 1990–2000

To recap: mutuality promised to remedy the divisive aspects of personal relationships between men and women. Mixing aimed to counter the unwholesome effects of segregation. Companionate marriage sought to collapse the power differences and emotional distance between spouses. And, with the man less inconsiderate and the woman less inert and with each partner being responsive to the other's every desire, shared sexual pleasure represented the apotheosis of the mutual ideal. Such was the promise of mutuality: boys and girls brought up together, mingling freely, appreciating the similarities and respecting the differences between them; then marrying and carrying that same delight in each other's company into a partnership of intimates and equals; and finally consummating their companionship in the tenderness of intercourse.

But counterbalancing this promise were problems aplenty: problems of transition, problems of implementation, problems of heightened expectation, problems of underlying inequality, problems stemming from the compromises and contradictions bound to occur when a model so comprehensive in its scope and ambitious in its aspirations made the awkward shift from pure principle to messy practice. The mixed youth clubs examined in chapter three demonstrate how *de jure* egalitarianism often failed to produce *de facto* equality. The male club members monopolized the best facilities and maintained their distance, leaving the girls listless and bored. In their late teens, girls tended to drift away for good, their disaffection confounding mutualist ambitions.

The problems in mixed youth clubs were child's play compared to those created by companionship in marriage: the subject of chapter four. Equality proved elusive under the sexual division of labour and unwelcome to those men and women reluctant to exchange the security of traditional marital roles for the uncertainty engendered by women's emancipation. Intimacy was difficult to accomplish thanks to the contrasting lives led by husbands and wives. And it was hard to cope with, with closeness threatening the individual identity of each spouse or else simply exposing intractable differences between the two. Sex, far from being the ultimate bond between couples, often proved anything but. For the unemancipated, burgeoning expectations of performance and pleasure regularly compounded pain and guilt. Conversely, wives whose thirst for sexual satisfaction went beyond what was deemed womanly either felt frustrated or else risked terrifying their husbands with their overweening demands.

Mutuality hit the rocks hardest, however, in the sixties and early seventies soft-core magazines discussed in chapter five. Their conversion to the mutualist cause lasted barely half a dozen years: first, because of the difficulty of squaring the reformation of masculinity with the retention of male power; then due to the emergence of a second-wave feminism that stressed autonomy over mutuality and insisted that women's sexuality did not mirror men's desires. Pornographers reacted bluntly. Their editorials railed against hairy-legged man-haters at every opportunity, while their pictorials replaced images of fresh-faced women possessing healthy sex drives with escapist fantasies replete with fetishism, objectification and lashings of sexual violence.

It took the women's liberation movement to expose the full flaws of the mutualist ideal. Chapter six has related how feminist critics of mutuality undermined its claims to represent a clean break with Victorianism, pointing to biological essentialism and sexual division of labour as unchanging elements of female subjugation. They reversed its assumption that the sexes possessed different capacities and identical interests. They questioned its affinity with women's emancipation by accusing it of masking strife behind a harmonious front and by advocating an anti-mutualist feminism of their own. Above all, they rejected mutuality's pretensions to having resolved the sexual politics of personal relationships, maintaining instead that inequality tainted all interactions between women and men.

Mutuality scarcely survived the twentieth century. At the turn of the millennium, its accomplishments were forgotten, its institutions pilloried, its basic assumptions overturned. Few now spoke up for complementarity between the sexes and those who did, such as the journalists Neil Lyndon and Melanie Phillips, paired it to a reactionary anti-feminism.[1] Public debate in the 1990s fixated instead on the contrasts between men and women and the conflicts that ensued. Feminists spoke of 'Twentieth-Century Man' falling out of synch with 'Twenty-First-Century Woman'.[2] Psychologists wrote of the sexes inhabiting not separate centuries but planets, the differing 'genderlects' and ethics of Martians and Venusians producing mutual incomprehension.[3] Sociobiologists hypothesized that the desire for variety by males and security by females turned seduction into an adversarial 'sexual chess game'.[4] Novelists used such disparities to comic effect, with Nick Hornby's and Helen Fielding's protagonists perpetually flummoxed by the other sex. To say that men and women were not 'seeing eye to eye', remarked fellow writer Tim Lott, was just about 'the least controversial statement one could make' at century's end.[5]

If the sexes were not complementary, then neither were they interdependent in the manner mutualists had envisaged. Popular commentary of the 1990s equated dependence with weakness and female autonomy evolved from being the battle-cry of second-wave feminists into a widely endorsed lifestyle choice.[6] Three archetypes predominated. The first were those 'self-sufficient urban girls' who had no wish to let a 'man virus' loose on their hard-won affluence. A pocket-size variant came in the form of Girl Power as the Spice Girls proclaimed that 'you don't necessarily need a man' to be fulfilled.[7] More controversial was the figure of the lone mother who, for some, personified self-determination. Newspaper columnist Barbara Ellen contended that single parents like herself got 'all the perks of being alone without feeling lonely':

> I've never enjoyed men coming into my home, spreading their 'guy vibes', wiping their big bloke-boots all over my psychic space, until everything is gone and nothing is mine. So, these days, they don't . . . . I get to make all my decisions myself, without having to kow-tow to some claustrophobic 'couple' committee.[8]

To their detractors, lone mothers overstepped the bounds of autonomy into pure wilfulness. To their defenders, they were anything but selfish in their decision to raise children without male assistance. Applauded or denigrated, lone motherhood appeared to be the logical conclusion of a wider societal shift towards women 'crav[ing] independence more than almost anything' as they entered a brave new 'Female-ennium'.[9]

As women sought to 'kick free', men appeared to be 'retreating deeper in their own virtual world.' Male autonomy was interpreted as selfishness on the part of 'Deadbeat Dads' deserting their children, 'workshy' husbands evading household chores and porn addicts spurning 'true companionship and intimacy' with women in favour of the ersatz kind.[10] Such irresponsibility amounted to a crisis of masculinity in the opinion of feminists and anti-feminists, psychotherapists and newspaper columnists, cultural critics and government ministers alike.[11] Male youths became an official concern, with the 2000 Queen's Speech targeting yobbishness, the then Education Secretary David Blunkett attributing exam failure to 'laddish culture' and Home Secretary Jack Straw labelling 'underskilled, undereducated young men' as 'the single most serious problem' in contemporary Britain.[12] Dysfunctional adolescence was apparently prolonged well into adulthood by such lads' mags as *FHM*, *Loaded* and *Maxim*, their retro formula of 'Sex, Sport, Ladies, Clothes, Gadgets, Beer [and] Skittles' being seen to signal men's preference to regress rather than embrace a 'new era of gender understanding'.[13] More disturbing still were claims of a backlash against women in general and feminism in particular. New Laddism, the men's rights movement, a 'flood' of misogyny, sexual and domestic violence: all were blamed on male resistance to change.[14]

With men and women seemingly so much at odds with one other, mutuality's solutions of mixing, marriage and sex were commonly portrayed as problems. The coeducational dream was all but dead. Its most famous product, Summerhill, narrowly escaped closure by educational watchdog Ofsted in 2000 and, after decades of being accused of discriminating against girls, mixed schooling was now adjudged by David Blunkett to disadvantage boys, leading him to tout single-sex classes as one possible solution to their underperformance.[15] Mixing between adults appeared to be scarcely more successful. From the right, sundry *Daily Mail* columnists pitted themselves against any such 'Unisex Nonsense' when lambasting the 'Blurring of the Sexes', proposing women-only railway carriages and declaring platonic friendships to be doomed by the 'state of semi-permanent unease' existing between the sexes. From the left, Germaine Greer advocated 'segregation' as the sole alternative to 'humiliation' at the hands of men.[16]

Marriage was by now too unstable an institution to bear the weight of mutualist hopes. Plummeting nuptuality rates revealed their mid-century rise to have been less tide than blip, and multiculturalism negated the wish for, let alone the possibility of, some single marital norm.[17] The alternatives of single life and cohabitation failed to provide deep union: the former self-evidently, the latter due to the 'contingent commitment' that distinguished many cohabiting from married couples.[18] Not that marriage was itself any guarantee of lasting bliss, as the highest divorce figures in Western Europe all too painfully indicated. Public debate on the issue polarized the sexes as some feminists declared marriage to be 'heaven for men and hell for women', prompting men's righters to attribute a 'marital holocaust' to 'female anger'.[19]

Then there was sex. Mutuality was in essence a pre-Freudian creed, the heir to a strain of nineteenth-century utopianism that stressed the benign nature of Eros freed from taboo. Such optimism rang hollow a century later. AIDS presented grave dangers to unchecked sexual behaviour. Internet porn exposed the dark side of desire. Saturation coverage of paedophilia and rape suggested that contemporary society suffered less from repression than its absence. It also implied that there was something in masculinity averse to blending sex with love. Apparent confirmation came from the text as much as the centrefolds of a new crop of men's magazines, with one 2000 issue of *Later* hoping that the new millennium would bring an end to foreplay, monogamy and conversation before or after intercourse.[20]

So the twentieth century ended, much as it had begun, in a riot of sex-antagonistic rhetoric. Yet there was something contrived about the latter-day '"War of the Sexes"... rag[ing] across the pages of glossy mags, best-sellers, academic studies and television screens', fuelled as it was by the most unscrupulous, if entertaining, press in the West.[21] The evergreen parlour game of exaggerating sex differences – responsible for *Lysistrata*, Punch and Judy and the Battle of the Sexes quiz on Heart 102.6 FM – was played with unrivalled ingenuity by newspapers hungry for sensation. Sex sold; war sold: sex war represented every sub-editor's dream. Nothing else explained why an estate agent's report on women's input into house-purchasing decisions was held to represent a 'Victory for Women in This Battle of the Sexes' or why a slight preponderance of female applicants was heralded in terms of 'Women Winning Oxford Sex War', as if university admission was some sort of team contest between the pinks and the blues.[22]

Alongside garbled reportage sat fanciful commentary. Trend features devised acronyms for this or that season's 'most talked-about social group'. One spring, the *Mail* introduced its readers to SINBADs ('Single Income, No Boyfriend and Absolutely Desperate') before turning its attention in the autumn to 'Perpetual Girlfriends – But Never Wives' or PEGIs (PGBNWs presumably being deemed a little too heavy on the consonants).[23] The same paper staged a debate over whether men or women were to blame for divorce, concocted a cod experiment to discover 'which sex triumphed' at DIY tasks and gave space to one loon's theory that 'Every Man Should Wear a Sword' as a 'Solution to the Nation's Masculinity Crisis'.[24] It also reflected the nineties fashion for rebarbative feminist columnists: the wit of the *Mail*'s Suzanne Moore, like that of the *Guardian*'s Julie Burchill and the *Independent*'s Jo Brand, questioning her serious intent. Flip comments that men stood a 'long way behind [women] in the evolutionary chain' and that their penises would 'always prevent them from thinking clearly' became the nineties equivalent of mother-in-law jokes.[25]

Humour likewise complicated the message of the lads' magazines which, as part of their puerility and calculated boorishness, sporadically flirted with backlash sentiments. A 'Sex Wars' edition of *GQ* launched a 'fightback' against men becoming the 'New Women', *Maxim* feared the creation of 'a nation of ladymen' and *FHM* was 'saddened to report that the fairer sex ... is dead.'[26] In one sense, these magazines were the true heirs to girlie mags of the 1960s and 1970s. Soft-core porn had changed its name but not its preference for femininity over feminism. Yet it was significant that nineties magazines did not dare to advance chauvinistic sentiments unless they were couched in humorous terms. Unravelling the layers of irony was no easy business, but they were most plausibly interpreted as a rueful acknowledgement that such opinions could no longer be uttered with a straight face, their nostalgic tinge confirming the impossibility of returning to some unreconstructed, PC-free age. Come the new century, the New Lad was himself consigned to history, with ex-*Loaded* editor James Brown castigating any man too 'set in his ways' to view woman as anything but an 'equal partner' and his successor Keith Kendrick considering a nipple ban in the flagging magazine. 'That was then, this is now,' he explained: 'Men and women are not the opposite sex ... We're friends with each other.'[27]

Ambivalence over whether the sexes were truly at loggerheads was not confined to men's magazines. The American author of *Men are from Mars, Women are from Venus* (1993) claimed that he highlighted differences between men and women in order to enhance 'mutual trust ... increased cooperation and greater love' between them.[28] The same could be said for sociobiologists, who hoped to 'minimise conflict and produce harmony between the sexes' through elucidating their differing mating strategies: behaviours which were in any case as likely to breed competition within the sexes as between them.[29] Girl Power, as might have been expected of feminism for five-year-olds, was anything but consistent in its separatism, displaying contradictory urges for romance and sisterhood, monogamy and autonomy from line to line and song to song.[30] Even sex warriors could be disarmingly conciliatory in the 1990s, the most scabrous anti-feminist and feminist respectively confessing to being 'wholly and unreservedly in favour of equality between men and women' and to liking men '*a lot!*'[31]

The nineties fashion for belabouring dissonance between the sexes, every bit as much as prior mutualist attempts to deny it, failed to do justice to the shape and texture of everyday personal relationships. Beneath the headline simplicities, behind the shadow-boxing and buried in polling data and sociological monographs lay a picture of men and women at once less sensational and more intriguing than any press hype. Take the case of women and their reputation for proud isolation. It was true that they felt more capable than ever of going it alone and the possibility of doing so became a matter of self-respect, with considerably more teenage girls than boys believing that one parent could care for a child as ably as two.[32] But that did not mean that most wanted to. Lifelong monogamy was the ideal of 95 per cent of women in one poll, and in another only one woman in twenty entertained the possibility of dumping her partner upon winning the lottery.[33] Singleness held attractions for some, especially those rich young metropolitans able to capitalize on the 'choice, freedom and independence' of an unfettered lifestyle.[34] But it was thrust upon many more. Widows formed a large proportion of the unattached, their numbers swelled by rising life-expectancy. The bulk of the rest comprised those to whom single life was the least worst alternative to a failed relationship.

Most lone mothers were little different. Some three-fifths of them, being separated or divorced, had not expected to bring up their children alone. The tiny number of thirty-something women who set out to become single parents did so only out of concern that their biological clocks would run down before they met Mr Right.[35] Moreover, for commentators to credit (or condemn) disadvantaged young unmarried mothers for their independence was to misconstrue a class of women radically different from themselves. Almost all become pregnant accidentally and proceeded to term not by choice, as they saw it, but because of their inability to contemplate abortion. Nor did they perceive their singleness to be a matter of preference, the fathers being deemed unsuitable marriage material either from the outset or after a period of unsatisfactory cohabitation.[36] Their lives transformed by absent or unreliable contraceptives and partners, these women manifested a fatalism and a dependence at odds with their autonomous image.[37] None of those interviewed by Louie Burges and Mark Brown took pride in their condition; all advised others not to follow their example. Their discontent reflected that of single women as a whole, who were half as likely as wives to be 'very satisfied' with their status.[38]

The male in crisis was another stereotype lacking substance, its oft-cited characteristics open to contrary interpretations. The feminization of the workforce did not prevent men from holding the most prestigious and lucrative positions, from dominating the full-time sector and from being most families' principal earners. Male workers were no less flexible than their female colleagues, if flexibility included a willingness to work overtime and travel on business.[39] It was debatable whether inferior examination results came from boys failing school or schools failing boys.[40] That suicide rates among young men rose in tandem with anorexia rates among young women indicated that self-loathing was not confined to one sex alone. And absent fathers were not as absent as all that, since almost half saw their children at least once a week. Just 7 per cent of those out of contact for a year or more avowedly chose to be so, the remainder mostly citing obstruction by the mothers, the courts or the children themselves.[41] Such matters could not be dismissed out of hand. Unemployment, suicide, educational underperformance and limited fatherly involvement were all subjects of acute concern. But the sheer range of the problems and the complexity of their origins defied reduction to a single syndrome of male angst.

Still less persuasive were claims of a masculine pathology advanced by the psychoanalytically inclined who, having long attracted flak for their views on women, switched tack by stigmatizing men. 'Womb envy' replaced penis envy and anxiety over 'phallic superiority' substituted sexual hysteria in models as categorical as they were unverifiable.[42] The one virtue of such arguments was their universality for, when researchers looked beyond their own time and place, it became evident how prevalent (hence redundant) were fears of a male crisis. Historians unearthed moral panics over masculinity in practically every period they studied, while American anthropologists identified a dizzying array of cultures that treated manhood as 'uncertain or precarious, a prize to be won or wrested through struggle.'[43] It seemed that masculinity was not *in* crisis so much as articulated *as* crisis, but quite how this related to the average man in late twentieth-century Britain was unclear. Not one of Heather Fourmaini's 120 interviewees identified with the term 'masculine' and a MORI poll found that just 3 per cent of young and middle-aged men claimed to be 'macho'. Such alpha male characteristics as being 'fearless', 'upwardly mobile' and 'highly sexed' clustered towards the bottom of their list of self-descriptors; being 'caring', 'intelligent' and 'sensitive' came top.[44]

That traditional manliness was of more significance as a cultural trope than a personally held aspiration helped to explain why men remained largely immune to anti-feminist reaction. Unlike America, birthplace of the backlash scare, Britain fostered no pseudo-penitential male crusades such as the Promise Keepers and the Million Man March, merely small fathers' rights groups and the cranky United Kingdom Men's Movement, which admitted to a complete 'lack of results' from its tireless, tiresome crusading.[45] Occasional broadsides against feminism represented back-handed compliments to its success. The most notorious of them, Neil Lyndon's No More Sex War (1992), brought its author modest sales, brickbats, an adverse divorce settlement and the ruination of his journalistic career.[46] Whereas a backlash would have produced a measurable drop in egalitarian attitudes, government surveys provided no evidence of a decline and many signs of an upsurge in support for women's rights among both sexes during the 1990s.[47] Men were marginally more cautious than women on these matters, yet only 6 per cent of eighteen- to forty-five-year-old males polled by MORI believed women to be unduly advantaged as against ten times that number thinking the same of men.[48] Attitudinal differences between career women and housewives and between the old and the young eclipsed those between men and women.[49]

Notwithstanding most media commentary, the outlook of men and women underwent 'convergence rather than divergence' on questions concerning personal relationships at the end of the twentieth century. The authoritative British Social Attitudes Survey discovered negligible differences between the sexes on all such matters other than single motherhood and male homosexuality. Hitherto divisive issues ceased to be so as men endorsed women's disapproval of adultery and women increasingly mirrored men in their acceptance of pre-marital sex.[50] Most young women strove for similarity in 'all but the superficial trappings of gender' as a matter of equality, and were supported in their ambitions by most young men. One poll of sixteen- to twenty-five-year-old men and women found that 94 per cent believed childcare to be an equal responsibility; a second of eighteen- to thirty-four-year-olds counted 92 per cent saying the same about housework.[51] Such ideals translated awkwardly into practice, leading sociologist Catherine Hakim to argue that experience would temper youthful enthusiasm for interchangeability.[52] However, the young had reason to think that an androgyny expressed in terms of 'sexual freedom' for women and 'hands-on' parenting for men gave them opportunities denied to their parents.[53] The 'surprisingly similar' jobs each sex performed in their twenties and the correspondingly small pay gap between them formed serious obstacles to any subsequent reversion to an orthodox sexual division of labour.[54]

The convergence between men and women in the workplace had a knock-on effect on their leisure activities. Such women-only organizations as the Mothers' Union and the Townswomen's Guilds, having already lost half their members in the 1970s and 1980s, found nineties career women still less inclined to join up.[55] While women lacked the time to socialize together, men lacked much inclination to do so. No true lads, they placed equal importance on friends of both sexes and only 31 per cent expressed a preference for their best friend to be male.[56] Mixing created tensions in the 1990s, much as it had before (see chapter three). A third of men reportedly felt threatened enough to restrict their wives' and girlfriends' friendships with other men. Women's concerns centred on sexual harassment, a subject on which the sexes failed to reach so much as a shared definition.[57] Even so, by the mid 1990s men had set about developing elaborate codes of conduct towards female colleagues. Making a comment about a woman's appearance was thought harmless, touching her shoulder ambiguous and enquiring about her private life downright unacceptable. Greater interaction of the sexes required renegotiation of the sexual boundaries between them.[58]

Men and women exhibited great and growing similarities within wedlock. Partners typically entered marriage possessing comparable sexual and occupational histories and a common desire for love, companionship and parenthood. 'No gender differences to speak of' regarding most marital issues emerged from one searching review of British Social Attitudes Survey data.[59] Dual careers reduced women's need for providers and introduced men to the novel allure of female 'power and financial independence'.[60] Overt patriarchal rule was rare, with 3 per cent of male partners dominating decision-making and 1 per cent curtailing their companions' careers, according to the women in question.[61] Nineties spouses made decisions jointly and performed almost equal amounts of labour, women's combination of paid work and housework slightly outweighing men's overall contribution.[62] Though parenthood still introduced the sharpest divisions between husbands and wives, the increasing number of couples delaying or deciding against having children, not to mention men's greater willingness to share parenting tasks, reduced the gulf commensurately.[63] Partners even achieved a rough equality in how much (though not how hard) they hit each other, a 1999 Home Office study reporting that 4.2 per cent of either sex considered themselves to be victims of domestic violence.[64]

Sexual congruence grew as the double standard waned. Older teenage girls engaged in more pre-marital sex than boys and largely abandoned customary female reservations about masturbation.[65] Women in one straw poll condemned male promiscuity more than their own, while in another four-fifths of men expressed indifference over their partners' tally of previous conquests and a mere 3 per cent objected to women making 'the first move'.[66] Pornography, once a male prerogative, became socially acceptable for women once sadomasochistic women's fiction found its way on to railway bookstalls, Company magazine ran 'Boy Next Phwoar!' spreads and The Full Monty legitimized male stripping. Even the Queen did not blanch when inadvertently exposed to full-frontal male nudity at the Royal Variety Performance of 2001. In ogling at least, the Observer noted, the sexes had achieved a 'measure of equality'.[67]

Sex research hinted at mutual accommodation in the bedroom. The mammoth National Survey of Sexual Attitudes and Lifestyles of 1990 revealed that a minority of couples confined themselves to vaginal intercourse and, of those performing oral sex, four-fifths practised reciprocity. Female orgasms received due attention, indeed a shade too much so from men, who were more inclined to view them as essential to women's enjoyment than were women themselves.[68] Despite such misunderstandings – and the curious finding that each sex believed that the other received the 'better "deal"' in bed – men and women expressed contentment with their sex lives. Men told MORI in 1991 that they relished intercourse from adolescence to senescence and dissatisfaction among women hovered at around 6 per cent before the age of 65, only after which point it trebled.[69]

Moreover, advances in reproductive technology looked set to reduce the significance of biological differences between the sexes. Whereas the Pill had enabled women to approximate male sexual behaviour, the imminent arrival of a male equivalent promised to allow men to prevent conception without recourse to the unpopular condom.[70] The diminishing gap between the time when an embryo could no longer be sustained in a test-tube and that when a foetus could safely be transferred into an incubator suggested that pregnancy would eventually be able to occur outside a woman's womb. Indeed, infertility expert Robert Winston accepted the feasibility of implanting an embryo and placenta within a male abdomen using existing medical techniques, albeit at great and pointless risk.[71] Much less speculatively, the practical implications of greater similarity between the sexes in reproductive matters were already apparent among the growing number of childless couples in their loosened adherence to the sexual division of labour. Identical proportions of men and women without children worked outside the home in their early thirties.[72]

As the sexes grew more similar, so did each sex fragment. Greater choices over whether to mother, to earn or to combine the two divided women between 'home-centred', 'work-centred' and 'adaptive' lifestyles which, as Catherine Hakim has shown, involved differing and even conflicting interests.[73] The obligation of breadwinning permitted no comparable divisions among men beyond those of status and income. They split instead in relation to fatherhood as family change and reproductive technology created a spectrum of involvement ranging from resident birth-fathers at one end to sperm donors at the other. As feminist writer Lynne Segal noted, such heterogeneity made it increasingly difficult to draw meaningful contrasts between the sexes.[74]

The convergence between the sexes and divergence within them was largely due to individualism, the ascendancy of which made new sense of the trajectory of relationships over the preceding three centuries. It had first converted marriages from kinship arrangements to love matches, then freed wives from their husbands' authority under the aegis of mutuality and women's liberation, before finally allowing men and women to become independent, almost interchangeable agents. The impact of individualism was readily apparent in nineties relationships: in their conceptualization as a means to self-fulfilment instead of an end in themselves; in individuals' reluctance to commit and readiness to split; in the give-and-take of fellatio and cunnilingus that allowed each partner to receive equal, if not concurrent, satisfaction.[75]

Trumpeting the virtues of individualism was 'third way' theorist Anthony Giddens, who welcomed the prospect of voluntary compacts between 'equal and autonomous' parties. Giddens defined a pure relationship as one unbeholden to 'kinship, social duty or traditional obligation' and unconstrained by 'institutionally-given gender roles', sustained instead by mutual disclosure and intrinsic rewards.[76] His views chimed with those of the young adults surveyed by the Demos think-tank, enthusiastic as they were about egalitarian partnerships characterized by 'positive experimentation' and 'greater discussion'.[77]

Coupledom and individualism nonetheless made strange bedfellows. The assertion of self-interest invited a self-absorption verging on selfishness. Those outside relationships proved reluctant to enter them if, like journalist Mariella Frostrup, they equated shared lives with a 'plethora of compromises' and 'regular bad sex'.[78] Those within them often resisted tying themselves down, the rationale behind many couples' decision to cohabit.[79] While parental love came to be valued for displaying an unconditionality uncommon in adult relationships, individualistic mothers and fathers tended to regard their offspring as an 'inertial drag' insufficient to rule out separation.[80] Those prepared to commit themselves fully to marriage reaped the greatest rewards in terms of health, wealth and pleasure.[81] But individuals dedicating themselves to their partners did so without any guaranteed reciprocity. Forming partnerships was a joint decision, ending them a unilateral one commonly taken by the party with less to lose from walking away. Choice privileged the fickle and punished the loyal.

The ambition of many women to 'assert their identity' through earning their own money formed another facet of individualism.[82] Whereas separate spheres and, to a lesser extent, mutuality insulated the private from the public through limiting female employment, dual careers provided no such defence against a market economy indifferent to the needs of 'family, parenthood and partnership'.[83] Yet the manner in which the sexual division of labour was discredited without being fully eradicated led to much bargaining-cum-bickering over what constituted a fair share of household labour for women and men.[84] Though heterosexual attraction romanticized sex difference, intercourse eroticized it, parenthood confirmed it and most marriages structured themselves around it, asymmetry unsettled a generation convinced that being male or female should have little or no bearing on an individual's activities. Quite why she did not act like him, and he like her, were questions underlying many a lovers' tiff and child-custody dispute.[85]

It was no wonder that nineties couples found their 'freer' relationships a little wanting in 'romance'.[86] What was lacking was commitment, a commodity reputedly at its rarest among British-born black men averse to 'facing up to their responsibilities'.[87] But their pat response that the other sex expected 'too much' of them was hardly unique. This, after all, was the decade in which *This Life* creator Amy

Jenkins saw nothing wrong in choosing 'not to compromise; to put herself first; not to be in love'.[88]

Some bonds between men and women nonetheless withstood the assault of individualism. The most fundamental was mutual attraction, with the National Sex Survey finding that 93.3 per cent of men and 93.6 per cent of women considered themselves exclusively heterosexual and an additional 4 per cent of each sex 'mostly' so.[89] The sexual division of labour, for all its drawbacks, kept alive a semblance of interdependence. Husband typically earned twice as much as wives, whose limited hours and responsibilities as secondary earners were intended to fit around domestic tasks.[90] Relationships also brought out elements of selflessness, with each sex adamant that 'the companionship of marriage' took precedence over 'personal freedom' and attached women stating that they put the needs of their children and partners before their own.[91] American research indicated that contented and durable marriages developed an anti-individualistic 'mutual family vision' of shared goals and a willingness to 'put their spouse before all other activities, people or things'.[92]

In an odd way, individualism also enhanced the attraction of partnership even as it reduced its likelihood. The vulnerability of relationships gave enduring ones a certain scarcity value. A thirst for self-gratification left individuals all the more dependent on others for its satisfaction. The loosening of kin networks made career women reliant on their husbands and unwilling to countenance juggling work and family without considerable spousal support.[93] An atomized society prized connection as an 'alternative to loneliness [and] doubt' and living alone remained a luxury resembling a privation, involving ceaseless single supplements as well as detrimental physical and psychological effects that especially, but not exclusively, afflicted men.[94] Furthermore, as psychoanalyst Adam Phillips remarked, the individualist conceit of there always being 'someone else who would love me more, understand me better, make me feel more sexually alive' served as the best justification for monogamy as well as infidelity.[95]

The question remained whether individualism and togetherness could be truly reconciled. Young couples had to believe so and denied any necessary conflict between 'self-development and commitment.' But their idea of 'commitment' excluded much of that sense of 'obligation' without which it remained shallow and brittle.[96] Should two go into one? Could hope triumph over experience? Would men and women find love together? A happy ending appeared far off.

Notes

Acknowledgements

1   Marcus Collins, 'Good Companions: Personal Relationships between Men and Women in Twentieth-Century Britain' (Columbia University PhD thesis, 2000). Other portions of this work have been published as *idem*, 'The Pornography of Permissiveness: Men's Sexuality and Women's Emancipation in Mid Twentieth-Century Britain', *History Workshop Journal* 47 (1999), 99–120; and *idem*, 'Trouble and Strife: Poor Marriages in Mid Twentieth-Century London', *Qwerty: Arts, Littératures et Civilisations du Monde Anglophone* 10 (2000), 225–236.

Prologue

1   Laurence Housman, 'A Peaceful Penetrator', *Edward Carpenter: In Appreciation*, ed. Gilbert Beith (London, 1931), 111; Edward Carpenter, *Love's Coming of Age: A Series of Papers on the Relations of the Sexes* (Manchester, 1896), 52, 80. For Edward Carpenter, see Samuel Hynes, *The Edwardian Turn of Mind* (Princeton, NJ, 1968), 149–154; Chushichi Tsuzuki, *Edward Carpenter, 1844–1929: Prophet of Human Fellowship* (Cambridge, 1980); Emile Delevenay, *D.H. Lawrence and Edward Carpenter: A Study in Edwardian Transition* (London, 1971); and Tony Brown (ed.), *Edward Carpenter and Late Victorian Radicalism* (London, 1990).
2   Carpenter, *Love's Coming of Age* [1896 edn], 102.
3   Ibid., 26, 81.
4   Ibid., 83, 75.
5   Ibid., 80, 43–46.
6   Ibid., 75, 74.
7   Ibid., 5, 73, 79.
8   *Idem, Love's Coming of Age: A Series of Papers on the Relations of the Sexes* [rev. edn] (London, 1913), 135–136.
9   *Idem, Love's Coming of Age* [1896 edn], 80, 48, 98, 5.
10   *Idem, Love's Coming of Age* [1913 edn], 115; *idem, Love's Coming of Age* [1896 edn], 39.
11   Ibid., 50.
12   Ibid., 48.
13   Ibid., 79, 102.
14   Ibid., 60, 37, 85.
15   Ibid., 72, 73, 90.
16   Ibid., 22, 5.
17   Ibid., 93, 15, 111.
18   Mary Wollstonecraft, *A Vindication of the Rights of Woman* (Harmondsworth, 1975), 296; William Thompson, *Appeal of Half the Human Race, Women, Against the Pretensions of the Other Half, Men* (London, 1825), 93, 94.
19   John Stuart Mill, 'The Admission of Woman to the Electoral Franchise' (1867), *Sexual Equality: Writings by John Stuart Mill, Harriet Taylor Mill and Helen Taylor*, ed. Ann

Robson and John M. Robson (Toronto, 1994), 238. For liberal feminist attitudes to marriage, see also Mary Lyndon Shanley, 'Marital Slavery and Friendship: John Stuart Mill's "The Subjection of Women",' *Political Theory* 9, 2 (1981), 229–247; and Kathryn Gleadle, *The Early Feminists: Radical Unitarians and the Emergence of the Women's Rights Movement, 1831–51* (Basingstoke, 1995), ch. 3.

20 David Tyack and Elizabeth Hansot, *Learning Together: A History of Coeducation in American Public Schools* (New Haven, CT, 1990); William Leach, *True Love and Perfect Union: The Feminist Reform of Sex and Society* (New York, 1980); Karen Lystra, *Searching the Heart: Women, Men and Romantic Love in Nineteenth Century America* (New York, 1989); Clelia Duel Mosher, *The Mosher Survey: Sexual Attitudes of Forty-five Victorian Women* (New York, 1980). For Ellen Key, see her *Love and Marriage* (New York, 1911); *The Woman Movement* (New York, 1912); and *Love and Ethics* (New York, 1911).

21 Holbrook Jackson, *The Eighteen Nineties: A Review of Art and Ideas at the Close of the Nineteenth Century* (London, 1913), 13, 12.

22 Edward Carpenter in Edith Ellis, *The New Horizon in Love and Life* (London, 1921), vii; Edith Ellis, *Essays* (Berkeley Heights, NJ, 1924), xv. For the relationship between Carpenter, Schreiner and the Ellises, see also Ruth Brandon, *The New Women and the Old Men: Love, Sex and the Woman Question* (London, 1990); Chris Nottingham, *The Pursuit of Serenity: Havelock Ellis and the New Politics* (Amsterdam, 1999), ch. 2; Sheila Rowbotham and Jeffrey Weeks, *Socialism and the New Life: The Personal and Sexual Politics of Edward Carpenter and Havelock Ellis* (London, 1977); Phyllis Grosskurth, *Havelock Ellis* (London, 1981); Edith Ellis, *Three Modern Seers*; *idem*, *Essays*; Carolyn Burdett, *Olive Schreiner and the Progress of Feminism: Evolution, Gender, Empire* (Basingstoke, 2001); and Ruth First and Ann Scott, *Olive Schreiner* (London, 1989).

23 Olive Schreiner to Havelock Ellis (2 May 1884) in '*My Other Self': The Letters of Olive Schreiner and Havelock Ellis, 1884–1920*, ed. Yaffa Claire Draznin (New York, 1992), 47; Nottingham, ch. 5.

24 Ibid., 252.

25 Cited in Bill Bryson, *The Mother Tongue: English and How It Got That Way* (New York, 1990), 19.

26 A. Herbert Gray, *Successful Marriage* (London, 1941), 6; Annie Keen, *Woman and Marriage* (London, 1929), 54; Conference on Christian Politics, Economics and Citizenship, 'The Relation of the Sexes', *COPEC Commission Report* 4 (London, 1924), 13; John Macmurray, *Reason and Emotion* (London, 1935), 127. For the twentieth-century denigration of 'Victorian' models of private life, see also Michael Mason, *The Making of Victorian Sexuality* (Oxford, 1994), 1–20; and Matthew Sweet, *Inventing the Victorians* (London, 2001), chs. 11 and 13.

27 Alison Neilans, 'Changes in Sex Morality', *Our Freedom and Its Results*, ed. Ray Strachey (London, 1936), 199; Jack Dominian, 'Are You Ready for Marriage?', *Getting Married, 1985* (London, 1985), 6; Olive Schreiner, *Woman and Labour* (London, 1911), 256. The deVictorianization in which mutuality was involved had implications for national identity. This, after all, was the nation that had provided the blueprint for separate spheres during the nineteenth century, exporting trousers and footballs to men and models of ladylike deportment to women in the West and beyond. Yet, if the figures of the lady and gentleman achieved greatest prominence in Britain, so did the opposition to them. No country produced a stronger first-wave women's movement, Richard Evans noting in his comparative history that Britain boasted in John Stuart Mill and Josephine Butler 'the most important theorist of feminism . . . and the most influential figure in international moral feminism' together with what was probably the biggest suffrage movement in the world. This ferment in turn drew an unrivalled array of intellectuals into the debate on women's emancipation, the names of George Bernard Shaw, H.G. Wells, Bertrand Russell and Virginia Woolf representing a roll-call of the era's foremost public intellectuals. DeVictorianization also provided Britain's sexual revolution with its particular fizz as the nation's reputation for repression was rudely contradicted by such strange novelties as the miniskirt and *Penthouse* magazine. Only with the derivativeness of the women's liberation movement in the 1970s does a distinctly British tradition of sexual politics show signs of faltering, as cultural supremacy at last passed to the United States. The Victorian legacy had finally been extinguished and with it Britain's singular

approach to matters of personal relationships (Richard J. Evans, *The Feminists: Women's Emancipation Movements in Europe, American and Australasia, 1840–1920* (London, 1977), 68).

28 A. Maude Royden, 'Modern Love', *The Making of Women: Oxford Essays in Feminism*, ed. Victor Gollancz (London, 1917), 43.

29 John Vincent, *An Intelligent Person's Guide to History* (London, 1995), 15. For similar doubts over the viability of studying the history of personal relationships, see Gertrude Himmelfarb, *The New History and the Old* (Cambridge, MA, 1987), ch. 1.

30 For oral histories of private life, see in particular Kate Fisher, 'An Oral History of Birth Control Practice, *c.* 1925–50: A Study of Oxford and South Wales' (University of Oxford DPhil thesis, 1997); Judy Giles, *Women, Identity and Private Life in Britain, 1900–50* (Basingstoke, 1995); Claire Langhamer, *Women's Leisure in England, 1920–60* (Manchester, 2000), ch. 4; Steve Humphries, *A Secret World of Sex* (London, 1988); Elizabeth Roberts, *A Woman's Place: An Oral History of Working-Class Women, 1890–1940* (Oxford, 1984); and *idem, Women and Families: An Oral History* (Oxford, 1995).

31 For historians' use of demographic data, see Simon Szreter, *Fertility, Class and Gender in Britain, 1860–1940* (Cambridge, 1996); Wally Seccombe, *Weathering the Storm: Working-Class Families from the Industrial Revolution to the Fertility Decline* (London, 1993); Hera Cook, 'The Long Sexual Revolution: British Women, Sex and Contraception in the Twentieth Century' (University of Sussex DPhil thesis, 1999), part ii; Edward Shorter, *The Making of the Modern Family* (London, 1976); and Mason, ch. 5.

32 See Mary Lyndon Shanley, *Feminism, Marriage and the Law in Victorian England, 1850–95* (Princeton, NJ, 1989); Susan Pedersen, *Family, Dependence and the Origins of the Welfare State: Britain and France, 1914–45* (Cambridge, 1993); Roderick Phillips, *Putting Asunder: A History of Divorce in Western Society* (Cambridge, 1988); and Jane Lewis, *The End of Marriage?: Individualism and Intimate Relations* (Cheltenham, 2001), chs. 5 and 8.

33 See Jean H. Hagstrum, *Esteem Enlivened by Desire: The Couple from Homer to Shakespeare* (Chicago, 1992); *idem, Sex and Sensibility: Ideal and Erotic Love from Milton to Mozart* (Chicago, 1980); Steven Marcus, *The Other Victorians: A Study of Sexuality and Pornography in Mid Nineteenth-Century England* (New York, 1966); and Elaine Showalter, *Sexual Anarchy: Gender and Culture at the Fin de Siècle* (New York, 1990). For historians drawing upon the techniques of literary criticism, see Peter Gay, *The Bourgeois Experience*, v vols. (New York, 1984–98); Judith Walkowitz, *City of Dreadful Delight: Narratives of Sexual Danger in Late Victorian London* (Chicago, 1992); G.J. Barker-Benfield, *The Culture of Sensibility: Sex and Society in Eighteenth-Century Britain* (Chicago, 1992); and Cook, ch. 16.

34 For historical analyses of personal writings, see Lawrence Stone, *The Family, Sex and Marriage in England, 1500–1800* (London, 1977); Amanda Vickery, *The Gentleman's Daughter: Women's Lives in Georgian England* (New Haven, CT, 1998); Leonore Davidoff and Catherine Hall, *Family Fortunes: Men and Women of the English Middle Class, 1780–1850* (London, 1987); John Tosh, *A Man's Place: Masculinity and the Middle-Class Home in Victorian England* (New Haven, CT, 1999); M. Jeanne Peterson, *Family, Love and Work in the Lives of Victorian Gentlewomen* (Bloomington, IN, 1989); Pat Jalland, *Women, Marriage and Politics, 1860–1914* (Oxford, 1986); Phyllis Rose, *Parallel Lives: Five Victorian Marriages* (London, 1984); A. James Hammerton, 'Pooterism or Partnership?: Marriage and Masculine Identity in the Lower Middle Class, 1870–1920', *Journal of British Studies* 38, 3 (1999), 291–321; and Lesley A. Hall, *Hidden Anxieties: Male Sexuality, 1900–39* (Cambridge, 1991). For the use of court records, see Lawrence Stone, *Road to Divorce: England, 1530–1987* (Oxford, 1992); *idem, Broken Lives: Separation and Divorce in England, 1660–1857* (Oxford, 1993); A. James Hammerton, *Cruelty and Companionship: Conflict in Nineteenth-Century Married Life* (London, 1992); and Shani D'Cruze, *Crimes of Outrage: Sex, Violence and Victorian Working Women* (London, 1998).

35 Anthony Giddens, *The Transformation of Intimacy: Sexuality, Love and Eroticism in Modern Societies* (Stanford, CA, 1992); Michel Foucault, *The History of Sexuality, i* (New York, 1978). For sociological overviews, see also Jeffrey Weeks, *Sexuality and Its Discontents: Meanings, Myths and Modern Sexualities* (London, 1985);

J.E. Goldthorpe, *Family Life in Western Societies: A Historical Sociology of Family Relationships in Britain and North America* (Cambridge, 1987); and Lynn Jamieson, *Intimacy: Personal Relationships in Modern Societies* (Cambridge, 1998).

36 See Lesley A. Hall, *Sex, Gender and Social Change in Britain since 1880* (Basingstoke, 2000); Angus McLaren, *Twentieth-Century Sexuality* (Oxford, 1999); Ina Zweiniger-Bargielowska (ed.), *Women in Twentieth-Century Britain* (Harlow, 2001), chs. 4 and 5; Joanna Bourke, *Working-Class Cultures in Britain, 1890–1960: Gender, Class and Ethnicity* (London, 1994), chs. 2 and 3; and Ross McKibbin, *Classes and Cultures: England, 1918–51* (Oxford, 1998), chs. 5 and 8.

37 For the history of sexual politics, see Jeffrey Weeks, *Sex, Politics and Society: The Regulation of Sexuality since 1800* [rev. edn] (Harlow, 1989); Susan Kingsley Kent, *Sex and Suffrage in Britain, 1860–1914* (Princeton, NJ, 1987); idem, *Making Peace: The Reconstruction of Gender in Interwar Britain* (Princeton, NJ, 1993); Sheila Jeffreys, *The Spinster and Her Enemies: Feminism and Sexuality, 1880–1930* (Melbourne, 1997); idem, *Anticlimax: A Feminist Perspective on the Sexual Revolution* (London, 1990); Margaret Jackson, *The Real Facts of Life: Feminism and the Politics of Sexuality, 1850–1940* (London, 1994); Lucy Bland, *Banishing the Beast: English Feminism and Sexual Morality, 1885–1914* (Harmondsworth, 1995); and Carol Dyhouse, *Feminism and the Family in England, 1880–1939* (Oxford, 1989).

38 For the relationship between welfare institutions and private life, see George K. Behlmer, *Friends of the Family: The English Home and Its Guardians, 1850–1940* (Stanford, CA, 1998); and Ellen Ross, *Love and Toil: Motherhood in Outcast London, 1870–1914* (Oxford, 1993).

39 For cultural treatments of personal relationships, see in particular Stephen Kern, *The Culture of Love* (Cambridge, MA, 1992); and Theodore Zeldin, *An Intimate History of Humanity* (London, 1994).

40 Peter Burke, *Varieties of Cultural History* (Cambridge, 1997), 170–173.

41 Ibid., 171, 212.

42 See, for example, Joseph McAleer, *Passion's Fortune: The Story of Mills and Boon* (New York, 1999); Michelene Wandor, *Look Back in Gender: Sexuality and the Family in Postwar British Drama* (London, 1987); and John Hill, *Sex, Class and Realism: British Cinema, 1956–63* (London, 1986).

43 While some working-class communities in England were tolerant of mixing between the sexes, others – particularly mining communities – enforced strict codes of segregation. Single-sex activities also seem to have been strong in Wales and Northern Ireland, famously manifested by the rugby teams and male voice choirs of the former and the Orange Order of the latter. Yet Scotland had a coeducational schooling system and higher levels of female paid employment, and as such may well have been a special case. It is curious, therefore, that the segregated youth clubs discussed in chapter three proved to be more entrenched in Scotland than elsewhere in Britain: a matter which, as with the regional and national impact of mutuality more generally, deserves further investigation (For the classic example of a segregated and patriarchal working-class community, see Norman Dennis, Fernando Henriques and Clifford Slaughter, *Coal is Our Life: An Analysis of a Yorkshire Mining Community* (London, 1956). For Scottish gender history, see Rosalind K. Marshall, *Virgins and Viragos: A History of Women in Scotland from 1080 to 1980* (London, 1983); Esther Breitenach and Eleanor Gordon (eds.), *Out of Bounds: Women in Scottish Society, 1800–1945* (Edinburgh, 1992); Helen Corr, 'Dominies and Domination: Schoolteachers, Masculinity and Women in Nineteenth-Century Scotland', *History Workshop Journal* 40 (1995), 148–164; Linda Mahood, *Policing Gender, Class and Family: Britain, 1850–1940* (London, 1995); and Leah Leneman, *'A Guid Cause': The Women's Suffrage Movement in Scotland* [rev. edn] (Edinburgh, 1995). The brevity of this list confirms T.C. Smout's observation (cited in Breitenach and Gordon, 2) that the neglect of Scottish women's history and family history is a 'historiographical disgrace').

44 For in-depth studies of sexual politics in the First and Second World Wars, see in particular Margaret Higonnet (ed.), *Behind the Lines: Gender and the Two World Wars* (New Haven, CT, 1987); Gail Braybon and Penny Summerfield, *Out of the Cage: Women's Experiences in Two World Wars* (London, 1987); Susan R. Grayzel, *Women's Identities at War: Gender, Motherhood and Politics in Britain and France during the First World War* (Chapel Hill, NC, 1999); Joanna Bourke, *Dismembering the Male:*

Men's Bodies, Britain and the Great War (Chicago, 1996); Kent, Making Peace, chs. 1–5; Angela Woollacott, On Her Their Lives Depend: Munitions Workers in the Great War (Berkeley, CA, 1994); Deborah Thom, Nice Girls and Rude Girls: Women Workers in World War One (London, 1998); John Costello, Love, Sex and War, 1939–45 (London, 1986); Penny Summerfield, Women Workers in the Second World War: Patriarchy and Production in Conflict (London, 1984); and idem, Reconstructing Women's Wartime Lives: Discourse and Subjectivity in Oral Histories of the Second World War (Manchester, 1998).

Chapter 1 – Common Cause

1 'Vir', 'Speculation on Sex War', The Freewoman 1, 4 (1911), 66. For the upsurge of interest in sexual politics at the end of the nineteenth century, see Judith Walkowitz, City of Dreadful Delight: Narratives of Sexual Danger in Late Victorian London (Chicago, 1992); Elaine Showalter, Sexual Anarchy: Gender and Culture at the Fin de Siècle (New York, 1990); Bram Dijkstra, Idols of Perversity: Fantasies of Feminine Evil in Fin de Siècle Culture (New York, 1986); Sally Ledger, The New Woman: Fiction and Feminism at the Fin de Siècle (Manchester, 1997); Lesley A. Hall, Sex, Gender and Social Change in Britain since 1880 (Basingstoke, 2000), chs. 2 and 3; and David Rubinstein, Before The Suffragettes: Women's Emancipation in the 1890s (Brighton, 1986).

2 Maud Churston Braby, Modern Marriage and How to Bear It (London, 1908), 10; Walter M. Gallichan (aka Geoffrey Mortimer), Modern Woman and How to Manage Her (London, 1909), 55, 110.

3 Frances Swiney, 'The Bar of Isis' (1912), The Sexuality Debates, ed. Sheila Jeffreys (London, 1987), 482. For the purity movement, see Judith Walkowitz, Prostitution and Victorian Society: Women, Class and the State (Cambridge, 1980); Lucy Bland, Banishing the Beast: English Feminism and Sexual Morality, 1885–1914 (Harmondsworth, 1995); Frank Mort, Dangerous Sexualities: Medico-Moral Politics in England since 1830 [rev. edn] (London, 2000), part ii; Margaret Jackson, The Real Facts of Life: Feminism and the Politics of Sexuality, 1850–1940 (London, 1994); Sheila Jeffreys, The Spinster and Her Enemies: Feminism and Sexuality, 1880–1930 (Melbourne, 1997); and Susan Kingsley Kent, Sex and Suffrage in Britain, 1860–1914 (Princeton, NJ, 1987).

4 See Cheryl R. Jorgensen-Earp, 'The Transfiguring Sword': The Just War of the Women's Social and Political Union (Tuscaloosa, AL, 1997). Brian Harrison would dispute whether suffragette militancy was essentially ideological in intent, viewing it as 'more pragmatic than theoretic, more institutional than inspirational', while Sandra Stanley Holton similarly argues ʀhat the major divisions between constitutional suffragists and militant suffragettes were tactical rather than intellectual. While such arguments have some validity for the 1900s, militancy acquired a clear doctrinal stance by 1911 at the very latest, insisting not only on the legitimacy of violence but on the pitfalls of cross-sex cooperation (Brian Harrison, Peaceable Kingdom: Stability and Change in Modern Britain (Oxford, 1982), 42; Sandra Stanley Holton, Feminism and Democracy: Women's Suffrage and Reform Politics in Britain, 1900–18 (Cambridge, 1986), 28).

5 Frances Swiney, for instance, was a local official in the non-militant National Union of Women's Suffrage Societies, while Martin Pugh notes the limited involvement of other purity campaigners in the wider suffrage cause (Martin Pugh, The March of the Women: A Revisionist Analysis of the Campaign for Women's Suffrage, 1866–1914 (Oxford, 2000), 30).

6 Christabel Pankhurst, The Great Scourge and How to End It (London, 1913), 37. For decidedly more conciliatory sentiments regarding men from supporters of militancy, see for example Elizabeth Robins, Way Stations (London, 1913); Laurence Housman, Sex War and Woman's Suffrage (London, 1912); and Sir Harry Johnston in Votes For Women, 6 March 1914. Both Robins and Housman cut ties wiʀh the WPSU soon after issuing these works.

7 L.H.M. Soulsby, A Woman's Movement (London, 1913), 29. For moderate anti-suffragism, see also Helen Bosanquet, The Family (London, 1906), 271–274; and John Sutherland, Mrs Humphry Ward: Eminent Victorian, Pre-eminent Edwardian (Oxford,

1990), ch. 25.

8 Anon., *Women and Other Enigmas* (London, 1914), 8.

9 Cicely Hamilton, *Marriage as a Trade* (London, 1909), 58; Frances Swiney, *The Awakening of Women: Woman's Part in Evolution* [rev. edn] (London, 1905), 193.

10 Christabel Pankhurst (1914) cited in David Mitchell, *Queen Christabel* (London, 1977), 224; Christabel Pankhurst, *The Great Scourge*, 98.

11 Swiney, *The Awakening of Women*, 106; *idem, The Mystery of the Circle and the Cross; or, The Interpretation of Sex* (London, 1908), 66. For Swiney's Theosophy, see Diana Burfield, 'Theosophy and Feminism: Some Explorations in Nineteenth-Century Biography', *Women's Religious Experience*, ed. Pat Holden (London, 1983), 36.

12 Frances Swiney, *Women among the Nations* (London, 1913), 70; *idem, The Awakening of Women*, 102.

13 Margaret Dalham, *Mere Man* (London, 1911), 81, 7.

14 Hamilton, *Marriage as a Trade*, 282; 'One Who Knows', *Wives and How to Manage Them* (London, 1904), 40.

15 Christabel Pankhurst, *The Great Scourge*, 17; Henry Phipps Denison, *The Mystery of Marriage* (London, 1916), 109.

16 T.W.H. Crosland, *The Lovely Woman* (London, 1903), 199; Francis Latham, *Is the British Empire Ripe for Government by Disorderly Women who Smash Windows and Assault the Police?* (London, 1911), 17, 18.

17 *A Message from the WSPU* (*c.* 1911–12), *Suffrage and the Pankhursts*, ed. Jane Marcus (London, 1987), 181; E. Belfort Bax, *The Fraud of Feminism* (London, 1913), 6. Even Christabel Pankhurst sometimes disavowed antagonism towards men; see her articles 'What Militancy Means' and 'The Marriage Ban, ii' in *The Suffragette*, 2 May 1913 and 8 May 1914.

18 Crosland, 200.

19 Christabel Pankhurst, 'A Matter of Conscience', *The Suffragette*, 17 July 1914; Mary R. Richardson, *Laugh A Defiance* (London, 1935), 12.

20 Brian Harrison, *Peaceable Kingdom*, 48; Millicent Garrett Fawcett cited in Leslie Parker Hume, *The National Union of Women's Suffrage Societies, 1897–1914* (New York, 1982), 36; National Union of Women's Suffrage Societies, *The Reform Bill and Woman Suffrage* (London, 1910), 4. The standard biography of Fawcett is David Rubinstein, *A Different World for Women: The Life of Millicent Garrett Fawcett* (Hemel Hempstead, 1991).

21 Helena Swanwick cited in Holton, *Feminism and Democracy*, 66; Helena Swanwick, *The Future of the Women's Movement* (London, 1913), 165.

22 Stella Browne cited in Sheila Rowbotham, *A New World for Women: Stella Browne, Socialist Feminist* (London, 1977), 61. Millicent Garrett Fawcett had once been involved with purity issues and issued an imperious rebuke to Grant Allen's sexual libertarianism in 1895 but, though she remained relatively conservative on matters of personal relationships, tended to avoid voicing her opinions on these subjects upon assuming the leadership of the NUWSS in 1900.

23 By way of examples of disagreement among mutualists, Olive Schreiner and Maude Royden condemned the sexual libertarians of *The Freewoman* journal for echoing 'the voice of the brutal self-indulgent male'. Nor did mutualists and suffragists always see eye to eye, Millicent Garrett Fawcett refusing to share a platform with Edward Carpenter on account of his open homosexuality (Schreiner (1912) cited in Bland, 265).

24 Havelock Ellis in introduction to Ellen Key, *The Woman Movement* (New York, 1912), xv.

25 A series of revisionist studies has thrown doubt on the rigid nature of personal relationships between Victorian men and women and, by implication, the revolutionary impact of mutuality. If separate spheres represented little more than a rhetorical construction and women were at liberty to mingle freely with men, then the subsequent growth of mixing must be nothing more than an optical illusion. If the period witnessed the 'full flowering' of companionship, then mutualists' denunciations of patriarchy in marriage appear inexplicable. And if Victorian women's passionlessness is 'largely a myth' contradicted by prescriptive literature and the personal testimony of happy, guiltless lovers, then the twentieth-century mutualist crusade for shared sexual pleasure seems at once belated and redundant (M. Jeanne Peterson, *Family, Love and Work in the Lives of Victorian Gentlewomen* (Bloomington, IN, 1989), 84; Peter Gay, *The Education of the Senses* (New York, 1984), 133).

Yet, when every allowance is made for the gap between rhetoric and reality, the concept of separate spheres retains considerable explanatory power. The great institutions of the age – the public school, the board room and the Houses of Parliament – were purposely male-only affairs, and studies such as Eve Kosofsky Sedgwick's *Between Men* (1985) have identified the importance of homosociality to Victorian gentlemen. Middle-class women, while not the sequestered innocents of popular imagination, nonetheless achieved most freedom of action through enlarging their own sphere rather than directly entering men's until late in the nineteenth century. The rules of chaperonage were more relaxed, the segregation of education less strict and social intercourse between the sexes somewhat easier among men and women of the urban poor. Yet it was precisely this which made them unrespectable in the eyes of their betters, Françoise Barret-DuCrocq noting that 'in the final analysis the immorality of the labouring classes was always linked to the mixing of the sexes' (Eve Kosofsky Sedgwick, *Between Men: English Literature and Male Homosocial Desire* (New York, 1985); Françoise Barret-DuCrocq, *Love in the Time of Victoria* (London, 1991), 24).

There is no question that love and mutual dependence underpinned the theory and practice of many Victorian marriages. However, as Peter Gay accepts, the idea that partners should marry for love alone was by no means wholly accepted. The correspondents in the mid-Victorian *Daily Telegraph* marriage debate analyzed by John Robson tended to value 'sense' over 'sentiment' and cautioned against love matches undertaken in disregard of economic considerations. Furthermore, mainstream Victorian marital ideals differed from those of the twentieth century in their tendency to see little or no contradiction between companionship and patriarchal power. A husband was expected by Lord Shaftesbury to exercise 'authority', a wife some lesser 'genial influence'. Those Victorian feminists who maintained that companionship could not exist in the absence of equality were a self-conscious minority all too aware that 'the generality of the male sex cannot yet tolerate the idea of living with an equal' (Peter Gay, *The Tender Passion* (New York, 1986), 102–103; John M. Robson, *Marriage or Celibacy?: The Daily Telegraph on a Victorian Dilemma* (Toronto, 1995), 264; Lord Shaftesbury cited in *The Victorian Family: Structures and Stresses*, ed. Anthony S. Wohl (London, 1978), 9–10; John Stuart Mill, *The Subjection of Women* (1869), *Sexual Equality: Writings by John Stuart Mill, Harriet Taylor Mill and Helen Taylor*, ed. Ann Robson and John M. Robson (Toronto, 1994), 350).

The debate on Victorian sexual repression is hindered by a lack of pertinent sources. To be sure, a large body of research has disabused us of the notion that Victorians were silent on the subject. American historians have also managed to make the leap from public debate to private practice, with Karen Lystra's analysis of love letters, Peter Gay's character study of Mabel Todd Loomis and Carl Degler's unearthing of the Mosher survey suggesting that middle-class Americans in the latter half of the nineteenth century saw sex as the 'ultimate expression of love'. But comparable material for Britain is only available for the London poor, via the testimony examined by Françoise Barret-DuCrocq of single mothers who sought help from the Thomas Coram Foundling Hospital. Pat Jalland and Jeanne Peterson contend that higher-class women experienced sexual satisfaction yet provide little corroborative evidence. As suggested below, the virtual absence of a respectable discourse on sexual pleasure throughout most of the Victorian period gave mutualist thinking its originality and moral force (Karen Lystra, *Searching the Heart: Women, Men and Romantic Love in Nineteenth Century America* (New York, 1989), 59; Gay, *The Education of the Senses*, 71–108; Carl N. Degler, 'What Ought to Be and What Was: Woman's Sexuality in the Nineteenth Century', *American Historical Review* 79, 5 (1974), 1467–1490; Pat Jalland, *Women, Marriage and Politics, 1860–1914* (Oxford, 1986), 130; Peterson, 66–68, 73–77).

26   Sarah Lewis, *Woman's Mission* [rev. edn] (London, 1839), 11. For a synthesis of current work on separate spheres, see Robert B. Shoemaker, *Gender in English Society, 1650–1850: The Emergence of Separate Spheres?* (London, 1998). For useful correctives against the indiscriminate use of the term, see Linda K. Kerber, 'Separate Spheres, Female Worlds, Woman's Place: The Rhetoric of Women's History', *Journal of American History* 75, 1 (1988), 9–39; and Amanda Vickery, 'Golden Age to Separate Spheres?: A Review of the Categories and Chronology of English Women's History', *Historical Journal* 36, 2 (1993), 383–414.

27   John Ruskin, *Sesame and Lilies* (Nelson, 2000), 87, 89, 87.

28 Sarah Stickney Ellis, *The Wives of England: Their Relative Duties, Domestic Influence and Social Obligations* (London, 1843), 65. For biological essentialism, see Cynthia Russett, *Sexual Science: The Victorian Construction of Womanhood* (Cambridge, MA, 1989).

29 Ruskin, 87.

30 Andrew Mearns, *The Bitter Cry of Outcast London* (London, 1883), 12.

31 Londa Schiebinger, 'Skeletons in the Closet: The First Illustrations of the Female Skeleton in Eighteenth-Century Anatomy', *The Making of the Modern Body: Sexuality and Society in the Nineteenth Century*, ed. Thomas Laqueur and Catherine Gallagher (Berkeley, CA, 1987).

32 Leonore Davidoff and Catherine Hall, *Family Fortunes: Men and Women of the English Middle Class, 1780–1850* (London, 1987); 'X.' in *Is Marriage a Failure?*, ed. Harry Quilter (London, 1888), 64.

33 Christabel Pankhurst, 'The Marriage Ban, ii', *The Suffragette*, 8 May 1914.

34 George Calderon, *Woman in Relation to the State* (London, 1908), 9; W. Lyon Blease, *The Emancipation of English Women* (London, 1910), 199, 200.

35 Havelock Ellis, 'Feminism and Masculism', *Essays in Wartime* (London, 1916), 96; Marie Stopes (1909) cited in June Rose, *Marie Stopes and the Sexual Revolution* (London, 1992), 64; Karen Offen, 'Defining Feminism: A Comparative Historical Approach', *Signs* 14, 1 (1988), 135. For contemporaneous Continental relational feminists, see *idem, European Feminisms, 1700–1950: A Political History* (Stanford, CA, 2000), ch. 8; and Ann Taylor Allen, 'Mothers of the New Generation: Adele Schreiber, Helene Stöcker and the Evolution of a German Idea of Motherhood', *Signs* 20, 3 (1985), 418–438.

36 Mrs Morgan-Dockrell, 'Is the New Woman a Myth?' (1896), *The Late Victorian Marriage Question, ii: The New Woman and Female Independence*, ed. Ann Heilmann (London, 1998), 348.

37 Edward Carpenter, *Love's Coming of Age* [rev. edn] (London, 1913), 79; C. Gasquoine Hartley, *The Truth about Women* (London, 1913), 268.

38 Ethel Snowden, *The Feminist Movement* (London, 1913), 16.

39 Carpenter, 114.

40 Olive Schreiner, *Woman and Labour* (London, 1911), 257–258, 274.

41 See Herbert Sussman, *Victorian Masculinities: Manhood and Masculine Poetics in Early Victorian Literature and Arts* (Cambridge, 1995); and Norman Vance, *The Sinews of the Spirit: The Ideal of Christian Manliness in Victorian Literature and Religious Thought* (Cambridge, 1985).

42 'A Member of the Aristocracy', *Manners and Tone of Good Society* [rev. edn] (London, 1888), 211. For the power of etiquette to regulate women's behaviour, see Michael Curtin, *Propriety and Position: A Study of Victorian Manners* (New York, 1987), ch. 8.

43 Hippolyte Taine, *Notes on England* (London, 1957), 44. For a groundbreaking analysis of middle-class male domesticity in this period, see John Tosh, *A Man's Place: Masculinity and the Middle-Class Home in Victorian England* (New Haven, CT, 1999).

44 Martha Vicinus (ed.), *A Widening Sphere: Changing Roles of Victorian Women* (Bloomington, IN, 1977); Walkowitz, *City of Dreadful Delight*, 68.

45 Swanwick, *The Future of the Women's Movement*, 173.

46 Editorial in *The Common Cause*, 22 July 1909; Schreiner, 257.

47 Alfred Corner, *The End of Male Ascendancy* (London, 1917), 10, 32.

48 Key, *The Woman Movement*, 114.

49 Henry Binns, 'A New Fellowship', *Seed-Time* 22 (1894), 7; Edith Ellis cited in Ruth Brandon, *The New Women and the Old Men: Love, Sex and the Woman Question* (London, 1990), 99. For a semi-fictional account of the Bloomsbury commune, see Edith Ellis, *Attainment* (London, 1909).

50 Roy Porter, *Enlightenment: Britain and the Creation of the Modern World* (London, 2000), 342–343; Mary Wollstonecraft, *A Vindication of the Rights of Woman* (Harmondsworth, 1992), 129, 283, 286–288, 292–294; Sheila R. Herstein, *A Mid Victorian Feminist: Barbara Leigh Smith Bodichon* (New Haven, CT, 1985), 59–64.

51 For general overviews of independent coeducation, see W.C. Stewart, *The Educational Innovators, ii: Progressive Schools, 1881–1967* (London, 1968); and Kevin Brehony, 'Coeducation: Perspectives and Debates in the Early Twentieth Century', *Coeducation Reconsidered*, ed. Rosemary Dean (Milton Keynes, 1984).

52   Annette M.B. Meakin, *Woman in Transition* (London, 1907), 294.

53   J.H. Badley, *Coeducation in Practice* (London, 1914), 4; *idem, Bedales School: Outline of Its Aims and System* (Cambridge, 1900), 16; Homer Lane, 'Introduction', *Advances in Coeducation*, ed. Alice Woods (London, 1919), xviii.

54   Mona Baird (pseud.), *Womanhood* (London, 1919), 43; Cecil Grant and Norman Hodgson, *The Case for Coeducation* (London, 1913), 142. For coeducationalists' relationship to first-wave feminism, see Katharine Reid and John Ablett, *Shall Women Be Enfranchised?* (London, 1897); and J.H. Badley, 'Coeducation and the Woman's Movement', *The Englishwoman*, August 1910, 21–30. For all their grand dreams of a post-feminist age, coeducationalists had trouble delivering equal opportunities to teachers in their own schools. Headmasters were almost universally preferred over headmistresses and women teachers generally received less money and lowlier positions than their male colleagues.

55   Walter M. Gallichan (aka Geoffrey Mortimer), *How to Love: The Art of Courtship and Marriage* (London, 1915), 35; Havelock Ellis, *Studies in the Psychology of Sex, ii* (New York, 1942), appendix b; John Ablett, *Why Boys and Girls Should be Coeducated* (London, 1897), 3.

56   Schreiner, 277–278. For Walter Gallichan's enthusiasm for women working alongside men, see *How to Love*, 96.

57   Elizabeth Sloan Chesser, *Woman, Marriage and Motherhood* (London, 1913), 248; Edith Ellis, 'The Maternal in Domestic and Political Life' (1911), *The New Horizon in Love and Life* (London, 1921), 125. For the ambivalence of Havelock Ellis on the subject of female employment, see *The Philosophy of Conflict and Other Essays in Wartime* (London, 1919), 182–184.

58   'An Appeal Against Female Suffrage' (1889), *The Opponents – The Anti-Suffragists: Controversies in the History of British Feminism,* ed. Marie Mulvey Roberts and Tamae Mizuta (London, 1995), 3.

59   Walter Heape, *Sex Antagonism* (London, 1913), 27; Ernest Crawley, *The Mystic Rose: A Study of Primitive Marriage and of Primitive Thought in Its Bearing on Marriage* [rev. edn] (London, 1965), 86. For anti-feminism in gentleman's clubs, see Brian Harrison, *Separate Spheres: The Opposition to Women's Suffrage in Britain* (London, 1978), ch. 5.

60   Mabel Hawtrey, *The Coeducation of the Sexes* (London, 1896), 55; Heber L. Hart, *Women's Suffrage and National Danger: A Plea for the Ascendancy of Man* (London, 1889), 187. Similar fears concerning female emancipation and male emasculation underlay G. Stanley Hall's opposition to coeducation in the United States, for which see David Tyack and Elizabeth Hansot, *Learning Together: A History of Coeducation in American Public Schools* (New Haven, CT, 1990), ch. 6.

61   See Martha Vicinus, *Independent Women: Work and Community for Single Women, 1850–1920* (Chicago, 1985).

62   Swiney, *Women among the Nations*, 43; 'J'Espere', 'The Co-Education of the Sexes', *Shafts*, 15 September 1894.

63   Hamilton, *Marriage as a Trade*, 160; 'Women's Clubs' in *Shafts*, October 1897.

64   Constance Lytton (1914) cited in Brian Harrison, *Peaceable Kingdom*, 43; Swiney, *The Awakening of Women*, 100. For the importance of sisterhood in the suffragette movement, see Ann Morley and Liz Stanley, *The Life and Death of Emily Wilding Davison* (London, 1988), ch. 6; and Vicinus, *Independent Women*, ch. 7.

65   Hartley, 268; H.M. Swanwick, *I Have Been Young* (London, 1935), 204.

66   Jane E. Harrison, *Homo Sum: Being a Letter to an Anti-Suffragist from an Anthropologist* (London, 1912), 26.

67   William Blackstone (1765) cited in Jalland, 58. For examples of patriarchal marriage literature, see A. Burch and J.J. Spark, *Marriage a Success* (Parkstone, 1891); and R.L. Tafel, *When Is Marriage a Failure?* (London, 1888).

68   Davidoff and Hall, 323; Tosh, 62; Anna Dawson (1875) and William Hall (1887) cited in Peter Ward, *Courtship, Love and Marriage in Nineteenth-Century English Canada* (Montreal, 1990), 156.

69   Joan Perkin, *Victorian Women* (London, 1993), 73, 75.

70   'A Successfully Married Man' in *Is Marriage a Failure?*, 87.

71   See Mary Lyndon Shanley, *Feminism, Marriage and the Law in Victorian England, 1850–95* (Princeton, NJ, 1989).

72   George Bernard Shaw, *The Quintessence of Ibsenism* (London, 1891), 35.
73   Walter M. Gallichan (aka Geoffrey Mortimer), *The Great Unmarried* (London, 1916), 84; Braby, 9. For emancipated woman's aversion to wedlock, see also Ella Hepworth Dixon, 'Why Women are Ceasing to Marry' (1899), *The Late Victorian Marriage Question, ii*.
74   George Bernard Shaw, *Getting Married and Press Cuttings* (Harmondsworth, 1986), 35, 26.
75   Schreiner, 272.
76   Robert Owen, *Lectures on the Marriages of the Priesthood in the Old Immoral World* [rev. edn] (Leeds, 1840), 89. See Barbara Taylor, *Eve and the New Jerusalem: Socialism and Feminism in the Nineteenth Century* (London, 1983), ch. 6.
77   Josephine E. Butler, 'Introduction', *Woman's Work and Woman's Culture: A Series of Essays*, ed. Josephine E. Butler (London, 1869), xv, xlviii.
78   John Allen Godfrey, *The Science of Sex: An Essay Towards the Practical Solution of the Sex Problem* (London, 1901), 280; Mona Caird in *Is Marriage a Failure?*, 42.
79   Wordworth Donisthorpe, *Love and Law: An Essay on Marriage* (London, 1893); W.L. George, *Woman and Tomorrow* (London, 1913), 184.
80   Carpenter, 90; Havelock Ellis, *My Life* (London, 1940), 229. For the failures of free love, see Brandon; and Taylor, ch. 8.
81   Charles J. Whitby, 'The Tragedy of the Happy Marriage', *The Freewoman*, 1, 2 (1911), 25, 26; Chesser, 33.
82   Schreiner, 246.
83   Gallichan, *The Great Unmarried*, 190; Carpenter, 94.
84   Jane Hume Clapperton, 'Reform in Domestic Life', *Shafts*, 15 June 1893.
85   Ellice Hopkins, *The Power of Womanhood; or, Mothers and Sons* [rev. edn] (London, 1900), 146–147; Christabel Pankhurst, 'The Marriage Ban, ii', *The Suffragette*, 8 May 1914; Hamilton, *Marriage as a Trade*, 265.
86   Hopkins, 149; Christabel Pankhurst, 'The Marriage Ban, ii', *The Suffragette*, 8 May 1914; Hamilton, *Marriage as a Trade*, 23; *idem* cited in Marie Mulvey Roberts and Tamae Mizuta (eds.), *The Wives: Perspectives on the History of British Feminism* (London, 1995), xi.
87   Swiney, *The Awakening of Women*, 89; Dalham, 120–121.
88   Cicely Hamilton, *Life Errant* (London, 1935), 65; *idem*, *Marriage as a Trade*, 255, 274. For the shift in feminist thinking on marriage, see Philippa Levine, *Feminist Lives in Victorian England: Private Roles and Public Commitment* (Oxford, 1990), 47; and A. James Hammerton, *Cruelty and Companionship: Conflict in Nineteenth-Century Married Life* (London, 1992), 159.
89   Christabel Pankhurst, 'The Marriage Ban, ii', *The Suffragette*, 8 May 1914; Lucy Re-Bartlett, *Sex and Sanctity* (London, 1912), 78.
90   Annie Kenney, *Memories of a Militant* (London, 1924), 110; Jihang Park, 'The British Suffrage Activists of 1913: An Analysis', *Past and Present* 120 (1988), 158. In contrast, a slight majority of NUWSS activists was married.
91   'A Misogynist', *The Celibate's Apology* (London, 1914); 'Grimaud', *The New Marriage* (London, 1904), 31–33; Tosh, ch. 8.
92   George Bainton, *The Wife as Lover and Friend* (London, 1895), 44; Harry Quilter, 'Marriage' (*c.* 1895), *Opinions on Men, Women and Things* (London, 1909), 271.
93   'Faith and Hope' in *Is Marriage a Failure?*, 69, 68.
94   James McGrigor Allan, *Woman Suffrage Wrong in Principle and Practice* (London, 1890), 24; Dalham, 7.
95   Henry C. Day, *Marriage, Divorce and Morality* (London, 1912), 19; Kenney, 110.
96   William Acton (1871) cited in Bland, 50; Frances Swiney, *The Bar of Isis; or, The Law of the Mother* (London, 1909), 38.
97   Carpenter, 85; Blease, 206; Josephine Pitcairn Knowles, *The Upholstered Cage* (London, 1912), xxix.
98   Shaw, 26.
99   Victor Gollancz, 'Introductory – A Restatement', *The Making of Women: Oxford Essays in Feminism*, ed. Victor Gollancz (London, 1917), 17; Wilma Meikle, *Towards a Sane Feminism* (London, 1916), 17.
100   Knowles, 37; Meikle, 96. For mutualist attacks on spinsterhood, see also Jeffreys, *The Spinster and Her Enemies*.

101 Zuzanna Shonfield, *The Precariously Privileged: A Professional Family in Victorian London* (Oxford, 1987), 64, 78; Michel Foucault, *The History of Sexuality, i* (London, 1979), 17.

102 Thomas Laqueur, *Making Sex: Body and Gender from the Greeks to Freud* (Cambridge, MA, 1990), viii; Roy Porter, 'Mixed Feelings: The Enlightenment and Sexuality in Eighteenth-Century Britain', *Sexuality in Eighteenth-Century Britain*, ed. Paul-Gabriel Boucé (Manchester, 1982), 21.

103 Lynda Nead, *Myths of Sexuality: Representations of Women in Victorian Britain* (Oxford, 1988), 179.

104 For contrasting opinions, see Steven Marcus, *The Other Victorians: A Study of Sexuality and Pornography in Mid Nineteenth-Century England* (New York, 1966); and Gay, *The Education of the Senses*.

105 Nancy F. Cott, 'Passionlessness: An Interpretation of Victorian Sexual Ideology, 1790–1850', *Signs* 4, 2 (1978), 219–236; Taine, 98.

106 Michael Mason, *The Making of Victorian Sexuality* (Oxford, 1994), 7; Havelock Ellis, *The Erotic Rights of Woman and the Objects of Marriage* (London, 1918), 19, 18. Mason's is the most comprehensive study to date of sexuality in nineteenth-century Britain.

107 Walter M. Gallichan (aka Geoffrey Mortimer), *The Psychology of Marriage* (London, 1917), 107; Edith Ellis, *Essays* (Berkeley Heights, NJ, 1924), 36. Historian Jane Lewis has noted that this quest to create a 'higher relationship' between men and women through intercourse distinguished the views of Havelock Ellis, Bertrand Russell and Ellen Key from the promiscuity promoted by H.G. Wells and, one might add, Grant Allen. As elsewhere, ideals did not always correspond to practice. Havelock Ellis was among the greatest proponents of the necessity of sex-love in marriage, yet found that he and his lesbian wife Edith 'scarcely missed' intercourse. Experience taught him that 'passionate intensity of love' could continue to grow 'even when the relationship of sex in the narrow sense has ceased to exist' (Jane Lewis, 'Intimate Relations between Men and Women: The Case of H.G. Wells and Amber Pember Reeves', *History Workshop Journal* 37 (1994), 80–81; Havelock Ellis, *My Life*, 292, 234, 293).

108 Gallichan, *How to Love*, 109; idem, *The Psychology of Marriage*, 105.

109 A. Maude Royden, 'Modern Love', *The Making of Women*, 42; Gallichan, *How to Love*, 67.

110 Havelock Ellis, *The Task of Social Hygiene* (London, 1912), 61; Royden, 39, 43.

111 Swanwick, *The Future of the Women's Movement*, 167.

112 Royden, 43, 39.

113 Ibid., 62; Gollancz, 25.

114 Margaret Jackson, 'Sexology and the Social Construction of Male Sexuality: Havelock Ellis', *The Sexuality Papers: Male Sexuality and the Social Control of Women*, ed. Lal Coveney *et al.* (London, 1984), 65; Havelock Ellis, *Studies in the Psychology of Sex, i* (New York, 1942), 82.

115 Jackson, 'Sexology and the Social Construction of Male Sexuality', 53; Sheila Jeffreys, 'Women and Sexuality', *Women's History: Britain, 1850–1945*, ed. June Purvis (London, 1995), 199; Havelock Ellis, *Studies in the Psychology of Sex, i*, 67.

116 *Idem, Sex in Relation to Society* (London, 1946), 322, 323; idem, *Studies in the Psychology of Sex, i*, 229.

117 Jeffreys, 'Women and Sexuality', 202; Havelock Ellis, *Studies in the Psychology of Sex, i*, 229; idem, *The Play-Function of Sex* (London, 1921), 6.

118 *Idem, Studies in the Psychology of Sex, i*, 240, 236.

119 Jeffreys, *The Spinster and Her Enemies*, ch. 9; Havelock Ellis, *Studies in the Psychology of Sex, i*, 194.

120 Ibid., 239, 323; idem, *The Erotic Rights of Woman*, 20. For more measured assessments of Ellis' sexual politics, see Chris Nottingham, *The Pursuit of Serenity: Havelock Ellis and the New Politics* (Amsterdam, 1999); and Paul Robinson, *The Modernization of Sex: Havelock Ellis, Alfred Kinsey, William Masters and Virginia Johnson* (London, 1976), ch. 1.

121 William Thompson, *Appeal of Half the Human Race, Women, Against the Pretensions of the Other Half, Men* (London, 1825), 93, 64. For an excellent discussion of these issues, see M.L. Bush, *What is Love?: Richard Carlile's Philosophy of Sex* (London, 1998).

122 Shelley cited in Michael Mason, *The Making of Victorian Sexual Attitudes* (Oxford, 1994), 11.

123 William Godwin, *Enquiry Concerning Political Justice and Its Influence on Morals and Happiness* [rev. edn] (London, 1796), 520; Wollstonecraft, 87.

124 Ibid., 252.

125 Hamilton, *Marriage as a Trade*, 80; Dalham, 74, 73.

126 Hopkins, 8; Swiney, *The Bar of Isis*, 38.

127 Hall, *Sex, Gender and Social Change*, 68; Sue Morgan, *A Passion for Purity: Ellice Hopkins and the Politics of Gender in the Late Victorian Church* (Bristol, 1999), ch. 7.

128 Christabel Pankhurst, *The Great Scourge*, 132, 8. For an adverse assessment of purity feminism, see Margaret Hunt, 'The Deeroticisation of Women's Liberation: Social Purity Movements and the Revolutionary Feminism of Sheila Jeffreys', *Feminist Review* 34 (1990), 33–34.

129 Heape, 127; James Corin (aka Sydney Savory Buckman), *Mating, Marriage and the Status of Woman* (London, 1910), vi; Bax, 29.

130 Heape, 127.

131 St George Mivart, 'The Degradation of Woman' (1896), *The Late Victorian Marriage Question, ii*, 256, 257; *idem*, 'Is It Degradation?: A Brief Restatement' (1896), *The Late Victorian Marriage Question, ii*, 419.

132 Havelock Ellis, *The Erotic Rights of Woman*, 7; Gollancz, 24.

133 Gallichan, *The Psychology of Marriage*, 125, 121.

134 Louise Creighton, *The Social Disease and How to Fight It: A Rejoinder* (London, 1914), 61, 67. Having hitherto opposed women's suffrage, Creighton embraced the cause in 1906; see James Covert, *A Victorian Marriage: Mandell and Louise Creighton* (London, 2000), 302.

135 Havelock Ellis, *Studies in the Psychology of Sex, ii*, 261; Martin Pugh, *The Pankhursts* (London, 2001), 311–315.

136 Godfrey, 88, 87; Maude Royden cited in Sheila Fletcher, *Maude Royden: A Life* (Oxford, 1989), 231; Stella Browne, *The Sexual Variety and Variability among Women and Their Bearing upon Social Reconstruction* (1917) in Rowbotham, 94; Hartley, 259.

137 Herbert Burrows, *The Future of Woman* (London, 1909), 8; Gallichan, *Modern Woman*, 116, 59, 57.

138 Vivian Grey (aka Elliott E. Mills) and Edward S. Tylee, *Boy and Girl: Should They Be Educated Together?* (London, 1906), 58–59.

139 Royden, 44, 38, 44.

140 Christabel Pankhurst cited in Mitchell, 162; Emmeline Pankhurst, *My Own Story* (New York, 1914), 279.

141 Ibid., n.p., 61; Christabel Pankhurst cited in Mitchell, 240.

142 Emmeline Pankhurst, *My Own Story*, 61; Christabel Pankhurst cited in Mitchell, 162. For the marginalization of men in the suffragette movement, see Laurence Housman, *The Unexpected Years* (London, 1937), 275; and Sandra Stanley Holton, 'Manliness and Militancy: The Political Protest of Male Suffragists and the Gendering of the "Suffragette" Identity', *The Men's Share?: Masculinities, Male Support and Women's Suffrage in Britain, 1890–1920*, ed. Angela V. John and Claire Eustance (London, 1997).

143 Editorial in *Votes for Women*, 26 June 1914.

144 Brian Harrison, *Separate Spheres*, 186–188.

145 Almroth Wright, 'Suffrage Fallacies' (1912), *The Opponents*, 4–5.

146 H.G. Wells, *What is Coming?: A Forecast of Things after the War* (London, 1916), 164; Christabel Pankhurst in *The Suffragette*, 7 August 1914.

147 Emmeline Pankhurst, *My Own Story*, n.p.; *idem* (1914) cited in Arthur Marwick, *Women at War, 1914–18* (London, 1977), 32; Christabel Pankhurst (1918) cited in Jacqueline de Vries, 'Gendering Patriotism: Emmeline and Christabel Pankhurst and World War One', *The Working Day World: Women's Lives and Culture(s) in Britain, 1914–45*, ed. Sybil Oldfield (London, 1994), 84.

148 Lord Curzon cited in Brian Harrison, *Separate Spheres*, 181.

149 Contributions by Sir Frederick Banbury, William Burdett-Coutts and Ramsay MacDonald to the debate on the Representation of the People Bill, *Parliamentary Debates: House of Commons* (19 June 1917), vol. 94, cols. 1648, 1665, 1692.

150 Susan R. Grayzel, *Women's Identities at War: Gender, Motherhood and Politics in Britain and France during the First World War* (Chapel Hill, NC, 1999), ch. 4. The

overall state of relations between the sexes in wartime remains a matter of dispute. Cultural historians have challenged the orthodox view of purposeful cooperation, advancing literary and psychohistorical evidence that the turmoil of war released 'female libidinal energies ... which men usually found anxiety-inducing and women often found exhilarating'. Social historians conversely find little indication that women felt so emancipated or men so emasculated as such studies suggest. Joanna Bourke argues that women were not so subservient to men before the war as to be empowered by war work, and in any case recognized that their new occupations, as with soldiering for men, were 'for the duration only'. The great majority of men, meanwhile, did not in her view become alienated misogynists, but rather yearned for 'domesticity and femininity' during the war and happily returned to them after it (Sandra M. Gilbert and Susan Gubar, *No Man's Land: The Place of the Woman Writer in the Twentieth Century, ii: Sexchanges* (New Haven, CT, 1989), 289; Joanna Bourke, *Dismembering the Male: Men's Bodies, Britain and the Great War* (London, 1996), 23. For further claims that the Great War exacerbated the sex war, see Susan Kingsley Kent, *Making Peace: The Reconstruction of Gender in Interwar Britain* (Princeton, NJ, 1993), chs. 1–5; and, for Germany, Klaus Theweleit, *Male Fantasies*, ii vols. (Minneapolis, MN, 1987)).

151 Helena Swanwick (1916) cited in Marwick, 119; Bertrand Russell (1917) cited in Fletcher, 232. Bertrand Russell was later to revise his opinion of women's sexual experimentation during the war, crediting it with having toppled the 'force of custom and mental inertia' sustaining traditional morality (Bertrand Russell, *Marriage and Morals* (London, 1929), 69).

152 British Society for the Study of Sex Psychology, *Policy and Principles and General Aims* (London, 1914), 14. For the BSSSP, see Lesley A. Hall, '"Disinterested Enthusiasm for Sexual Misconduct": The British Society for the Study of Sex Psychology, 1913–47', *Journal of Contemporary History* 30, 4 (1995), 665–687. Membership of the BSSSP was not confined to mutualists, if the presence of Cicely Hamilton is any indication.

153 *Idem*, 'Uniting Science and Sensibility: Marie Stopes and the Narratives of Marriage in the 1920s', *Rediscovering Forgotten Radicals: British Women Writers, 1889–1939*, ed. Angela Ingram and Daphne Patai (Chapel Hill, NC, 1993), 130; Gollancz, 33.

154 Wells, 184.

155 Vera Brittain (1915) in *idem, Testament of Youth* (Harmondsworth, 1989), 213.

Chapter 2 – The Great Experiment

1 A.T. Schofield, *The Mind of a Woman* (London, 1919), 91; Naomi Mitchison, *You May Well Ask: A Memoir* (London, 1979), 277.

2 Contributions by Philip Snowden, Nancy Astor and Stanley Baldwin to the debate on the second reading of the Representation of the People (Equal Franchise) Bill, *Parliamentary Debates: House of Commons* (29 March 1928), vol. 15, cols. 1376, 1452, 1475, 1476–1477. For the passage of the 1928 Act, see Cheryl Law, *Suffrage and Power: The Women's Movement, 1918–28* (London, 1997); Martin Pugh, *Women and the Women's Movement in Britain, 1914–59* (London, 1993), chs. 2–6; and Harold L. Smith, *The British Women's Suffrage Campaign, 1866–1928* (London, 1998), ch. 6. Smith argues that there was in fact much less enthusiasm for full female suffrage than the parliamentary debate suggested, since the heavyweights opposed to an equal franchise had already been silenced within Cabinet. Even so, Tory diehards recognized that if they did not pass the reform, Labour was sure to do so when it next came to power, meaning that their opposition was effectively redundant.

3 Stanley Baldwin, *Parliamentary Debates: House of Commons* (29 March 1928), vol. 15, col. 1475; Board of Education Consultative Committee, *Differentiation of the Curriculum for Boys and Girls Respectively in Secondary Schools* (London, 1923).

4 Sylvia Anthony, *Women's Place in Industry and Home* (London, 1932), 1; Cynthia Russett, *Sexual Science: The Victorian Construction of Womanhood* (Cambridge, MA, 1989), 186, 169, 46.

5 A.G. Pite, *Christian Marriage and Modern Practice* (London, 1931), 5; Conference on Christian Politics, Economics and Citizenship, 'The Relation of the Sexes', *COPEC Commission Report* 4 (London, 1924), 19. For the confused nature of sexual politics in

this period, see Lesley A. Hall, 'Impotent Ghosts from No Man's Land, Flappers' Boyfriends or Crypto-Patriarchs?: Men, Sex and Social Change in 1920s Britain', *Social History* 21, 1 (1996), 54–70.

6   Alison Neilans, 'Changes in Sex Morality', *Our Freedom and Its Results*, ed. Ray Strachey (London, 1936), 221.

7   For the decline in the rhetoric of sex antagonism, see Denise Riley, *Am I That Name?* (Basingstoke, 1988), 59; and Susan Kingsley Kent, *Making Peace: The Reconstruction of Gender in Interwar Britain* (Princeton, NJ, 1993), 136.

8   The stemming of male emigration after 1914 more than offset soldiers' deaths in the Great War, resulting in a closer balance between the sexes after the war than before it. However, for concerns over the dearth of eligible bachelors, see A. Maude Royden, *Sex and Commonsense* (London, 1921), ch. 1; and Billie Melman, *Women and the Popular Imagination in the Twenties: Flappers and Nymphs* (Basingstoke, 1988), 17–20.

9   H.G. Wells, *Experiment in Autobiography* (New York, 1934), 409. Though Wells had been fearful in 1924 that sex antagonism would become of 'increasing importance in our world', he was content a decade later that it had 'slowly...died down' (H.G. Wells, *A Year of Prophesying* (London, 1924), 256; *idem, Experiment in Autobiography*, 409).

10   Elsie M. Lang, *British Women in the Twentieth Century* (London, 1929), 14; Willa Muir, *Women: An Inquiry* (London, 1925), 36.

11   Wells, *Experiment in Autobiography*, 409.

12   Besides the supporters listed above, Havelock Ellis, Winifred Holtby, Laurence Housman and Alec Craig pledged their support for the FPSI's sexual programme, Dora Russell and Stella Browne wrote for its journal *Plan* and its Man-Woman Relationship Group invited virtually every prominent mutualist thinker to lecture to them after World War Two.

13   J.B. Coates, *Educational Policy of the Federation of Progressive Societies and Individuals* (London, *c.* 1930s), 1; C.E.M. Joad, 'The FPSI', *Manifesto: The Book of the Federation of Progressive Societies and Individuals*, ed. C.E.M. Joad (London, 1934), 32; Eden Paul, *Chronos: The Future of the Family* (London, 1930), 37. For the FPSI, which was renamed the Progressive League in 1940, see also J.H. Badley *et al.*, *Experiments in Sex Education* (London, 1935); and *Plan*, 1934–79.

14   Bronislaw Malinowski (1931) in Robert Briffault and Bronislaw Malinowski, *Marriage: Past and Present* (Boston, 1956), 27; Edward Westermarck, *The Future of Marriage in Western Civilisation* (London, 1936), 81.

15   J.J. Findlay, *The Foundations of Education: A Survey of Principles and Projects, ii: The Practice of Education* (London, 1930), 137; Frank E. Moreton, 'Attitudes of Teachers and Scholars towards Coeducation', *British Journal of Educational Psychology* 16, 2 (1946), 82–95. Some British authorities still supported G. Stanley Hall's arguments for segregation during adolescence, for which see chapter three.

16   John Macmurray, *Freedom in the Modern World* [rev. edn] (London, 1935), 140; Ian Suttie, *The Origins of Love and Hate* (London, 1935), 80, 81, 95. Mutuality's relationship to psychoanalysis, to which we shall return in chapter four, was a complex affair. Suttie was one of a number of mutualists severely critical of Freud, Ellis thinking him an 'amateur' and Stopes being repelled by his 'aberrant mind'. Such thinkers as A.S. Neill, however, found affinities between the two doctrines over the ill-effects of single-sex environments and men's tendency to separate sex from love, and incorporated psychoanalytic teachings into the jumble of ideas collectively labelled the 'New Psychology'. British psychoanalysts were somewhat aloof and in any case too preoccupied with matters of early childhood to engage fully with mutuality between the wars, though psychiatrist and founder of the Tavistock Clinic J.R. Rees put in a good word for one best-selling Christian mutualist sex manual. Their critique of companionate marital problems did not appear until after the Second World War (Suttie, ch. 13; Havelock Ellis, *Sex and Marriage: Eros in Contemporary Life* (London, 1951), 205; Stopes cited in Christina Hardyment, *Dream Babies: Child Care from Locke to Spock* (London, 1983), 166; J.R. Rees in foreword to Leslie D. Weatherhead, *The Mastery of Sex through Psychology and Religion* (London, 1931), xii. For the diffusion of Freudian ideas, see Deam Rapp, 'The Early Discovery of Freud by the British General Public, 1912–19', *Social History of Medicine* 3, 2 (1990), 217–243. For British psychoanalytic theory on adult personal relationships in this period, see J.C. Flügel, 'Psychological Aspects of Marriage and the Family', *Psychology and Modern Problems*,

ed. Morris Ginsburg *et al.* (London, 1935); and M. Esther Harding, *The Way of all Women: A Psychological Interpretation* (London, 1933)).

17 'Report on Marriage and Sex', *Lambeth Conference, 1930* (London, 1930), 85, 89–90. Another important Christian endorsement of mutuality came from the Conference on Christian Politics, Economics and Citizenship of 1924, for which see *COPEC Commission Reports* 2–4 (London, 1924); *The Proceedings of COPEC* (London, 1924); Edward Shillito, *Christian Citizenship: The Story and Meaning of COPEC* (London, 1924); and E.R. Norman, *Church and Society in England, 1770–1970: A Historical Study* (Oxford, 1976), ch. 7.

18 For interwar Christian perspectives on personal relationships, see Jane Lewis, *The End of Marriage?: Individualism and Intimate Relations* (Cheltenham, 2001), 82–85.

19 Havelock Ellis, *Studies in the Psychology of Sex*, i (New York, 1942), 192.

20 Dora Russell, *Hypatia: Woman and Knowledge* (London, 1925), 14; Bertrand Russell, *Marriage and Morals* (London, 1929), 44.

21 Dora Russell, *The Right to be Happy* (London, 1927), 128, 132.

22 Solomon Herbert, *Fundamentals in Sexual Ethics* (London, 1920), 130; Bertrand Russell, *Principles of Social Reconstruction* (London, 1927), 191.

23 Kenneth Ingram, *Christianity and Sexual Morality: A Modernist View* (London, 1944), 19.

24 *Idem, The Unreasonableness of Anti-Christianity* (London, 1928); Edward F. Griffith, *Sex and Citizenship* (London, 1941), 34.

25 Claud Mullins, *Marriage, Children and God* (London, 1933), 55; John Middleton Murry, *Adam and Eve: An Essay Towards a New and Better Society* (London, 1944), 90; Weatherhead, xxv.

26 George Ryley Scott, *Scott's Encyclopaedia of Sex* (London, 1939), 129; Havelock Ellis, *Marriage Today and Tomorrow* (San Francisco, 1929), 2.

27 John Macmurray, *Reason and Emotion* (London, 1935), 102; Norman Haire, *Hymen: The Future of Marriage* (London, 1928), 15, 6. A Quaker, Macmurray was a rare example of a religious sex radical.

28 COPEC, 'The Relation of the Sexes', 12, 13, 24, 14.

29 Herbert, 289; A. Herbert Gray, *The Mysteries, Beauties and Perplexities of Sex* (London, 1936), 4. For the sceptical attitude of some sex radicals towards innate sex differences, see Dora Russell, *Hypatia*, 53; and *idem, The Right to be Happy*, 144. Conversely, for mutualist discomfort over masculinized women, see Austin Harrison, *Pandora's Hope: A Study of Woman* (London, 1925), 209; and Schofield, 90–96. These writers' fears about Amazons were less pronounced than those exhibited in such anti-feminist works as Alfred Summers, *What's Wrong with England* (London, 1928), ch. 7; Mary Moore, *The Defeat of Woman* (London, 1935), 7–8; and Meyrick Booth, *Woman and Society* (London, 1929), ch. 2. For anti-feminists on the degeneration of manhood, a subject about which mutualists had little to say, see D.H. Lawrence, *Assorted Articles* (London, 1930), 39, 62–65, 79–81; *idem, Selected Essays* (Harmondsworth, 1950), 33–34; and Anthony M. Ludovici, *Man: An Indictment* (London, 1927), chs. 6–7.

30 Paul B. Bull, *A Man's Guide to Courtship and Marriage* (London, 1932), viii; Douglas White, *Modern Light on Sex and Marriage* (London, 1932), 120.

31 A.S. Neill, *Hearts Not Heads in the School* (London, 1945), 133.

32 W.B. Curry, *The School and a Changing Civilisation* (London, 1934), 65; Dora Russell, 'Beacon Hill', *The Modern Schools Handbook*, ed. Trevor Blewitt (London, 1934), 39; Neill, 85.

33 *Idem* in preface to Ethel Mannin, *Commonsense and the Adolescent* [rev. edn] (London, 1945), 8; Kenneth Barnes and Frances Barnes, *Sex, Friendship and Marriage* (London, 1938); Weatherhead, 37. The misgivings of Christian mutualists over radical plans for coeducation were well illustrated in COPEC's report on education. Even though it was written by a former headmaster of Clifton and Rugby, the report condemned 'monastic' schooling and hoped that coeducation would introduce a familial atmosphere into school life. However, it withheld its unreserved support for mixed schools, arguing that they were unsuitable for those adolescents experiencing a sudden 'awakening to sex life' and, by way of compromise, suggesting that they be introduced on an experimental basis until their full effects were known (Conference on Christian Politics, Economics and Citizenship, 'Education', *COPEC Commission Report* 2 (London, 1924), 58, 61. For Christian mutualist doubts about coeducation, see also Marie Carmichael Stopes, *Sex and the Young* (London, 1926), ch. 11).

34   COPEC, 'The Relation of the Sexes', 21, 215, 20.

35   Bertrand Russell, *Principles of Social Reconstruction*, 190; Ben B. Lindsey and Evans Wainwright, *The Companionate Marriage* (New York, 1928); Havelock Ellis, *More Essays of Love and Virtue* (London, 1931), 42; Bertrand Russell, *Marriage and Morals*, 129–133; Macmurray, *Reason and Emotion*, 109; Irene Clephane, *Towards Sex Freedom* (London, 1935), 221; Ethel Mannin, *Commonsense and Morality* (London, 1942), 62; Vera Brittain, *Halcyon: The Future of Monogamy* (London, 1929); J.D. Unwin, *Hopousia: The Sexual and Economic Foundations of a New Society* (London, 1940), 17.

36   Bertrand Russell (1929) in *Is Modern Marriage A Failure?: A Debate*, ed. Margaret Moran (North Walsham, 1983), 14; Dora Russell, *The Right to be Happy*, 261.

37   G.E. Newsom, *The New Morality* (London, 1932), 293, 294.

38   Robert V. Storer, *Adolescence and Marriage* (London, 1934), 208; W.F. Lofthouse, *The Family and the State* (London, 1944), 122. For conflicting Christian mutualist views on divorce, see A. Herbert Gray, *Men, Women and God: A Discussion of Sex Questions from the Christian Point of View* [rev. edn] (London, 1945), 142; and COPEC, 'The Relation of the Sexes', 173.

39   Royden, *Sex and Commonsense*, 35. As Edward Bristow has noted, the purity movement jettisoned much of its old baggage after the First World War. This involved aligning itself with the new psychology, repudiating the 'rotten foundation' of the 'old purity literature', issuing guidance on how to achieve simultaneous orgasms and, of course, ditching the anti-male rhetoric of the prewar radical feminist purity crusade (Edward J. Bristow, *Vice and Vigilance: Purity Movements in Britain since 1700* (Dublin, 1977), 146–147).

40   Weatherhead, 211, xviii, 213. For revised Christian teachings on sexuality, see also T.W. Pym, *The Place of Sex in Life* [rev. edn] (London, 1931).

41   Herbert, 202, 214.

42   Walter M. Gallichan (aka Geoffrey Mortimer), *Letters to a Young Man on Love and Health* (London, 1919), 11; Bertrand Russell, *Marriage and Morals*, 99.

43   COPEC, 'The Relation of the Sexes', 214; Royden, *Sex and Commonsense*, 50–51. Awkwardly, however, Christian mutualists tended to believe that men were naturally more polygamous than women, making the higher sexual standard harder for them to attain.

44   COPEC, 'The Relation of the Sexes', 95.

45   Janet Chance, *The Cost of English Morals* (London, 1931), 18; Bertrand Russell, *Marriage and Morals*, 69.

46   Ibid., 72; William A. Brend, *Sacrifice to Attis: A Study of Sex and Civilisation* (London, 1936), 43.

47   Clephane, 224.

48   Michael Fielding, *Parenthood – Design or Accident?: A Manual of Birth Control* (London, 1928), 38, 39, 31. For the birth control question in this period, see Richard Allen Soloway, *Birth Control and the Population Question in England, 1877–1930* (Chapel Hill, NC, 1982).

49   Lambeth Conference proceedings (1930) cited in Weatherhead, 100; Murry, 131.

50   Ellis, *Sex and Marriage*, 56; Clephane, 220. Not all mutualists before the Great War had dealt with contraception, Edward Carpenter for one circumventing the issue by extolling a non-ejaculatory method of love-making known as *karezza*; see Jeffrey Weeks, *Coming Out: Homosexual Politics from the Nineteenth Century to the Present* [rev. edn] (London, 1990), 76.

51   Newsom, 23; Bull, 20.

52   Edward Charles (aka Charles Edward Hempstead), *An Introduction to the Study of the Psychology and Physiology and Biochemistry of the Sexual Impulse among Adults in Mental and Bodily Health* (London, 1935), 240. Lesley Hall has also noted the manner in which the purity and sex reform movements did not represent 'two embattled camps' in the interwar period, but rather formed two forces within a 'spectrum of opposition to conventional assumptions of the day about sexual relations and the role of women' (Lesley A. Hall, 'Suffrage, Sex and Science', *The Women's Suffrage Movement: New Feminist Perspectives*, ed. Maroula Joannou and June Purvis (Manchester, 1998), 198).

53   Les Garner, *Stepping Stones to Women's Liberty: Feminist Ideas in the Women's Suffrage Movement, 1900–18* (London, 1984), 52. For the dilemmas faced by interwar feminism,

see in particular Law; Pugh, *Women and the Women's Movement in Britain*; Susan Pedersen, *Family, Dependence and the Origins of the Welfare State: Britain and France, 1914–45* (Cambridge, 1993); Shirley M. Eoff, *Viscountess Rhondda: Equalitarian Feminist* (Columbus, OH, 1991); Harold L. Smith (ed.), *British Feminism in the Twentieth Century* (Aldershot, 1990); Johanna Alberti, *Beyond Suffrage: Feminists in War and Peace, 1914–28* (Basingstoke, 1989); Barbara Caine, *English Feminism, 1780–1980* (Oxford, 1997), ch. 5; Caitriona Beaumont, 'The Women's Movement, Politics and Citizenship, 1918–1950s', *Women in Twentieth-Century Britain*, ed. Ina Zweiniger-Bargielowska (Harlow, 2001); Jane Lewis, 'In Search of a Real Equality: Women between the Wars', *Class, Culture and Social Change: A New View of the 1930s*, ed. Frank Gloversmith (Brighton, 1980); and Brian Harrison, *Prudent Revolutionaries: Portraits of British Feminism between the Wars* (Oxford, 1987).

54 Martin Pugh, *The Pankhursts* (London, 2001), 393; Lady Rhondda, *This Was My World* (London, 1933), 299.

55 Kent, *Making Peace*; Sheila Jeffreys, *The Spinster and Her Enemies: Feminism and Sexuality, 1880–1930* (Melbourne, 1997), ch. 10.

56 Walter M. Gallichan (aka Geoffrey Mortimer), *Sexual Apathy and Coldness in Women* (London, 1927), 12–13. For the equation of women's emancipation with sexual liberation, see also Clephane; Alec Craig, *Sex and Revolution* (London, 1934), 13; Hugh Northcote, *The Social Value of the Study of Sex Psychology* (London, 1920), 4; Havelock Ellis, *The Erotic Rights of Woman and the Objects of Marriage* (London, 1918); Dora Russell, *Hypatia*, 32; Scott, *Scott's Encyclopaedia of Sex*, 129–130; G. Pitt-Rivers, 'Sex-Phobia and Marriage', *World League for Sexual Reform: Proceedings of the Third Congress*, ed. Norman Haire (London, 1930), 20; and Herbert, 2–4.

57 Dora Russell, *Hypatia*, 26; Bertrand Russell, *Marriage and Morals*, 69.

58 Doris Langley Moore, *The Vulgar Heart: An Enquiry into the Sentimental Tendencies of Public Opinion* (London, 1945), 167; Dorothy Ellen Abb, *What Fools We Women Be!* (London, 1937), 4, 1.

59 Irene Clyde (aka Thomas Baty), *Eve's Sour Apples* (London, 1934), 45; Abb, 108. For Baty, see Daphne Patai and Angela Ingram, 'Fantasy and Identity: The Double Life of a Victorian Sexual Radical', *Rediscovering Forgotten Radicals: British Women Writers, 1889–1939*, ed. Angela Ingram and Daphne Patai (Chapel Hill, NC, 1993); and for his refutation of sex differences, see Thomas Baty, *Alone in Japan* (Tokyo, 1959), 189–191; and Alison Oram, '"Sex is an Accident": Feminism, Science and the Radical Sexual Theory of Urania, 1915–40', *Sexology in Culture: Labelling Bodies and Desires*, ed. Lucy Bland and Laura Doan (Cambridge, 1998), 222.

60 Vera Brittain, 'What Talkers Men Are' (1929), *Testament of a Generation: The Journalism of Vera Brittain and Winifred Holtby*, ed. Paul Berry and Alan Bishop (London, 1985), 115; Winifred Holtby, 'The Man Colleague' (1929), *Testament of a Generation*, 63.

61 Maude Royden, 'Doubts and Difficulties', *Advances in Coeducation*, ed. Alice Woods (London, 1919), 1, 5.

62 Clyde, 11; Baty, 190–191; Clyde, 11.

63 Ibid., 14, 13.

64 Doris Langley Moore, 171, 169.

65 Abb, 263.

66 Kent, *Making Peace*, 136.

67 Clyde, 71–76; Abb, 267, 20.

68 For Ludovici, see R.B. Kerr, *Our Prophets* (Croydon, 1932), ch. 6; and Dan Stone, 'The Extremes of Englishness: The "Exceptional" Ideology of Anthony Mario Ludovici', *Journal of Political Ideologies* 4, 2 (1999), 191–218. For a droll overview of interwar anti-feminist writing, see Virginia Woolf, *A Room of One's Own* (1929), *A Room of One's Own and Three Guineas* (London, 1984), ch. 2.

69 Arabella Kenealey, *Feminism and Sex-Extinction* (London, 1920), vii; Ludovici, *Man: An Indictment*, 42, 44.

70 Idem, *Woman: A Vindication* (London, 1923), vii; C.K. Munro, *The True Woman: A Handbook for Husbands and Others* (London, 1932), 28. The necessity of maintaining sexual differentiation explained anti-feminists' universal hostility to female contraception in that it made women's sexuality more closely approximate men's and thereby undercut their insistence upon separate spheres and a double sexual standard

based upon women's maternal function. See Anthony M. Ludovici, *The Night-Hoers: The Case Against Birth Control and an Alternative* (London, 1928); and A.H. Henderson-Livesey, *Sex and Public Life* (London, 1926).

71 Anthony M. Ludovici, *Lysistrata: Woman's Future and Future Woman* (London, 1924), 108.

72 Theodore Besterman, *Men Against Women: A Study of Sexual Relations* (London, 1934), 175.

73 Wyndham Lewis, *Rude Assignment* (London, 1950), 176; Ludovici, *Woman: A Vindication*, 278.

74 Kenealey, *Feminism and Sex-Extinction*, 249; Reginald de Heaton, *What Every Man Should Know* (London, 1938), 21.

75 Kenealey, *Feminism and Sex-Extinction*, 269, 249.

76 D.H. Lawrence cited in Charlotte Cowdroy, *Wasted Womanhood* (London, 1933), 119. For anti-feminist opposition to coeducation, see also Cowdroy, 118–120; de Heaton, 26; and Newcastle-upon-Tyne Association of Schoolmasters, *Coeducation or Separation?* (Newcastle, 1924). See Meyrick Booth, *Youth and Sex: A Psychological Study* (London, 1932), ch. 11, for a rare instance of an anti-feminist willing to accept a degree of mixing in schools.

77 Munro, 212.

78 Lawrence, *Assorted Articles*, 69; Booth, *Woman and Society*, 68.

79 Boswell King, *Sex and Human Nature: Studies* (London, 1933), 234; 'Baital' (aka G.W. Harris?), *Man the Mutt* (Aylesbury, 1934), 64.

80 Ludovici, *Woman: A Vindication*, 179; Munro, 219.

81 Ludovici, *Woman: A Vindication*, 169, 212; Grace Ellison, *The Disadvantages of Being a Woman* (London, 1922), 78. Like Kenealey, Ellison appears to have been an apostate feminist. See *idem*, *An Englishwoman in a Turkish Harem* (London, 1915); and Arabella Kenealey, 'The Dignity of Love' (1896), *The Late Victorian Marriage Question, ii: The New Woman and Female Independence*, ed. Ann Heilmann (London, 1998).

82 Ludovici, *Woman: A Vindication*, 147, 83.

83 Munro, 183; Ludovici, *Woman: A Vindication*, 147.

84 W.R. Inge, *Christian Ethics and Modern Problems* (London, 1930), 356; Ludovici, *Lysistrata*, 102. Though Lawrence was identified to be a force – perhaps *the* force – behind sex reform in this period, his views on sexuality differed from those of mutualist sex radicals in important respects. What he shared with mutualists (as a result of an early infatuation with the ideas of Edward Carpenter) was a belief in the complementarity of men's and women's sexuality: what he called the 'connection, almost unification, of the genitals' occurring between the 'two complementary parts' of the male and the female. He differed in his conviction that intercourse was practically the sole positive point of contact between the two. Whereas mutualists saw sex as the culmination of a great friendship formed through mixing and marriage, Lawrence insisted that the 'sex-activity is, and always was and will be, in some way hostile to the mental, *personal* relationships between man and woman.' And even when, as in the posthumous pamphlet *We Need One Other* (1933), he appealed for deeper affectional ties between the sexes, he nonetheless expected woman to display an 'instinctive … submission' to man. As Sheila Macleod observes, the prospect of women demanding an intimate and equal relationship with men threatened the proud if fragile model of masculinity to which he clung. The efforts by sex radicals to claim him as one of their own, most conspicuously in the postwar *Lady Chatterley* trial, involved a good deal of wishful thinking on their part (D.H. Lawrence, 'Study of Thomas Hardy' (1914), *Study of Thomas Hardy and Other Essays* (Cambridge, 1985), 127; *idem*, 'A Propos of *Lady Chatterley*', cited in Sheila Macleod, *Lawrence's Men and Women* (London, 1987), 202; D.H. Lawrence, *We Need One Another* (New York, 1933), 45; Macleod, 202. For Carpenter's influence on Lawrence, see Emile Delevenay, *D.H. Lawrence and Edward Carpenter: A Study in Edwardian Transition* (London, 1971). For the (possibly deliberate) misinterpretation of Lawrence in the *Chatterley* trial, see John Sutherland, *Offensive Literature: Decensorship in Britain, 1960–82* (London, 1982), 26).

85 Kenealey, *Feminism and Sex-Extinction*, 166.

86 Ludovici, *Woman: A Vindication*, 179; King, 216; Ludovici, *Woman: A Vindication*, 172. For further arguments in favour of the double standard, see James James (aka Arthur Henry Adams), *Guide Book to Women* (London, 1921), 131–132.

87   Kenealey, *Feminism and Sex-Extinction*, 166; Anthony M. Ludovici, *Enemies of Women: The Origins of Anglo-Saxon Feminism* (London, 1948), 201.

88   Contributions by Sir Charles Oman, William Joynson-Hicks and Stanley Baldwin to the debate on the second reading of the Representation of the People (Equal Franchise) Bill, *Parliamentary Debates: House of Commons* (29 March 1928), vol. 15, cols. 1434, 1361, 1474. For the controversy over enfranchising young women, see Adrian Bingham, '"Stop The Flapper Vote Folly": Lord Rothermere, the *Daily Mail*, and the Equalisation of the Franchise, 1927–28', *Twentieth-Century British History* 13, 1 (2002), 17–37; and Melman, ch. 1.

89   Ray Strachey, *The Cause: A Short History of the Women's Movement in Great Britain* (London, 1978), 385. For the National Association of Schoolmasters, see Alison Oram, 'Embittered, Sexless or Homosexual: Attacks on Spinster Teachers, 1918–39', *Not A Passing Phase: Reclaiming Lesbians in History, 1840–1985*, ed. Lesbian History Group (London, 1989); and Joanna Bourke, *Dismembering the Male: Men's Bodies, Britain and the Great War* (London, 1996), 193–198. For *Men Only*, see Jill Greenfield, Sean O'Connell and Chris Reid, 'Fashioning Masculinity: *Men Only*, Consumption and the Development of Marketing in Interwar Britain', *Twentieth-Century British History* 10, 4 (1999), 457–476.

90   Ludovici, *Woman: A Vindication*, 364.

91   'Anonymous' (aka Beckles Wilson), *England, by an Overseas Englishman* (London, 1922), ch. 13; Anthony Ludovici cited in Kerr, 97; Ludovici, *Enemies of Women*, 69; 'Baital', 77, 21, 77.

92   J. Linden Spencer, *What Men Really Want* (London, 1924), 7; Ludovici, *Lysistrata*.

93   *Idem, The Future of Woman* (London, 1936), 150. Historians who identify an 'accentuation of anti-feminist feeling' between the wars base their claims less upon the power of self-confessed chauvinists than the notion that mutualists themselves formed an anti-feminist fifth column. The most influential formulation of this argument comes from Susan Kingsley Kent, who characterizes sex reformers' advocacy of a 'domestic harmony' based on complementarity as serving to justify a 'return to "traditional" sex roles [and] separate spheres' after the destabilizing effects of World War One. The difficulty with Kent's thesis lies not in her identification of 'sexual peace' as a *leitmotif* of interwar thinking – this chapter has provided evidence of that – but whether this constituted any sort of 'backlash'. First of all, Kent's overstatement of the transgressive and antagonistic motives of pre-1914 feminists naturally, if misleadingly, makes their successors seem conservative by comparison. Given that many prewar feminists neither denied sex differences nor incited sex antagonism (see chapter one), the 'difference' feminism advanced by interwar mutualists and 'new' feminists cannot be considered particularly novel or, by extension, a reaction to wartime trauma (Olive Banks, *The Politics of British Feminism, 1918–70* (Aldershot, 1993), 73; Susan Kingsley Kent, 'Gender Reconstruction after the First World War', *British Feminism in the Twentieth Century*, 73; *idem, Gender and Power in Britain, 1640–1990* (London, 1999), 295, 299. For claims of an anti-feminist backlash between the wars, see also Pugh, *Women and the Women's Movement in Britain*, ch. 4; Deirdre Beddoe, *Back to Home and Duty: Women between the Wars, 1918–39* (London, 1989), 3–4; Martha Vicinus, *Independent Women: Work and Community for Single Women, 1850–1920* (Chicago, 1985), 281; and Sheila Jeffreys, 'Sex Reform and Anti-Feminism in the 1920s', *The Sexual Dynamics of History: Men's Power, Women's Resistance*, ed. London Feminist History Group (London, 1983)).

It is also the case that the 'conservative and reactionary' impulses Kent discerns in ostensibly progressive thinking were not regarded as such either by their proponents or their opponents. It was avowed anti-feminists who defended all that was 'respectable and Victorian' and despised mutualists for their fashionability. Mutualists for their part savaged anti-feminists and rubbished the 'Victorian Marriage', the 'Victorian attitude to sex' and what they understood by the term 'separate spheres'. Elements of her characterization of Havelock Ellis as an anti-feminist stem from misapprehensions. Neither he nor, for that matter, 'all' sexologists of the period espoused the pro-natalist view that procreation was the 'chief and central aim' of intercourse, for Ellis categorically decried such 'animal' motives and expressed his 'contempt' for women who viewed sex solely in these terms (Kent, *Making Peace*, 140; Booth, *Youth and Sex*, 17; Marie C. Stopes, *Marriage in My Time* (London, 1935), ch. 4; Kenneth Ingram, *The*

Modern Attitude to the Sex Problem (London, 1930), 27; *idem, Sex Morality Tomorrow* (London, 1940), 157; Kent, *Gender and Power*, 295; Havelock Ellis, 'Love as an Art', *The Book of Marriage*, ed. Hermann Keyserling (New York, 1926), 374, 382. For the foremost advocate of 'new' feminism, whose critical view of men in families contradicts the idea that 'difference' feminism was necessarily conciliatory in tone, see Susan Pedersen, 'Eleanor Rathbone: The Victorian Family under the Daughter's Eye', *After the Victorians: Private Conscience and Public Duty in Modern Britain,* ed. Susan Pedersen and Peter Mandler (London, 1994)).

Kent's difficulties in finding British reactionaries of import may explain her unusual reliance on foreign authorities in support of her central contention that sexologists 'sought to resolve the anxieties and political turmoil caused by the Great War by establishing harmonious marital relationships'. To cite the Austrian Sigmund Freud, the German Magnus Hirschfeld, the Dutchman Theodore van de Velde, the Norwegian K.A. Weith Knudsen and the mysterious H.C. Fischer and E.X. Dubois (who, we may surmise from their names, were probably not 'British sexologists') is to suggest that Britain participated in a pan-European backlash. Yet, compared to any other major European country, interwar Britain was remarkable for escaping the worst of anti-feminism. British marriage reformers sought to reconcile female emancipation to family responsibilities in contrast to the inability of French intellectuals to envisage any common ground between the traditional mother and the irresponsible 'new woman'. Though sexology in interwar Britain outgrew its utopian socialist origins after 1918, its equivalent in Weimar Germany conspicuously failed to do the same. And, besides being insignificant, British fascism was inconsistent in its anti-feminism compared to its German and Italian counterparts, which reduced the status of women to that of brood mares. For all these reasons, interwar mutuality and anti-feminism represented schools of thought both distinct from and antagonistic to each other, and were conceived of as such at the time (Kent, *Making Peace*, 107, 105–106. For the complex attitudes of British fascists towards feminism, see Oswald Mosley, *The Greater Britain* (London, 1932), 38–42; and Julie Gottlieb, 'Suffragette Experience Through the Filter of Fascism', *A Suffrage Reader: Charting Directions in British Suffrage History*, ed. Claire Eustance, Joan Ryan and Laura Ugolini (London, 2000). For France, see Mary Louise Roberts, *Civilization without Sexes: Reconstructing Gender in Postwar France, 1917–27* (Chicago, 1994). For Germany, see Atina Grossmann, *Reforming Sex: The German Movement for Birth Control and Abortion Reform, 1920–50* (New York, 1995); and Claudia Koonz, *Mothers in the Fatherland* (New York, 1987). For Italy, see Victoria de Grazia, *How Fascism Ruled Women* (Berkeley, CA, 1992)).

94 Ethel Mannin, *Young in the Twenties: A Chapter of Autobiography* (London, 1971), 64.
95 Ross McKibbin, *Classes and Cultures: England, 1918–51* (Oxford, 1998), 88. For all-female organizations, see Jill Julius Matthews, '"They Had Such a Lot of Fun": The Women's League of Health and Beauty between the Wars', *History Workshop Journal* 30 (1990), 22–55; Frank Prochaska, 'A Mother's Country: Mothers' Meetings and Family Welfare in Britain, 1850–1950', *History* 74, 242 (1989), 379–399; and Maggie Andrews, *The Acceptable Face of Feminism: The Women's Institute as a Social Movement* (London, 1997). The ancient universities were scarcely more mixed than the schools. Oxford University conceded university membership to women in the 1920s but limited their numbers to one fifth of the undergraduate body, while the 1922 Asquith Commission on Cambridge University recommended that it remain 'a men's university, though of a mixed type'. It shamefully denied full degrees to women until after the Second World War.
96 Eustace Chesser, *Love Without Fear* (London, 1940), 13; Norman Haire in preface to C.B.S. Evans, *Man and Woman in Marriage* (London, 1932), 8. In his iconoclastic article 'Victorian Britain, 1837–1963', Simon Szreter argues that sex reformers had every reason to feel marginalized due to the persistence of nineteenth-century sexual attitudes and practices well beyond the Second World War. This claim for the primacy of continuity over change is as speculative as it is startling. The meticulous number-crunching of census data supporting his contention that abstinence formed the principal means of birth control in the period up to 1911 contrasts sharply with the anecdotal evidence advanced for its continued primacy thereafter and is questioned by Kate Fisher's interviews with working-class couples. The generalization that 'sex remained a classic taboo' throughout British society until the 1950s and 1960s, while applying to

such specific cases as the lower working-class families examined in chapter four, nonetheless jars with the fact that under 1 per cent of respondents refused to participate in the sex survey conducted by Mass-Observation in 1949. Nor was it the case that censorship seriously inhibited the publication of information (as opposed to titillation) concerning heterosexual intercourse during this period. His assessment of the influence of sex writers is contradictory, portraying them on the one hand as 'mavericks' and on the other as traditionalists 'retaining more than a vestige of Victorian concern for public proprieties and respectability.' Yet, as Lesley Hall points out, it was the very manner in which Marie Stopes 'blended old and new thinking' that appealed to so many of her contemporaries. While these writers were evidently not 'typical representatives of their age', the wide dissemination of their works represented a decisive 'change in public codes' over a generation before Szreter allows (Simon Szreter, 'Victorian Britain, 1837–1963: Towards a Social History of Sexuality', *Journal of Victorian Culture* 1, 1 (1996), 136–149; *idem, Fertility, Class and Gender in Britain, 1860–1940* (Cambridge, 1996), esp. ch. 10; Kate Fisher, 'An Oral History of Birth Control Practice, *c.* 1925–50: A Study of Oxford and South Wales' (University of Oxford DPhil thesis, 1997), 100–108; Szreter, 'Victorian Britain', 142; Liz Stanley, *Sex Surveyed, 1949–94* (London, 1995), 71; Szreter, 'Victorian Britain', 144, 145; Lesley A. Hall, 'Uniting Science and Sensibility: Marie Stopes and the Narratives of Marriage in the 1920s', *Rediscovering Forgotten Radicals*, 123; Szreter, 'Victorian Britain', 145, 143. For evidence on the relative use of abstinence and contraception in the interwar period, see Claire Davey, 'Birth Control in Britain during the Interwar Years: Evidence from the Stopes Correspondence', *Journal of Family History* 13, 3 (1988), 329–345; and Angus McLaren, *Twentieth-Century Sexuality* (Oxford, 1999), 83)).

97   J.F. Worsley-Boden, *Mischief of the Marriage Law: An Essay in Reform* (London, 1932), 338.

98   Dora Russell, *The Right to be Happy*, 175; *idem, The Tamarisk Tree, i: My Quest for Liberty and Love* (London, 1975), 156–157.

99   Cicely Hamilton, *The Englishwoman* (London, 1940); Maude Royden, *Women's Partnership in the New World* (London, 1941), 49. For Nazi chauvinism, see J.B. Priestley, *Postscripts* (London, 1940), 77; David R. Mace, *Marriage Crisis* (London, 1948), 26; and Douglas Griffiths in *The Times*, 21 April 1947.

100   Geoffrey Thomas, *Women at Work* (London, 1944), 28. For wartime female employment, see in particular Penny Summerfield, *Women Workers in the Second World War: Patriarchy and Production in Conflict* (London, 1984); and Harold L. Smith, 'The Effect of the War on the Status of Women', *War and Social Change: British Society in the Second World War*, ed. Harold L. Smith (Manchester, 1986).

101   A.S. Neill in preface to Mannin, *Commonsense and Morality*, 4; Griffith, *Sex and Citizenship*, 11; Mace, 68. For the relationship between sex and war, see also George Ryley Scott, *Sex Problems and Dangers in Wartime* (London, 1940); Alex Comfort, *Barbarism and Sexual Freedom: Lectures on the Sociology of Sex from the Standpoint of Anarchism* (London, 1948), 16–18; John Costello, *Love, Sex and War, 1939–45* (London, 1986); and Sonya O. Rose, 'Sex, Citizenship and the Nation in World War II Britain', *American Historical Review* 103, 4 (1998), 1147–1176.

102   Griffith, *Sex and Citizenship*, 9; *Final Report of the Committee on Procedure in Matrimonial Cases* (London, 1947), 5.

103   Mace, 12; *idem* in *Marriage Guidance* 1, 6 (1947), 1.

104   For government policy on coeducation in the 1940s, see Madeleine Arnot, 'A Cloud Over Coeducation: An Analysis of the Forms of Transmission of Class and Gender Relations', *Gender, Class and Education*, ed. Stephen Walker and Len Barton (Lewes, 1983), 69–70.

Chapter 3 – All Mixed Up

1   For uniformed youth organizations, see in particular Tim Jeal, *Baden-Powell* (London, 1989); Michael Rosenthal, *The Character Factory: Baden-Powell and the Origins of the Scout Movement* (New York, 1986); John Springhall *et al., Sure and Stedfast: A History of the Boys' Brigade, 1883–1983* (London, 1983); John Springhall, *Youth, Empire and*

Society: British Youth Movements, 1883–1940 (London, 1977); and Paul Wilkinson, 'English Youth Movements, 1908–30', *Journal of Contemporary History* 4, 2 (1969), 3–23.

2   For commercial youth culture, see David Fowler, *The First Teenagers: The Lifestyle of Young Wage-Earners in Interwar Britain* (London, 1995), chs. 4 and 5; Ross McKibbin, *Classes and Cultures: England, 1918–51* (Oxford, 1998), chs. 10 and 11; Claire Langhamer, *Women's Leisure in England, 1920–60* (Manchester, 2000), chs. 3 and 4; Bill Osgerby, *Youth in Britain since 1945* (Oxford, 1998); John Springhall, *Coming of Age: Adolescence in Britain, 1860–1970* (Dublin, 1986); Andrew Davies, *Leisure, Gender and Poverty: Working-Class Culture in Salford and Manchester, 1900–39* (Milton Keynes, 1992); Penny Tinkler, *Constructing Girlhood: Popular Magazines for Girls Growing up in England, 1920–50* (London, 1995); *idem*, 'Girlhood and Growing Up', *Women in Twentieth-Century Britain*, ed. Ina Zweiniger-Bargielowska (Harlow, 2001); and Angela McRobbie, *Feminism and Youth Culture* (Basingstoke, 1991).

3   For the attempts of youth clubs to counteract unsupervised youth activity, see Mary Morse, *The Unattached* (Harmondsworth, 1965). The conflictual models of adult–youth interaction utilized in much research on youth subcultures are not readily transferable to the study of youth clubs for three principal reasons. First of all, neither the adults nor the adolescents involved in the clubs formed homogeneous categories. The leaders of boys' clubs and mixed clubs demonstrated through their dispute over mixing that adult society possessed no uniform standards it wished to impose upon the young, regardless of its ability to do so. For their part, youth club members defined themselves less against adult authority figures than against each other, the boys and girls dividing along lines of sex over what they wanted from club life. Secondly, social control models tend to conflate conformity with conservatism. While both boys' clubs and mixed clubs strove to impose prescriptive models of social behaviour on their charges, only the former's mission was conservative according to contemporary norms. The ambition of mixed clubs to further cooperation between the sexes was, within its own terms, progressive. Third, the concept of social control does not capture the reactive nature of much youth work. Although mixed clubs were set up by girls' clubs and the government, they strove to meet a demand emanating from the young. This coincidence of youth demand and mixed club supply demonstrates how youth club leaders and members could possess surprisingly compatible agendas. In cases of conflict, as when boys' clubs opposed mixing in defiance of their members' preferences, the voluntary nature of youth club membership – together with the increasing abundance of alternative forms of leisure provision – provided young people with the power simply to leave. Most of the time, however, the mutual recognition by club leaders and adolescents that each needed the other impelled them to reach an accommodation. Hence the reactionary and liberal schemes of social engineering respectively entertained by boys' clubs and mixed clubs were heavily diluted by the desires of the young, who mixed more than boys' club leaders would have wished but not in the manner preferred by mixed club leaders. Adolescents in turn generally put up with the irksome supervision that was part and parcel of the youth club experience. Compromise, not confrontation, governed most encounters between teenagers and those nominally in charge of them in mid twentieth-century Britain. For social control and youthful resistance, see in particular Stanley Cohen, *Folk Devils and Moral Panics: The Creation of the Mods and the Rockers* (London, 1972); Stuart Hall and Tony Jefferson (eds.), *Resistance through Rituals: Youth Subcultures in Postwar Britain* (London, 1976); Dick Hebdige, *Subculture: The Meaning of Style* (London, 1979); Paul Willis, *Learning to Labour: How Working-Class Kids Get Working-Class Jobs* (Aldershot, 1978); John Davis, *Youth and the Condition of Britain: Images of Adolescent Conflict* (London, 1990); and Stephen Humphries, *Hooligans or Rebels?: An Oral History of Working-Class Childhood and Youth, 1889–1939* (Oxford, 1981).

4   For the history of boys' clubs, see W. McG. Eagar, *Making Men: The History of Boys' Clubs and Related Movements in Great Britain* (London, 1953); Frank Dawes, *A Cry from the Streets: The Boys' Club Movement in Britain from the 1950s to the Present Day* (Hove, 1975); L.L. Loewe, *Basil Henriques: A Portrait* (London, 1976); Martin John Dedman, 'Economic and Social Factors Affecting the Development of Youth Organisations for Civilian Boys in Britain between 1880 and 1914' (London School of Economics PhD thesis, 1985), esp. ch. 5; Victor Bailey, *Delinquency and Citizenship:*

Reclaiming the Young Offender, 1914–48 (Oxford, 1987); Harry Hendrick, *Images of Youth: Age, Class and the Male Youth Problem, 1880–1920* (Oxford, 1990); David Williams, *Stanley Nairne: The Boys' Club Pioneer* (Perth, 1990); Seth Koven, 'From Rough Lads to Hooligans: Boy Life, National Culture and Social Reform', *Nationalisms and Sexualities*, ed. Andrew Parker *et al.* (London, 1992); and Fowler, ch. 6. For girls' clubs and allied organizations, see Iris Dove, 'Sisterhood or Surveillance?: The Development of Working Girls' Clubs in London, 1880–1939' (University of Greenwich PhD thesis, 1996); Jane Dixon, 'A Short History of the Girls' Club Movement in London' (typescript, 1981); Carol Dyhouse, *Girls Growing Up in Late Victorian and Edwardian England* (London, 1981), 104–114; Brian Harrison, 'For Church, Queen and Family: The Girls' Friendly Society, 1874–1920', *Past and Present* 61 (1973), 107–138; and Mica Nava, 'Youth Service Provision, Social Order and the Question of Girls', *Gender and Generation*, ed. Angela McRobbie and Mica Nava (London, 1984).

5   For mixed clubs, see Sidney Bunt and Ron Gargrave, *The Politics of Youth Clubs* (Leicester, 1980), 77–91; Emma Latham, 'The Liverpool Boys' Association and the Liverpool Union of Youth Clubs: Youth Organisations and Gender, 1940–70', *Journal of Contemporary History* 35, 3 (2000), 423–437; and Val Carpenter and Kirsty Young, *Coming in from the Margins: Youth Work with Girls and Young Women* (Leicester, 1986).

6   Margaret Bone, *The Youth Service and Similar Provision for Young People* (London, 1972), 35. This figure would have included some youngsters who had attended clubs unaffiliated to the two principal national organizations.

7   Ibid., 25, 44. Pearl Jephcott's 1954 survey of fourteen- to seventeen-year-olds in Southern England and the Midlands found youth club membership to be double that of the uniformed organizations. By Margaret Bone's calculation fifteen years later, four times as many fourteen- to twenty-year-olds attended youth clubs as uniformed and academic organizations. Furthermore, using the statistics provided in 1973 by the organizations themselves, we find that approximately 110,000 boys and 60,000 girls aged fourteen and above were members of single-sex uniformed youth organizations as compared to the 175,000 boys belonging to boys' clubs and the 375,000 boys and girls belonging to mixed clubs. This gives a ratio of non-uniformed to uniformed organization membership of over three to one (Pearl Jephcott, *Some Young People* (London, 1954), 105; Bone, 52; Kenneth R. Matthews, *Youth Club Leadership: A Guide to Principles and Practice* (London, 1975), 29–30; National Association of Boys' Clubs (henceforth NABC), *Annual Report* (1972–3); National Association of Youth Clubs (henceforth NAYC), *Annual Report* (1972–3)).

8   Bernarr F. Atherton, 'The Relative Merits of Coeducational and Single-Sex Schools with Special Reference to the Happiness of Marriage of Former Pupils' (University of Wales, Swansea MSc Thesis, 1970), 494–495. Identical proportions of men and women stated that their attendance at mixed clubs had aided their marriages. In contrast, 30 per cent of men and 26 per cent of women who had formerly attended segregated clubs said likewise.

9   Scotland is an exceptional case deserving separate study, since its single-sex youth organizations bucked the trend towards mixing elsewhere in Britain. In addition, although their religious foundation excludes them from the present study, it is also worth drawing attention to a parallel movement towards mixing undertaken by Methodists during this period. Persuaded by the Christian mutualist dogma that 'the essential character of Christian teaching ... implies the breakdown of all barriers (including that of sex)', the Methodist Association of Youth Clubs was committed to mixing from its establishment in 1945. The organization was a great success, in the early sixties claiming 110,000 members in 3,400 clubs, some 99 per cent of which were mixed (Douglas S. Hubery, *The Emancipation of Youth* (London, 1963), 83, 82).

10   B. Paul Neuman, *The Boys' Club* (London, 1900), 73; Bailey, 3. For the connection between boys' club leaders and the juvenile justice system, see also George K. Behlmer, *Friends of the Family: The English Home and Its Guardians, 1850–1940* (Stanford, CA, 1998), ch. 5; Bailey, 9–12, 62–3 and 199–202; and Hendrick, ch. 6.

11   Basil L.Q. Henriques, *Club Leadership* (London, 1933), 176.

12   G. Stanley Hall, *Adolescence: Its Psychology and Its Relations to Physiology, Anthropology, Sociology, Sex, Crime, Religion and Education*, ii vols. (New York, 1904).

13   NABC, *Principles and Aims of the Boys' Club Movement* (London, 1930), 14; NABC, *Annual Report* (1930–1), 3.

14   NABC, *Principles and Aims*, 6; NABC, *A Guide to Starting a Boys' Club* [rev. edn] (London, 1932), 6; NABC, *What is a Boys' Club?* (London, 1932), n.p.

15   Henriques, *Club Leadership* [1933 edn], 53; NABC, *Principles and Aims*, 7.

16   NABC, *Clubs for Boys* (London, 1932), n.p.

17   Ibid., n.p.; C.E.B. Russell and Lilian B. Russell, *Lads' Clubs: Their History, Organisation and Management* (London, 1932), 267.

18   Basil Henriques cited in Loewe, 85; W. McG. Eagar, 'Plainer Principles and Clearer Aims', *The Boy* 12, 1 (1938), 15.

19   Fowler, 140.

20   Hubert Llewellyn Smith (ed.), *New Survey of London Life and Labour, ix: Life and Leisure* (London, 1935), 159.

21   Fowler, 143; NABC, *Principles and Aims*, 8; Springhall *et al.*, 129.

22   S.F. Hatton, *London's Bad Boys* (London, 1931), 85.

23   Neuman, 73; Henriques, *Club Leadership* [1933 edn], 1.

24   Maude Stanley, *Clubs for Working Girls* [rev. edn] (London, 1904), 123; Federation of Working Girls' Clubs, *In Perils in the City* (London, 1909); National Union of Women Workers, *Girls' Clubs* [rev. edn] (London, 1905), 4.

25   *New Survey of London Life and Labour, ix*, 200–201; Margaret Simey, *The Disinherited Society: A Personal View of Social Responsibility in Liverpool during the Twentieth Century* (Liverpool, 1996), 73.

26   National Council of Girls' Clubs (henceforth NCGC), *Annual Report* (1936–7), 11; NCGC, *Club Leaders' News (News Sheet)* 1, 1 (1938).

27   Madeleine Rooff, *Youth and Leisure: A Survey of Girls' Organisations in England and Wales* (Edinburgh, 1935), 99; NCGC, *Annual Report* (1929), 14.

28   Basil L.Q. Henriques, *Club Leadership* [rev. edn] (London, 1942), 245; Katharine C. Dewar, *The Girl* (London, 1920), 72. Interestingly, it appears that boys' club leaders were if anything less favourable towards mixing in the interwar period than previously. In 1913, Alexander Paterson applauded the 'comradeship' obtained in a mixed evening institute (which was, admittedly, not strictly speaking a club), while Charles Russell in 1905 had not been overly concerned by the sight of boys consorting with girls. It seems possible that the antipathy to mixing so evident in the interwar boys' club movement formed part of the move towards stricter standards signalled by the founding of the NABC in 1925 and its issuing of a *Principles and Aims* document five years later (Alexander Paterson in 'Boys in Girls' Clubs', *Girls' Club News* 24 (1914), 6; Charles E.B. Russell, *Manchester Boys: Sketches of Manchester Lads at Work and Play* (Manchester, 1905), 116–117).

29   K. Gallwey, 'Barnsbury Club', *Girls' Club News* 92 (1920), 14; Public Record Office (henceforth PRO) ED 24/2110, evidence of Miss M. McN. Sharpley to the Juvenile Organisations Committee, 13 February 1919.

30   E.J. Urwick, 'Conclusion', *Studies of Boy Life in Our Cities*, ed. E.J. Urwick (London, 1904), 308; *idem*, 'Introduction', *Studies of Boy Life in Our Cities*, xii.

31   Lily H. Montagu, 'The Girl in the Background', *Studies of Boy Life in Our Cities*, 244; Stanley, 218.

32   'Clubs and the War', *Girls' Club Journal* 7, 19 (1915), 17.

33   PRO ED 24/2110, evidence of Mrs Potter to the Juvenile Organisations Committee, 14 March 1918; B.E. Lewarne, 'A War-Time Club', *Girls' Club Journal* 7, 21 (1915), 63. For wartime clubs for female factory workers, see Dove, 124; and Angela Woollacott, *On Her Their Lives Depend: Munitions Workers in the Great War* (Berkeley, CA, 1994), 155–160.

34   Ruth Lousada, 'Music in Girls' Clubs', *Girls' Club News* 1 (1912), 3. For the Woodcraft Folk and its ilk, see Leslie A. Paul, *The Folk Trail: An Outline of the Philosophy and Activities of Woodcraft Fellowships* (London, 1929); and Springhall, *Youth, Empire and Society*, ch. 7. For the Youth Hostels Association, see Bernard Trayner, *A Short History of the YHA* [rev. edn] (St. Albans, 1979).

35   Isabel O'Hanlon, 'About a Mixed Club', *Girls' Club Journal* 26, 81 (1935), 3; A.E. Morgan, *The Needs of Youth: A Report Made to the King George's Jubilee Trust Fund* (London, 1939), 340.

36   Basil L.Q. Henriques, *The Indiscretions of a Warden* (London, 1937), 79; *idem* cited in *Girls' Club News* 109 (1922), 84.

37 Russell and Russell, 204; H. Justin Evans, *First Steps to Club Leadership* (London, 1938), 33.

38 Valentine Bell, 'Hostile Forces: Dance Halls', *The Boy* 5, 1 (1932), 3.

39 Morgan, 335. Club leaders' concerns about the distracting effect of female influence were far from baseless. A confidential NABC survey of old boys issued in 1949 found that 'The most frequent reason for leaving is, in one form or another, "Girls"' (PRO ED 124/162, NABC Research Office Report on Further Study of Leakage, March 1949).

40 Stanley Nairne, *The Starting and Organising of a Boys' Club* (London, 1928), 40; Henriques, *Indiscretions*, 78.

41 *Idem, Club Leadership* [rev. edn] (London, 1934), 186–187. Similar disapproval of fast women can be found in Robert Baden-Powell's risible *Rovering to Success* (London, 1922), 122.

42 Lewarne, 63. The most prominent opponent of mixing in the interwar girls' club movement was Lily Montagu, who retained her concern that girls lacked the necessary self-control to remain composed in the presence of boys. 'The unhealthy aspects of sex excitement' would, she feared, thoroughly 'spoil club life' and would make girls so 'dependent on the society of boys [that] they will not study or amuse themselves alone.' Such scepticism about mixing was, however, very much a minority opinion within the girls' club movement and reflected Montagu's comparatively more conservative attitude towards sex roles (Lily Montagu in 'Mixed Clubs or Girls' Clubs?: A Discussion', *Girls' Club News* 85 (1920), 11; *idem*, 'The Boy Element in Girls' Clubs', *Girls' Club Journal* 12, 35 (1920), 8. For Lily Montagu's club work, see also *idem, My Club and I: The Story of the West Central Jewish Club* (London, 1944); and Ellen M. Umansky, *Lily Montagu and the Advancement of Liberal Judaism: From Vision to Vocation* (Lewiston, NY, 1983), 117–125).

43 Sally Alexander, *Becoming a Woman and Other Essays* (London, 1994), 21; NCGC, *Annual Report* (1936–7), 16. For an analogous, earlier shift towards mixing in American leisure activities, see Kathy Peiss, *Cheap Amusements: Working Women and Leisure in Turn-of-the-Century New York* (Philadelphia, 1986), ch. 8.

44 Louise Creighton, 'The Women's Movement', *Girls' Club News* 20 (1913), 2; Jane Black of the Daffodil Club in 'Chivalry between Men and Women', *Girls' Club News* 73 (1918), 9; 'The "Mixed" Club', *Girls' Club Journal* 14, 40 (1922), 8. For Louise Creighton's feminist beliefs, see Louise Creighton, *The Social Disease and How to Fight It: A Rejoinder* (London, 1914); and James Covert, *A Victorian Marriage: Mandell and Louise Creighton* (London, 2000), 302–304.

45 Katharine C. Dewar, 'The Place of Women in Boys' Clubs', *The Boy* 1, 3 (New Series) (1928), 7; 'The "Mixed" Club', 9.

46 Lady Emmott in 'Mixed Clubs or Girls' Clubs?', 11; Miss H.E. Davis cited in Dewar, *The Girl*, 70; W.H.M. Jackson, 'A Plea for Cooperation between Boys' and Girls' Clubs, ii', *Girls' Club Journal* 25, 77 (1934), 19.

47 Catherine Green, *In The Service of Youth: A History of the National Council for Voluntary Youth Services, 1936–86* (Leicester, 1986), 6.

48 For the negotiations between girls' and boy's clubs on the subject of mixing, see NCGC and NABC, *Mixed Activities in Clubs* (London, 1938).

49 Mass-Observation, 'Drinking Habits', *File Report* 3029 (August 1948), 46.

50 *Club News* (August 1942), 5; Henriques, *Club Leadership* [1942 edn], 246.

51 Liverpool Youth Organisations Committee, *Youth in the Changing World* (Liverpool, 1945), 14; PRO ED 124/14, 'Preliminary Report of the Investigation into Leisure Time Activities of Young People', *Youth Advisory Council Paper* 50 (1944).

52 Board of Education, *The Service of Youth* (London, 1942). State intervention in youth leisure had been prefigured to some extent in the 1930s by the fitness drive and youth initiatives in the deprived 'Special Areas'. However, while such schemes had been handicapped by financial constraints and suspicions concerning their militaristic motives, war removed such obstacles. For an overview of governmental policy on youth leisure in wartime, see P.H.J.H. Gosden, *Education in the Second World War: A Study in Policy and Administration* (London, 1976).

53 Board of Education, *Juvenile Offences* (London, 1941), 4. For governmental attitudes to the pre-service organizations, see PRO ED 124/60; War Office, *Report of the Committee on the Officer Training Corps and Cadet Force* (London, 1939); and Joanna Bourke,

Dismembering the Male: Men's Bodies, Britain and the Great War (London, 1996), 180–192.

54 Home Office, *Judicial Statistics*, 1939–47; Board of Education, *Juvenile Offences*, 4; 'Girls, 16 to 18, "Running Wild"', *The People*, 19 January 1941; Board of Education, *Juvenile Offences*, 8. For wartime misbehaviour, see John Costello, *Love, Sex and War, 1939–45* (London, 1986).

55 See PRO ED 124/60; and PRO ED 124/90.

56 Penny Tinkler, 'Sexuality and Citizenship: The State and Girls' Leisure Provision in England, 1939–45', *Women's History Review* 4, 2 (1995), 193–217; *idem*, 'An All-Round Education: The Board of Education's Policy for the Leisure-Time Training of Girls, 1939–50', *History of Education* 23, 4 (1994), 385–403. For wartime concerns about young women's sexuality, see also Sonya O. Rose, 'Sex, Citizenship and the Nation in World War II Britain', *American Historical Review* 103, 4 (1998), 1147–1176.

57 PRO ED 124/14, Summary of Views Expressed at First Meeting of the Youth Advisory Council, 3 July 1942; PRO ED 124/15, note by 'P.C.C.', 25 September 1940.

58 L.J. Barnes, *Youth Service in an English County* (London, 1945), 30.

59 Ibid., 48.

60 NABC, War Time Policy Committee minutes, undated memorandum by Mr Rickerby; Mary Nicholson, *Clubs for Citizens: A Wartime Experiment* (London, 1945).

61 Mass-Observation Topic Collection on Youth, box 3, file A. For a case study of one Youth Recreation Centre, see Board of Education, 'Youth in a City: An Account of an Experiment of Youth Service in Its Initial Stages', *Board of Education Educational Pamphlets* 117 (London, 1943).

62 NABC, *Boys' Clubs in War-time: Hints for Activities* (London, 1939), 4; NABC, War Time Policy Committee minutes, undated memorandum by Mr Rickerby.

63 'London Youth Recreation Centres', *The Boy* 13, 4 (1940), 161; R.E. Hill, 'Mixed Clubs: A Personal Experience', *The Boy* 24, 2 (1951), 38; London Federation of Boys' Clubs cited in 'London Youth Recreation Centres', 161.

64 'Sub', 'Men of Little Faith', *The Boy* 13, 2 (1939), 65.

65 Israel Feldman, 'A Doctor on Mixed Clubs', *The Boy* 15, 2 (1941–2), 215; Henriques, *Club Leadership* [1942 edn], 246; NABC, Executive Council agenda, Executive Council statement on mixing, 1944.

66 Editorial in *The Boy* 17, 2 (1944), 44; Valentine Bell in *The Boy* 13, 4 (1940), 169.

67 PRO ED 124/70, Katharine Elliot to Kenneth Lindsay, 29 November 1939; PRO ED 124/70, Honoria Harford to B.L. Pearson, 6 August 1941; PRO ED 124/70, H. Ramsbotham to Katharine Elliot, 5 March 1941. Katharine Elliot was also a Tory of note, becoming chair of the party and, as Baroness Elliot of Harwood, the first woman to speak in the House of Lords.

68 PRO ED 124/70, B.H. Pearson to Miss Goodfellow, 7 August 1941; Mass-Observation Topic Collection on Youth, box 3, file A, interview with secretary of the London Federation of Boys' Clubs.

69 J. Macalister Brew, *In the Service of Youth* (London, 1943), 17; J. Macalister Brew (ed.), *Clubs and Club-Making* (Bickley, 1943), 37.

70 Brew, *In the Service of Youth*, 62, 56.

71 NAGC, *Annual Report* (1941–2), 2; PRO ED 124/70, NAGC confidential report on mixing, February 1944, 5.

72 Katharine Elliot in *Club News* (January 1944), 2.

73 NAGC, *Annual Report* (1943–4), 1.

74 Brew, *In the Service of Youth*, 253, 256.

75 NABC, *Boys' Clubs in War-time*, 5; B.L.Q. Henriques, 'A Case for Mixed Clubs', *The Boy* 13, 4 (1940), 166. For Henriques' reversion to type, see *idem*, *Club Leadership* [1942 edn], 245–248. For indications of the NABC's willingness to compromise, see Hubert Llewelyn Smith in *Club Leaders' News* (October 1941), 4; and editorial in *The Boy* 17, 2 (1944), 43.

76 For NCGC overtures towards the NABC, see 'Joint Training Course: NABC and NAYC', *Club News* (July 1942), 1; and 'A Plan for Youth', *Club News* (December 1942), 1.

77 Henriques, *Club Leadership* [1942 edn], 245; NAGC, *Annual Report* (1941–2), 2.

78 NABC, Executive Council agenda, draft letter to directors of education and chairs of Youth Committees, 6 June 1944; PRO ED 124/70, NAGC confidential report on mixing, February 1944, 7; NAGC, *Annual Report* (1943–4), 4.

79   Editorial in *The Boy* 17, 2 (1944), 43; Leeds and West Riding Association of Girls' Clubs and Mixed Clubs cited in Bunt and Gargrave, 83; London Union of Girls' Clubs, *Annual Report* (1941), 4; London Union of Girls' Clubs, *Annual Report* (1944–5), 10; London Union of Mixed Clubs and Girls' Clubs, *Annual Report* (1946–7), 4.

80   NABC, Executive Council minutes, 8 January 1946.

81   Lord Aberdare in NABC, *Annual Report* (1949–50), 21–22.

82   Basil L.Q. Henriques, *The Home-Menders: The Prevention of Unhappiness in Children* (London, 1955), 14; Lord Aberdare in NABC, *Annual Report* (1947–8), 17.

83   NABC, *The Contribution of Boys' Clubs to the Life of Our Time* (London, 1948), 10; NABC, *The Development of Boys' Clubs* (London, 1954); NABC, *Boys' Clubs, The Way Ahead: A Policy Statement by the National Association of Boys' Clubs* (London, 1975). In the scouting movement, only Venture Scouts fully embraced mixing. Younger Scouts were excused wholesale mixing although a report recommended mixed activities for them 'where there is demand for them and competent leaders are available.' As for the other uniformed organizations for boys, the Jewish Lads' Brigade launched its first girls' section in 1963, which proved such a boon to recruitment that it was widely imitated. The Boys' Brigade, meanwhile, admitted in 1964 that it was 'questionable whether an organisation so definitely mono-sexual as [itself was] entirely suitable to the modern Boy of the later teenage years'. Its 'Seniors' of sixteen and up were therefore to be offered 'every opportunity…to enjoy normal relationships between the sexes' (Boy Scouts Association, *Advance Party Report* (London, 1966), 40, 34; Sharman Kadish, '*A Good Jew and a Good Englishman': The Jewish Lads' and Girls' Brigade, 1895–1995* (London, 1995), 155–166; Boys' Brigade, *The Report of the Haynes Committee on the Work and Future of the Boys' Brigade* (London, 1964), 38, 42).

84   NABC, *Annual Report* (1971–2), 1; Field-Marshal Montgomery cited in *The Times*, 30 October 1946; Clement Attlee cited in *The Times*, 1 December 1945.

85   Lord Aberdare in NABC, *Annual Report* (1951–2), 15; NABC, *The Development of Boys' Clubs*, 4; Eagar in *The Boy*, 26,3 (1953), 89; 'A well-known figure in the movement' cited in *News Service* 4 (1961), n.p.

86   PRO ED 124/163, G.W.W. Browne to E.B.H. Baker, 10 October 1953; Lord Aberdare in NABC, *Annual Report* (1948–9), 22.

87   For postwar relations between the NABC and the Ministry of Education, see PRO ED 124/162 and PRO ED 124/163. Buoyed by the success of its 'Brunswick' campaign to build new clubs, the NABC decided in 1947 to enrol no fewer than a million men to run them. The 'Bridge-Builders' appeal was endorsed in advance of its publication by Rab Butler and Clement Davies, James Griffiths and Chuter Ede, the vice-chancellors of Oxford and Cambridge, the captains of the England cricket and football teams, half of the press barons, dozens of mayors and a huge haul of financiers and industrialists. Yet two vital signatories – the Secretary of State for Education and the Archbishop of Canterbury – withheld their support simply because the scheme excluded girls, a matter over which the NABC refused to compromise. It was a momentous rejection. With the minister's backing, the NABC would have undertaken a recruitment drive to dwarf all others with the support of the entire British establishment and could have expected to attract, if not one million men, then at least enough to establish itself as the paramount youth organization. Without it, they felt unable to proceed with the scheme and instead issued a general fund-raising appeal in May 1948, supported by a *Times* editorial: a bathetic conclusion to a scheme of immense promise brought down by the NABC's ideological intransigence (PRO ED 124/162, Lord Aberdare to George Tomlinson, 17 September 1947; Tomlinson to Aberdare, 24 September 1947; Aberdare to Tomlinson, 12 November 1947; Tomlinson to Aberdare, 19 November 1947; *The Times*, 28 May 1948).

88   PRO ED 124/163, G.W.W. Browne to E.B.H. Baker, 10 October 1953; NABC, Executive Committee minutes, 23 March 1967.

89   NABC, Executive Council minutes, 5 January 1965; London Federation of Boys' Clubs, *Boys' Clubs and Girls* (London, 1962), 8; NABC, *Boys' Clubs, The Way Ahead*, n.p.

90   PRO ED 124/163, memorandum by K.A. Kennedy, 28 June 1955; Eagar, *Making Men*, 9.

91   Ashley Smith in *The Boy* 13, 4 (1940), 167.

92   Editorial in *The Boy* 23,3 (1950) 98.

93   C.M. Fleming, *Adolescence: Its Social Psychology* (London, 1958), 241; John Barron Mays, *The Young Pretenders: A Study of Teenage Culture in Contemporary Society* [rev. edn] (New York, 1967), 130.

94 A.T.M. Wilson, 'Some Reflections and Suggestions on the Prevention and Treatment of Marital Problems', *Human Relations* 2, 3 (1949), 242; Gwilym O. Roberts, *The Road to Love: Avoiding the Neurotic Pattern* (London, 1950), xiii, 172, 72.

95 'A Mortal Danger', *The Boy* 30, 3 (1957), 3; Reg Goodwin in *News Service* 16 (November/December 1963), n.p; Malcolm Munthe, *The Bunty Boys* (London, 1961), 144. For examples of innovative work by boys' clubs in the field of anti-delinquency, see John Barron Mays, *On the Threshold of Delinquency* (Liverpool, 1949); and M. Lloyd Turner, *Ship without Sails: An Account of the Barge Boys' Club* (London, 1953). The famous 'Barge Boys Experiment', however, foundered on a 'mutiny' from the older boys who went off to join a mixed club.

96 NAYC, *Annual Report* (1963–4), 20; NABC, Executive Committee minutes, 28 November 1968; ; NABC, *Boys' Clubs: Under 14s* (London, 1974), 7; NABC, *Boys' Clubs, The Way Ahead*, n.p.

97 Eric Keown in *Punch*, 12 April 1950, 398.

98 NABC, *Boys' Clubs, The Way Ahead*, n.p.; NABC, Executive Council minutes, 28 May 1963, 23 January 1953, 27 February 1964 and 26 March 1964.

99 National Association of Mixed Clubs and Girls' Clubs (henceforth NAMC&GC), *Girls' Interests* (London, 1956), 3; Liverpool Union of Girls' and Mixed Clubs, *Annual Report* (1963–4), 3. For a typical example of why girls' clubs closed (i.e. lack of space and lack of interest), see Albion House, Everton, *Annual Report* (1953).

100 *Eighty Thousand Adolescents* (London, 1950), 71; NAMC&GC, *Girls' Interests*, 3.

101 Ministry of Education, *The Youth Service in England and Wales* (London, 1960), 64, 61, 64. For evidence of governmental sympathy for mixing in the 1960s, see *The Sunday Times*, 7 November 1965; and Department of Education and Science, *Youth and Community Work in the 1970s* (London, 1969), 57).

102 PRO ED 124/203, E.B.H. Baker to R.N. Heaton, 23 March 1959; PRO ED 124/333, submissions by NAYC to Youth Service Development Council, 1965. Talks between the two organizations spasmodically continued in the postwar period before breaking down when the NABC dismissed the NAYC's proposals for amalgamation as being premised upon 'the entirely false assumption that there was a similarity between a boys' club and a mixed club, and hence between the NABC and the NAGC&MC' (NABC, Executive Committee minutes, 24 July 1952).

103 PRO ED 124/163, H.J. Edwards to R.D. Salter-Davis, June 1955; PRO ED 149/252, report on Speke Boys' Club, 1965.

104 Roberts, 72; Eagar cited in *The Boy* 26, 3 (1953), 89. For endorsements of Margaret Mead, see Marjorie Tait in *Mixed Clubs* (London, *c.* 1945), 12; NAMC&GC, *Girls' Interests*, 6; Josephine Klein, *Human Behaviour and Personal Relations* (London, 1963), 43; and Julia Hanmer, *Girls at Leisure* (London, 1964), 75.

105 See NABC, *Boys' Clubs: Under 14s*; and NCGC, *News Sheet* (1948).

106 *News Service* 8 (May 1962), n.p.; J. Macalister Brew, *The Young Idea* (London, 1958), 15.

107 NCGC, *Annual Report* (1929), 14; NAYC, *Annual Report* (1963–4), 20.

108 Marjorie Tait in *Mixed Clubs*, 5.

109 Brew, *In the Service of Youth*, 260; NAYC, *Annual Report* (1970–1), 13.

110 NAMC&GC, *Annual Report* (1957–8), 14; NAMC&GC, *Annual Report* (1959–60), 10; Ray Gosling, *Lady Albemarle's Boys* (London, 1961), 18. For postwar innovations in youth club practice, see L.J. Barnes, *The Outlook for Youth Work* (London, 1948).

111 National Association of Girls' Clubs and Mixed Clubs (henceforth NAGC&MC), *How to Run a Mixed Club* (London, 1952), 7; Brew, *The Young Idea*, 25.

112 Eric Keown in *Punch*, 7 March 1951, 307; Marjorie Tait in *Mixed Clubs*, 10–11.

113 NAGC&MC, *Planning a Mixed Club* (London, *c.* late 1940s), 3; Pearl Jephcott, *Rising Twenty: Notes on Some Ordinary Girls* (London, 1948), 170.

114 G.M. Johnson in *Mixed Clubs*, 17; J. Macalister Brew, *Youth and Youth Groups* (London, 1957), 156.

115 Eric Keown in *Punch*, 7 March 1951, 306; Kathleen Goldsmith in *Mixed Clubs*, 24; NAYC, 'Sex Education in the Youth Club', *Programme Paper* 13 (London, *c.* 1967), n.p.

116 Marjorie Tait in *Mixed Clubs*, 5.

117 London Union of Mixed Clubs and Girls' Clubs, *Annual Report* (1952–3), 15; Margareta Berger-Hammerschlag, *Journey into a Fog* (London, 1955), 71. For another crackdown on petting, see Mary Blandy, *Razor Edge: The Story of a Youth Club* (London, 1967), 119.

118 NAGC&MC, *The Mixed Club: A Statement of Its General Aim and Functions* (London, 1948), 6; J.B. Chapman, 'Home Making', *Club Leaders' Notes* 3, 8 (1955), 1.

119 Berger-Hammerschlag, 137.

120 NAGC&MC, *How to Run a Mixed Club*, 7.

121 Unnamed social worker cited in T.R. Fyvel, *The Insecure Offenders: Rebellious Youth in the Welfare State* (London, 1961), 23.

122 Hanmer, 19; Fyvel, 336.

123 Margaret G. Allen, *A Survey of Mixed Clubs* (London, 1948), 8; *Youth in a Dockland Community: A Survey of Wapping Carried Out by Members of the London School of Economics* (London, 1950), 16.

124 Hanmer, 46; J. Macalister Brew, *Hours Away from Work: Boys in Mixed Clubs* (London, 1949), 45; NAGC&MC, *Club Girls and Their Interests* (London, c. late 1940s), 51.

125 Elizabeth Stucley, *Teddy Boys' Picnic* (London, 1958), 118; Anne Foster, *These Our Children* (London, 1945), 79.

126 NAGC&MC, *Annual Report* (1950–1), 8; Val Carpenter *et al.*, 'Working with Girls', *Women in Collective Action* (London, 1982), 140; Hanmer, 60. Among the NAYC's leaders, Honoria Harford, Organising Secretary during the Second World War, and Lesley Sewell, General Secretary in the 1950s and 1960s, were both unmarried. For the impact of professionalization upon women's philanthropic activity, see Jane Lewis, 'Women, Social Work and Social Welfare in Twentieth Century Britain: From (Unpaid) Influence to (Paid) Oblivion?', *Charity, Self-Interest and Welfare in the English Past*, ed. Martin Daunton (London, 1996).

127 Mary Stewart, *The Leisure Activities of School Children* (London, 1960), 11; *Eighty Thousand Adolescents*, 154.

128 Brew, *Hours Away from Work*, 43–44; Hanmer, 51.

129 Foster, 82; London Federation of Boys' Clubs, *Boys' Clubs and Girls*, 7.

130 Eleanor E. Maccoby, *The Two Sexes: Growing Up Apart, Coming Together* (Cambridge, MA, 1998).

131 Stucley, 121.

132 Foster, 82; Hanmer, 60; Berger-Hammerschlag, 29.

133 Hanmer, 46, 48; Mass-Observation, 'Teenage Girls', *File Report* 3150 (August 1949), 7.

134 Hanmer, 60; Stucley, 121–122.

135 Mass-Observation, 'A Report on Voluntary Services', *File Report* 2507 (August 1947), 52; Pearl Jephcott, *Time of One's Own: Leisure and Young People* (Edinburgh, 1967), 69; Stewart, 12. For girls' love of dancing, see also McRobbie, ch. 7.

136 Hanmer, 40; Jephcott, *Time of One's Own*, 69; Fyvel, 126.

137 NAMC&GC, *Girls' Interests*, 6, 10, 6.

138 PRO ED 124/333, NAYC submission on experimental projects with girls, c. 1965; Allen, 7.

139 NAGC&MC, *How to Run a Mixed Club*, 7; Kathleen Goldsmith in *Mixed Clubs*, 24. The provision of segregated activities has led historian Emma Latham to claim that mixed clubs were complicit with boys' clubs in upholding a 'conservative gender ideology'. The manner in which mixed clubs 'train[ed] the two sexes to appreciate and respect what they believed to be their innate differences' succeeded in her view in reinforcing rather than questioning 'established messages about gender relations.' Latham's argument rests upon the debatable assumption that boys' and mixed clubs promoted the same conception of male and female nature and that a belief in inherent sex differences is invariably conservative. As we have already seen, it was the two organizations' divergence over what constituted natural development in boys and girls that divided them most profoundly. The NABC's chairman thought it 'natural and normal' for adolescents to cultivate their sex roles apart from one another and their vice-president held mixing to be a 'defiance of nature'. What seemed 'perfectly normal [and] natural' to mixed club leaders, however, was that boys and girls grew up together and so were spared an 'artificial' segregation. Latham's preoccupation with separate activities makes her overlook the fact that young Liverpudlians valued mixed clubs for their recognition that 'the sexes have ... a great range of common interests': a vision of sex roles alien to single-sex clubs. The biological essentialism of boys' club leaders was avowedly conservative. Because boy nature 'probably never will' change, Henriques argued, postwar boys' clubs 'required very little modification.' The opposite view

pertained in the mixed clubs. They embraced the 'modern psychology [and] sociology' so despised within boys' clubs and sought to overhaul the aims and methods of youth club provision. To regard mixed clubs as conservative institutions is to assess them by the standards not of their age but of ours. (Latham, 424, 432; Lord Aberdare cited in *The Times*, 19 March 1947; Eagar, *Making Men*, 427; *Clubs and Club-Making*, 36; Brew, *Youth and Youth Groups*, 154; Liverpool Youth Organisations Committee, *Youth in the Changing World*, 14; Basil L.Q. Henriques, *Club Leadership Today* (London, 1951), xiii; Eagar, *Making Men*, 427).

Latham's failure to distinguish between the sex roles promoted by the NABC and NAYC on a national level leaves her at a loss to explain why the NABC spent 25 years campaigning against the merger of its affiliated bodies in Liverpool. Since amalgamation was proposed on administrative grounds and since Liverpool's mixed clubs were no different from boys' clubs in 'training young people to conform to a specific gender identity', she considers its opposition to have been simply misplaced. Yet the pragmatic stance of the Liverpool Boys' Association stood in defiance of the NABC line that boys could not be adequately catered for in mixed clubs. The NABC had every reason to view a merger as the beginning of the end for boys' clubs in a city in which mixed clubs were favoured by the bulk of adolescents and an 'overwhelming majority' of their parents; in which the Ministry of Education officials and the local Youth Organisation Committee urged 'every effort' to meet this demand; in which the mixed body was solvent while the boys' one was not; and in which those boys' clubs seeking to meet their arrears through mixed dances faced demands from inspectors to take proper responsibility for their female guests. Only once we recognize that the NABC believed boy nature to be threatened by a whole medley of social forces acting in the name of progress does its conservatism and its opposition to amalgamation make sense (Latham, 433; Liverpool Youth Organisations Committee, *Youth in the Changing World*, 14; *idem*, *The Changing Service of Youth* (Liverpool, *c.* 1947), 15; Ministry of Education, *A Survey of Youth Service in Liverpool Held during November 1946* (London, 1947), 2; Liverpool Youth Organisations Committee, *The Changing Service of Youth*, 15; PRO ED 149/38, report on Florence Institute for Boys, 1953).

140 H.E. Howes, *The Mixed Club: Getting Your Second Wind* (London, 1955), 16.
141 'Celia' cited in Jephcott, *Rising Twenty*, 164; Hanmer, 60; NAYC, *Girls in Two Cities* (London, 1967), 20.
142 NAMC&GC, *Girls' Interests*, 11; Mary Robinson, *Girls in the Nineteen Sixties* (London, 1963), 9.
143 NAMC&GC, *Girls' Interests*, 3; Hanmer, 19; NAMC&GC, *Girls' Interests*, 3, 13.
144 Hanmer, 70.
145 Baroness Elliot of Harwood in *Parliamentary Debates: House of Lords* (11 February 1970), vol. 307, col. 957; E. Parkinson Smith and A. Graham Ikin, *Morality – Old and New* (Derby, 1964), 41.
146 NABC, *Newsom and Boys' Clubs* (London, 1967), 39.
147 The boys' club movement formally accepted mixing in 1992, half a century after the opportunity had first presented itself. By this time it had entirely lost its focus on adolescence, claiming to cater for all between the ages of eight and twenty-five. It had also lost almost all its government grants which, because of policies against funding single-sex youth work, now accounted for some 10 per cent or less of its expenditure. The decision to mix took the form of a deathbed conversion at a time when its finances were perilous, its membership figures were no longer released, its annual reports were printed on a single sheet of paper and its purpose was questioned by a government inspectorate report. Its pamphlets trumpeted its new-found commitment to sexual equality almost to the point of parody. Single-sex activities were retained, though not to boost virility and femininity. Instead, girls were encouraged to 'Challeng[e] Sexism' and to combat the 'roles and assumptions' of conventional femininity. And boys, or rather 'young men', were offered gender-awareness workshops designed to combat 'oppressive attitudes and behaviour' and 'break through the boundaries of masculinity' within a 'single gender setting.' The boys' club ideal was now quite dead (NABC-Clubs for Young People, *Partners with the Youth Service* (London, *c.* early 1990s), n.p.; NABC, *Development Review* (London, 1988); HM Inspectorate of the Department of Education and Science, *The National Association of Boys' Clubs, September 1988–June 1989* (London, 1990); NABC-Clubs for Young People, *Girls' Work* (London, *c.* early 1990s),

n.p.; NABC-Clubs for Young People, *Boys' Work* (London, *c.* early 1990s), n.p.).
148 NAMC&GC, *Girls' Interests*, 14; Hanmer, 60.

Chapter 4 – Marriage for Moderns

1   Barbara Drake, *Women in the Postwar World* (London, 1943), 22.
2   For the history of mid twentieth-century sex and marriage manuals, see Hera Cook, 'The Long Sexual Revolution: British Women, Sex and Contraception in the Twentieth Century' (University of Sussex DPhil thesis, 1999), chs. 6–8; Angus McLaren, *Twentieth-Century Sexuality* (Oxford, 1999), ch 3; Roy Porter and Lesley Hall, *The Facts of Life: The Creation of Sexual Knowledge in Britain, 1650–1950* (New Haven, CT, 1995), ch. 9; M.E. Melody and Linda M. Peterson, *Teaching America about Sex: Marriage Guides and Sex Manuals from the Late Victorians to Dr Ruth* (New York, 1999); and Michael Bush, 'The Rise of the Sex Manual', *History Today* 49, 2 (1999), 36–42. For rare exceptions to mutualist orthodoxy in the genre, see T.A.A. Hunter (ed.), *Newnes Manual of Sex and Marriage* (London, 1964); and Shaw Desmond, *Adam and Eve: A Guide to Sex and Marriage* (London, 1954).
3   The original London-only Marriage Guidance Council was launched by Gray and Griffith in 1938. For historical analyses of marriage guidance, see Christopher Lasch, *Haven in a Heartless World: The Family Besieged* (New York, 1979); Nikolas Rose, *Governing the Soul: The Shaping of the Private Self* (London, 1990), ch. 13; *idem, The Psychological Complex: Psychology, Politics and Society in England, 1869–1939* (London, 1985), ch. 7; Elizabeth Wilson, *Only Halfway to Paradise: Women in Postwar Britain, 1945–68* (London, 1980), 90–95; and George K. Behlmer, *Friends of the Family: The English Home and Its Guardians, 1850–1940* (Stanford, CA, 1998), ch. 3.
4   Edward Westermarck, *A Short History of Marriage* (London, 1926), 51; Solomon Herbert, *Fundamentals in Sexual Ethics* (London, 1920), 291.
5   Lawrence Stone, *Broken Lives: Separation and Divorce in England, 1660–1857* (Oxford, 1993), 12.
6   B.M. Spinley, *The Deprived and the Privileged: Personality Development in English Society* (London, 1953), 59; Mary Farmer, *The Family* (London, 1970), 58.
7   W.F. Lofthouse, *The Family and the State* (London, 1944), 123; Walter M. Gallichan (aka Geoffrey Mortimer), *Pitfalls of Marriage* (London, 1926), 60; Hugh Lyon, *Happy Ever After?* (London, 1950), 8.
8   David R. Mace, *Marriage Crisis* (London, 1948), 28, 30.
9   National Marriage Guidance Council (henceforth NMGC), *Syllabus for the Training of Marriage Counsellors* (London, 1949), 11; Annie Keen, *Woman and Marriage* (London, 1929), 54–55.
10 A. Joseph Brayshaw, *The Stability of Marriage* (London, 1953), 5; David R. Mace, *Does Sex Morality Matter?* (London, 1943), 95.
11 *Idem, Marriage Crisis*, 31.
12 Mary Macaulay, *The Art of Marriage* [rev. edn.] (London, 1956), 73; Colin Rosser and Christopher Harris, *The Family and Social Change* (London, 1965), 290; Michael Young and Peter Willmott, *The Symmetrical Family* (New York, 1973); Elizabeth Bott, *Family and Social Networks* (London, 1957), 95; Ernest W. Burgess and Harvey J. Locke, *The Family: From Institution to Companionship* [rev. edn] (New York, 1953), 23. Burgess' and Locke's was the most famous formulation of companionship.
13 For the dating of companionship, see respectively Janet Finch and Penny Summerfield, 'Social Reconstruction and the Emergence of Companionate Marriage, 1945–59', *Marriage, Domestic Life and Social Change*, ed. David Clark (London, 1992), 7–8; Leonore Davidoff *et al., The Family Story: Blood, Contract and Intimacy, 1830–1960* (London, 1999), 190; Jose Harris, *Private Lives, Public Spirit: Britain, 1870–1914* (Harmondsworth, 1994), 79; A. James Hammerton, *Cruelty and Companionship: Conflict in Nineteenth-Century Married Life* (London, 1992), ch. 3; Randolph Trumbach, *The Rise of the Egalitarian Family* (New York, 1978); Lawrence Stone, *The Family, Sex and Marriage in England, 1500–1800* (New York, 1977), ch. 8; and Alan Macfarlane, *Marriage and Love in England: Modes of Reproduction, 1300–1840* (Oxford, 1986), 331. See also the work of the early modern historians Keith Wrightson

and Ralph Houlbrooke, who dispute the idea that companionship had a starting-point as such and that it can be clearly distinguished from patriarchal marriage (Keith Wrightson, *English Society, 1580–1680* (London, 1982), ch. 4; Ralph Houlbrooke, *The English Family, 1400–1700* (London, 1984), chs. 4 and 5).

14 For evidence of eighteenth- and nineteenth-century companionship, see Stone, *Family, Sex and Marriage*; Trumbach; Amanda Vickery, *The Gentleman's Daughter: Women's Lives in Georgian England* (New Haven, CT, 1998); M. Jeanne Peterson, *Family, Love and Work in the Lives of Victorian Gentlewomen* (Bloomington, IN, 1989); and Leonore Davidoff and Catherine Hall, *Family Fortunes: Men and Women of the English Middle Class, 1780–1850* (London, 1987). For the different conditions of working-class marriages in this period, see Anna Clark, *The Struggle for the Breeches: Gender and the Making of the British Working Class* (Berkeley, CA, 1995).

15 Barbara Cartland, *Husbands and Wives* (London, 1961), 44. Cartland's enthusiasm for companionship chimed with that of romance fiction more generally, for which see Joseph McAleer, *Passion's Fortune: The Story of Mills and Boon* (New York, 1999), 158.

16 Edward Charles (aka Charles Edward Hempstead), *An Introduction to the Study of the Psychology and Physiology and Biochemistry of the Sexual Impulse among Adults in Mental and Bodily Health* (London, 1935), 153; Kenneth Walker, *Preparation for Marriage* (London, 1940), 4.

17 John Middleton Murry, *Adam and Eve: An Essay Towards a New and Better Society* (London, 1944), 133; Arthur Belleville MacCoid, *Husbands and Wives* (London, 1922), 48.

18 Walter M. Gallichan (aka Geoffrey Mortimer), *Letters to a Young Man on Love and Health* (London, 1919), 110.

19 Mary Denham (pseud.), *Modern Views on Sex: An Aid to Happiness* [rev. edn] (London, 1948), 140; Ronald Fletcher cited in Christopher Walker and Robert Chester, 'Marital Satisfaction amongst British Wives', *Marriage Guidance* 17, 1 (1977), 220.

20 J.H. Wallis, *Marriage Observed* (London, 1970), 30; William Beveridge *et al.*, *Changes in Family Life* (London, 1932), 133; Eustace Chesser, *Marriage and Freedom* [rev. edn] (London, 1952), 66.

21 Gallichan, *Letters to a Young Man*, 116; William Robinson, *Christian Marriage: A Manual for Those About to be Married* (London, 1945), 22.

22 David R. Mace, *Success in Marriage* (London, 1958), 31; Margaret Leonora Eyles, *The Woman in the Little House* (London, 1922), 146–147.

23 Ibid., 95; S.G. Tuffill, *Sexual Stimulation in Marriage* (London, 1971), 17. For the controversy surrounding 'suburban neurosis', see Judy Giles, *Women, Identity and Private Life in Britain, 1900–50* (Basingstoke, 1995), 78–85.

24 Denham, 110; Edward Kaufmann, *You and Your Marriage* (London, 1951), 80; Edward Westermarck, *The Future of Marriage in Western Civilisation* (London, 1936), 91. For the reform of housework, see Carol Dyhouse, *Feminism and the Family in England, 1880–1939* (Oxford, 1989).

25 John Newsom and Elizabeth Newsom, *Infant Care in an Urban Community* (London, 1964), 133; Drake, 21; A. Herbert Gray, *Men, Women and God: A Discussion of Sex Questions from the Christian Point of View* [rev. edn] (London, 1945), 102.

26 E.D. Hutchinson, *Creative Sex* (London, 1936), 42; Marie Carmichael Stopes, *Radiant Motherhood* (London, 1920), 63, 68, 63.

27 Vera Brittain, *Lady into Woman: A History of Women from Victoria to Elizabeth II* (London, 1953), 10. The importance placed on fatherhood by marriage counsellors contrasted with the focus on maternal attachment of such psychologists as John Bowlby and D.W. Winnicott, for which see chapter six and Denise Riley, *War in the Nursery: Theories of the Child and Mother* (London, 1983).

28 *The Marriage Book* (London, 1937), 50–52. For mid twentieth-century sexual ideals, see in particular Lesley A. Hall, *Hidden Anxieties: Male Sexuality, 1900–39* (Cambridge, 1991).

29 Rennie MacAndrew (aka Andrew George Elliot), *The Red Light: Intimate Hygiene for Men and Women* [rev. edn] (London, 1949), 63; Eustace Chesser, *Love Without Fear* (London, 1940), 13.

30 Walter M. Gallichan (aka Geoffrey Mortimer), *The Poison of Prudery: An Historical Survey* (London, 1929), 187; G. Courtenay Beale (pseud.), *Wise Wedlock* (London, 1921), 69. See also Edward F. Griffith, *The Pioneer Spirit* (Upton Grey, 1981), 57.

31 Kenneth Walker and Peter Fletcher, *Sex and Society* (Harmondsworth, 1955), 127;

Walter M. Gallichan (aka Geoffrey Mortimer), *Sexual Apathy and Coldness in Women* (London, 1927), ch. 7; NMGC, *Sex Difficulties in the Wife* (London, 1953), 3.

32   Beale, *Wise Wedlock*, 48; Chesser, *Love Without Fear*, 129.

33   Ross McKibbin, *Classes and Cultures: England, 1918–51* (Oxford, 1998), 320; NMGC, *Over the Seas – and Far Away* (London, 1955), 11; NMGC, *Sex in Marriage* (London, 1947), 3, 7.

34   Norman Haire *et al.*, *The Encyclopaedia of Sex Practice* [rev. edn] (London, 1951), 726.

35   Kenneth Walker, *Sex and a Changing Civilisation* (London, 1955), 95.

36   Robert Chartham, *Sex Manners for Men* (London, 1967), 15; Edward F. Griffith, *Sex and Citizenship* (London, 1941), 73; Rennie MacAndrew (aka Andrew George Elliot), *Encyclopaedia of Sex and Love Technique* [15th impression] (London, 1955), 211; NMGC, *Sex Difficulties in the Wife*, 9; Kenneth Walker, 'Why Marriages Fail: The Personal Aspect', *Sex in Social Life*, ed. Sybil Neville-Rolfe (London, 1949), 379.

37   Evelyn Home (aka Peggy Makins), *Handbook of Marriage* (London, 1953), 11. See Sheila Jeffreys, *The Spinster and Her Enemies: Feminism and Sexuality, 1880–1930* (Melbourne, 1997); *idem*, *Anticlimax: A Feminist Perspective on the Sexual Revolution* (London, 1990); and Margaret Jackson, *The Real Facts of Life: Feminism and the Politics of Sexuality, 1850–1940* (London, 1994).

38   Chesser, *Marriage and Freedom*, 89; NMGC, *Marriage Preparation through Group Discussion* (London, 1955), 18; J.H. Wallis, *Sexual Harmony in Marriage* (London, 1964), 89.

39   Edward F. Griffith, *Morals in the Melting Pot* (London, 1938), 86; Beale, *Wise Wedlock*, 44.

40   Edward F. Griffith, *Sex in Everyday Life* (London, 1938), 234; Mace, *Success in Marriage*, 40.

41   'Medica' (aka Joan Graham), *Any Wife or Any Husband* [rev. edn] (London, 1955), 97; Kenneth C. Barnes and G. Frances Barnes, *Sex, Friendship and Marriage* (London, 1938), 84. Positions other than the missionary could be tried on occasion on the grounds that 'variety is the spice of love'. Also encouraged were new techniques such as the 'Crimean Tartar's method', recommended by Arthur Koestler when moonlighting as a sexologist (MacAndrew, *The Red Light*, 67; Norman Haire, A. Costler (aka Arthur Koestler) and A. Willy (pseud.), *Encyclopaedia of Sexual Knowledge* (London, 1934), 208).

42   Macaulay, *The Art of Marriage*, 73; Beveridge *et al.*, 105.

43   Mary Agnes Hamilton, 'Changes in Social Life', *Our Freedom and Its Results*, ed. Ray Strachey (London, 1936), 276.

44   Ralph de Pomerai, *Marriage: Past, Present and Future* (London, 1930), 228; Eyles, 142. Elizabeth Bott, Peter Willmott and Michael Young sought to finesse the crude association of the working class with patriarchy, Bott arguing that the segregation of conjugal roles was not necessarily related to class and Willmott and Young rejecting the old stereotype of the tyrannical working-class husband. But it was apparent in Bott's work that the most segregated couples were working class and all of the 'Joint Conjugal–Loose Knit' (i.e. companionate) couples were some sort of professionals. Equally, Willmott and Young acknowledged in their later work, *The Symmetrical Family*, that the division of labour evident in traditional working-class marriages did not produce equality between man and wife (Liz Stanley, *Sex Surveyed, 1949–94* (London, 1995), 115, 114; Bott, 112; Michael Young and Peter Willmott, *Family and Kinship in East London* (London, 1957), 4; *idem*, *The Symmetrical Family*, 30).

45   The FWA's reputation as a charity of last resort confined its clientele to the very poor until the latter part of the 1950s, when its increasing involvement in family therapy attracted a few upper working-class and lower middle-class couples. As regards ethnic composition, seven out of the 68 families studied for this chapter contained Irish members, one couple had emigrated from Africa, another consisted of an African wed to an Afro-Caribbean and one was a 'mixed race' marriage. For the history of the Family Welfare Association in the twentieth century, see Jane Lewis, *The Voluntary Sector, the State and Social Work in Britain: The Charity Organisation Society/Family Welfare Association* (Aldershot, 1995); Madeline Rooff, *A Hundred Years of Family Welfare: A Study of the Family Welfare Association, 1869–1969* (London, 1972); Robert Humphreys, *Poor Relief and Charity, 1869–1945: The London Charity Organisation Society* (Basingstoke, 2001); Magali Gente, 'Family Ideology and the Charity

Organization Society in Great Britain during the First World War', *Journal of Family History* 27, 3 (2002), 255–272. For the Victorian period, see Helen Bosanquet, *Social Work in London, 1869–1912: A History of the Charity Organisation Society* (London, 1912); Robert Humphreys, *Sin, Organised Charity and the Poor Laws in Victorian England* (New York, 1995); and Gertrude Himmelfarb, *Poverty and Compassion: The Moral Imagination of the Late Victorians* (New York, 1991), ch. 13.

46   In her authorized history of the Family Welfare Association, Jane Lewis describes how the organization became increasingly interested in psychodynamic methods from the 1940s onwards. This was partly in response to intellectual fashions and, as the welfare state began to deal effectively with cases of immediate material hardship, partly due to the changing nature of the problems it encountered (Lewis, ch. 5). For FWA case-work methods, see also Michael Peplar, *Family Matters: A History of Ideas about Family since 1945* (Harlow, 2002), 57–67; and John E. Mayer and Noel Timms, *The Client Speaks: Working-Class Impressions of Casework* (London, 1970).

47   For the use of working-class autobiography, see Joanna Bourke, 'Housewifery in Working-Class England', *Past and Present* 143 (1994), 167–197; and John Burnett (ed.), *Destiny Obscure: Autobiographies of Childhood, Education and Family from the 1820s to the 1920s* (London, 1982). For oral history on marriage, see in particular Carl Chinn, *They Worked All Their Lives: Women of the Urban Poor in England, 1880–1939* (Manchester, 1988); Diana Gittins, *Fair Sex: Family Size and Structure, 1900–39* (London, 1982); Trevor Lummis, 'The Historical Dimension of Fatherhood: A Case Study', *The Father Figure*, ed. Lorna McKee and Margaret O'Brien (London, 1982); Elizabeth Roberts, *A Woman's Place: An Oral History of Working-Class Women, 1890–1940* (Oxford, 1984); *idem, Women and Families: An Oral History* (Oxford, 1995); Jerry White, *The Worst Street in the World: Campbell Bunk, Islington, between the Wars* (London, 1986); and Pat Ayers and Jan Lambertz, 'Marriage Relations, Money and Domestic Violence in Working-Class Liverpool, 1919–39', *Labour and Love: Women's Experience of Home and Family, 1850–1940*, ed. Jane Lewis (Oxford, 1986).

48   Mayer and Timms, 25; FWA Study Group Report (*c.* early 1970s) cited in Lewis, 134; Florence Mitchell, 'Marriage Counselling in a Family Casework Agency', *Social Work* 14, 2 (1957), 309.

49   Considerations of confidentiality likewise prevent me from providing citations for the FWA files quoted in this section. These will, however, be made available to researchers who have received the FWA's permission to consult the files housed in the London Metropolitan Archives.

50   Most family histories are in fact regional in focus. For London, see White; Ellen Ross, *Love and Toil: Motherhood in Outcast London, 1870–1914* (Oxford, 1993); and Anna Davin, *Growing Up Poor: Home, School and Street in London, 1870–1914* (London, 1996). For Liverpool, see Ayers and Lambertz; for Birmingham, Chinn; for Lancashire, Roberts, *A Woman's Place; idem, Women and Families;* and Gittins; and for East Anglia, Lummis. For the contrasting dynamics of *petit bourgeois* marriages, see A. James Hammerton, 'Pooterism or Partnership?: Marriage and Masculine Identity in the Lower Middle Class, 1870–1920', *Journal of British Studies* 38, 3 (1999), 291–321.

51   For the impact of the Second World War on family life, see in particular Geoffrey Field, 'Perspectives on the Working-Class Family in Wartime Britain, 1939–45', *International Labor and Working-Class History* 38 (1990), 3–28.

52   B.E. Astbury, T.E. Lloyd and R. Saunderson, 'A Plea for the Husband', *Charity Organisation Quarterly* 8, 1 (1934), 32. The reluctance of female FWA case-workers to side with wives is all the more remarkable considering that the mostly male probation officers involved in very similar marriage guidance work were twice as likely to criticize husbands than wives (Beatrice E. Pollard, *Social Casework for the State: A Study of the Principle of Client Independence in the Matrimonial Work of Probation Officers* (London, 1962), 90–91).

53   For a statistical breakdown of marriage rates, see David Coleman, 'Population and Family', *Twentieth-Century British Social Trends*, ed. A.H. Halsey and Josephine Webb (Basingstoke, 2000).

54   Eliot Slater and Moya Woodside, *Patterns of Marriage: A Study of Marriage Relationships in the Urban Working Classes* (London, 1951), 117.

55   For more on the unromantic attitudes of working-class men and women, see John R. Gillis, *For Better, For Worse: British Marriages, 1600 to the Present* (New York, 1985),

302; and Judy Giles, '"You Meet 'Em and That's It": Working-Class Women's Refusal of Romance between the Wars in Britain', *Romance Revisited*, ed. Lynne Pearse and Jackie Stacey (London, 1995).

56   Young and Willmott, *Family and Kinship*; Peter Townsend, *The Family Life of Old People: An Inquiry in East London* (London, 1957), xiv; Richard Hoggart, *The Uses of Literacy: Changing Patterns in English Mass Culture* (Fair Lawn, NJ, 1957).

57   Melanie Tebbutt, *Women's Talk: A Social History of 'Gossip' in Working-Class Neighbourhoods, 1880–1960* (Aldershot, 1995), 173.

58   For the double-edged nature of neighbourliness, see also McKibbin, *Classes and Cultures*, 181.

59   Ferdynand Zweig, *Women's Life and Labour* (London, 1952), 18.

60   *Idem*, *Life, Labour and Poverty* (London, 1949), ch. 2. For the seminal text on income maldistribution in working-class families, see Eleanor F. Rathbone, *The Disinherited Family: A Plea for the Endowment of the Family* (London, 1924), ch. 3.

61   Townsend, 68.

62   For the drawbacks of female responsibility for the family purse, see also Ayers and Lambertz, 201.

63   Zweig, *Life, Labour and Poverty*, 21, 23.

64   H.B. Grant, *Marriage, Separation and Divorce* [rev. edn] (London, 1948), 43. My findings offer, if anything, a conservative estimate of domestic violence when compared to other studies of the poor in early twentieth-century London. Jerry White found evidence of chronic wife-beating in half of the families he interviewed in the Islington slum of Campbell Bunk, while Ellen Ross believes working-class husbands to have been 'practically by definition violent' towards their wives (White, 139; Ross, 84). For Victorian domestic violence, see Nancy Tomes, 'A "Torrent of Abuse": Crimes of Violence between Working-Class Men and Women in London, 1840–75', *Journal of Social History* 11, 3 (1978), 328–345; Shani D'Cruze, *Crimes of Outrage: Sex, Violence and Victorian Working Women* (London, 1998); and Hammerton, *Cruelty and Companionship*, ch. 2.

65   Slater and Woodside, 167; A.F. Philp, *Family Failure: A Study of 129 Families with Multiple Problems* (London, 1963), 137.

66   Madeleine Kerr, *The People of Ship Street* (London, 1958), 77.

67   For conflicting evidence on family limitation in this period, see Simon Szreter, *Fertility, Class and Gender in Britain, 1860–1940* (Cambridge, 1996); Kate Fisher, '"She Was Quite Satisfied with the Arrangements I Made": Gender and Birth Control in Britain, 1920–50', *Past and Present* 169 (2000), 161–193; Richard Allen Soloway, *Birth Control and the Population Question in England, 1877–1930* (Chapel Hill, NC, 1982); Deborah A. Cohen, 'Private Lives in Public Spaces: Marie Stopes, the Mothers' Clinics and the Practice of Contraception', *History Workshop Journal* 35 (1993), 95–116; and Claire Davey, 'Birth Control in Britain during the Interwar Years: Evidence from the Stopes Correspondence', *Journal of Family History* 13, 3 (1988), 329–345.

68   Townsend, 75; Slater and Woodside, 168.

69   For examples of mothers' possessiveness towards children, see McKibbin, *Classes and Cultures*, 175; and Gittins, 142.

70   Mrs Pember Reeves, *Round About a Pound a Week* (London, 1913), 115.

71   Spinley, 57, 23; Zweig, *Women's Life and Labour*, 45.

72   Ibid., 82.

73   For the operation of the law in working-class marital disputes, see Behlmer, ch. 4.

74   For an influential attack on working-class patriarchy predating mutuality, see Frances Power Cobbe, 'Wife Torture in England' (1878), *The Wives – Controversies in the History of British Feminism*, ed. Marie Mulvey Roberts and Tamae Mizuta (London, 1995), 2. For critiques of this tradition of social commentary, see M. Loane, *The Queen's Poor: Life as They Find It in Town and Country* (London, 1905); and Young and Willmott, *Family and Kinship*, ch. 1.

75   Roberts, *A Woman's Place*, chs. 3–4; Joanna Bourke, *Working-Class Cultures in Britain, 1890–1960: Gender, Class and Ethnicity* (London, 1994), ch. 3; *idem*, 'Housewifery in Working-Class England'; McKibbin, *Classes and Cultures*, 169–176.

76   Gittins, 129–130; Lummis, 44.

77   Bourke, *Working-Class Cultures*, 96; Ross McKibbin, *The Ideologies of Class: Social Relations in Britain, 1880–1950* (Oxford, 1990), ch. 5; Lummis, 52.

78 White, 95–96; Ross, 56; Chinn, 16, 23.

79 Bourke, *Working-Class Cultures*, 80, 74, 78.

80 Gittins, 145; Roberts, *Women and Families*, 84.

81 McKibbin, *Classes and Cultures*, 176.

82 Kathleen Bannister *et al.*, *Social Casework in Marital Problems: The Development of a Psychodynamic Approach* (London, 1955), 173; W.G. Fox, 'The Family Discussion Bureau', *Case Conference* 1, 11 (1955), 22–26.

83 J.H. Wallis and H.S. Booker, *Marriage Counselling: A Description and Analysis of the Remedial Work of the National Marriage Guidance Council* (London, 1958), 127–130; Jill Heisler, 'Some of Our Clients', *Marriage Guidance* (July/August 1974), 132; Henry V. Dicks, *Marital Tensions: Clinical Studies towards a Psychological Theory of Interaction* (London, 1967), 279. What Dicks attributed to ignorance may have been the indifference to talking cures of working-class clients seeking concrete solutions to primarily material problems, for which see Mayer and Timms; and Geoffrey Parkinson, 'Marriages on Probation' (1969), *One for Sorrow, Two for Joy: Ten Years of New Society*, ed. Paul Barker (London, 1972).

84 David Mace, *Marriage Counselling* (London, 1948), 177. For the FDB (later known as the Tavistock Institute of Marital Studies), see also Isabel E.P. Menzies, 'Factors Affecting Family Breakdown in Urban Communities: A Preliminary Study Leading to the Establishment of Two Pilot Family Discussion Bureaux', *Human Relations* 2, 4 (1949), 363–373; Kathleen Bannister, 'The Development of a Professional Marriage Counselling Service', *Social Work* 14, 2 (1957), 312–317; Family Discussion Bureau, *The Marital Relationship as a Focus for Casework* (London, 1962); Lily Pincus (ed.), *Marriage: Studies in Emotional Conflict and Growth* (London, 1960); Christopher Clulow and Janet Mattinson, *Marriage Inside Out: Understanding Problems of Intimacy* (Harmondsworth, 1989); Christopher Clulow (ed.), *Marriage, Disillusion and Hope: Papers Celebrating the Forty Years of the Tavistock Institute of Marital Studies* (London, 1990); Christopher Clulow (ed.), *Rethinking Marriage: Public and Private Perspectives* (London, 1993); and Stanley Ruszczynski (ed.), *Psychotherapy with Couples: Theory and Practice at the Tavistock Institute of Marital Studies* (London, 1993). For the Marital Unit, see Dicks, *Marital Tensions*; and *idem*, *Fifty Years of the Tavistock Clinic* (London, 1970). For the NMGC, see Wallis and Booker; Jane Lewis, David Clark and David Morgan, *Whom God Hath Joined Together: The Work of Marriage Guidance* (London, 1992); and Jennifer Chapman, *Made in Heaven: Ordinary and Extraordinary People Talk about Marriage* (London, 1993). The Catholic Marriage Advisory Council and the Jewish Education Marriage Council are excluded from this discussion since they promoted a patriarchal model of marriage, for which see Catholic Marriage Advisory Council, *Beginning Your Marriage* (London, 1963); and Jewish Marriage Education Council, *Jewish Marriage, i–iv* [rev. edn] (London, 1964–6). Also omitted are the Family Service Units on account of their catering exclusively for lower working-class 'problem' families. See Pat Starkey, *Families and Social Workers: The Work of the Family Service Units, 1940–85* (Liverpool, 2000); and Alan Cohen, *The Revolution in Postwar Family Casework: The Story of Pacifist Service Units and Family Units, 1940–59* (Lancaster, 1998).

85 Bannister *et al.*, 168; Dicks, *Marital Tensions*, 14; *Marriage: Studies in Emotional Conflict*, 231, 233.

86 The lack of case-notes for companionate marriages in mid twentieth-century Britain appears to be an insuperable problem. The Tavistock Institute of Marital Studies (*née* FDB) shredded all its records of clients predating the mid seventies and every branch of Relate diligently destroys its files after five years.

87 Rhona Rapoport and Robert N. Rapoport, *Dual Career Families Reconsidered: New Integrations of Work and Family* (London, 1976), 11; Rhona Rapoport, 'The Study of Marriage as a Critical Transition', *The Predicament of the Family*, ed. Peter Lomas (London, 1967), 201.

88 J.M. Pahl and R.E. Pahl, *Managers and the Wives: A Study of Career and Family Role in the Middle Class* (Harmondsworth, 1972), 235; Hannah Gavron, *The Captive Wife: Conflicts of Housebound Mothers* (London, 1966), 129.

89 Rapoport and Rapoport, 318. For a summary of contemporary research on male housework, see Victor George and Paul Wilding, *Motherless Families* (London, 1972), 3.

90 Mary Macaulay, *Marriage for the Married* (London, 1964), 118; Dicks, *Marital Tensions*, 148, 55, 57.

91   J.H. Wallis, *Thinking About Marriage* (Harmondsworth, 1963), 42.
92   *Idem, Sexual Harmony in Marriage*, 46; *idem, Thinking About Marriage*, 105.
93   Bannister *et al.*, 80.
94   Drucilla Beyfus, *The English Marriage* (London, 1968), xii; A. Herbert Gray, *Successful Marriage* (London, 1941), 113, 114.
95   *Marriage: Studies in Emotional Conflict*, 77; Dicks, *Marital Tensions*, 64, 63, 64.
96   'The Cruelty of Silence', *Marriage Guidance* (July 1953), 4; Dicks, *Marital Tensions*, 61.
97   Roger Pilkington, 'Like Attracts Like', *Getting Married, 1965* (London, 1965), 72; Eustace Chesser, *Unquiet Minds: Leaves from a Psychologist's Casebook* (London, 1952), 165; Beyfus, 99.
98   *Marriage: Studies in Emotional Conflict*, 127.
99   David R. Mace, *Whom God Hath Joined: A Book of Christian Marriage* (London, 1953), 34, 33.
100 Rapoport, 200; *Marriage: Studies in Emotional Conflict*, 232; E.M. Goldberg, *Family Influences and Psychosomatic Illness: An Inquiry in the Social and Psychological Background of Duodenal Ulcer* (London, 1958), 124.
101 Bannister *et al.*, 128; *Marriage: Studies in Emotional Conflict*, 152.
102 Talcott Parsons, 'The Kinship System of the Contemporary United States' (1943), *Essays in Sociological Theory* [rev. edn] (New York, 1964), 193. See also *idem*, 'The American Family', *Family Socialisation and Interaction Process* (London, 1956).
103 Kaufmann, 71, 81.
104 Dicks, *Marital Tensions*, 259, 75, 177.
105 Ibid., 48.
106 Bannister *et al.*, 80; Dicks, *Marital Tensions*, 62.
107 Ibid., 60, 61.
108 Ibid., 57; *Marriage: Studies in Emotional Conflict*, 115.
109 For 'masculinized' women, see Chesser, *Love Without Fear*, 27; John Macmurray, 'Conditions of Marriage Today', *Marriage Guidance* (December 1965), 379; Anthony Mann, *The Human Paradox: Counselling in the Context of Human Experience* (London, 1973), 120; Bannister *et al.*, 130; Dicks, *Marital Tensions*, 20, 48, 158; Leonard Friedman, *Virgin Wives: A Study of Unconsummated Marriages* (London, 1962), 56; and *Marriage: Studies in Emotional Conflict*, 98–99.
110 Dicks, *Marital Tensions*, 60; *Marriage: Studies in Emotional Conflict*, 99; Dicks, *Marital Tensions*, 250.
111 Florida Scott-Maxwell, *Women and Sometimes Men* (London, 1957), 7; Bannister *et al.*, 166.
112 *Marriage: Studies in Emotional Conflict*, 185, 184; L.P.D. Tunnadine, *Contraception and Sexual Life: A Therapeutic Approach* (London, 1970), 70.
113 *Marriage: Studies in Emotional Conflict*, 54, 56.
114 Gray, *Successful Marriage*, 6; Eustace Chesser, 'Social Influences on Marriage', *Marriage Guidance* (July 1952), 4; Bannister *et al.*, 166.
115 Wallis, *Thinking About Marriage*, 80; Bannister *et al.*, 131.
116 Wallis, *Marriage Observed*, 100; Beyfus, 89. Viola Klein found that wives underestimated the extent of husbandly hostility towards their going out to work (Viola Klein, *Britain's Married Women Workers* (London, 1965), 63–66).
117 Eustace Chesser, *An Outline of Human Relationships* (London, 1959), 149; Bannister *et al.*, 131.
118 Ann Mullins, 'The Best Sort of Marriage', *Getting Married, 1964* (London, 1964), 66.
119 Dicks, *Marital Tensions*, 177, 60.
120 Heather Jenner and Muriel Segal, *Men and Marriage* (London, 1970), 43; Dicks, *Marital Tensions*, 145; *Marriage: Studies in Emotional Conflict*, 45. For husbands shirking their responsibilities, see also G.M. Carstairs, *This Island Now* (London, 1963), 70–71.
121 Wallis, *Marriage Observed*, 100.
122 Wallis, *Sexual Harmony in Marriage*, 39; Bannister *et al.*, 119; Dicks, *Marital Tensions*, 254; Bannister *et al.*, 129. For women's reluctance to claim their right to equal sexual pleasure, see also Eustace Chesser, *The Sexual, Marital and Family Relationships of the English Woman* (London, 1956), 379; and Geoffrey Gorer, *Exploring English Character* (London, 1955), 116.
123 W.L. Herbert and F.V. Jarvis, *A Modern Approach to Marriage Counselling* (London, 1959), 70; *Marriage: Studies in Emotional Conflict*, 115; Sandra McDermott, *Studies in*

Female Sexuality (London, 1970), 94. However, two-fifths of the women surveyed by Eustace Chesser in the early 1950s believed that they could make a success of their marriages even if they did not themselves enjoy intercourse (Chesser, *The Sexual, Marital and Family Relationships*, 379).

124 Mann, 119; Michael Courtenay, *Sexual Discord in Marriage: A Field for Brief Psychotherapy* (London, 1968), 53.

125 Nancy Holt, *Counselling in Marriage Problems* (London, 1971), 94, 93.

126 Kathleen Bannister and Lily Pincus, *Shared Phantasy in Marital Problems: Therapy in a Four Person Relationship* (London, 1965), 66; Dicks, *Marital Tensions*, 153.

127 *Marriage: Studies in Emotional Conflict*, 111; Wallis, *Sexual Harmony in Marriage*, 83.

128 *Marriage: Studies in Emotional Conflict*, 149, 124; Beyfus, 78; *Marriage: Studies in Emotional Conflict*, 111.

129 Wallis, *Sexual Harmony in Marriage*, 39; Edward F. Griffith, *Ups and Downs in Married Life* (London, 1966), 49.

130 Dicks, *Marital Tensions*, 156, 99, 156.

131 Griffith, *Ups and Downs in Married Life*, 58; Tunnadine, 55; Wallis, *Sexual Harmony in Marriage*, 83.

132 Tunnadine, 42, 71.

133 David Mace, *Sexual Difficulties in Marriage* [rev. edn] (Rugby, 1983), 6; David R. Mace, *The Christian Response to the Sexual Revolution* (London, 1971), 76.

134 'Medica', *Any Wife or Any Husband* [rev. edn], 85; *idem*, *Any Wife or Any Husband* (London, 1950), 92; Esther Adams, 'Eros and Agape', *Marriage Guidance* 4, 2 (1950), 6.

135 Griffith, *Ups and Downs in Married Life*, 165, 163. For the claims made for vaginal orgasms, see also Cook, 151–155. An important exception to marriage counsellors' antipathy towards clitoral orgasms is to be found in the work of Helena Wright. In her groundbreaking *More about the Sex Factor in Marriage*, she questioned the 'efficacy of the penis-vagina combination for producing an orgasm for the woman' and presented the case for the clitoris as 'an organ of unique sensitiveness' functionally equivalent to the penis (Helena Wright, *More about the Sex Factor in Marriage* [rev. edn] (London, 1954), 49, 61).

136 NMGC, *Sex Difficulties in the Wife*, 8.

137 Bannister *et al.*, 98; *Marriage: Studies in Emotional Conflict*, 131, 137.

138 Dicks, *Marital Tensions*, 153.

139 Robert Chartham, *Mainly for Wives: A Guide to Practical Love-Making* (London, 1964), 52; Holt, 60–61.

140 Griffith, *Ups and Downs in Married Life*, 24; *Marriage: Studies in Emotional Conflict*, 143.

141 Wallis, *Marriage Observed*, 79.

142 Tuffill, 38; Lorna Guthrie and Janet Mattinson, *Brief Casework with a Marital Problem* (London, 1971), 30.

143 Mace, *Sexual Difficulties*, 6.

144 Mann, 122; Courtenay, 47, 48.

145 Wallis, *Sexual Harmony in Marriage*, 97, 93.

146 Edmund Leach, *A Runaway World?* (New York, 1968), 44.

147 Dicks, *Marital Tensions*, 19; Bannister *et al.*, 69.

148 Macaulay, *Marriage for the Married*, 94; Dicks, *Marital Tensions*, 160.

149 Cartland, 165–166; Holt, 61; Martin Richards, 'The Companionship Trap', *Women, Men and Marriage: Talks from the Tavistock Marital Studies Institute*, ed. Christopher Clulow (London, 1995), 61–62.

150 Stanley, 121; Chesser, *The Sexual, Marital and Family Relationships*, 397. However, Rhona Rapoport reported that between a third and a half of her sample experienced problems in their first year of marriage (Rapoport, 197–198).

151 Richard A. Mackey and Bernard A. O'Brien. *Lasting Marriages: Men and Women Growing Together* (Westport, CN, 1995), 52; Jessica Weiss, *To Have and to Hold: Marriage, the Baby Boom and Social Change* (Chicago, 2000), 225, ch. 5. For further American parallels, see Elaine Tyler May, *Great Expectations: Marriage and Divorce in Post-Victorian America* (Chicago, 1980); *idem*, *Homeward Bound: American Families in the Cold War Era* (New York, 1988); Barbara Ehrenreich, *The Hearts of Men: American Dreams and the Flight from Commitment* (Garden City, NY, 1984), chs. 1 and

2; and Sharon R. Ullman, *Sex Seen: The Emergence of Modern Sexuality in America* (Berkeley, CA, 1997), ch. 4.

152 Stanley, 197, 121.

153 Gavron, 58, 134; Bott, 28.

154 Gavron, 142; Bott, 83; Gavron, 58; Bott, 84.

155 Bannister *et al.*, 168.

156 Elizabeth Sloan Chesser, 'The Honeymoon and the Years Which Follow', *Love, Marriage, Jealousy*, ed. A. Forbath (London, 1938), 169.

157 Mayo Wingate, *Human Problems of Today: Sex, Courtship and Marriage* (London, 1964), 75–76; Dicks, *Marital Tensions*, 138.

158 Wingate, 54; Dicks, *Marital Tensions*, 217.

159 Helena Wright, *The Sex Factor in Marriage* (London, 1930), ch. 5; A. Herbert Gray, *Love: The One Solution* (London, 1938); A.G. Thompson in introduction to *Marriage: Studies in Emotional Conflict*, 3; Dicks, *Marital Tensions*, 133, 129.

160 E.M. Goldberg, 'The Normal Family: Myth and Reality' (1959), *Social Work with Families*, ed. Eileen Younghusband (London, 1971), 14, 26, 15.

161 Dicks, *Marital Tensions*, 20; Bannister *et al.*, 167.

162 Dicks, *Marital Tensions*, 158.

163 Macaulay, *Marriage for the Married*, 8; Mace, *Marriage Crisis*, 49; Dicks, *Marital Tensions*, 3.

164 David Mace and Vera Mace, *We Can Have Better Marriages, If We Really Want Them* (London, 1975), 84; Angela Willans (aka 'Mary Grant'), 'Expectations of Marriage', *Marriage Guidance* (January 1973), 213; Wallis, *Marriage Observed*, 78.

165 Mace, *Sexual Difficulties*, 4.

166 *Idem*, *Marriage Counselling*, 17; Jill Heisler and Alan Whitehouse, 'The NMGC Client, 1975', *Marriage Guidance* 16, 6 (1976), 191; NMGC cited in Home Office, *Marriage Matters* (London, 1979), 8; David R. Mace, *Marriage: The Art of Lasting Happiness* (London, 1952); Angela Reed, *The Woman on the Verge of Divorce* (London, 1970).

167 Ibid., 5, 27, 9.

168 Ibid., 7, 8.

Chapter 5 – Porn Free

1 Philip Larkin, 'Annus Mirabilis', *Collected Poems* (London, 1988), 167; *King* (Winter 1964), 2. Since the *Pirelli Calendar* was not a magazine and *Forum* not strictly speaking pornographic, they fall outside of the present discussion. For the former, see *The Complete Pirelli Calendar Book* (London, 1975); and for the latter, see Lal Coveney, Leslie Kay and Pat Mahony, 'Theory into Practice: Sexual Liberation or Social Control – *Forum* Magazine, 1968–81', *The Sexuality Papers: Male Sexuality and the Social Control of Women*, ed. Lal Coveney *et al.* (London, 1984). For the origins of *Penthouse*, see John Heidenry, *What Wild Ecstasy: The Rise and Fall of the Sexual Revolution* (New York, 1997), 40–47. The comparative unadventurousness of *Playboy* was exposed by the new pornographic magazines, which displayed more women (and more of the women) – three or four photo-sets against Hefner's one or two. They also presented the women in a radically altered fashion, as a comparison between the first cover of *Penthouse* and that of the concurrent issue of *Playboy* readily demonstrates. The *Playboy* cover was of a girl in grey slacks and sandals, one hand on hip and the other waving a sparkler for Independence Day. Against this cheerleader pose and cheeky smile, the *Penthouse* woman was wearing only a sweater, had her hands clasped in front of her and was staring unashamedly into the camera lens.

2 See *Pornography: The Longford Report* (London, 1972).

3 *Mayfair* 1, 1 (1966), 38; *Penthouse* 1, 2 (1965), 5, 9. For the utopian aspects of pornography, see also Robert Darnton, *The Literary Underground of the Old Regime* (Cambridge, MA, 1982), 199–208; Peter Wagner, *Eros Revived: Erotica of the Enlightenment in England and America* (London, 1990), 6; Steven Marcus, 'Pornotopia', *Encounter* (August 1966), 9–18; and Barbara Ehrenreich, *The Hearts of Men: American Dreams and the Flight from Commitment* (Garden City, NY, 1984), 50.

4 For a groundbreaking analysis of pre-permissive gay pornography, see Thomas Waugh,

Hard to Imagine: Gay Male Eroticism in Photography and Film from the Beginnings to Stonewall (New York, 1996); and for representative samples of the same, see *Adonis: The Male Physique Pin-up, 1870–1940* (London, 1989); and John Barrington, *Art and Anatomy* (London, 1951). The history of pornographic films has also been thoroughly researched, for which see David McGillivray, *Doing Rude Things: The History of the British Sex Film, 1957–81* (London, 1992); and Linda Williams, *Hard Core: Power, Pleasure and the 'Frenzy of the Visible'* (London, 1990). For Victorian pornography, see Lisa Z. Sigel, *Governing Pleasures: Pornography and Social Change in England, 1815–1914* (New Brunswick, NJ, 2002).

5   George Orwell, *Nineteen Eighty-Four* (London, 1974), 69. See also his 'Raffles and Miss Blandish', *Collected Essays, Journalism and Letters*, iii (Harmondsworth, 1968) for the authoritarian overtones of sadomasochistic detective novels. Orwell's ideas are clearly developed from D.H. Lawrence's *Pornography and Obscenity* (London, 1929). Interestingly, Aldous Huxley's *Brave New World* (1932) also featured government-controlled erotica. For conservative moralism, see William Joynson-Hicks (Viscount Brenford), *Do We Need a Censor?* (London, 1929).

6   For masturbation, see Lesley A. Hall, 'Forbidden by God, Despised by Man: Masturbation, Medical Warnings, Moral Panic and Manhood in Great Britain', *Forbidden History*, ed. John C. Fout (Chicago, 1992); and *idem, Hidden Anxieties: Male Sexuality, 1900–39* (Cambridge, 1991), 129–134, which describe how male masturbators writing to Marie Stopes presented themselves as being in the grip of a compulsion and feared for the damage that masturbation might cause to their marriages, their organs and their 'nerves'. For calls for the freedom to publish sexual literature, see Bernard Causton and G. Gordon Young, *Keeping it Dark; or The Censor's Handbook* (London, 1930); Holbrook Jackson, *The Fear of Books* (London, 1932); Bertrand Russell, *Marriage and Morals* (London, 1976), ch. 8; and George Ryley Scott, *Into Whose Hands: An Examination of Obscene Libel in Its Legal, Sociological and Literary Aspects* (London, 1945). However, while these sex radicals were generally prepared to tolerate a certain amount of pornography, they were careful to distinguish between it and both erotica and instructive sexual literature, and never failed to express the hope that the availability of the latter would extinguish the demand for the former.

7   Waugh, 216. For the difficulty in obtaining hard-core porn, see the memorandum by the Metropolitan Police Commissioner in *Minutes of Evidence from the Select Committee on the Obscene Publications Bill* (London, 1958), 71, 73. For a study of the most famous hard-core house of its day, Maurice Girodias' Olympia Press, see John de St Jorre, *The Good Ship Venus: The Erotic Voyage of the Olympia Press* (London, 1994); and for a sample of its predominantly sadomasochistic output, see Maurice Girodias (ed.), *The Best of Olympia* (London, 1966).

8   *Health and Efficiency*, February 1968, 9; *Health and Efficiency Summer Annual* (1957), 17; *Health and Efficiency*, December 1970, 10; *Health and Efficiency*, May 1968, 8, 11. For representative naturist erotica, see Charles Sennet, *Sunshine and Naturism* (London, 1946); and Michael Rutherford, *British Naturism* (London, 1946).

9   For Walter Bird, see *Beauty's Daughters* (London, 1938). For John Everard, see *Adam's Fifth Rib* (London, 1935); and *Artist's Model* (London, 1951). For 'Roye' (aka Horace Narbeth), see *Perfect Womanhood* (London, 1938); and *Nude Ego* (London, 1955). For a rare collaborative venture, see Walter Bird, John Everard and 'Roye' (aka Horace Narbeth), *Eves Without Leaves* (London, 1940). For an analysis of the female nudes in *Men Only*, see Jill Greenfield, Sean O'Connell and Chris Reid, 'Fashioning Masculinity: *Men Only*, Consumption and the Development of Marketing in Interwar Britain', *Twentieth-Century British History* 10, 4 (1999), 468.

10   See 'Roye' (aka Horace Narbeth), *Unique Editions* (London, 1958); and *idem, Unique Verdict* (London, 1960).

11   Eric Howe, *How to Draw Pin-ups* (London, 1963), 17; Peter Bailey, 'Parasexuality and Glamour: The Victorian Barmaid as Cultural Prototype', *Gender and History* 2, 2 (1990), 148.

12   Diana Dors, *Swingin' Dors* (London, 1960), 121, 183.

13   Mark Gabor, *The Pin-up: A Modest History* (London, 1972), 112; Reginald Arkell in *Eves Without Leaves*, 9.

14   *Men Only* 76, 301 (1961), 41; *Men Only* 77, 309 (1961), 19.

15   These escapist settings compare with the 'pornotopias' famously described by Steven

Marcus in *The Other Victorians: A Study of Sexuality and Pornography in Mid Nineteenth-Century England* (New York, 1966).

16 Richard Hoggart, *The Uses of Literacy: Changing Patterns in English Mass Culture* (Harmondsworth, 1958), 233.

17 For Harrison Marks, see his autobiography *She Walks in Beauty* (London, 1964). For a sampling of this sort of porn, see *Peep* (1959), *Cuddles* (1960) and *Pin-Ups* (1963).

18 Hoggart, 246, 213, 253, 232, 233.

19 For general discussions of permissiveness, see in particular Christie Davies, *Permissive Britain: Social Change in the Sixties and Seventies* (London, 1975); National Deviancy Conference, *Permissiveness and Control: The Fate of the Sixties Legislation* (New York, 1980); Jeffrey Weeks, *Sex, Politics and Society: The Regulation of Sexuality since 1800* [rev. edn] (London, 1989); John Seed and Bart Moore-Gilbert (eds.), *Cultural Revolution?: The Challenge of the Arts in the 1960s* (London, 1992); Anthony Aldgate, James Chapman and Arthur Marwick (eds.), *Windows on the Sixties: Exploring Key Texts of Media and Culture* (London, 2000); Arthur Marwick, *The Sixties: Cultural Revolution in Britain, France, Italy and the United States, c. 1958–74* (Oxford, 1998); and Tim Newburn, *Permission and Regulation: Law and Morals in Postwar Britain* (London, 1992). For the debate on obscenity in this period, see in particular John Sutherland, *Offensive Literature: Decensorship in Britain, 1960–82* (London, 1982); Norman St John-Stevas, *Obscenity and the Law* (London, 1956); Progressive League, *Memoranda of Evidence Submitted to the Select Committees of the House of Commons on Obscene Publications* (London, 1958); Kenneth Allsop and Robert Pitman, *A Question of Obscenity* (Northwood, 1960); C.H. Rolph (ed.), *Does Pornography Matter?* (London, 1961); Lord Radcliffe, *Censors* (London, 1961); John Trevelyan, *Censorship* (London, 1962); *Pornography and Public Morals* (London, 1963); H. Montgomery Hyde, *A History of Pornography* (London, 1964); Arts Council Working Party, *The Obscenity Laws* (London, 1969); and Donald Thomas, *A Long Time Burning: The History of Literary Censorship in England* (London, 1969).

20 *Club International* 2, 5 (1973).

21 For a Stateside perspective on the 'Pubic Wars', see Russell Miller, *Bunny: The Real Story of Playboy* (London, 1984), ch. 9.

22 Alan Herbert in *Minutes of Evidence from the Select Committee on the Obscene Publications Bill*, 100, 43. For Alan Herbert's second thoughts, see his autobiography *A.P.H.: His Life and Times* (London, 1970), 238–240. 'Wives and servants' were notoriously the people whom prosecutor Mervyn Griffith-Jones wished to shield from the filth contained in *Lady Chatterley's Lover*; see C.H. Rolph (ed.), *The Trial of Lady Chatterley* (Harmondsworth, 1961), 17.

23 H.J. Eysenck, *Sex and Personality* (London, 1976), 81. A majority was also against all censorship and only a quarter of each sex thought that reading girlie magazines 'suggests failure to achieve adult attitudes to sex' (83, 85). See Geoffrey Robertson, *Obscenity* (London, 1979), 207, 209 for polling evidence of tolerance for pornography in the early seventies; and Steven Harding, 'Trends in Permissiveness', *British Social Attitudes: The Fifth Report*, ed. Roger Jowell *et al.* (Aldershot, 1988) for the subsequent hardening of attitudes.

24 For consumerism in *Playboy*, see Ehrenreich, ch. 4; Gail Dines, '"I Buy It for the Articles": *Playboy* Magazine and the Sexualization of Consumerism', *Gender, Race and Class in Media: A Text-Reader* (Thousand Oaks, CA, 1995); and Thomas Weyr, *Reaching for Paradise: The Playboy Vision of America* (New York, 1978).

25 *Mayfair* 4, 1 (1969), 4; *Mayfair* 4, 7 (1969), 4; *Mayfair* 4, 8 (1969), 4; *Mayfair* 4, 11 (1969), 4; *Mayfair* 4, 12 (1969), 4.

26 Mary Quant in *The Permissive Society: The Guardian Inquiry* (London, 1969), 21. For the relationship between fashion and pornography, Emma Peel's catsuit included, see Valerie Steele, *Fetish: Fashion, Sex and Power* (New York, 1996).

27 For erotica in the counterculture, see issues of *Oz* and *IT (International Times)* prior to the eruption of the women's liberation movement; but for countercultural objections to the inauthenticity of pornography, see Theodore Roszak, *The Making of a Counter Culture* (London, 1970), 14–15; Germaine Greer, *The Female Eunuch* (London, 1970), 258; and *idem*, 'Seduction is a Four-Letter Word' (1973), *The Madwoman's Underclothes: Essays and Occasional Writings, 1968–85* (London, 1987), 164. For sexologists' earlier attempts to dissociate themselves from porn, see Alec Craig's

discomfort at the 'unhappy juxtaposition' of sexology with pornography on the shelves of 'disreputable' booksellers and George Ryley Scott's attempt to restrict the sale of his *Encyclopaedia of Sex* to 'members of the Medical and Legal Professions, Scientists, Anthropologists, Psychologists, Sociologists, Criminologists and Social Workers' (Alec Craig, *The Banned Books of England* (London, 1937), 169; George Ryley Scott, *Scott's Encyclopaedia of Sex* (London, 1939), frontispiece).

28 *King* (August 1965), 71; *Club International* 2, 4 (1973); *Penthouse* 1, 1 (1965), 7.

29 Graham Chapman *et al*; *Monty Python's Flying Circus: Just the Words, i* (London, 1989), 99; Ken Baynes, *Art and Society: Sex* (London, 1972), 34. For the relationship between art and pornography, see Lynda Nead, *The Female Nude: Art, Obscenity and Sexuality* (London, 1992); Edward Lucie-Smith, *Sexuality in Western Art* (London, 1991); Janet Hobhouse, *The Bride Stripped Bare: The Artist and the Nude in the Twentieth Century* (London, 1988); John Berger *et al.*, *Ways of Seeing* (London, 1972), 55; Laura Mulvey, 'You Don't Know What is Happening, Do You, Mr Jones?' (1973) in Rozsika Parker and Griselda Pollock, *Framing Feminism: Art and the Women's Movement, 1970–85* (London, 1987); and Peter Webb, *The Erotic Arts* (London, 1975). For the 'pornographisation of the mainstream' in subsequent decades, see Brian McNair, *Mediated Sex: Pornography and Postmodern Culture* (London, 1996); Laura Kipnis, *Bound and Gagged: Pornography and the Politics of Fantasy in America* (New York, 1996); and Stephen Heath, *The Sexual Fix* (London, 1982), 108–110.

30 *King* (Winter 1964), 31–33.

31 For an example of the comparative primness of Britain's pre-permissive sexual culture, see the purposefully cosmopolitan *Fiesta*, whose demure British edition of March 1960 included Anne Heywood in a full length gown.

32 John D'Green, *Birds of Britain* (London, 1967), introduction. *Birds of Britain* was serialized in *King* (December 1967).

33 *Penthouse* 1, 2 (1965), 6; *King* (July 1965), 8.

34 *Mayfair* 2, 11 (1967), 23; *Penthouse* 1, 2 (1965), 6.

35 *Penthouse* 1, 6 (1965), 60; *Penthouse* 3, 11 (1968), 22.

36 *Lords* 1, 1 (1968), 17.

37 *Mayfair* 1, 1 (1966), 3; *Penthouse* 1, 1 (1965), 55. For an example of the Bond influence, see *King* (March 1967), 17–21. For the centrality of Bond in sixties culture, see Tony Bennett and Janet Woollacott, *Bond and Beyond: The Political Career of a Popular Hero* (Basingstoke, 1987).

38 *Penthouse* 1, 11 (1966), 70–71; *Mayfair* 1, 1 (1966), 3.

39 *Penthouse* 2, 3 (1966), 34; *Penthouse* 1, 2 (1965), 9; *Mayfair* 4, 8 (1969), 67.

40 *Mayfair* 4, 7 to 4, 11 (1969).

41 *Mayfair* 1, 1 (1966), 3; *Penthouse* 3, 11 (1968), 22. For the Playboy Club in London, see Victor Lownes, *Playboy Extraordinaire* (London, 1982).

42 *Penthouse* 1, 6 (1965), 66. For the sexual philosophy of Alan Hull Walton, see his *New Vistas* (London, 1945).

43 *Mayfair* 3, 11 (1968), 68–69.

44 *Mayfair* 3, 11 (1968), 67; *Mayfair* 5, 1 (1970), 68.

45 *Mayfair* 3, 11 (1968), 68.

46 *Mayfair* 5, 7 (1970), 66, 68; *Mayfair* 7, 1 (1973), 73.

47 *Penthouse* 1, 1 (1965), 44; *Penthouse* 1, 2 (1965), 70; *Penthouse* 1, 1 (1965), 44, 69.

48 *Mayfair* 4, 2 (1969), 68, 73.

49 *Mayfair* 2, 10 (1967), 27; Rodney Bennett-England, *Dress Optional: The Revolution in Menswear* (London, 1967), 32, 29; *Penthouse* 5, 1 (1970), 43. Bennett-England was *Penthouse*'s fashion editor.

50 *Lords* 1, 1 (1968), 17; *Penthouse* 5, 2 (1970), 46; *Penthouse* 1, 9 (1966), 52; *Penthouse* 1, 12 (1966), 47; *King* (July 1966), 20.

51 Frank Mort and Peter Thompson, 'Retailing, Commercial Culture and Masculinity in 1950s Britain: The Case of Montague Burton, the "Tailor of Taste"', *History Workshop Journal* 38 (1994), 106–128; Sean Nixon, *Hard Looks: Masculinities, Spectatorship and Contemporary Consumption* (London, 1996), 168–179, 191–192.

52 *Penthouse* 5, 1 (1970), 46; *Penthouse* 4, 4 (1969), 48.

53 Bennett-England, 32.

54 *Men Only* 36, 1 (1971), 23; *Club International* 1, 1 (1972).

55 *Mayfair* 2, 1 (1967), 74.

56 Williams, 267.
57 Andy Moye, 'Pornography', *The Sexuality of Men*, ed. Andy Metcalf and Martin Humphries (London, 1985), 55–57.
58 Miller, 191.
59 Stills from *The Brides of Fu Manchu* printed in *Penthouse* 1, 9 (1966) were the only bondage pictures in any of the magazines before 1969, after which *Mayfair* published three items in 1969 and 1970 (4, 7, 61; 4, 9, 58–61; 93; and 5, 3, cover) with *Penthouse* following with one in 1970 (5, 3, 56–57) and another in 1971 (6, 3, 54–59).
60 For the objectifying aspects of pornography, see Andrea Dworkin, *Pornography: Men Possessing Women* (London, 1981), 223; Catherine A. MacKinnon, *Only Words* (London, 1994), 12, ix; Susanne Kappeler, *The Pornography of Representation* (Cambridge, 1986), 61, 104; Shere Hite, *The Hite Report on Male Sexuality* (London, 1990), 789–791; and Alison Assiter, *Pornography, Feminism and the Individual* (London, 1989), 134–135.
61 *Penthouse* 1, 5 (1965), 34; *Penthouse* 8, 3 (1973), 46.
62 *Penthouse* 1, 2 (1965), 36; *Penthouse* 1, 2 (1965), 58.
63 *Penthouse* 1, 2 (1965), 58; *Penthouse* 1, 3 (1965), 56; *Penthouse* 1, 2 (1965), 36; *Penthouse* 1, 2 (1965), 58; *Penthouse* 1, 1 (1965), 33.
64 *Mayfair* 3, 10 (1968), 36; *Mayfair* 4, 1(1969), 24, 26.
65 *Mayfair* 7, 3 (1972), 61; *Mayfair* 6, 1 (1971), 37; *Penthouse* 8, 4 (1973), 47, 51–52. For the child-woman, see also *Penthouse* 8, 1 (1973), 43.
66 *Penthouse* 2, 1 (1966), 90; *Mayfair* 4, 6 (1969), 73.
67 *King* (October 1966), 49; *Mayfair* 4, 7 (1969), 4.
68 *Mayfair* 5, 3 (1970), 4. *Penthouse* displayed a certain nervousness about sixties dress, condemning the rapidity of changing tastes and assuring its readers that 'despite transitory fads and fashions, despite Mary Quant, *Vogue* and the Silver Screen, a girl is a girl is still a girl.' But this did not prevent its models from sporting that month's hairstyle and the most modish of outfits, when wearing anything at all (*Penthouse* 1, 11 (1966), 33).
69 *Mayfair* 5, 1 (1970), 68; *Penthouse* 1, 3 (1965), 11–14, 60–61; *Penthouse* 3, 9 (1968), 66.
70 *Penthouse* 3, 9 (1968), 66; *Penthouse* 3, 5 (1968), 69.
71 *Penthouse* 4, 11 (1969), 66; *Mayfair* 1, 1 (1966), 36.
72 *Men Only* 1, 1 (1935), 23; *Men Only* 1, 3 (1935), 99–102. For like-minded sentiments in American men's magazines of this period, see Kenon Breazeale, 'In Spite of Women: *Esquire* Magazine and the Construction of the Male Consumer', *Signs* 20, 1 (1994), 1–22.
73 *Mayfair* 6, 2 (1971), 73; *Mayfair* 4, 10 (1969), 62; *Mayfair* 2, 11 (1967), 23.
74 *King* (June 1965), 44; *King* (July 1965), 7.
75 *Penthouse* 3, 6 (1968), 36; *Penthouse* 1, 5 (1965), 34.
76 *Penthouse* 1, 3 (1965), 34.
77 *Lords* 1, 1 (Winter 1968), 17.
78 *Penthouse* 5, 1 (1970), 51; *Penthouse* 3, 11 (1968), 22; *Penthouse* 5, 1 (1970), 51.
79 *Mayfair* 4, 1 (1969), 73; *Mayfair* 5, 12 (1970), 6.
80 *Mayfair* 4, 1 (1969), 13; *Mayfair* 5, 6 (1970), 68.
81 *Mayfair* 5, 3 (1970), 73; *Mayfair* 4, 7 (1969), 73; *Mayfair* 5, 6 (1970), 68, 67, 68.
82 *Mayfair* 4, 1 (1969), 4.
83 *Penthouse* 1, 2 (1965), 69; *Mayfair* 4, 1 (1969), 13.
84 *Penthouse* 1, 2 (1965), 68; *Mayfair* 1, 1 (1966), 37; *Mayfair* 1, 3 (1966), 64.
85 *Penthouse* 1, 1 (1965), 62; *Penthouse* 1, 2 (1965), 58.
86 *Mayfair* 5, 12 (1970), 6; *Mayfair* 5, 11 (1970).
87 *Penthouse* 7, 8 (1972). The back-to-nature theme was, of course, a commonplace of late sixties and early seventies disillusionment with modernity.
88 *Penthouse* 8, 4 (1973), 47; *Penthouse* 7, 5 (1972), 37; *Penthouse* 5, 4 (1970), 37.
89 *Penthouse* 5, 4 (1970), 32, 37.
90 *Penthouse* 6, 5 (1971), 38; *Penthouse* 6, 7 (1971), 42; *Penthouse* 6, 4 (1971), 38.
91 *Penthouse* 6, 9 (1971), 64; *Penthouse* 6, 3 (1971), 35.
92 *Penthouse* 6, 5 (1971), 37; *Penthouse* 8, 1 (1973), 49.
93 *Penthouse* 8, 2 (1973), 33; *Penthouse* 8, 7 (1973), 92; *Penthouse* 8, 1 (1973), 49.
94 *Penthouse* 6, 5 (1971), 38; *Penthouse* 6, 8 (1971), 41.

95   *Penthouse* 8, 1 (1973), 49; *Penthouse* 8, 3 (1973), 51.

96   *Penthouse* 8, 8 (1973), 33; *Penthouse* 6, 7 (1971), 42; *Penthouse* 6, 3 (1971), 35.

97   *Penthouse* 6, 12 (1972), 13; *Penthouse* 8, 2 (1973), 19; *Penthouse* 8, 4 (1973), 19.

98   *Penthouse* 6, 12 (1972), 13; *Penthouse* 7, 6 (1972), 44.

99   *Penthouse* 8, 3 (1973), 19; *Penthouse* 6, 6 (1971), 92; *Penthouse* 7, 6 (1972), 44.

100 *Penthouse* 6, 6 (1971), 91.

101 *Men Only* 36, 1 (1971), 23–25.

102 *Men Only* 36, 1 (1971), 23–25.

103 For homophobia, *Men Only* 37, 7 (1972), 21–23. For sadomasochism, see also the accompanying stories 'Women in Captivity' and 'Miss de Sade' in *Men Only* 36, 6 and 36, 7 (1971). For quantitative studies of the rise of sadomasochism in soft-core pornography, see Bill Thompson, *Soft Core: Moral Crusades against Pornography in Britain and America* (London, 1994), 160–166; Neil Malamuth and Barry Spinner, 'A Longitudinal Content Analysis of Sexual Violence in the Best-Selling Erotic Magazines', *Journal of Sex Research* 16, 3 (1980), 226–237; and Joseph E. Scott and Steven J. Cuvelier, 'Sexual Violence in *Playboy* Magazine: A Longitudinal Content Analysis', *Journal of Sex Research* 23, 4 (1987), 534–539.

104 *King* (Winter 1964), 2; *Men Only* 36, 1 (1971), 3.

105 Larkin, 167.

106 Hugh Hefner cited in Miller, 192–193.

107 For an excellent analysis of men's 'heteroerotic dilemma', see Simon Hardy, *The Reader, The Author, His Woman and Her Lover: Soft-Core Pornography and Heterosexual Men* (London, 1998). For the contrast between men's and women's sexual fantasies, see Bruce J. Ellis and Donald Symons, 'Sex Differences in Sexual Fantasy: An Evolutionary Psychological Approach', *Journal of Sex Research* 27, 4 (1990), 527–555.

108 Dworkin, *Pornography*, 68. For the notion that pornography represents a backlash against women's liberation, see Andrea Dworkin, 'Why So-Called Radical Men Love and Need Pornography', *Take Back the Night: Women on Pornography*, ed. Laura Lederer (New York, 1982); Ellen Willis, 'Feminism, Moralism and Pornography', *Powers of Desire: The Politics of Sexuality*, ed. Ann Snitow et al. (New York, 1983), 461; and Joan Hoff, 'Why Is There No History of Pornography?', *For Adult Users Only: The Dilemma of Violent Pornography*, ed. Susan Gubar and Joan Hoff (Bloomington, IN, 1989), 25–26, 29.

109 For anxiety and alienation in pornography, see Marcus, *The Other Victorians*; Alan Soble, *Pornography: Marxism, Feminism and the Future of Sexuality* (New Haven, CT, 1986); Bernard Arcand, *The Jaguar and the Anteater: Pornography Degree Zero* (London, 1993); Roger Horrocks, *Male Myths and Icons: Masculinity in Popular Culture* (New York, 1995), ch. 7; and Lynne Segal's many works, including *Straight Sex: The Politics of Pleasure* (London, 1994).

Chapter 6 – Fallout

1   Eva Hubback cited in Elizabeth Wilson, *Only Halfway to Paradise: Women in Postwar Britain, 1945–68* (London, 1980), 48; Vera Brittain, *Lady into Woman: A History of Women from Victoria to Elizabeth II* (London, 1953), 10. In her excellent overview of the period immediately before women's liberation, Wilson identifies 'reasonable feminism' as the sole surviving form of feminism in this period. For mutualist feminism, see also Birmingham Feminist History Group, 'Feminism as Femininity in the 1950s?', *Feminist Review* 3 (1979), 48–63.

2   Kenneth G. Greet, *The Mutual Society: Aspects of the Relationship of Men and Women* (London, 1962), 4, 166; Alex Comfort, *Sex in Society* (London, 1963), 31–32.

3   Alastair Heron (ed.), *Towards a Quaker View of Sex* (London, 1963); John A.T. Robinson, *Honest to God* (Philadelphia, 1963), ch. 6. For the change of heart among Christian authorities on sexual matters, see Jane Lewis and Kathleen Kiernan, 'The Boundaries between Marriage, Nonmarriage and Parenthood: Changes in Behaviour and Policy in Postwar Britain', *Journal of Family History* 21, 3 (1996), 373–378; and Douglas Rhymes, *No New Morality: Christian Personal Values and Sexual Morality* (London, 1964). For Catholic rethinking in response to Vatican II, see Jock Dalrymple,

Jack Dominian: Lay Prophet? (London, 1995), 2–6.

4   For changing pub culture, see Daniel E. Vasey, *The Pub and English Social Change* (New York, 1990); Joyce O'Connor, *The Young Drinkers* (London, 1978); and Raphael Samuel, *Theatres of Memory, i: Past and Present in Contemporary Culture* (London, 1994), 75.

5   Anthony Sampson, *Anatomy of Britain* (New York, 1962), 74. For the decline in football attendances (and the concomitant increase in terrace aggro), see Eric Dunning *et al.*, *The Roots of Football Hooliganism: An Historical and Sociological Study* (London, 1988).

6   Robin Pedley, *The Comprehensive School* [rev. edn] (Harmondsworth, 1969), 88; Bernarr F. Atherton, 'The Relative Merits of Coeducational and Single-Sex Schools with Special Reference to the Happiness of Marriage of Former Pupils' (University of Wales, Swansea MSc Thesis, 1970), 4. That coeducational state secondary schools retained the style but lost the substance of the original mutualist vision helps to explain why one 1960s survey of teachers adjudged A.S. Neill's influence on the practice of coeducation to be next to nil. Coeducation became the norm because it was considered to be the most obvious and administratively convenient manner of arranging things, much as segregation had been fifty years before. Furthermore, the comprehensivizers' concentration on class inequality allowed them to overlook the severe underperformance of girls and the *de facto* segregation of schools in which the sexes led 'largely separate lives'. Stripped of its radical purpose of instituting an intimate equality between the sexes, coeducation happily coexisted with all manner of overt and covert discrimination between boys and girls (Ray Hemmings, *Fifty Years of Freedom: A Study of the Development of the Ideas of A.S. Neill* (London, 1972), 166; Ministry of Education, *Half Our Future* (London, 1963), 61).

7   Royston Lambert, *The Chance of a Lifetime: A Study of Boys' and Coeducational Boarding Schools in England and Wales* (London, 1975), 244. For mixing in public schools, see John Rae, *The Public School Revolution: Britain's Independent Schools, 1964–79* (London, 1981), 131–143.

8   Fred Halliday, 'Students of the World Unite', *Student Power: Problems, Diagnosis, Action*, ed. Alexander Cockburn and Robin Blackburn (Harmondsworth, 1969), 318. For mixing in universities, see Christopher N.L. Brooke, *A History of the University of Cambridge, iv: 1870–1990* (Cambridge, 1993), 528–531; and Janet Howarth, 'Women', *The History of the University of Oxford, viii: The Twentieth Century*, ed. Brian Harrison (Oxford, 1994).

9   Ferdynand Zweig, *Women's Life and Labour* (London, 1952), 18; *idem*, *The Worker in an Affluent Society* (London, 1961), 208, 31.

10   Ronald Fletcher, *Britain in the Sixties: The Family and Marriage* (Harmondsworth, 1962), 124; *idem*, *The Family and Marriage in Britain* [rev. edn] (Harmondsworth, 1973), 252.

11   Liz Stanley, *Sex Surveyed, 1949–94* (London, 1995), 72, 73, 63; Geoffrey Gorer, *Exploring English Character* (London, 1955), 94, 111, 116.

12   *Idem, Sex and Marriage in England Today* (London, 1971), 113, 123; 1963 *New Society* poll cited in Robert Millar, *The New Classes* (London, 1966), 31.

13   Michael Young and Peter Willmott, *The Symmetrical Family* (New York, 1973), 20; Stanley, *Sex Surveyed*, 114, 115, 76. Kate Fisher likewise finds that, even among those few mid-century working-class couples who had read Marie Stopes, fewer still fully understood her arguments (Kate Fisher, 'An Oral History of Birth Control Practice, *c.* 1925–50: A Study of Oxford and South Wales' (University of Oxford DPhil thesis, 1997), 89–92). For further indication of class differences over romance, see Jacqueline Sarsby, *Romantic Love and Society* (Harmondsworth, 1983), ch. 7.

14   Arthur Wesley Helweg, *Sikhs in England: The Development of a Migrant Community* (Delhi, 1979), 118, 127; Clifford Hill, *Immigration and Integration: A Study of the Settlement of Coloured Minorities in Britain* (Oxford, 1969), 120.

15   Juliet Cheetham, *Social Work with Immigrants* (London, 1972), 130. For one portrait of the libidinous West Indian male, see O.R. Dathorne, *Dumplings in the Soup* (London, 1963), 92.

16   Public Record Office CO 876/39, report by Phyllis Young on male immigrants in Stepney (1943).

17   Elspeth Huxley, *Back Street New Worlds: A Look at Immigrants in Britain* (London, 1964), 90; Clifford Hill, *Black and White in Harmony: The Drama of West Indians in*

the Big City from a London Minister's Notebook (London, 1958), 77.

18   See Surjit Singh Kalra, *Daughters of Tradition: Adolescent Sikh Girls and Their Accommodation to Life in British Society* (Birmingham, 1980), 69, 44.

19   Dilip Hiro, 'The Coloured Man's View of the British', *New Society*, 22 February 1968, 263–264.

20   Helweg, 127; Rashmi Desai, *Indian Immigrants in Britain* (London, 1963), 143, 123–124.

21   Sheila Patterson, *Dark Strangers* (London, 1963), 337; Ari Kiev, 'Psychiatric Illness Among West Indians in London', *Race* 5, 3 (1964), 53.

22   Katrin Fitzherbert, *West Indian Children in London* (London, 1967), 38.

23   Leary Constantine, *Colour Bar* (London, 1954), 89. Both the Notting Hill and Nottingham race riots of 1958 erupted over white fury at one of 'their' women consorting with a black man.

24   Kenneth Barnes, 'Coeducation and Sex', *Who are the Progressives Now?: An Account of an Educational Confrontation*, ed. Maurice Ash (London, 1969), 206; A.S. Neill cited in Robert Skidelsky, *English Progressive Schools* (Harmondsworth, 1969), 50; Maurice Punch, *Progressive Retreat: A Sociological Study of Dartington Hall School and Some of Its Former Pupils* (Cambridge, 1977), 159.

25   Margherita Rendel *et al.*, 'Equality for Women', *Fabian Research Series* 268 (London, 1968), 24. For paid work for women, see Alva Myrdal and Viola Klein, *Women's Two Roles* [rev. edn] (London, 1968); and Jane Lewis, 'Myrdal, Klein, Women's Two Roles and Postwar Feminism, 1945–60', *British Feminism in the Twentieth Century*, ed. Harold L. Smith (Aldershot, 1990).

26   Viola Klein, *Britain's Married Women Workers* (London, 1965), 77, 59, 76; Michael P. Fogarty, Rhona Rapoport and Robert N. Rapoport, *Sex, Career and Family* (London, 1971), 474.

27   Janet Saltzman Chafetz, 'Chicken or Egg?: A Theory of the Relationship between Feminist Movements and Family Change', *Gender and Family in Industrialised Countries*, ed. Karen Oppenheim Mason and An-Magrit Jensen (Oxford, 1995), 73.

28   John Newsom and Elizabeth Newsom, *Infant Care in an Urban Community* (London, 1964), 213.

29   B.D. Hendy, 'Parenthood', *Sex in Social Life*, ed. Sybil Neville-Rolfe (London, 1949), 194; D.W. Winnicott, *The Child and the Family: First Relationships* (London, 1957), 84. For maternal deprivation theory, see Denise Riley, *War in the Nursery: Theories of the Child and Mother* (London, 1983).

30   'J.B.H.', 'Bored By My Children', *The Guardian*, 16 September 1959. For more of the same, see the 'Bored Mothers' collection in the Mary Stott archive at the Women's Library.

31   G.W. Johnson, *The Evolution of Woman: From Subjection to Comradeship* (London, 1926), 238; Royal Commission on Marriage and Divorce, *Report* (London, 1956), 9; Fletcher, *The Family and Marriage in Britain*, 16–17; *idem* cited in Jennifer Chapman, *Made in Heaven: Ordinary and Extraordinary People Talk about Marriage* (London, 1993). For Christian attitudes to divorce, see G.I.T. Machin, 'British Churches and Social Issues, 1945–60', *Twentieth-Century British History* 7, 3 (1996), 345–370; Jane Lewis and Patrick Wallis, 'Fault, Breakdown and the Church of England's Involvement in the 1969 Divorce Reform', *Twentieth-Century British History* 11, 3 (2000), 308–332; and Archbishop of Canterbury Group, *Putting Asunder: A Divorce Law for Contemporary Society* (London, 1966).

32   Contribution of Bruce Campbell to the debate on the Divorce Reform Bill, *Parliamentary Debates: House of Commons* (16 December 1968), vol. 756, col. 2044; Edith Summerskill, *A Woman's World* (London, 1967), 143.

33   Sir Dugald Baird in *Abortion in Britain: Proceedings of a Conference held by the Family Planning Association at the University of London Union on 22 April 1966* (London, 1966), 20; Michael Schofield, *Promiscuity* (London, 1976), 179. Though Schofield may well have overestimated the extent of men's disquiet about the Pill, such sentiments reflected how dramatically oral contraception reversed couples' previous reliance on the male-directed birth control techniques of condoms and withdrawal. Even so, Lara Marks points out that swallowing a tablet many hours before sex 'allowed women to preserve the appearance of passivity' by dissociating the act of intercourse from their precautions against pregnancy (Lara Marks, *Sexual Chemistry: A History of the*

Contraceptive Pill (New Haven, 2001), 193).

34   G.B. Bentley, 'The New Morality: A Christian Comment', *Sexual Morality: Three Views*, ed. Richard Sadler (London, 1965), 58. See Eustace Chesser, *Is Chastity Outmoded?* (London, 1960); and John Robinson, *Honest to God*, 118.

35   Dora Russell, 'In A Man's World: The Eclipse of Woman' (1965), *The Dora Russell Reader* (London, 1983), 165. For sex radical attitudes to pornography, see George Ryley Scott, *Into Whose Hands: An Examination of Obscene Libel in Its Legal, Sociological and Literary Aspects* (London, 1945), 5.

36   John Osborne, 'The Fifties' (1959), *Damn You, England: Collected Prose* (London, 1994), 193. Examples of male pals include Cliff in *Look Back in Anger*, Atkinson and Beesley in *Lucky Jim*, Charles in *Room at the Top* and Harry in *A Kind of Loving*.

37   Colin MacInnes, 'Pop Songs and Teenagers' (1958), *England, Half English* (New York, 1961), 53.

38   Derek Allcorn in *Universities and Left Review* 4 (Summer 1958), 57; Kenneth C. Barnes, *He and She* (London, 1958), 129, 131.

39   Stan Barstow, *A Kind of Loving* (London, 1960), 202; Alan Sillitoe, *Saturday Night and Sunday Morning* (London, 1958), 142. For the sexual politics of the Angry Young Men, see Lynne Segal, *Slow Motion: Changing Masculinities, Changing Men* [rev. edn] (London, 1997), ch. 1; and, for a contemporaneous male revolt in the United States, see Barbara Ehrenreich, *The Hearts of Men: American Dreams and the Flight from Commitment* (Garden City, NY, 1984).

40   John Osborne, *Look Back in Anger* (London, 1957), 37; Barstow, 33; John Braine, *Room at the Top* (Boston, 1957), 175.

41   Paul E. Willis, *Profane Culture* (London, 1978), 20; Ferdynand Zweig, *The Student in the Age of Anxiety: A Survey of Oxford and Manchester Students* (London, 1963), 128. Willis was writing about the 'motor bike boys' he encountered in 1969.

42   Marty Wilde cited in Frank Clews, *Teenage Idols* (London, 1962), 59. Wilde came to regret his devotion to marriage and parenthood when he found himself deserted by heartbroken female fans. Little did he know that the next generation of popsters would be grateful for his daughter Kim.

43   Richard Neville in *Days in the Life: Voices of the English Underground, 1961–71*, ed. Jonathon Green (London, 1988), 424; Richard Neville, *Play Power* (London, 1970), 72.

44   Liz Hodgkinson, *Unholy Matrimony: The Case for Abolishing Marriage* (London, 1988), 88; Neville, *Play Power*, 74.

45   Sara Maitland in *Very Heaven: Looking Back at the 1960s*, ed. Sara Maitland (London, 1988), 15. The connections of prominent second-wave feminists to the counterculture were many and varied. Juliet Michell taught at the Anti-University and Sue O'Sullivan was active in the anti-Vietnam campaign. Germaine Greer was involved with *Oz* and *Suck* and Sheila Rowbotham worked for *Black Dwarf*. Rosie Boycott wrote for *Frendz*, Rosalind Delmar for *7 Days*, Bea Campbell for *Idiot* and both Anna Coote and Alison Fell for *Ink*. Marsha Rowe had worked on *Oz* in Australia with Louise Ferrier, then Richard Neville's partner, while Michelene Wandor contributed to *Time Out*. For non-countercultural origins of second-wave feminism in the National Joint Action Committee for Women's Equal Rights and the far left, see Anna Coote and Beatrix Campbell, *Sweet Freedom: The Struggle for Women's Liberation* [rev. edn] (Oxford, 1987), 9–10; and Nigel Fountain, *Underground: The London Alternative Press, 1966–74* (London, 1988), 102–103. As will be evident from the footnotes, this section is particularly indebted to Fountain's analysis.

46   Sheila Rowbotham, *Woman's Consciousness, Man's World* (Harmondsworth, 1973), 13; Mary Ingham, *Now We Are Thirty: Women of the Breakthrough Generation* (London, 1981), 67.

47   Bryan Wilson, 'The Hippies' (1967), *The Youth Culture and the Universities* (London, 1970), 201; David Widgery cited in Fountain, 126.

48   Statement of aims of *Spare Rib* cited in Richard Neville, *Hippie Hippie Shake* (London, 1995), 349; Sheila Rowbotham, 'The Beginnings of Liberation in Britain' (1972), *Dreams and Dilemmas* (London, 1983), 26.

49   David Widgery cited in Fountain, 106; Nicola Lane in *Days in the Life*, 420.

50   Michelene Wandor, 'The Conditions of Illusion', *Conditions of Illusion: Papers from the Women's Movement*, ed. Sandra Allen *et al.* (Leeds, 1974), 188; Louise Ferrier cited in Neville, *Hippie Hippie Shake*, 246.

51   Dale Spender in *Women Who Do and Women Who Don't Joint the Women's Movement*, ed. Robyn Rowland (London, 1984), 206; Lynne Segal, 'Sexual Uncertainty', *Sex and Love: New Thoughts on Old Contradictions*, ed. Sue Cartledge and Joanna Ryan (London, 1983), 31.

52   Sara Maitland in *Very Heaven*, 4. For an important meditation on the relationship between women's emancipation and sexual liberation, see Juliet Mitchell, 'Women: The Longest Revolution' (1966), *Women: The Longest Revolution – Essays in Feminism, Literature and Psychoanalysis* (London, 1984).

53   Unnamed feminist cited in Fountain, 144; Caroline Coon in *The Guardian*, 9 August 1999.

54   Sheila Rowbotham, *Promise of a Dream: Remembering the Sixties* (London, 2000), 230; *idem*, diary entry for 1967 in *Dreams and Dilemmas*, 45.

55   Sara Maitland in *Very Heaven*, 4.

56   Sheila Rowbotham cited in Arthur Marwick, *The Sixties: Cultural Revolution in Britain, France, Italy and the United States, c. 1958–74* (Oxford, 1998), 689.

57   Rosie Boycott in *Days in the Life*, 409; Angela Carter in *Very Heaven*, 4.

58   Belsize Lane Women's Group, 'Nine Years Together' (1978), *The Spare Rib Reader*, ed. Marsha Rowe (Harmondsworth, 1982), 570.

59   'Organising Ourselves', *Shrew* 3, 2 (1971), 2.

60   Juliet Mitchell, *Women's Estate* (Harmondsworth, 1971), 57; Erin Pizzey cited in Suzanne Lowry, *The Guilt Cage: Housewives and a Decade of Liberation* (London, 1980), 100.

61   'Organising Ourselves', 2; Belsize Lane Women's Group, 562.

62   Jill Tweedie, *In the Name of Love* (London, 1979), 7; Rosie Boycott, *A Nice Girl Like Me* (London, 1985), 60. For the emergence of American second-wave feminism from sixties radicalism, see Sara Evans, *Personal Politics: The Roots of Women's Liberation in the Civil Rights Movement and the New Left* (New York, 1980). For general histories of the women's liberation movement, see Eve Setch, 'The Women's Liberation Movement in Britain, 1969–79: Organisation, Creativity and Debate' (University of London PhD thesis, 2001); Elizabeth Arledge Ross and Miriam L. Bearse, *A Chronology of the Women's Liberation Movement in Britain, 1969–79* (Bradford, 1996); Olive Banks, *Faces of Feminism: A Study of Feminism as a Social Movement* (Oxford, 1981), part iv; David Bouchier, *The Feminist Challenge: The Movement for Women's Liberation in Britain and the USA* (London, 1983); April Carter, *The Politics of Women's Rights* (London, 1988); Coote and Campbell; Joni Lovenduski and Vicky Randall, *Contemporary Feminist Politics: Women and Power in Britain* (Oxford, 1993); Marwick, ch. 13; Angela Neustatter, *Hyenas in Petticoats: A Look at Twenty Years of Feminism* (London, 1989); Sheila Rowbotham, *The Past is Before Us: Feminism in Action since the 1960s* (Harmondsworth, 1990); and Imelda Whelehan, *Modern Feminist Thought: From the Second Wave to 'Post Feminism'* (Edinburgh, 1995).

63   Rowbotham, *Woman's Consciousness*, 12; *idem*, *Promise of a Dream*, 159.

64   Emma Tennant, 'The Rise of Capitalism and the Fall of Woman', *Woman on Woman*, ed. Margaret Lang (London, 1971), 187; Eva Figes, *Patriarchal Attitudes: Women in Society* [rev. edn] (Basingstoke, 1986), 168.

65   Ann Oakley, *Sex, Gender and Society* (London, 1972), 208; Sheila Rowbotham cited in Lynne Segal, *Why Feminism?: Gender, Psychology, Politics* (Cambridge, 1999), 17.

66   Jane Lewis, 'From Equality to Liberation: Contextualising the Emergence of the Women's Liberation Movement', *Cultural Revolution?: The Challenge of the Arts in the 1960s*, ed. Bart Moore-Gilbert and John Seed (London, 1992), 111.

67   Sue O'Sullivan, 'My Old Man Said Follow the Vanguard', *Very Heaven*, 126. An aversion to sex antagonism was especially pronounced among communist feminists who feared that 'man-haters' within the women's movement would fracture the proletariat along lines of sex. Their defence of men's right to attend women's meetings fatally compromised their feminism in the eyes of others within the movement. Germaine Greer was for her part profoundly contradictory on the possibility of cooperation with men when denouncing men as 'the enemy' and those women who 'characterise men as the enemy' at one and the same time (unnamed Maoist cited in Sue O'Sullivan, 'Passionate Beginnings: Ideological Politics, 1969–72', *Feminist Review* 11 (1982), 78; Germaine Greer, 'The Slag-Heap Erupts' (1970), *The Madwoman's Underclothes: Essays and Occasional Writings, 1968–85* (London, 1987), 28; *idem, The Female Eunuch* (London,

1970), 17. For Greer, see Christine Wallace, *Germaine Greer: Untamed Shrew* (London, 1999)).

68   Greer, *The Female Eunuch*, 14; Lee Comer, *Wedlocked Women* (Leeds, 1974), 273.

69   O.R. McGregor cited in Hannah Gavron, *The Captive Wife: Conflicts of Housebound Mothers* (London, 1966), 17; Comer, *Wedlocked Women*, 223–224, 227.

70   Rozsika Parker, 'Images of Men' (1980), *No Turning Back: Writings for the Women's Liberation Movement, 1975–80*, ed. Feminist Anthology Collective (London, 1981), 232; Ann Oakley, *Subject Women* (Oxford, 1981), 245.

71   Hodgkinson, *Unholy Matrimony*, 76, 10; *idem*, *Sex is Not Compulsory: Giving Up Sex for Better Health and Greater Happiness* (London, 1986), 115.

72   Elizabeth Wilson, *What is to be Done about Violence against Women?* (Harmondsworth, 1983), 235; Angie in Campaign for Homosexual Equality, *Women Together: Report of a Meeting of Women from the Gay Movement and from the Women's Movement* (Manchester, 1973), 16.

73   Sheila Rowbotham, 'Women's Liberation and the New Politics' (1969), *Dreams and Dilemmas*, 7.

74   Greer, *The Female Eunuch*, 142. For an extended feminist critique of single-sex male institutions, see Barbara Rogers, *Men Only: An Investigation into Men's Organisations* (London, 1988).

75   Maggie Havergal in *Scottish Women's Liberation Journal* 1, 4 (1977), 4; Ann Oakley, *Taking It Like A Woman* (London, 1985), 197.

76   Tough and Tender Collective, *A Plan for Action* (London, *c.* 1975), 2.

77   Una in Nell Dunn (aka Nell Mary Sandford), *Living Like I Do* (London, 1979), 61. For female deference, see Sally Cline and Dale Spender, *Reflecting Men at Twice Their Natural Size* (London, 1987).

78   Wendy Collins *et al.*, *Women: The Directory of Social Change* (London, 1978), 230; 'Organising Ourselves', 2.

79   Department of Education and Science, *Education Survey 21: Curricular Differences for Boys and Girls* (London, 1975), 7.

80   Michelle Stanworth, *Gender and Schooling: A Study of Sexual Divisions in the Classroom* (London, 1983), 47; Dale Spender, *Invisible Women: The Schooling Scandal* (London, 1982), 118. Coeducation was by now so mainstream that even its most severe opponents accepted that a return to segregation was 'not a realistic possibility'. Despite some talk of establishing a segregated school of their own, the most that feminists could do was to defend the few remaining girls' schools and press for the creation of anti-sexism groups for coeducated girls (Spender, *Invisible Women*, 125; *London Women's Liberation Movement Newsletter* 56 (15 March 1978), n.p.; Jane L. Thompson, *All Right for Some!: The Problem of Sexism* (London, 1986), 87).

81   Ann Oakley, *The Sociology of Housework* (London, 1974), 164, 146; *idem*, *Subject Women*, 246; Michaela Nava, 'The Family: A Critique of Certain Features' (1971), *The Body Politic: Writings from the Women's Liberation Movement in Britain, 1969–72*, ed. Michelene Wandor (London, 1972), 36.

82   Angela Hamblin, 'And They Lived Happily Ever After', *Shrew* 4, 6 (1972), 9; Ann Oakley, *Housewife* (London, 1974), 237.

83   Oakley, *The Sociology of Housework*, 164, 146; Margaret Elphinstone, 'Living with a Man', *Spare Rib* 140 (1984), 52. See Jessie Bernard, *The Future of Marriage* [rev. edn] (New Haven, CT, 1982), chs. 1–3.

84   Angela Hamblin, 'Ultimate Goals', *Women's Liberation Review* 1 (1972), 37; Lee Comer, 'The Act of Forgetting', *Women's Liberation Review* 1 (1972), 13.

85   Beatrix Campbell, 'A Feminist Sexual Politics: Now You See It, Now You Don't', *Feminist Review* 5 (1980), 5; *idem*, 'Sexuality and Submission', *Conditions of Illusion*, 102, 103.

86   *Shrew* 5, 4 (1973), 5; Irene Fick, 'Wot No Orgasm', *Red Rag* 3 (1973), 8; Rosalind Coward, *Female Desire* (London, 1984), 240.

87   Germaine Greer, 'The Politics of Female Sexuality' (1970), *The Madwoman's Underclothes*, 37; *idem*, *The Female Eunuch*, 280, 46.

88   Women's Liberation Workshop, *Women's Liberation: A Beginning* (London, 1970), 2; 'Organising Ourselves', 2; Oakley, *Taking It Like a Woman*, 196; Dale Spender in *Women Who Do*, 207.

89   Bronwen in *Shrew* (Autumn 1974), 7; Spitfire in *Bread and Roses* 6 (Winter 1976–7), 7;

Alison in *Bread and Roses* 6 (Winter 1976–7), 10.

90 Debby Gregory in 'Consciousness Raising: Back to Basics', 54; Sue O'Sullivan, 'From 1969', '68, '78, '88: *From Women's Liberation to Feminism*, ed. Amanda Sebestyen (Bridport, 1988), 53.

91 John Wilcock in *Days in the Life*, 403; *Spare Rib* 24 (1974), 23. For early anti-sexist events, see *Men Against Sexism* (1973–4). For the belated conversion of the underground press, see *Oz* 29 (1970) and 48 (1973); and Richard Neville in *The Trials of Oz*, ed. Tony Palmer (London, 1971), 234. For men's liberation, see Victor J. Seidler (ed.), *The Achilles Heel Reader: Men, Sexual Politics and Socialism* (London, 1991), introduction; Harry Christian, *The Making of Anti-Sexist Men* (London, 1994); and Ehrenreich, chs. 9 and 11.

92 Carolyn, 'Fuck the Family', *Come Together* 7 (1971), 3. For mixed consciousness-raising groups, see Collins *et al.*, 231, 233.

93 Maggie in *Women Together*, 16; Liz Stanley, '"Male Needs": The Problems of Working with Gay Men', *On the Problem of Men: Two Feminist Conferences*, ed. Scarlet Friedman and Elizabeth Sarah (London, 1982), 191. For general accounts of gay liberation, see Lisa Power, *No Bath but Plenty of Bubbles: An Oral History of the Gay Liberation Front, 1970–73* (London, 1995), ch. 10; and Jeffrey Weeks, *Coming Out: Homosexual Politics from the Nineteenth Century to the Present* [rev. edn] (London, 1990), ch. 16.

94 Dave Leon in *Men Against Sexism* 2 (1973), 1; Amanda Sebestyen, 'Thinking about Men', *Spare Rib* 94 (1980), 23. Men's liberationists divided into two broadly distinct 'men's rights' and 'men against sexism' camps in response to feminist criticism. The men's rights faction underplayed men's power and emphasized their pain in a manner epitomized by Neil Lyndon's *No More Sex War* (1992). Yet the abuse which greeted his plea for the recognition of 'complementary, mutual and inseparable' interests between the sexes as an antidote to the 'failures of feminism' indicated the impossibility of returning to the mutuality of old. Shunned by women's liberationists, men's righters shuffled off into men-only bonding and activism centred on the iniquities of family law. The men against sexism crowd tried the opposite tack of conciliation with scarcely greater success. Hamstrung by being unable to challenge women's opinions or even relate their own experiences 'without being, or feeling we are being, oppressive', their willingness to accept personal responsibility for patriarchal injustice became an almost Maoist exercise in self-mortification. Discussions of sexuality revealed 'confusion', violence left them 'paralysed' with guilt and efforts to curb their aggression made them feel 'very lost'. And their attempts to apply these muddy insights to relationships with women often courted despair. Ken Smith and 'B.' tried to be perfect New Men, only for their partners to leave them respectively for a lesbian and a 'male chauvinist' prepared to administer a 'good hard bang'. For his part, Brian, concluding that feminist sisterhood placed straight men like himself in an 'impossible situation', flirted first with homosexuality before opting for the safe if ultimately barren act of masturbation: 'And I get more afraid as I get older' (Neil Lyndon, *No More Sex War: The Failures of Feminism* (London, 1992), 235, 174; Fred cited in Collins *et al.*, 233; *Spare Rib* 24 (1974), 23; *Achilles Heel* editorial (1982) in *Men, Sex and Relationships*, ed. Victor J. Seidler (London, 1992), 127; *Spare Rib* 24 (1974), 23; Ken Smith in Yvonne Roberts, *Man Enough: Men of 35 Speak Out* (London, 1984), 264; 'B.' and Brian in *Men, Sex and Relationships*, 70, 84).

95 Eva Figes, 'Marriage Today and Tomorrow', *Marriage Guidance* (January 1973), 215; Peckham Rye Women's Liberation, 'Happily Ever After', *Black Dwarf* 14, 37 (5 September 1970), 13.

96 Deborah Gregory, 'From Where I Stand: A Case for Feminist Bisexuality', *Sex and Love: New Thoughts*, 152, 153; Joyce Nicholson, *What Society Does to Girls* (London, 1977), 49. Male partners of feminists felt neglected by their quest for autonomy and profoundly threatened by their sexual demands, according to an American survey conducted by Natalie Gittelson in the late 1970s (Jerry L. Rodnitzky, *Feminist Phoenix: The Rise and Fall of a Feminist Counterculture* (Westport, CN, 1999), 196).

97 Joanna Watt cited in Liz Heron, *Changes of Heart: Reflections on Women's Independence* (London, 1986), 136.

98 Greer, *The Female Eunuch*, 17; Comer, *Wedlocked Women*, 222; Oakley, *Housewife*, 236.

99   Sue Bruley, 'Women Awake: The Experience of Consciousness Raising' (1976), *No Turning Back*, 65; Women's Liberation Movement manifesto (1971), *The Body Politic*, 2. For American feminists' take on motherhood, see Lauri Umansky, *Motherhood Reconceived: Feminism and the Legacies of the Sixties* (New York, 1996).

100 Jo Sutton and Scarlet Friedman, 'Fatherhood: Bringing it All Back Home', *On the Problem of Men*, 121. For single motherhood, see Kathleen Kiernan, Hilary Land and Jane Lewis, *Lone Motherhood in Twentieth-Century Britain: From Footnote to Front Page* (Oxford, 1998).

101 'H.R.', 'Sex and Procreation: Its Political Relevance', *Harpies Bizarre* (1969), 5; *Shrew* 5, 2 (1973), 6–8; Angela Stewart-Park and Jules Cassidy in *We're Here: Conversations with Lesbian Women*, ed. Angela Stewart-Park and Jules Cassidy (London, 1977), 3.

102 Beatrix Campbell, 'Sexuality and Submission', *Red Rag 5* (1973), 12; Michèle Barrett and Mary McIntosh, *The Anti-Social Family* (London, 1982), 74; Hamblin, 'And They Lived', 10.

103 'The Suppressed Power of Female Sexuality', *Shrew* 4, 6 (1972), 1.

104 Greer, *The Female Eunuch*, 318; Angela Hamblin, 'Taking Control of Our Sex Lives', *Spare Rib* 104 (1981), 19; Greer, *The Female Eunuch*, 318.

105 Gregory, 'From Where I Stand', 147; Germaine Greer, 'The Slag-Heap Erupts', 28.

106 Jeanette Winterson, *Fit for the Future: The Guide for Women Who Want to Live Well* (London, 1986), 108.

107 Hodgkinson, *Sex is Not Compulsory*, 87; Loulou Brown, 'Heterosexual Celibacy', *Heterosexuality*, ed. Sue Wilkinson and Celia Kitzinger (Newbury Park, CA, 1993), 91.

108 Elizabeth Wilson, *Mirror Writing: An Autobiography* (London, 1982), 90; Helen Liddy in *Inventing Ourselves: Lesbian Life Stories*, ed. Hall-Carpenter Archives Lesbian Oral History Group (London, 1989), 113.

109 Tasmin Wilton, 'Sisterhood in the Service of Patriarchy: Heterosexual Women's Friendships and Male Power', *Heterosexuality*, 273. For varieties of lesbianism, see E.M. Ettorre, *Lesbians, Women and Society* (London, 1980), 110; and Celia Kitzinger, *The Social Construction of Lesbianism* (London, 1987).

110 Susan Cartledge and Susan Hemmings, 'How Did We Get This Way?', *Spare Rib* 86 (1979), 46.

111 Campaign for Homosexual Equality, *Everything You Wanted to Know About… Lesbians* (Manchester, 1976), n.p.

112 Ruth in *Women Together*, 20; 'Lesbians Come Together' (1971) in *Come Together: The Years of Gay Liberation, 1970–73*, ed. Aubrey Walter (London, 1980), 97.

113 Suzie Fleming, 'Women's Liberation', *Enough* 3 (*c.* 1971), 10; Mitchell, *Women's Estate*, 57.

114 For the best account of the events at the 1971 Skegness conference, see O'Sullivan, 'Passionate Beginnings'.

115 Lovenduski and Randall, 67. For a fine history of American radical feminism, see Alice Echols, *Daring to be Bad: Radical Feminism in America, 1967–75* (Minneapolis, MN, 1989). In an important challenge to conventional classifications of feminists into rival 'radical' and 'socialist' camps, historian Eve Setch has drawn attention to overlaps between the two. She observes that radical feminists did not necessarily practise outright separatism, while socialist feminists accepted some degree of separatism in the form of women-only activism. Setch also draws attention to the divisions existing within radical feminism. There were different types of separatism and distinctions between self-described 'radical' and 'revolutionary' feminists, while cultural feminists' celebration of womanliness did not translate into hostility to men. It is clearly the case that a movement so disputatious and fissiparous as women's liberation contained a plethora of viewpoints unamenable to crude taxonomies. Any ten feminists could be relied on to produce eleven different opinions. It remains useful, however, to distinguish the wood from the trees. Setch acknowledges that 'radical and socialist feminists *did* exist and *were* divisive – they were and are central terms of self-definition for many feminists'. 'Radical feminist' also entered common parlance, as witnessed by the manner in which the female celebrities interviewed by Naim Attallah used the phrase to connote 'lesbians' and 'separatists', 'living without men' and a 'total rejection of the male'. Revolutionary feminists were not distinct from radical feminists, but rather the most radical of radicals, responsible for setting the pace on issues of personal relationships. Conversely, the lack of interest manifested by cultural feminists in this matters excludes them from the present

discussion save to note that the wise womanhood preached by the Matriarchy Study Group privileged female solidarity without wholly ruling out relationships with men (Eve Setch, 'The Face of Metropolitan Feminism: The London Women's Liberation Workshop, 1969–79', *Twentieth-Century British History* 13, 2 (2002), 187–189; *idem*, 'The Women's Liberation Movement in Britain, 1969–79', 12–13, 236–240, 26; Carmen Callil, Penny Perrick, Bel Mooney and Pamela Armstrong in Naim Attallah, *Women* (London, 1987), 512, 452, 458, 523; Matriarchy Study Group, *Politics of Matriarchy* (London, 1978)).

116 CLIT Statement cited in Campbell, 'A Feminist Sexual Politics', 15.

117 *Catcall* editorial collective (1979) cited in Ross and Bearse, 32.

118 The turning point for *Spare Rib* was its refusal to publish an anti-separatist article by Ann Pettitt in 1980. The following year, it signalled its sympathy with the radical feminist agenda by publishing articles on the Leeds sexual violence conference, the sexual abuse of Linda Lovelace, the age of consent, rape, the Yorkshire Ripper and paedophilia. And in 1982, by means of counteracting the 'heterosexual propaganda' that made lesbians a minority, it declared that 'the more we print on lesbian politics, the better' (*Spare Rib* 98–100 (1980), 103–6 and 108–9 (1981); editorial in *Spare Rib* 116 (1982), 4).

119 Amanda Sebestyen, 'Tendencies in the Movement: Then and Now', *Feminist Practice: Notes for the Tenth Year* (London, 1979), 22; Susan Ardill and Sue O'Sullivan, 'Upsetting an Applecart: Difference, Desire, and Lesbian Sadomasochism', *Sexuality: A Reader*, ed. Feminist Review (London, 1987), 286.

120 Sheila Jeffreys, 'The Need for Revolutionary Feminism', *Scarlet Women* 5 (1977), 12; Leeds Revolutionary Feminist Group, 'Political Lesbianism: The Case Against Heterosexuality' (1979), *Love Your Enemy?: The Debate between Heterosexual Feminism and Political Lesbianism* (London, 1981), 6.

121 Sebestyen, 'Tendencies in the Movement', 22; Nora Joanchild, 'All Women Think Their Male Children Are Different', *London Women's Liberation Movement Newsletter* 149 (12 December 1979), n.p.

122 Janet Dixon, 'Separatism: A Look Back in Anger', *Radical Records: Thirty Years of Lesbian and Gay History, 1957–87*, ed. Bob Cant and Susan Hemmings (London, 1988), 81, 70; Sheila Jeffreys *et al.* in *London Women's Liberation Movement Newsletter* 76 (21 July 1978), n.p.

123 Maggie Christie in *Footsteps and Witnesses: Lesbian and Gay Lifestyles from Scotland*, ed. Bob Cant (Edinburgh, 1993), 126; Radical Feminists (Miscellaneous), *Thoughts on Feminism* (London, 1972), 16.

124 Ibid., 8; unidentified contributor to 'Why We Are Revolutionary Feminists' in *Report Back from Third London Area Women's Liberation Conference* (London, 1980), n.p; Dixon, 82.

125 Lovenduski and Randall, 361.

126 *Breaching the Peace: The Women's Liberation Movement versus the Women's Peace Movement* (London, 1983). For general accounts of the Greenham campaign, see Sasha Roseneil, *Disarming Patriarchy: Feminism and Political Action at Greenham* (Buckingham, 1995); *idem, Common Women, Uncommon Practices: The Queer Feminism of Greenham* (London, 2000); Anna Coote and Polly Pattullo, *Power and Prejudice: Women and Politics* (London, 1990), ch. 7; Lovenduski and Randall, 113–122; Jill Liddington, *The Long Road to Greenham* (London, 1989), chs. 11–13; and Beth Junor, *Greenham Common Women's Peace Camp: A History of Non-Violent Resistance, 1984–95* (London, 1995).

127 Roseneil, *Common Women, Uncommon Practices*, ch. 7, 294, 297; Jean Freer, *Raging Womyn – In Reply to* Breaching the Peace: *A Comment on the Women's Liberation Movement and the Common Womyn's Peace Camp at Greenham* (London, 1984), 7.

128 Caroline Taylor cited in *Greenham Common: Women at the Wire*, ed. Barbara Harford and Sarah Hopkins (London, 1984), 22; Connie Masnueto, 'Take the Toys from the Boys: Competition and the Nuclear Arms Race', *Over Our Dead Bodies: Women Against the Bomb*, ed. Dorothy Thompson (London, 1983).

129 Freer, 8; Penny Gulliver cited in Roseneil, *Disarming Patriarchy*, 158; Roseneil, *Disarming Patriarchy*, 45.

130 'Shameless Hussies' (sung to the tune of 'Dixie') in *Chant Down Greenham* (London, *c.* 1986), n.p.

131 For non-radical feminist involvement in campaigns against sexual violence, see Erin Pizzey, *Scream Quietly or the Neighbours will Hear* [rev. edn] (Harmondsworth, 1979); Erin Pizzey and Jeff Shapiro, *Prone to Violence* (London, 1982); Select Committee on Violence in Marriage, *Minutes of Evidence* (London, 1976); Greer, 'A Needle for Your Pornography' (1971) and 'Seduction is a Four-Letter Word' (1973), *The Madwoman's Underclothes*; Tweedie, 18–19, 56; Elizabeth Wilson, *What is to be Done about Violence against Women?*; and Bea Campbell, *Unofficial Secrets: Child Sexual Abuse – The Cleveland Case* (London, 1988).

132 For rape, see Susan Brownmiller, *Against Our Will: Men, Women and Rape* (New York, 1975); *Women at W.A.R.: Women Against Rape* (Bristol, 1978); Kathleen Hudson, *Woman Against Rape* (Bognor Regis, 1982); London Rape Crisis Centre, *Sexual Violence: The Reality for Women* (London, 1984); Ruth E. Hall, *Ask Any Woman: A London Inquiry into Rape and Sexual Assault* (Bristol, 1985); and Cathy Roberts, *Women and Rape* (Hemel Hempstead, 1989). For sexual harassment, see Ann Sedley and Melissa Benn, *Sexual Harassment at Work* (London, 1982).

133 See Nigel Parton, *The Politics of Child Abuse* (Basingstoke, 1985).

134 For an excellent analysis of the discourses on sexual violence, see Philip Jenkins, *Intimate Enemies: Moral Panics in Contemporary Great Britain* (New York, 1992).

135 For an account of the 1980 Leeds conference, see the epilogue to Judith Walkowitz's *City of Dreadful Delight: Narratives of Sexual Danger in Late Victorian London* (Chicago, 1992). For transcripts of papers delivered at this conference as well as those from the Women Against Violence Against Women conference held in London in 1981 and the Male Power and the Sexual Abuse of Girls conference held in Manchester in 1982, see Dusty Rhodes and Sandra McNeill (eds.), *Women Against Violence Against Women* (henceforth *WAVAW*) (London, 1985).

136 For anti-pornography campaigns, see in particular Home Office, *Report of the Committee on Obscenity and Film Censorship* (London, 1979); Andrea Dworkin, *Pornography: Men Possessing Women* (London, 1981); Susanne Kappeler, *The Pornography of Representation* (Cambridge, 1986); Catherine Itzin (ed.), *Pornography: Women, Violence and Civil Liberties* (Oxford, 1992); and Bill Thompson, *Soft Core: Moral Crusades against Pornography in Britain and America* (London, 1994).

137 London Rape Crisis Centre, ix.

138 Annie Smith, 'Sexual Initiation as Rape', *WAVAW*; Sheila Jeffreys, 'Prostitution', *WAVAW*, 61; Sandra McNeill, 'In Steering Women...', *WAVAW*; Lesley H., 'Sex Therapy', *WAVAW*; Sheila Jeffreys, 'Indecent Exposure', *WAVAW*, 84; anon., 'Fashion as Violence Against Women', *WAVAW*; Sally, 'Language as Violence', *WAVAW*; Women Against Violence Against Women in *Spare Rib* 119 (1982), 55; Ginny Cook, 'Psychiatry as Male Violence', *WAVAW*; Anna Briggs' 'Gynaecology, Obstetrics: A Refined Form of Violence?', *WAVAW*; Al Garthwaite, 'Mixed Wards: A Form of Sexual Violence against Women', *WAVAW*; Leeds Revolutionary Feminist Group, 'Political Lesbianism', 6.

139 London Rape Action Group, 'Towards a Revolutionary Feminist Analysis of Rape', *On the Problem of Men*, 43; Leeds Revolutionary Feminists, 'Incest as an Everyday Event in the Normal Family', *WAVAW*, 202. See also Rachel Adams, 'How All Men Benefit From Rape', *WAVAW*.

140 Bernadette Manning, 'The London Rape Crisis Centre: A Feminist Response from the Voluntary Sector', *Child Sexual Abuse after Cleveland: Alternative Strategies*, ed. Family Rights Group (London, 1988), 29.

141 Kappeler, 62; London Revolutionary Feminist Group, 'How Do Men See You?' (1978), *WAVAW*, 19.

142 Ibid., 19; London Rape Crisis Centre, ix; Ruth Hall, 'Up from Under', *Women at W.A.R.*, 20.

143 The Soho Sixteen, 'The Soho Sixteen and Reclaim the Night' (1978), *No Turning Back*, 221; Sheila Jeffreys *et al.*, introduction to *WAVAW*, 6.

144 Jeffreys, 'The Need for Revolutionary Feminism', 11; Astrid Torud, 'But Everybody Is Against Sexual Terrorism Against Women', *Scarlet Woman* (December 1979), 6.

145 Greer, *The Female Eunuch*, 19; Gregory in 'Consciousness Raising', 53.

146 Alison Fell, 'Notes on Ideology', *Conditions of Illusion*, 68; Lee Comer, 'Medical Mystifications', *Conditions of Illusion*, 45.

147 Greer, *The Female Eunuch*, 90; Figes, 'Marriage Today and Tomorrow', 213; Greer, *The Female Eunuch*, 19.

148 Kerry Yeung, *Working with Girls: A Reader's Route Map* [rev. edn] (Leicester, 1985), 26; Val Marshall, 'Girls Are People Too!', *Working with Girls Newsletter*, Newsletter Omnibus 1–6 (1981), 5.

149 Marshall, 5; National Association of Youth Clubs, *Working with Girls Film and Video Review List* (Leicester, c. 1983), 3.

150 Val Carpenter and Kirsty Young, *Coming in from the Margins: Youth Work with Girls and Young Women* (Leicester, 1986), 49, 52; *Working with Girls Newsletter* 37 (1987), 24.

151 Marshall, 4. For official investigations into youth clubs, see Department of Education and Science, *Experience and Participation: Report of the Review Group on the Youth Service in England* (London, 1982); and Inner London Education Authority, *Implementing the ILEA's Anti-Sexist Policy* (London, 1986). While generally endorsing the substance of the feminist case, most official reports rejected the solution of single-sex provision for girls; see *Experience and Participation*, 63.

152 Natalie St John, 'A Wintry Tale', *Through the Break: Women in Personal Crisis*, ed. Pearlie McNeill, Marie McShea and Pratibha Parmar (London, 1986), 227; Lovenduski and Randall, 95; *The London Women's Handbook* (London, 1986), 9. For feminist involvement in local government, see Jim Barry, *The Women's Movement and Local Politics* (Aldershot, 1991).

153 Oakley, *Housewife*, 83; Greer, *The Female Eunuch*, 50. For an important feminist text on the nature–nurture debate, see Oakley, *Sex, Gender and Society*. Only in the 1990s did sociobiologists gain widespread attention for restating the significance of sex differences. See Glenn Wilson, *The Great Sex Divide: A Study of Male–Female Differences* (London, 1989) for an early formulation of their case.

154 Charlotte Brunsdon, 'It Is Well Known', *Women Take Issue: Aspects of Women's Subordination*, ed. Birmingham Women's Studies Group (London, 1978), 31; Sheila Rowbotham, *A New World for Women: Stella Browne, Socialist Feminist* (London, 1977), 73; Margaret Jackson, 'Sexual Pleasure and Women's Liberation', *WAVAW*, 221; Campbell, 'A Feminist Sexual Politics', 5.

155 Comer, *Wedlocked Women*, 67. Equally telling was the breach between father Richard Titmuss and daughter Ann Oakley, two of the most influential sociologists of their respective generations. The mutualist Titmuss had celebrated how 'the idea of companionship in marriage is being substituted for the more sharply defined roles and codes of behaviour set by the Victorian patriarchal system'. The feminist Oakley did not acknowledge much difference between the two so long as the 'traditional oppression to domesticity' in marriage and the 'Victorian' expectation of passivity in sex continued to plague wives' lives. Ronald Fletcher and a fellow sociologist of the family, Michael Young, eventually struck back against women's liberationists in print, but by this point their reputations had been damaged beyond full repair (Richard Titmuss, 'The Position of Women' (1952), *Essays on the Welfare State* (London, 1958), 98; Oakley, *Housewife*, 236; idem, *Subject Women*, 258; Ronald Fletcher, T*he Abolitionists: The Family and Marriage under Attack* (London, 1988); Michael Young, 'Declaration of Peace between the Genders', *Rewriting the Sexual Contract*, ed. Geoff Dench (London, 1997)).

156 Elizabeth A. Stanko, *Intimate Intrusions: Women's Experience of Male Violence* (London, 1985), 48. For significant early contributions to feminist social science on personal relationships, see Sue Sharp, *'Just Like a Girl': How Girls Learn to be Women* (Harmondsworth, 1976); Carol Smart and Barry Smart (eds.), *Women, Sexuality and Social Control* (London, 1978); Julia Brannen and Jean Collard, *Marriages in Trouble: The Process of Seeking Help* (London, 1982); and R. Emerson Dobash and Russell Dobash, *Violence against Wives: A Case against the Patriarchy* (London, 1979). For the absorption of radical feminist critiques of sexual violence into media reporting and professional practice since the mid 1980s, see Julie Bindel, 'Never Give Up', *On The Move: Feminism for a New Generation*, ed. Natasha Walter (London, 1999).

157 Some women's liberationists naturally wrote their own manuals, at once attracted by their self-help ethos and antagonized by the 'passivity and subservience' they were thought to inculcate in women. The resulting products were nonetheless few in number and moderate in tone (Myra Connell *et al.*, 'Romance and Sexuality: Between the Devil and the Deep Blue Sea?', *Feminism for Girls: An Adventure Story*, ed. Angela McRobbie and Trisha McCabe (London, 1981), 159. For feminist-inflected self-help manuals, see Anne Hooper, *The Body Electric* (London, 1984); Sheila Kitzinger, *Woman's Experience*

of Sex (London, 1983); Anne Dickson, *A Woman in Your Own Right* (London, 1982); and Sandra Horley, *Love and Pain: A Survival Handbook for Women* (London, 1988)).

158 Miriam Stoppard, *Every Woman's Lifeguide* (London, 1982), 382. For marriage counselling literature in this period, see Martin P.M. Richards and B. Jane Elliott, 'Sex and Marriage in the 1960s and 1970s' and Janet Finch and David Morgan, 'Marriage in the 1980s: A New Sense of Realism?', both in *Marriage, Domestic Life and Social Change*, ed. David Clark (London, 1992).

159 Robert Morley, 'Separate but Together: The Essential Dichotomy of Marriage', *Change in Marriage*, ed. National Marriage Guidance Council (Rugby, 1982), 13; Shirley Conran, *Futurewoman* (aka *Futures*) (Harmondsworth, 1981), 13, 148.

160 Gyles Brandreth, *The Complete Husband* (London, 1978), 11, 12.

161 Tony Bradman, *The Essential Father* (London, 1985); Martin Francis, *Fathering for Men: Every Man's Guide to the First Years of Fatherhood* (Bristol, 1986), 223; Bradman, 19.

162 Schofield, 101; Alex Comfort, *The Joy of Sex: A Cordon Bleu Guide to Lovemaking* (New York, 1972), 103. For an excellent dissection of seventies sex manuals, see Stephen Heath, *The Sexual Fix* (London, 1982).

163 G.L. Simons, *Sex Tomorrow* (London, 1971), ch. 9; James Hemming and Zena Maxwell, *Sex and Love* (London, 1973), 140.

164 Arianna Stassinopoulos, *The Female Woman* (London, 1973); Claire Rayner, *Claire Rayner's Marriage Guide* (London, 1984), 6.

165 Jack Dominian, *Make or Break: An Introduction to Marriage Counselling* (London, 1984), 23; Stoppard, 16.

166 David Mace and Vera Mace, *We Can Have Better Marriages, If We Really Want Them* (London, 1975), 84, 36.

167 Brandreth, 11.

168 Bradman, 7; Peter Fenwick and Elizabeth Fenwick, *The Baby Book for Fathers* (London, 1978), 180. For an intelligent analysis of the dilemmas of fatherhood in this period, see Maureen Green, *Goodbye Father* (London, 1976).

169 Bradman, 262.

170 Fenwick and Fenwick, 3, 184; Francis, xii, 140.

171 Hemming and Maxwell, 47; Stuart Holroyd and Susan Holroyd, *The Complete Book of Sexual Love* (London, 1980), 11.

172 Jane Firbank in *Forum* 6, 10 (1973), 36; John Taylor, 'The Sexual Revolution', *Forum* 5, 3 (1972), 20, 19. For further examples of anti-feminism in sex radical literature, see Lal Coveney, Leslie Kay and Pat Mahony, 'Theory into Practice: Sexual Liberation or Social Control? – *Forum* Magazine, 1968–81', *The Sexuality Papers: Male Sexuality and the Social Control of Women*, ed. Lal Coveney *et al.* (London, 1984); and Rosalind Brunt, '"An Immense Verbosity": Permissive Sexual Advice in the 1970s', *Feminism, Culture and Politics*, ed. Rosalind Brunt and Caroline Rowan (London, 1982).

173 Robert Chartham, 'The Unsensuous Woman', *Forum* 4, 3 (1971), 5, 8.

174 Hemming and Maxwell, 94; Schofield, 217; Hemming and Maxwell, 57.

175 For Lesbian Left, see 'Lesbianism as a Model of Feminism: A Critique of Radical Feminism', *A Collection of Papers by Women in Lesbian Left – A Socialist-Feminist Group*, ed. Lesbian Left (London, 1979). Other occasional lesbian revisionists included Bea Campbell and Elizabeth Wilson. American feminism spawned a contemporaneous revisionist movement best represented by Betty Friedan's attacks on the 'ludicrous fulminations of radical feminists' against men and the family. Though critics regarded Friedan's ideas for a 'Second Stage' to be a *volte face* on her part, they are better understood as a return to the 'equal partnership of the sexes' she had favoured at the outset of the National Organization of Women in 1966 (Betty Friedan, *The Second Stage* (London, 1982), 54; *idem* cited in Marwick, 679).

176 Leeds Revolutionary Feminist Group, 'Political Lesbianism', 7. For the row over lesbian sadomasochists in the London Lesbian and Gay Centre, see Ardill and O'Sullivan.

177 Anne Eadington *et al.* in *London Women's Liberation Movement Newsletter* 46 (11 January 1978), n.p.; Gail Chester, 'I Call Myself A Radical Feminist', *The Woman Question: Readings on the Subordination of Women*, ed. Mary Evans (London, 1982), 58.

178 Victoria Robinson, 'Heterosexuality: Beginnings and Connections', *Heterosexuality*, 80; Ardill and O'Sullivan, 294.

179 Rowbotham, *The Past Is Before Us*, 252, 9; Ardill and O'Sullivan, 284.
180 Lynne Segal, *Is the Future Female?: Troubled Thoughts on Contemporary Feminism* (London, 1987), 70; Rowbotham, *The Past Is Before Us*, 9.
181 London Lesbian Offensive Group, 'Anti-Lesbianism in the Women's Liberation Movement' (1982), *Sweeping Statements: Writings from the Women's Liberation Movement, 1981–83*, ed. Hannah Kanter *et al.* (London, 1984), 260; Yvonne Roberts, *Mad about Women: Can There Ever Be Fair Play between the Sexes?* (London, 1992), 22; Audrey Battersby in *Once A Feminist: Stories of a Generation*, ed. Michelene Wandor (London, 1990), 117.
182 Campbell, 'A Feminist Sexual Politics', 3.
183 Editorial in *Spare Rib* 98 (1980), 3; A Woman's Place Collective in *London Women's Liberation Movement Newsletter* 45 (4 January 1978), n.p.; Lorna Mitchell, 'A Subjective View on Radical Feminism', *Scottish Women's Liberation Journal* 1, 2 (1977), 23. For the demise of sisterhood at the 1978 conference, see Catherine Hall in *Once a Feminist*, 173. For separatists' isolation from other women, see Ettorre, 109–111; Penny Holland, 'Still Revolting', *'68, '78, '88*, 139; and Dixon, 79–80.
184 Griselda Pollock, 'Feminism and Marriage', *'68, '78, '88*, 128; Lowry, 214.
185 Elizabeth Wilson, 'Forbidden Love', *Hidden Agendas: Theory, Politics and Experience in the Women's Movement* (London, 1986), 182.
186 Maria Katyachild, 'Fighting Porn', *WAVAW*, 19; Angela Carter, *The Sadeian Woman: An Exercise in Cultural History* (London, 1979), 19–20; Marion Bower, 'Daring to Speak Its Name: The Relationship of Women to Pornography', *Feminist Review* 24 (1986), 47. For slightly later revisionist critiques of the radical feminist line on pornography, see in particular Gillian Rogerson and Elizabeth Wilson, *Pornography and Feminism: The Case against Censorship* (London, 1991); and Lynne Segal and Mary McIntosh (eds.), *Sex Exposed: Sexuality and the Pornography Debate* (London, 1992).
187 Leeds Revolutionary Feminist Group, 'Political Lesbianism', 5; Lilian Mohin cited in Melissa Benn, 'The Passion of Decency: Thoughts on Feminism and Bisexuality', *Spare Rib* 198 (1989), 19; Angie Weir cited in Power, 242.
188 Campbell, 'A Feminist Sexual Politics', 1; Debby Gregory in *London Women's Liberation Movement Newsletter* 155 (14 Feb 1980), n.p.
189 Sheila Rowbotham in *Beyond The Fragments: Feminism and the Making of Socialism* (London, 1979), 41.
190 Jo Somerset, 'I Was A Teenage *Jackie* Reader', *'68, '78, '88*, 225, 227; Boycott, 78; Frankie Rickford, 'No More Sleeping Beauties and Frozen Boys', *The Left and the Erotic*, ed. Eileen Phillips (London, 1983), 144.
191 Ingham, 174, 175.
192 Pollock, 129.
193 Judy Barrington in *We're Here*, 37.
194 Erin Pizzey, *Wild Child* (Siena, 1995), 178; Boycott, 83.
195 Elizabeth Wilson, 'Forbidden Love', 173; Lisa in Dunn, 57–58.
196 Somerset, 225; Joyce Wilkinson, 'One Woman Speaks About Monogamy', *Red Herring: Scottish Lesbian Feminist Newsletter* 3 (1975), n.p.
197 Sue Bruley, *Women Awake: The Experience of Consciousness-Raising* (London, 1976), 12.
198 Elizabeth Wilson, 'I'll Climb the Stairway to Heaven: Lesbianism in the Seventies', *Sex and Love: New Thoughts*, 192, 180.
199 See Roseneil, *Disarming Patriarchy*, 95–96; and Wilmette Brown, *Black Women and the Peace Movement* [rev. edn] (Bristol, 1984).
200 Lovenduski and Randall, 98.
201 Nira Yuval-Davis in *Heterosexuality*, 53; Kathy, 'A Message to all Women – and Men Too', *Bread and Roses* 6 (Winter 1976–7), 3.
202 Pollock, 130, 126; Rickford, 146.
203 Hamblin, 'Is A Feminist Heterosexuality Possible?', *Sex and Love: New Thoughts*, 105; Helen Franks, *Goodbye Tarzan: Men After Feminism* (London, 1984), 42.
204 Susie Orbach and Luise Eichenbaum, *What Do Women Want?* (London, 1983), 15. It was Orbach's half-digested ideas that Diana used so memorably in her 1995 *Panorama* interview with Martin Bashir.
205 Edward Carpenter, *Love's Coming of Age: A Series of Papers on the Relations of the Sexes* [rev. edn] (London, 1913), v; Orbach and Eichenbaum, *What Do Women Want?*, 176.

206 Idem, Understanding Women (aka Outside In... Inside Out) (Harmondsworth, 1985),
       197–198. Not all revisionists subscribed to Eichenbaum's and Orbach's solution of
       shared parenting, Lynne Segal fearing that it conflated femininity with motherhood and
       abandoned collective efforts to change women's place in society (Segal, Is the Future
       Female?, 138–140, 161, 215).
207 Sheila Rowbotham, 'Women, Power and Consciousness' (1981), Dreams and Dilemmas,
       159; Yvonne Roberts, Mad about Women, 13; Rickford, 142.
208 Tweedie, 180.
209 Liz Heron, 38, 57.

Epilogue

1   Neil Lyndon, No More Sex War: The Failures of Feminism (London, 1992); Melanie
       Phillips, The Sex-Change Society: Feminised Britain and the Neutered Male (London,
       1999). See also Geoff Dench (ed.), Rewriting the Sexual Contract (London, 1997).
2   Harriet Harman, The Century Gap: Twentieth-Century Man, Twenty-First-Century
       Woman (London, 1993).
3   Deborah Tannen, You Just Don't Understand: Women and Men in Conversation
       (London, 1991), 42; Carol Gilligan, In A Different Voice: Psychological Theory and
       Women's Development [rev. edn] (Cambridge, MA, 1993); John Gray, Men are from
       Mars, Women are from Venus (London, 1993). For an analysis of the methodological
       problems in such studies of sex differences, see Elizabeth Aries, Men and Women in
       Interaction: Reconsidering the Differences (New York, 1996).
4   Matt Ridley, The Red Queen: Sex and the Evolution of Human Nature (London, 1993),
       204.
5   Nick Hornby, Fever Pitch (London, 1992); idem, High Fidelity (London, 1995); Helen
       Fielding, Bridget Jones's Diary (London, 1996); idem, Bridget Jones: The Edge of
       Reason (London, 1999); Tim Lott in The Mail on Sunday, 7 March 1999.
6   See 'Just What Do You Think about Life in Britain Today?', Nova, June 2000, in which
       men were adjudged the 'weaker sex' for being thought to need women more than women
       needed them.
7   Amy Jenkins in The Daily Mail, 18 May 2000; Mel C. in Spice Girls, Girl Power!
       (London, 1997), 31.
8   Barbara Ellen in The Observer, 5 November 2000.
9   'Welcome to the Female-ennium: Why the Future Belongs to Women', Cosmopolitan,
       January 2000.
10   Germaine Greer, The Whole Woman (London, 1999), 320; Suzanne Moore in The Mail
       on Sunday, 23 May 1999; Greer, 93.
11   For representative texts on the crisis of masculinity, see Roger Horrocks, Masculinity in
       Crisis (Basingstoke, 1994); Lynne Segal, Slow Motion: Changing Masculinities,
       Changing Men [rev. edn] (London, 1997); Dave Hill, The Future of Men (London,
       1997); Jenni Murray, 'Men's Lib for the Millennium?', The Female Odyssey: Visions for
       the Twenty-First Century, ed. Charlotte Cole and Helen Windrath (London, 1999); and,
       for America, Susan Faludi, Stiffed: The Betrayal of the Modern Man (London, 1999).
12   David Blunkett in The Daily Mail, 21 August 2000; Jack Straw cited in Melanie Phillips,
       3.
13   Cover of Maxim, January 2000; Suzanne Franks, Having None of It: Women, Men and
       the Future of Work (London, 1999), 170.
14   Jane Phillimore in The Observer, 2 July 2000. For the backlash thesis, see Susan Faludi,
       Backlash: The Undeclared War against American Women (New York, 1991); Ann
       Oakley and Juliet Mitchell (eds.), Who's Afraid of Feminism?: Seeing Through the
       Backlash (London, 1997); and Imelda Whelehan, Overloaded: Popular Culture and the
       Future of Feminism (London, 2000).
15   David Blunkett in The Daily Mail, 21 August 2000.
16   Angela Lambert in The Daily Mail, 5 May 2000; Lynda Lee-Potter in The Daily Mail,
       23 June 1999; Robyn Sisman in The Daily Mail, 28 September 2000; Greer, 328.
17   For an excellent overview of the literature on contemporary marriage, see Jane Lewis,
       The End of Marriage?: Individualism and Intimate Relations (Cheltenham, 2001), chs.

1 and 2. For the diversity of family mores among ethnic groups in Britain, see Geoff Dench, *The Place of Men in Changing Family Cultures* (London, 1997).

18   Carol Smart and Pippa Stevens, *Cohabitation Breakdown* (London, 2000), 24. For growing public acceptance of cohabitation, see Anne Barlow *et al.*, 'Just a Piece of Paper?: Marriage and Cohabitation', *British Social Attitudes: The Eighteenth Report*, ed. Alison Park *et al.* (London, 2001), 32–33.

19   Julie Burchill, *I Knew I Was Right: An Autobiography* (London, 1998), 146; David Thomas in *The Daily Mail*, 10 February 2000.

20   'If *Later* Ruled the Millennium', *Later*, January 2000.

21   Neil Spencer in *The Observer*, 20 June 1999. For parallels between gender politics in the 1890s and 1990s, see Caroline Wright and Gill Jagger, 'End of Century, End of Family?: Shifting Discourses of Family "Crisis"', *Changing Family Values*, ed. Caroline Wright and Gill Jagger (London, 1999).

22   Lynne Bateson in *The Daily Mail*, 26 November 1999; Alison Gordon in *The Mail on Sunday*, 21 November 1999.

23   Sarah Ivens in *The Daily Mail*, 20 April 1999; Alex Reed in *The Daily Mail*, 7 September 1999.

24   Vanessa Lloyd Pratt *et al.* in *The Daily Mail*, 9–11 February 2000; Rachel Snowden in *The Daily Mail*, 1 February 1999; Eric Bailey in *The Mail on Sunday*, 6 August 2000.

25   Suzanne Moore in *The Mail on Sunday*, 7 February 1999; Julie Burchill in *The Guardian*, 29 April 2000.

26   'Are Men the New Women?', *GQ*, March 2000; 'She's Out to Change You', *Maxim*, February 2000; Chris Bell in *FHM*, September 2000.

27   James Brown in *Cosmopolitan*, February 2000; Keith Kendrick cited in *The Guardian*, 29 January 2001.

28   Gray, 4. See also Tannen, 18–19.

29   David M. Buss, *The Evolution of Desire: Strategies of Human Mating* (New York, 1994), 13; Ridley, 168.

30   See Jude Davies, '"It's Like Feminism, But You Don't Have to Burn Your Bra": Girl Power and the Spice Girls' Breakthrough, 1996–7', *Living Through Pop*, ed. Andrew Blake (London, 1999).

31   Lyndon, 12; Julie Burchill in *The Guardian*, 17 November 1999.

32   See Industrial Society, *Speaking Up, Speaking Out!* (London, 1997), 99; Ann Oakley, 'Gender Matters: Man the Hunter', *Having Their Say: The View of 12–19 Year-Olds*, ed. Helen Roberts and Darshan Sachdev (Ilford, 1996), 25; and Helen Wilkinson and Geoff Mulgan, *Freedom's Children* (London, 1995), 74.

33   Christina Hardyment, *The Future of the Family* (London, 1998), 27; ICM, *Millennium Women Survey* (London, 1999), 6.

34   Ray Hall *et al.*, 'Living Alone: Evidence from England and Wales and France for the Last Two Decades', *Changing Britain: Families and Households in the 1990s*, ed. Susan McRae (Oxford, 1999), 296.

35   Amanda Riley-Jones in *The Guardian*, 10 June 2000.

36   Esther Addley and Crystal Mahey in *The Guardian*, 16 November 2000; Isobel Allen and Shirley Bourke Dowling, 'Teenage Mothers: Decisions and Outcomes', *Changing Britain*, 337.

37   Ibid., 339, 347.

38   Louie Burghes and Mark Brown, *Single Lone Mothers: Problems, Prospects and Policies* (London, 1995), 60, 55; ICM, 4–5.

39   Sara Horrell, Jill Rubery and Brendan Burchell, 'Working-Time Patterns, Constraints and Preferences', *The Social and Political Economy of the Household*, ed. Michael Anderson, Frank Bechhofer and Jonathan Gershuny (Oxford, 1994), 122.

40   For a range of opinions on boys' underperformance at school, see Adrienne Katz *et al.* in *The Daily Telegraph*, 18 August 2000.

41   Jonathan Bradshaw *et al.*, *Absent Fathers?* (London, 1999), 81, 90.

42   John Mander Ross, *What Men Want: Mothers, Fathers and Manhood* (Cambridge, MA, 1994); Anthony Clare, *On Men: Masculinity in Crisis* (London, 2000), 129. For the use and abuse of psychoanalysis, see also Adam Jukes, *Why Men Hate Women* (London, 1993); and *idem*, *Men Who Batter Women* (London, 1999).

43   David D. Gilmore, *Manhood in the Making: Cultural Concepts of Masculinity* (New Haven, CT, 1990), 1. For further anthropological work on the subject, see Gilbert H.

Herdt, *Guardians of the Flute: Idioms of Masculinity* (New York, 1987), while for historical crises of masculinity, see Mark Breitenberg, *Anxious Masculinity in Early Modern England* (Cambridge, 1996); and Geoffrey Pearson, *Hooliganism: A History of Respectable Fears* (Basingstoke, 1983).

44   Heather Fourmaini, *Men: The Darker Continent* (London, 1990), 8; John Nicholson and Fiona Thompson, *Men on Sex: The* Esquire *Report* (London, 1992), 96. For the disparity between male archetypes and men's self-perceptions, see also John MacInnes, *The End of Masculinity* (Buckingham, 1998), 15.

45   United Kingdom Men's Movement, 'About the UKMM', http://www.ukmm.org.uk. For the contrast between Britain and America, see Sylvia B. Bashevkin, *Women on the Defensive: Living Through Conservative Times* (Chicago, 1997), 45.

46   For Lyndon's downfall, see Jim White in *The Guardian*, 15 December 2000.

47   Jacqueline Scott, Duane F. Alwin and Michael Braun, 'Generational Changes in Gender-Role Attitudes: Britain in a Cross-National Perspective', *Sociology* 30, 3 (1996), 489. For polling evidence contradicting the idea of a backlash, see also Jacqueline Scott, 'Family Change: Revolution or Backlash in Attitudes?', *Changing Britain*; and Kathleen Kiernan, 'Men and Women at Work and at Home', *British Social Attitudes: The Ninth Report*, ed. Roger Jowell *et al.* (Aldershot, 1992).

48   Nicholson and Thompson, 4.

49   Jacqueline Scott, 'Women and the Family', *British Social Attitudes: The Seventh Report*, ed. Roger Jowell *et al.* (Aldershot, 1990), 62; Catherine Hakim, *Female Heterogeneity and the Polarisation of Women's Employment* (London, 1996), 88; Scott, 'Family Change', 86.

50   Kerstin Hinds and Lindsey Jarvis, 'The Gender Gap', *British Social Attitudes: The Seventeenth Report*, ed. Roger Jowell *et al.* (London, 2000), 115, 112.

51   Helen Wilkinson, Vicki Cook and Deborah Mattinson, 'Continuity and Change amongst 18–34 Year-Olds: A Qualitative Research Study', *The Seven Million Project Working Paper* 9 (London, 1995), 36; Industrial Society, 122; MORI Socioconsult poll cited in Wilkinson and Mulgan, 76.

52   Catherine Hakim, *Work–Lifestyle Choices in the Twenty-First Century: Preference Theory* (Oxford, 2000), ch. 5.

53   Wilkinson, Cook and Mattinson, 18, 22.

54   Heather Joshi and Pierella Paci, 'Life in the Labour Market', *Twenty-something in the 1990s: Getting On, Getting By, Getting Nowhere*, ed. John Bynner, Elsa Ferri and Peter Shepherd (Aldershot, 1997), 43, 48.

55   Gerda Siann and Helen Wilkinson, 'Gender, Feminism and the Future', *The Seven Million Project Working Paper* 3 (London, 1995). See also Jane Grant, 'Where Have all the Women Gone?: The Experience of Women Aged 18–34 in Women's Organisations', *The Seven Million Project Working Paper* 6 (London, 1995).

56   Nicholson and Thompson, 12, 8.

57   See details of Carol Tully's experiment at Columbia University, in which she found her female subjects to be three times more likely than their male counterparts to identify sexual harassment in identical scenarios (cited by Ben Taylor in *The Daily Mail*, 9 August 2000). For tensions between the sexes at work, see also Eleanor E. Maccoby, *The Two Sexes: Growing Up Apart, Coming Together* (Cambridge, MA, 1998), ch. 9.

58   'The GQ Poll', *GQ*, January 1995.

59   Eric Jacobs and Robert Worcester, *Typically British?: The Prudential MORI Guide* (London, 1991), 27; Scott, 'Women and the Family', 63.

60   Janet Reibstein in *The Daily Mail*, 14 May 1999; Mary Balfour cited in *The Daily Mail*, 18 February 2000.

61   NSM Research, *Millennium Woman Survey* (Summertown, 1998), table 27; Gallup, *Marriage/Partnership Survey: Summary Report* (London, 1990), 39.

62   For the division of household labour, see Jonathan Gershuny, 'Sexual Divisions and the Distribution of Work in the Household', *Rewriting the Sexual Contract*; and Jonathan Gershuny, Michael Godwin and Sally Jones, 'The Domestic Labour Revolution: A Process of Lagged Adaptation', *The Social and Political Economy of the Household*. See also NSM Research, table 31, in which attached women estimated their leisure time to be almost identical to that of their partners.

63   A quarter of women born in 1973 was expected never to bear children; see Family Policy Studies Centre, 'Family Change: Guide to the Issues', *Family Briefing Paper* 12 (2000), 1.

64   Cited in Melanie Phillips, 150.
65   Office for National Statistics survey cited by Paul Kelso in *The Guardian*, 29 June 2000.
66   Susan Quilliam, *Women on Sex* (London, 1994), 49; 'The GQ Poll', *GQ*, January 1995. For men's preference for assertive women in bed, see also Nicholson and Thompson, 63–65.
67   Editorial in *The Observer*, 19 November 2000.
68   Kaye Wellings *et al.*, *Sexual Behaviour in Britain: The National Survey of Sexual Attitudes and Lifestyles* (Harmondsworth, 1994), 151, 265.
69   Wilkinson, Cook and Mattinson, 18; Eric Jacobs and Robert Worcester, *We British: Britain under the MORIscope* (London, 1990), 150–159.
70   Anything between two-fifths and two-thirds of men expressed interest in using a male Pill, which was due to be launched in 2005; see Roger Henderson in *The Sunday Times*, 11 March 2001; and Frank O'Donnell in *The Daily Mail*, 23 February 2000.
71   David Bainbridge and Robert Winston interviewed in 'Women's Hour' on BBC Radio 4, 22 February 1999.
72   Elsa Ferri, *Life at Thirty-Three: The Fifth Follow-up of the National Child Development Study* (London, 1993), 28.
73   Hakim, *Work–Lifestyle Choices*, 6, 10. See also *idem*, *Female Heterogeneity*.
74   Margrit Eichler, *Family Shifts: Families, Policies and Gender Equality* (Toronto, 1997), 72; Lynne Segal, *Why Feminism?: Gender, Psychology, Politics* (Cambridge, 1999), 160–162.
75   Two key works on the impact of individualism on relationships are Lewis, *The End of Marriage?*; and Ulrich Beck and Elisabeth Beck-Gernscheim, *The Normal Chaos of Love* (Cambridge, 1995).
76   Anthony Giddens and Christopher Pierson, *Conversations with Anthony Giddens: Making Sense of Modernity* (Cambridge, 1998), 125; Anthony Giddens, *Modernity and Self-Identity: Self and Society in the Late Modern Age* (Stanford, CA, 1991), 6; Giddens and Pierson, 124. See also Anthony Giddens, *The Transformation of Intimacy: Sexuality, Love and Eroticism in Modern Societies* (Stanford, CA, 1992). For feminist critiques of Giddens, see Wendy Langford, *Revolutions of the Heart: Gender, Power and the Delusions of Love* (London, 1999); and Lynn Jamieson, *Intimacy: Personal Relationships in Modern Societies* (Cambridge, 1998).
77   Wilkinson, Cook and Mattinson, 17–18.
78   Mariella Frostrup in *The Observer*, 5 November 2000.
79   See Stein Ringen, *The Family in Question* (London, 1998), 47. However, for evidence that cohabitation is becoming a more long-term arrangement, see Michael Murphy, 'The Evolution of Cohabitation in Britain, 1960–95', *Population Studies* 54, 1 (2000), 50.
80   Giddens, *Modernity and Self-Identity*, 89. For the detrimental effects of family breakdown on some children, see Monica Cockett and John Tripp, *The Exeter Family Study: Family Breakdown and Its Impact on Children* (Exeter, 1994).
81   See Penny Mansfield, 'Good Relations', *The Good Life*, ed. Ian Christie and Lindsay Nash (London, 1998), 40; and Andrew Oswald cited by Geraldine Bedell in *The Observer*, 11 February 2001.
82   Jane Lewis, Jessica Datta and Sophie Sarre, *Individualism and Commitment in Marriage and Cohabitation* (London, 1999), 42.
83   Beck and Beck-Gernscheim, 144.
84   Lewis, Datta and Sarre, 54.
85   Over four-fifths of twelve- to nineteen-year-olds did not think that a person's sex was important in determining his or her chances of succeeding in life (Oakley, 38).
86   Wilkinson, Cook and Mattinson, 17, 12.
87   Jenny McLeod, 'Still Rising', *On The Move: Feminism for a New Generation*, ed. Natasha Walter (London, 1999), 128.
88   Alwin Peter, *From The Mouths of Men: Black Men Speak Freely and Frankly about Black Women, Relationships, Love and Sex* (London, 1998), 47; Amy Jenkins in *The Daily Mail*, 18 May 2000.
89   Anne M. Johnson *et al.*, *Sexual Attitudes and Lifestyles* (Oxford, 1994), 187.
90   See Hakim, *Female Heterogeneity*; *idem*, 'Five Feminist Myths about Women's Employment', *British Journal of Sociology* 46, 3 (1995), 429–455.
91   Scott, 'Women and the Family', 63; NSM Research, table 81.
92   Fran C. Dickson, 'Ageing and Marriage: Understanding the Long-term, Later-life Marriage', *Clinical Handbook of Marriage and Couples Interventions*, ed. W. Kim

Halford and Howard J. Markman (Chichester, 1997), 262. See also Steven L. Nock, *Marriage in Men's Lives* (New York, 1998), 133–136.

93   Francis McGlone, Alison Park and Ceridwen Roberts, 'Relative Values; Kinship and Friendship', *British Social Attitudes: The Thirteenth Report*, ed. Roger Jowell (Aldershot, 1996), 59–61; Diane M. Houston, 'Employment Choices for Mothers of Pre-School Children: A Psychological Perspective', talk at Family Policy Studies Centre, 29 November 2000.

94   Beck and Beck-Gernscheim, 191–192; Fiona McAllister (ed.), *Marital Breakdown and the Health of the Nation* [rev. edn] (London, 1995). For a critique of earlier American studies which claimed that marriage disadvantaged women, see Linda J. Waite and Maggie Gallagher, *The Case for Marriage: Why Married People are Happier, Healthier and Better Off Financially* (New York, 2000), ch. 12.

95   Adam Phillips, *Monogamy* (London, 1996), n.p.

96   Lewis, Datta and Sarre, 3–4, 44.

Index